American Visions ▪ Readings in American Culture

Consulting Editors

Michael Barton
Associate Professor of American Studies and History
Pennsylvania State University at Harrisburg, Capital College

Nancy A. Walker
Professor of English
Vanderbilt University

This unique series consists of carefully assembled volumes of seminal writings on topics central to the study of American culture. Each anthology begins with a comprehensive overview of the subject at hand, written by a noted scholar in the field, followed by a combination of selected articles, original essays, and case studies.

By bringing together in each collection many important commentaries on such themes as humor, material culture, architecture, the environment, literature, politics, theater, film, and spirituality, American Visions provides a varied and rich library of resources for the scholar, student, and general reader. Annotated bibliographies facilitate further study and research.

Volumes Published

Nancy A. Walker, editor
What's So Funny? Humor in American Culture (1998).
Cloth ISBN 0-8420-2687-8   Paper ISBN 0-8420-2688-6

Robert J. Bresler
*Us vs. Them: American Political and Cultural Conflict
from WW II to Watergate* (2000).
Cloth ISBN 0-8420-2689-4   Paper ISBN 0-8420-2690-8

Jessica R. Johnston, editor
The American Body in Context: An Anthology (2001)
Cloth ISBN 0-8420-2858-7   Paper ISBN 0-8420-2859-5

Richard P. Horwitz, editor
The American Studies Anthology (2001)
Cloth ISBN 0-8420-2828-5   Paper ISBN 0-8420-2829-3

Chris J. Magoc
*So Glorious a Landscape: Nature and the Environment
in American History and Culture* (2002)
Cloth ISBN 0-8420-2695-9   Paper ISBN 0-8420-2696-7

THE AMERICAN BODY
IN CONTEXT

THE
AMERICAN BODY
IN CONTEXT

AN ANTHOLOGY

Edited by
JESSICA R. JOHNSTON

American Visions ▪ Readings in American Culture
▪
Number 3
▪
A Scholarly Resources Inc. Imprint ▪ Wilmington, Delaware

Scholarly Resources Inc.
104 Greenhill Avenue
Wilmington, DE 19805-1897
www.scholarly.com

Library of Congress Cataloging-in-Publication Data

The American body in context : an anthology / edited by Jessica R. Johnston.
    p. cm.—(American visions ; no. 3)
  Includes bibliographical references (p.   )
  ISBN 0-8420-2858-7 (alk. paper)—ISBN 0-8420-2859-5 (pbk. : alk. paper)
  1. Body, Human—Social aspects—United States. I. Johnston, Jessica R.,
1952– II. American visions (Wilmington, Del.) ; no. 3.

GT497.U6A447 2001
391.6'0973–dc21   00-066104

♾ The paper used in this publication meets the minimum requirements of the American National Standard for permanence of paper for printed library materials, Z39.48, 1984.

To Betty, for her wisdom and guidance

ABOUT THE EDITOR

JESSICA JOHNSTON is a lecturer at the University of Canterbury in New Zealand where she teaches courses on contemporary American culture, deviance in America, power and knowledge in corporate America, and issues of identity and qualitative methodologies. Her current research is focused on two areas of the body—a ten-year study of people with body issue concerns, and the computer antivirus industry and its conceptualization of infection of the body politic.

ACKNOWLEDGMENTS

A number of people have helped this book through its many stages. John Caughey has been an invaluable source of intellectual and professional guidance throughout my career. Michael Barton originally contacted me about the concept of a reader on the body and through our many discussions has shown enthusiasm, patience and faith. Nancy Walker offered encouragement for and understanding of my vision of this book. And my editors at Scholarly Resources, Matthew Hershey and Linda Pote Musumeci, provided high standards for and keen insights into the entire process. Nick FitzGerald contributed his time, his critical proofreading, and emotional support, all of which made the production of this book an enjoyable endeavor. And finally, I want to extend my gratitude to the students of American culture whose responses and insights continue to inspire my desire to investigate the social circumstances in which we live.

CONTENTS

JESSICA R. JOHNSTON

Introduction

In a classic episode of *Star Trek: The Next Generation*, the starship *Enterprise* battles with the Borg—cybernetic beings whose only purpose appears to be the conquest and assimilation of others. The Borg capture the captain of the *Enterprise*, Jean-Luc Picard. Before he is incorporated into the Borg collective consciousness and his body transformed into a cyborg, Captain Picard and a Borg voice enter into what is now a well-known exchange:

> *Picard:* I will resist you with my last ounce of strength.
> *Borg voice:* Strength is irrelevant. Resistance is futile. We wish to improve ourselves. We will add your biological and technological distinctiveness to our own. Your culture will adapt to service ours.
> *Picard:* Impossible. My culture is based on freedom and self-determination.
> *Borg voice:* Freedom is irrelevant. Self-determination is irrelevant. You must comply.
> *Picard:* We would rather die.
> *Borg voice:* Death is irrelevant.

In the next scene, Picard's body and mind have been reengineered into a cybernetic being. Now called Locutus, the body has been penetrated and punctured by multiple mechanical devices and prosthetics. Picard's knowledge has been incorporated into the Borg collective consciousness. His individuality has been erased. Bioengineering and advanced technology have eliminated the essence of Picard's humanity.

There is a rationale for beginning this book on the body with the transformation of Picard into the cyborg Locutus. The anthropologist Mary Douglas suggests that a culture's views of the human body are intimately connected to its concerns and fears of the world at large (Douglas, 1970). The body is, in Douglas's words, "good to think with." Adopting Douglas's perspective, there are three topical areas in which we can use the Picard/Locutus body to "think with" in the analysis of the larger social structure. This science fiction portrayal of the merging of human beings and technology illustrates current issues and concerns about human individuality, social control and conformity, and gender and ethnicity.

What makes the human being superior to a machine? The transformation of Picard into Locutus highlights a future in which physical changes in the human body are accomplished through bioengineered transformations. The Borg are stronger than humans and more physically adapted to a technological world. Their prosthetic arms have the ability to directly "jack into" computers, to download and share all information simultaneously. Dissolving the boundaries between human and machine, cyborgs highlight the union between animate beings and information technologies. Yet, they are presented as intellectual automatons, individually vegetative and unaware of a sense of self. Individual minds and bodies are exchanged/sacrificed for a heightened communal awareness. This construction of a potential human future is presented as something to be feared. Picard's individuality and humanity have been lost in Locutus.

Similar to the fate that befalls Picard, the bodies and minds of other beings are absorbed into the Borg collective consciousness. The Borg have the power to technologically discipline all individuals into conformity and compliance. According to the Borg, individual resistance to this bodily incorporation is futile; the concept of freedom is irrelevant. All will be assimilated. This part of the storyline suggests that no matter how strong-willed, the lone individual cannot fight the advances of bioengineering and technological oppression. Conformity to the will and social control of advanced technology is ensured. Even the strong-willed Picard cannot resist working for and with the advanced technology of the Borg.

As individuality is incorporated and eliminated in this episode, so too are gender and ethnicity. All Borg are seemingly standardized white human male bodies. There are no overweight or skinny, short or tall, female or nonwhite or even alien versions. The construction of a crisis of technological incorporation is not applied to females or various ethnic groups. The show highlights the use of external forces and powers that eliminate men's freedom and the ability to resist. Yet, women and nonwhite ethnic groups have long had to deal with external forces that transform them into servicing agents for others. They have continually been "incorporated" into white male visions of appropriate minds and bodies. The traditional oppression of nonwhites and women in Western societies, particularly their loss of autonomy over their bodies to the power of white men, is basically invisible. Significantly, as women and ethnic groups gain a voice and articulate historical perspective on their loss of autonomy, the white male is now articulating a fear of his incorporation. Indeed, in this *Star Trek* episode, the powerful white man is in crisis as his body is threatened with total incorporation and the total elimination of his individuality. In the fictional construction of the Borg's technologically determined future, issues regarding gender and ethnicity are subsumed into the white male perspective. These represented white male fears ignore the experiences of gender and race and leave unexplored the intersections of gender and race with technology.

The Picard/Locutus division thus demonstrates the seemingly contradictory assumptions grounding our interpretations of the body. The body is simultaneously a physical, biological entity and a symbolic artifact. A body is both created in the world of nature and also physically reconstructed by a culture. The body is both an internal, subjective environment and simultaneously is an object for others to observe and evaluate. The body is a physical entity over which we labor. In this sense we serve our bodies. Our everyday life is tacitly dominated by the details of our corporeal existence, immersing us in a perpetual labor of bodily maintenance. We eat, we drink, we sleep, and we spend time concerned about the proper amounts of each. By commanding much of our daily attention, the requirements of physical maintenance ultimately structure the experience of others, our environment, and ourselves.

These bodily practices, while performed by the individual in response to biological needs, also weave the individual within a dense web of social relationships. What an individual eats, how much an individual drinks, and where and with whom an individual sleeps locates a body within race, class, and gender determinants. Bodily practices are then both individual and collective, the individual body expressing cultural values, rules, and regulations in the daily routines of living.

Americans today continually search within themselves for the self-control, the self-discipline, and the willpower to achieve their goals, seemingly fighting with themselves and against themselves for what they desire, for what they want. Whether they want to exercise more, eat less, stop smoking, drink less, study more, or realize some of the other common self-improvement goals, they must deal with competing, and sometimes conflicting, yearnings that lead in opposite directions.

This book is devoted to exploring the foundations of these seeming contradictions. While the *Star Trek* episode may be only one television show, it highlights how the body can be used as a symbol to explore cultural tensions surrounding technology, gender, race, and social control and resistance to that control. Exploring these issues in their various manifestations and relationships to the body will illuminate past and present tensions in American culture. With that end in mind, the book is divided into four interrelated sections. The first section analyzes the conventional distinction between the mind and the body. Does the body have a "mind of its own"? Does the human mind or consciousness distinguish itself through its self-awareness and its ability to control the body? Or is this mind/body split merely a socially constructed concept unique to Western viewpoints? Through this exploration of the connections between the mind and the body, the reader will come to recognize some of the social and cultural contradictions complicating the construction of a consistent body/self.

The second section focuses on the media's construction of the body. In American culture today, the values drawn upon in making decisions in almost any area of life are conflicting. Buying a car generates a desire for a vehicle that is either luxurious yet economical, or compact yet spacious. In a magazine advertisement, a perfume is sold to "bring out the beast in him," next to an article about date rape. Commercials and advertisements continually direct consumers to both eat and consume, and to lose weight and be thin. Friends and relatives encourage people to eat, "just this once," then critique them for not being able to stick to a weight loss program. From the larger culture through to intimate family and friends, mixed messages are sent about what is important, what is success, what our accomplishments should be.

From Marilyn Monroe to the Spice Girls, from Arnold Schwarzenegger to O. J. Simpson, from William Taft to Bill Clinton, to your own naked form reflected in the mirror each morning, we are taught to read bodies as symbols displaying and revealing hidden "truths" about the individual and his or her behaviors. Any discussion of the body becomes complex and muddled as one tries to analyze how and why certain body types are attributed certain meanings.

While the first section of this book investigates the philosophical distinctions between the mind and the body, the second section analyzes the body as a symbol and metaphor, and discusses who has the power to define and influence characteristics attributed to certain bodies. Specifically, it explores how advertising constructs "ideal bodies" and considers the stigmas attached to bodies not meeting those ideals. The articles investigate differences between male and female, and black and white constructions of the perfect body and show how the body becomes a "text" that can be read and interpreted by others.

The third section explores the various forms of discipline applied to the body. While the Borg had the ability to technologically restructure bodies and minds into docile and cooperative laborers for the collective whole, several of the authors in this section suggest that current social institutions are accomplishing this feat without technological intervention. As an example, within the classroom individuals are taught to control themselves in order to be "good" students, to be part of the collective student body. Educational disciplinary techniques train a child to be quiet, compliant, and cooperative. Acquiring the necessary self-discipline to monitor and control one's behavior renders the individual a "good student." Similarly, medicine advocates certain rules and standards through which individuals will achieve and maintain a "healthy body." Using the body for pure pleasure and sensation is to be regulated. The enjoyment of sex, drugs, alcohol, and food are all to be managed and disciplined by the individual for the individual's own "good health." In both medicine and education then, individuals learn to monitor themselves, to keep themselves under their own surveillance in order to meet a cultural standard. It is suggested that, in this way, the techniques learned and used to control the self, whether one is acquiring "good health" or becoming a "good student," are ultimately forms of social control. Obedience and compliance are accomplished as one becomes a "good" citizen—part of the collective.

Yet, can we resist this form of social control? The last section focuses on individual's acts of resistance to, and negotiation with, seemingly oppressive "collective" structures. Individuals do assert their own interpretations of the body, interpretations that are in opposition to the dominant way of thinking and knowing the body. The authors in this section demonstrate how individuals confront the assumptions displayed in advertisements and the medical literature with their real world experiences, challenging the projected images of "good" and "healthy" male and female bodies. Institutional directives at times seem contradictory, suggesting conflicting methods and goals toward which we should be progressing to meet our "potentials." By recognizing the conflicts between the various discourses, several of the authors illustrate how individuals can free themselves from the imposition of structures that would discipline them. Individuals can resist; freedom is not irrelevant.

Yet one last set of questions must be asked about our ability to resist. Stepping back from the assertion of freedom and individuality inherent in Picard's speech before being incorporated by the Borg, we need to question whether the concept of a unique and identifiable mind/body is merely part of our collective consciousness. Are resistance strategies, enacted to maintain ourselves as single entities, just part of our programming? Is our belief in "freedom" merely part of our incorporation into a different type of "collective consciousness"? Is the concept of "choice," and our "decision" to be a "good" or "bad" student merely a disciplinary "technique" that keeps us monitoring our bodies and our behaviors, a "decision" that ultimately ensures that we "voluntarily" keep ourselves part of the collective?

As an illustration of the consequences of these questions, consider this: If a "smart pill" was offered that did not have side effects, a kind of healthy steroid for the brain, would you be tempted to take it? Why? After taking it, could you afford to go back to being less smart? Would you want to? In what way would you be "free" not to take it? What would the consequences of that "free" choice mean in a world where most people did change themselves, their bodies, in order to succeed? In contemplating methods of changing our bodies, we need to be aware of the invisible pressures formed through our current "collective consciousness." What are the values toward which we strive and where do these values come from? Why do we consider it "good" to change our minds and bodies to meet social standards? Is our collective consciousness really that different from the Borg? Is resistance merely an elusive concept that allows us to assume we are participating "freely"? This book raises these questions about the boundaries of the self, the boundaries of the body, and our sense of ourselves at the beginning of a new millennium when transformations of the body and mind are becoming more and more of a reality.

A short popular culture article on the body is included at the end of each section. Each of these popular articles is very "ordinary" in that it addresses body issues in circulation within the popular press. Questions have been included to connect the more scholarly articles to these popular pieces. By thinking about and answering the questions, the relationships between institutions such as advertising, medicine, and education and how they construct the body will become more obvious. Realizing the power of these institutions to influence what is taken for granted as "natural" about the body can contribute to alternative and resistant readings of the body. The "collective" construction of the body becomes easier to see and understand, and the ability to resist the imposition of disciplinary techniques by the "collective consciousness" becomes more effective through the active probing of popular assumptions.

So, is resistance futile? The answer is no if we take the Picard/Locutus body as an example. Picard, with the help of his crew, through technological insight and his own self-determination, was able to break free of the Borg control of his mind and body. He was able to release himself from a technologically determined future of obedience and compliance. With help, he liberated himself from life within a predator community. No longer a mere cog reproducing the will of the collective consciousness, Picard was set free to continue the struggle. This book is constructed with this type of resistance in mind.

JESSICA R. JOHNSTON

I | Minds and Bodies

Where is the boundary between the "outside" of you and the "inside" of you? What does it mean when something or someone "gets inside" you? Does your body ever do things your mind doesn't want it to? At times does your body have a "mind of its own"? Who is that "you" that is held responsible for the actions of your body?

There has been much academic debate recently on this mind/body problem, on how and where individuals locate a sense of themselves within the body. Mainstream Western philosophical thought assumes a common view of "man" as formed through two opposed characteristics: mind and body. The French mathematician and philosopher René Descartes is cited most often for articulating this mind-body dualism, for the phrase, "I think, therefore I am." According to Descartes, the actual thinking process, the "I think," grants a privileged status to the observing reflexive mind over the more instrumental and mechanical body. The ability to think and be reflexive elevates the status of the mind to the definition of the person (Turner, 1984, p. 48). In this sense, you are your mind, and the body is merely an instrument for the mind to control. This observing and reflexive mind is seen as continually subjecting the "mindless"

1

body to analysis, measurement, and discipline. Since the mind is thought to exercise intimate rulership over the body, a person cannot be easily excused by saying, "my body did it." The mind is seen as a self-contained, self-enclosed inner realm, separate from nature and the body. This mind/body division is known as the Cartesian dualism.

The extension of this mind/body dualism can be seen in the disciplines within which both the mind and body are studied. Generally, physiology, biology, and medicine analyze the body. In these natural, or life, sciences, the body's sensations, activities, and processes are part of an interconnected chain of organic forms. The body is viewed as similar to, though a more complex version of, other kinds of biological organisms. On the other hand, psychology, the humanities, and the social sciences explore the mind and emotions of human beings more than the physical body.

The social sciences specifically view the body as a tool for the mind to use, as an instrument at the disposal of consciousness. In social Darwinism and the functionalism of Talcott Parsons, the body enters social theory as the "biological organism"; in Marxism, the presence of the body is signified by "need" and "nature"; in symbolic interactionism, the body appears as the presentational self; in Freudianism, the body is rendered as a field of energy in the form of desire; in postmodernism, the body is a text to be "read." The social sciences are littered with discourses on the drives, needs, and instincts of the body. Because of its "unconsciouness," the body is acted upon, coerced, or constrained by external forces, including the mind. Body without mind is seen as static and inert, ultimately lifeless. In this respect, much of the social science exploration of the body is essentially Cartesian by implicitly accepting and reinforcing a mind/body dichotomy.

Inherent within the mind/body dualism is the body-as-machine metaphor. The body-as-machine metaphor suggests the body is similar to a system of moving parts with an outside energy/power source. The spring in a clock, or the heat of a steam engine, or the combustion of fuel are all familiar metaphors to explain how the body works. For example, metabolism would be interpreted as an efficient fueling of the body-machine with energy inputs and outputs measured in calories. Or the heart is like a pump, the brain is like a computer, people can be turned on or off.

Cyborgs are the epitome of this body-as-machine metaphor. Samantha Holland analyzes the pervasiveness of this aspect of the mind/body dualism in the first reading in this section, "Descartes Goes to Hollywood: Mind, Body, and Gender in Contemporary Cyborg Cinema." Holland suggests the Hollywood production of cyborg films illuminates the assumed distinctiveness and supremacy of the human mind over the body. In contests between human beings and cyborgs, men are constructed as mind while cyborgs are merely reactive, preprogrammed body/machines. The machine-enhanced bodies of the cyborgs grant them greater physical prowess and strength. While men are threatened by the technologically enhanced bodies, it is still man's mind that ultimately triumphs over the cyborg's body-as-machine. The ability to think and be reflexive elevates the status of the mind to the definition of a human being, while bodies are conquered and controlled. Cyborg films are the late twentieth century's Western interpretation and reaffirmation of the basic foundations of Cartesian dualism.

Objections to Mind/Body Dualism

There are philosophical objections though to the assumed universality of mind/body split and to its mechanistic interpretation of the body. The machine metaphor is seen as ignoring the body's ability to grow, to regenerate, and to decay. Instead, alternative propositions highlight the identifying characteristic of the body as its continual processes of transformation, suggesting the body is a self-constituting organism. The body is not a mere static machine, but is, from conception through continual decomposition after death, in a perpetual exchange process with the environment. An alternative metaphor perceives the body through the lens of a flame: "As in a burning candle, the permanence of the flame is a permanence, not of substance but of process. . . . [A]t each moment the 'body' with its 'structure' of inner and outer layers is reconstituted of materials different from the previous and following ones, so the living organism exists as a constant exchange of its own constituents and has its permanence and identity in the continuity of this process" (Jonas, 1970, p. 55).

The flame metaphor is not focused on the function of a machine in a closed system, but on the continual reconstitution of outer and inner layers. The candle and the flame are in a constant exchange of elements. The hierarchy of outer and inner is less significant than the exchange and identity formed through that exchange. The body within this metaphor is in a series of processes of becoming, inter-acting, exchanging, and producing. It is also, like the flame, frag-mented and consuming.

From this perspective, the lived body is active and helps both to create itself and to organize systems of meaning. "Consciousness" or mind is part of that created system of meaning. Bodies construct and are constructed by an interior consciousness. The philosopher Friedrich Nietzsche specifically suggests that consciousness itself should be regarded as the direct product or effect of reactive forces within the body. In his books, *On the Genealogy of Morality* and *The Will to Power*, he interprets the individual's "psychological interior" as merely the interplay of the body's forces and instincts, energies incorporated into a seemingly self-contained unit, and then second-arily constructed as the origin of thought. Nietzsche suggests that the ability to look inward, as is expected in introspection, psychology, and self-reflection, is an illusion or a fiction. The "psychic interior" is a product of the body that has been mistakenly named "mind." According to Nietzsche, Western philosophers have confused "mind" with the effects of the body, attributing cause to "mind" when in reality, consciousness is merely the outgrowth or product of the body and its energies.

Another challenge to mind/body dualism is Maurice Merleau-Ponty's exploration of the interconnections between consciousness and the body, between concepts of interiority and exteriority of the body. Three areas of Merleau-Ponty's philosophical insights are pertinent here: the examination of perception; examination of touch; and the bodily confusion experienced through "phantom limbs."

Merleau-Ponty suggests the idea of external space is understood only through its relationship to the body. Space is not grasped directly or through the senses. Instead, space is experienced through the body in its relation to objects. The movements are not simple successive mechanics of the Cartesian body-machine. Merleau-Ponty claims "the senses communicate with each other . . . my body is not a collection of adjacent organs, but a synergic system, all the func-tions of which are exercised and linked together in the general action of being in the world" (Merleau-Ponty, 1962, p. 232). For example, without mindfully thinking about each step in the process, I am able to scratch an itch or pet the cat sitting in my lap. This is true even if I extend my reach with a stick. Merleau-Ponty claims that the stick is no longer just an object for me but has been absorbed or incorporated into my perceptual field or body parts. For Merleau-Ponty, the senses can be translated into each other, or at least understood in the terms of the other senses, specifically because the body and mind are active and united. The body then is not a passive "unconscious" object.

And the same is true with the sensation of touch. The example Merleau-Ponty gives is the experience of one hand touching the other. It becomes a double sensation. They are irreducible to each other, experienced as the transformation of one position into another. (For a philosophical debate on the hierarchy or mutuality of this position, see Irigaray, 1991.) Merleau-Ponty concludes again, that the body is not an object like other objects in the world. The body senses, feels, and is aware of itself.

Merleau-Ponty's analysis of phantom limbs is the classic example of bodily awareness. A phantom limb is identified when an amputee suffers pain where a limb once was. Traditional psychology and physiology assume a fundamentally passive body, one on which the senses and perception of objects produce a reaction. Merleau-Ponty instead suggests that the body is active insofar as it gives form and sense to its own component parts and to its relations with objects in the world. A phantom limb indicates that our experiences are organized not by real objects and relations, but by the expectations and meaning objects have for the body's movements and capacities. The phantom limb indicates a fictional or fantasy construction of the body outside of or beyond its neurological structure.

Kay Toombs, author of "The Lived Experience of Disability," explores many of these issues in the second article in this section. She articulates the extendable or elastic senses of the body in her discussion of her experiences with multiple sclerosis. Her sense of space, distance, and objects, seemingly concrete and unchangeable facts of reality, is transformed for her as her physical condition both improves and deteriorates. Her wheelchair becomes a real extension of her body, her judgment of space and distances relative to the wheelchair's position and her bodily strength on that day. Her body is actively interacting with the environment. Following Merleau-Ponty's theoretical views, her body and mind are necessarily linked together in the general action of being in the world.

Sociobiology and
Evolutionary Psychology

There are other challenges to Cartesian dualism, challenges that focus on a biological explanation of the body/mind development. Instead of the philosophical position of Nietzsche or Merleau-Ponty, where the body is active in producing consciousness or "mind," there are other explanations grounded in biology where mind and consciousness are interpreted in terms of the biological brain or central nervous system. Sociobiologists and evolutionary psychologists suggest that a significant amount of human behavior, thought, and emotion is hormonally controlled or determined by our neurological structures, which are themselves genetically based and the result of evolution. These theorists assert that biological foundations generate the essential differences between human beings—differences between men and women, differences in IQs—and even provide an understanding of violence and criminal behavior.

Both disciplinary orientations maintain that the human body and mind were, in their essentials, established millions of years ago. Humans today possess the emotional and behavioral repertoire of their remote hunter-gatherer ancestors, a repertoire which is in turn shared with primates and other animals. The human brain is designed to adjust to social circumstances and, most significantly, this adjustive program is in our genes and thus shaped by natural selection. Genes are the bedrock of the relationship among mind, culture, and biology.

General critiques of sociobiology and evolutionary psychology are both methodological (doing "bad science") and ideological (ignoring cultural and social determinants). Critiquing these disciplines is not the focus of this book (but see Gowaty, 1997), yet a short summary of the critic's position is offered here. Critics assert that not all behaviors are adaptations or natural outcomes of biological evolution, and that these interpretations are in effect promoting biological determinism. Where sociobiologists or evolutionary psychologists argue for specific genetic bases for male dominance, class bias, sexual coercion, war, religion, or xenophobia, critics suggest these theorists are ignoring the pivotal role socialization and culture play in the development of human behavior. They are seen as operating on the assumption that all human behaviors are natural and immutable, that all behaviors must have had some adaptive function in the past. They are critiqued for grounding their analysis of human behavior on genes, natural selection, and evolution to explain and thus justify the status quo of patriarchy, sexism, racism, and class bias, valuing behaviors that support these structures as natural outcomes of human evolutionary history.

The basic theoretical assumptions of sociobiology and evolutionary psychology have been applied to and focused on specific human groups. A recent high-profile subject of evolutionary psychological research is the role of serotonin, a biochemical in the body which has a variety of functions. An increase or decrease in levels of serotonin is associated with a range of behaviors and conditions, including depression and links between impulsive aggressive behaviors. The theorists suggest that natural selection designed serotonin to generate certain types of behaviors. Violence and aggressive behavior were especially functional for men, who must compete and conquer other males in order to impregnate females and pass on their genes.

The serotonin thesis became controversial when it was suggested as a way to identify inner-city young men at risk of becoming violent criminals (Spallone, 1998). Inner-city violence was interpreted as the reassertion of "ancient" ways of being male in an environment where the civilized structures of society had broken down. For inner-city youths, a bad socioeconomic environment produced low serotonin levels. It was suggested that measurement of serotonin levels could be used diagnostically to identify young men inclined to violence. Once low serotonin levels were identified, intervention would become possible. A drug that raises serotonin levels could be administered. With the serotonin thesis, biological factors are considered important, in interaction with the environment and social conditions.

There are many critiques of this serotonin thesis. The solution to the problem of inner-city violence is presented as artificially raising an individual's serotonin levels. This medicalized solution is generated without questioning existing institutions and socioeconomic conditions. The site of intervention is the individual. The solution is promoted as politically neutral, offering a drug therapy to offenders or possible ones, treating the "at-risk" individual. The war on violence is played out in physiological terms, looking inward at the biological body for explanation and solutions to the human condition (Spallone, 1998).

Grouping individuals in this way raises questions about the ideology grounding the categorizations inherent in both sociobiology and evolutionary psychology. Such categories fail to recognize the variation that occurs within other categories and groups. For example, low serotonin levels in women, the upper classes, politicians, or doctors are not factors in this analysis. The practice of excluding and including is inherently social and political.

There are critics who challenge the assumptions behind both this concept of biological determinism and the opposing orientation of cultural determinism. Social theorists who focus on this nature/nurture debate are now suggesting a reworking of the debate itself. Theorists are analyzing how the boundaries between mind and body, between nature and culture, are constructed. They suggest that dividing behavior into innate or acquired traits, focusing on one or the other, prevents examination of how life experiences shape anatomy and physiology, and the ways in which physiological and anatomical differences shape behavior and experience (see Turner, 1984). These divisions constrain our ability to perceive reciprocal and mutually constructive origins. Instead of analyzing our universal biological human nature beneath the veneer of cultural diversity, these social theorists suggest we need to look at the social within the biological, and the way in which body is an interactive physiological and social entity. (For more detailed analysis of the contestation of these boundaries, see Grosz, 1994.)

Alternatives to the Mind/Body Duality

The Western division of the rational mind and mechanical body is not a universal or dominant human conceptualization. Indeed, one of the better-known representations of a balanced or complementary system is the ancient Chinese yin/yang cosmology. Here holistic thinking emphasizes the relationship of the parts to the whole instead of the hierarchy of mind over body. Harmony and interdependence is highlighted with the focus on inclusive interactions. Hierarchy is replaced with the concept of interrelationship and balance. No one entity is seen as dominating.

The Cuna Indians of Panama provide another example of alternative conceptualizations of a mind/body duality. For the Cuna, an individual's temperament is governed by a specific body part. A thief is dominated by the hand, the romantic by the heart, the intellectual by the head. In all, there are eight selves, each associated with different parts of the body (Scheper-Hughes & Lock, 1986).

While there are over five hundred tribes with variations in culture, language, and beliefs, traditional Native American conceptualization of the body generally varies from dominant Western perspectives. Carol Locust, in her exploration of the divergent systems of meaning between conventional medicine and Native American belief systems, investigated some Native Americans' perceptions of the body (Locust, 1995). She suggests that for some Navajo, the Western transplantation of donor organs such as hearts, lungs, kidneys, or corneas would be considered a crime against nature, the Creator, and fellow human beings. The recipient would be stigmatized for existing with a dead person's parts. The recipient would also be considered selfish for taking another person's body part for themselves, thus rendering the donor unable to return a body to the Creator with all its parts. Believing that bodies are merely lent to individuals for their time on Earth, the "gift" should be returned in as nearly a perfect condition as possible. Within this conceptualization, "human" is not split between a "rational" mind and an "unconscious" body, but is a unification of mind, body, and spirit. The body is not conceptualized within the mechanistic framework, a framework that emphasizes "function" as the ultimate value of the body and its organs. The body is viewed more holistically, and not merely as a mechanical device with interchangeable parts.

Another potential alternative to the mind/body dualism is emerging within the interactions in cyberspace. The body, or its absence, is central to contemporary notions of cyberspace and computer-mediated communication. It is the ability to interact with others, not as a physical presence, but as an "essence" crossing temporal, geographic, and spatial boundaries, that is one of the defining characteristics of cyberspace. Identity is performed independently of fixed bodily attributes because your physical body no longer limits who you are or can be. You are able to (re)present yourself as young or old, male or female, attractive or ugly, abled or disabled, of any color or size, in any part of the world. By losing the concreteness of the physical body and its connection to supposed naturalness and the taken-for-granted givenness of real life bodies, the assumptions guiding Western conceptualizations of the mind/body dualism can be challenged as the definition of the person. The "real" body is no longer an anchor for the mind, an instrument needing to be controlled by the mind. The discipline of the body is no longer significant when the mind can be unencumbered by physical reality. The infamous *New Yorker* cartoon, "On the internet, nobody knows you are a dog," succinctly encapsulates this challenge to unembodied presences.

Significantly though, research is showing that Cartesian dualism is not effectively challenged either in the real or virtual worlds. Studies have shown that much of the potential for online communication to challenge conventional interpretation is not realized as interactions are geared toward "re-connecting and re-fixing bodies and identities" (Slater, 1998, p. 92). For instance, individuals and online communities put their photos on Web sites, or people who meet in chat rooms exchange electronic images of themselves. People online also seek each other out to meet in real life, either individually or in groups. And as is analyzed in this section's first reading, "Descartes Goes to Hollywood: Mind, Body, and Gender in Contemporary Cyborg Cinema," science fiction is also reproducing the status quo, reestablishing the mind as the definition of the person. Identity is still constructed through the mind/body dualism. While people may form bonds through disembodied interaction in cyberspace, the concreteness of the body is still sought. Bodily attributes such as gender markers are still perceived as stable identifiers. The markers are used to anchor the disembodied voice, the "real" body perceived as manifesting the outcome of the battle between temptations, sensations, indulgences, and the mind's control of rational thought. RoboCop, Terminator, Picard/Locutus, and most of the various chat rooms all reinforce the mind/body duality and the accompanying gender distinctions. At the beginning of the twenty-first century, mind/body and gender distinctions are being reproduced despite the challenges that have been made to those constructs.

SAMANTHA HOLLAND

1 Descartes Goes to Hollywood

Mind, Body, and Gender in Contemporary Cyborg Cinema

Cyborgs are cybernetic beings, a technologically in-
spired combination of the human body and machine.
Samantha Holland applies insights from analyses of
the Cartesian mind/body dualism to this genre of
science fiction films, focusing specifically on the
formulaic distinctions displayed between humans
and cyborgs. Analysis of the films illustrates how
the machine basis of the cyborgs, while they may
be physically stronger and faster, are represented
as ultimately inferior to the human soul/mind.
Through her analysis, Holland highlights the taken-
for-granted assumptions that support the mind/
body dualism, demonstrating how the films continually reaffirm the human mind as containing the
unique identity of the human being. Holland shows
how cyborgs, because they are portrayed as just
bodies, become merely animated automatons that
ultimately fail to eliminate humanity. The male
rational mind, the epitome of Cartesianism, is
shown to conquer both male and female cyborg
bodies every time.

From Samantha Holland, "Descartes Goes to Hollywood: Mind, Body, and Gender
in Contemporary Cyborg Cinema," in *Cyberspace/Cyberbodies/Cyberpunk:
Cultures of Technological Embodiment (Theory, Culture, and Society)*, ed.
Michael Featherstone and Roger Burrows (Thousand Oaks, CA: Sage Publications, 1995), 157–61, 162–74. Reprinted by permission of Sage Publications.

Many contemporary films take up and enter into the traditionally philosophical debates surrounding the so-called "mind-body problem" and the nature of the human "self," but few do so more explicitly than those centering on the representation of what is popularly referred to as a cyborg.[1] With their human/machine hybrids, these films foreground questions of dualism and personal identity especially clearly and highlight contemporary concerns about the effects of technology on the human "self" in the present and the future. The cyborg film is particularly interesting when considering the relationship between the Cartesian (or Cartesian-influenced) dualisms of traditional philosophy and those dualisms of gender that, arguably, underlie and inform such a conceptual division.

The cyborg film is a generic hybrid that draws primarily on the genres of science fiction, action, and horror and uses images of the technologized body to investigate questions of "self"-hood, gender, the "mind-body problem" and the threats posed to such concepts by postmodern technology and AI (artificial intelligence). Of course the current fascination with cyborgs per se is not limited to the cinema: there are numerous "cyberpunk" comics, novels, and video games in circulation, for example. I will be concentrating on films in my discussion, though—primarily because they epitomize so well the contemporary concerns about strong AI, or technology more generally, "taking over" and rendering humans and humanness in some sense redundant.[2] Further, while I will discuss a number of cyborg films in this paper—*RoboCop 3, Cyborg, R.O.T.O.R., RoboC.H.I.C., Hardware, Cherry 2000, Universal Soldier*—my arguments will focus on the *Terminator* films, the first two *RoboCop* films, and *Eve of Destruction*.

In concentrating on the cyborg film, I will be addressing questions of what it is, or means, to be human in an age where the boundaries between humans and machines are becoming increasingly difficult to define and sustain (Best, 1989). The relevance of such images to the "mind-body problem" is self-evident, with a proliferation of central questions such as that of whether the individual "self" remains when his (*sic*)[3] brain and central nervous system are transplanted into a mechanical body, or whether a "completely artificial" cyborg can be in any sense human: these are, indeed, the central questions of *Terminator 2, Eve of Destruction,* and the *RoboCop* films. I will also be highlighting the way in which no longer self-evident gender differences are displaced "on to the more remarkable difference between the human and the other" (Penley, 1990, 123) in the cyborg film, as part of its attempt to reaffirm and secure the basis of traditional dualisms. A central concern of this paper, in fact, is to show that the cyborg film's continuing engagement with the "mind-body problem" and concepts of the "self" reveals a great deal about the issues of gender at stake in the traditional philosophical positions it often (re)presents,[4] and to which it sometimes represents a challenge.

Representations of Dualism and Materialism

At *RoboCop's* most obvious level of narrative, the "bad guys," Omni Consumer Products (OCP), are identified with an unquestioning, strongly materialist position, and it is OCP against which Murphy/RoboCop (Peter Weller) has to battle to recuperate and reassert his "self"-identity. OCP assumes that once Murphy has been recycled as RoboCop, they can eradicate his personal identity by programming it out of existence (by re/programming his brain). Some weight is given to this materialist view because it is articulated when RoboCop has just failed to arrest the corrupt Jones, and this inability is because such an attempt is a "product violation" which causes automatic shutdown. However, the (Cartesian) point *is* that although he is limited by his programming, he nevertheless retains the *will* to arrest Jones: the sequence in fact ultimately restores the dualistic position, as it is RoboCop's *body* that is actually disabled by the "product violation," while his mental desire to resist appears to be unaffected.

At the end of *RoboCop*, the Old Man has to sack Jones to enable RoboCop to shoot him. This shows that RoboCop is still partly controlled by OCP's programming, despite his emphatic closing assertion that he is "Murphy." In *RoboCop 2*, however, RoboCop finally finds a way to eradicate all his programming: after being reprogrammed to the point of uselessness (with directives like "Avoid making premature value judgments," and "Avoid interpersonal conflicts"), he apparently retains so strong a will to escape that he "fries" himself on power cables when he hears that a huge electric current—while potentially fatal—might rid his brain of all the programmed directives. This clearly implies that RoboCop has an "inner" desire to break free from his programming, although that very programming has rendered him unable to *articulate* such feelings. The suggestion that there is something which will enable humans to maintain control over their own bodies and technology in the face of such extreme adversity as the *RoboCop* films represent is a common one in contemporary cinema (Best, 1989).

The *Terminator* also asserts a very Cartesian picture of the mind-body problem, although it uses the cyborg in a very different way. The Terminator is *not* endowed with the status of human precisely because it is a purely *material*(ist) object with no self-identity. While *Terminator 2* makes some attempt to "humanize" one of the Terminators by concentrating on how it can learn from human companions, the type of autonomous self-identity of the Cartesian "self" constantly eludes it, as it always relies on its programming. Significantly, it never really *understands* why John Connor will not let it kill human beings, although it obeys his orders and refrains from so doing. This is hardly surprising, given the film's own Cartesianism: after all, a Cartesian "self" (or "soul") cannot be *acquired*—it is a mysterious "something" that comes from "elsewhere" to inhabit the body.[5] Also, the T1000 model—the antagonist in *Terminator 2*—emphatically embodies the superficial nature of a cyborg's "identity" by constantly changing its appearance.

The cyborg-wife in *Cherry 2000* is in this sense very similar to the Terminators: her whole "identity" is held in one (very expensive) microchip, and while her husband in some sense sees a particular *type* of body as necessary to her continued identity, the *particular* body is clearly no more an integral or constitutive part of her than are clothes and makeup. Here, we can begin to see exactly how much the bodies of cyborgs *do* in fact matter. After all, if we look at the Terminator, RoboCop, Eve 8 (in *Eve of Destruction*), or Cherry 2000, it is clear that each and everyone of them has a highly gendered appearance in addition to the fact that they *have* bodies—rather than just minds/computers—at all. While it may be understandable that cyborgs have humanoid bodies and even the appearance of human beings—especially when they are used as "infiltration units"—this does *not* in itself fully explain or justify the highly muscled and exaggeratedly gendered nature of their bodies. Rather, the cyberbodies are represented in such a highly gendered way to counter the threat that cyborgs indicate the loss of human bodies, where such a loss implies the loss of the gendered distinctions that are essential to maintaining the patriarchal order (which is based on exploiting difference)—a point to which I will return later.

The fears concerning technology in the cyborg film appear to be two-fold—representing both fears that human beings will be *replaced* by, and that we are *becoming*, machines (Best, 1989, 51). However, as both Steve Best and J. P. Telotte point out, the films simultaneously operate to deny the possibility of these things actually occurring by dramatizing the resilience of the subject, and juxtaposing "the *dystopic* projection of a hyperalienated future . . . with a *utopic* hope for spiritual survival, salvation, and redemption" (Best, 1989, 51). The films endow pure consciousness with some kind of "redemptive power," and visualize a "testimony to the ghost in the machine" (Telotte, 1988, 256). But as Yvonne Tasker (1993, 151) has noted, "[w]hen all else fails, the body of the hero, and not his voice, or his capacity to make a rational argument, is the place of last resort"—the sole space that is safe, as it were. And this—the last resort to the body—remains "even" in cyborg films (and others) that ostensibly work to (re)assert the Cartesian superiority of the "mind" over the body.

The cyborg film represents purely mechanical/technological alternatives to cyborgs as inferior—especially when comparing them to cyborgs with a "self." This again suggests the importance attributed to the body on a *visual* level despite ostensive narrative concerns to remain with the "mind." For instance, the *RoboCop* films represent all the purely robotic alternatives to RoboCop as inferior: an ED 209 malfunctions, killing Kinney, shortly after Jones introduces him as "the future of law-enforcement" in OCP's board room. It is further coded as inferior when it is unable to navigate the stairs to follow RoboCop, and ends up falling down them, flailing helplessly. ED 209s are compared with RoboCop in *RoboCop 2*, as well, where they are implemented throughout the city during the police strike despite "widespread complaints of their malfunction." In *RoboCop 3*, an ED 209 is further ridiculed; a young girl hooks up her PC to it, and thus takes control of it—saving her fellow citizens and turning it against the police. Also—and significantly for the role of masculinity in these films—the other cyborgs in *RoboCop 2* are far less (coded as) male/masculine than RoboCop: the two whose "suicides" we see briefly on videotape have recognizably human-shaped "bodies," but lack the excessively masculine coding of the original RoboCop. And Cain's robotic body is also less masculine-looking—it is bigger than RoboCop's, but more like an ED 209 than a man.

"Things Are Not Always What They Seem"

An implication of the cyborg film is that being human is anything but *simply* a matter of appearance. In most cases a "genuine" human mind is identified as the essential element of a human person: and a mind is precisely what we are told RoboCop and the Universal Soldiers have retained, and what the Terminators and Cherry 2000 never had and cannot acquire. The whole issue of appearance and its (un)reliability is central to the cyborg film, of course, which ostensibly operates to warn us that "Things are not always what they seem" (McQuade [Gregory Hines] in *Eve of Destruction*). Despite such narrative assertions, however, the films' own attitude to the importance of bodies makes their position ambivalent: after all, the body does seem to provide some level of certainty insofar as it *is* the site on and over which battles for "self"-hood are fought.

The Terminator's otherness is already apparent because of the *computerized* images that represent its point of view. This emphasizes the extent to which the Terminators do not "see" as we do—where "seeing" has both literal and metaphorical weight. In the case of RoboCop and the protagonists of *Universal Soldier*, a computerized image is not always used to represent their point of view. Rather, as the narratives progress, and the protagonists become "more human," computerized imagery gives way to a more "normal" representation of vision. This "normal" vision that is a mark of humanness is shared by Eve 8. Also, once the (original) Terminator has lost its human appearance and its machine-skeleton is revealed (after Kyle blows it up), its point of view shots are no longer computerized. This is primarily because we no longer need this kind of "proof" that the Terminator is a machine because we can now *see* that to be so. However, the change still provides a problematic: there is no simplistic and generalized way in which to read the use of computerized versus "normal" vision in the cyborg film. One constant feature, though, is that only cyborgs endowed with a "self" by the narrative have dreams and/or flashbacks—which are always represented as uncomputerized images with epistemological authority. *None* of the Terminators are allowed this kind of "vision." This lack brands them as inhuman, where humanness is apparently marked by having (or "being," in Eve 8's case) an unconscious and/or conscious memory to provide such images—images like those experienced by RoboCop, who, in *RoboCop 3*, thanks Dr. Lazarus for not erasing his "memories". . . .[6]

The Pain of Being Human

The concept of pain—a common theme in the philosophy of "mind"—is invoked as a sure signifier of humanness in the cyborg film. RoboCop feels both emotional and physical pain. He suffers anguish when he sees or remembers his wife and son, and is clearly upset whenever he finds his actions restricted by his programming. In addition, physical pain is something that is blatantly foregrounded in the *RoboCop* films. The most insistent instances are of RoboCop's pain in each of the first two films' mutilation sequences: in the original *RoboCop*, the entire cyborg narrative is initiated when Boddicker's gang tortures Murphy almost to death, allowing for his recycling as "RoboCop." In *RoboCop 2,* the scenes in which RoboCop is ripped apart by Cain's gang echo this original sequence, and as some oil-like substance splatters from his mechanical insides onto his baby-like face, RoboCop's screams leave us in little doubt as to whether or not he still feels pain. Moreover, RoboCop's technician rejects OCP's claim that he's "just a piece of equipment," saying "Don't tell me he can't suffer," and responding to the argument that he's merely "electrical" with a vehement "Bullshit." She further insists that "He's suffering" because "his pain centers are alive" and "lit up like Christmas tree lights."

In direct contrast, the human-*looking* cyborgs in the *Terminator* films feel no pain of any sort. This is asserted very clearly in the first film, and its significance as a differentiating factor between humans and machines is underlined when Sarah bites Kyle (Michael Biehn) and he tells her that "Cyborgs don't feel pain. I do." Emotional pain is also used as a signifier of humanness in *The Terminator*. Sarah is horrified when Kyle says that "Pain can be controlled. You just disconnect." She asks him, then, "So you feel nothing?"—to which he responds with a declaration of love, saying: "John Connor gave me a picture of you once . . . I came across time for you, Sarah. I love you—I always have." This display of emotion—sited in a context of discussing human pain—reveals what it is that the cyborg film identifies as a central difference between humans and machines: that is, human desire (where this is something that the Terminators, along with Cherry 2000 and the *Hardware* cyborg, clearly do not have, while cyborgs who were created "from" human subjects—such as RoboCop, Eve 8, and the cyborg in *Cyborg*—do retain it in some form). In *Terminator 2*, cyborgs' inability to feel pain is overtly articulated when John Connor asks the "good" Terminator whether he feels pain. The cyborg's response is that "I sense injuries. The data could be called pain"—but it precisely *isn't* pain in the human sense that John means it. The same applies to emotional pain in the films, where both "bad" Terminators clearly have no feelings at all (not even of aggression), and the limits of the "good" Terminator's ability to learn about such things are revealed when he tells John that "I know now why you cry, but it is something that I can never do."

Whatever the individual cyborg's inability to feel pain in these movies, it *always* has the ability to *inflict* pain through physical violence. The cyborg film constantly foregrounds physical violence—and especially physical violence directed towards *bodies*. This points to the cyborg film's concern with the human body, where the *visual* nature of this theme is paramount, as "physical pain defies language" (Codell, 1989, 12) in the way that so many of our experiences of "self" seem to do.

The significance of gender to the inability to feel pain in the cyborg film cannot be ignored. While bullets bounce off the masculine-coded Terminators and RoboCops (although they are not invincible),[7] and the Universal Soldiers deal with their wounds by cauterizing them with cigarette lighters, Eve 8 feels pain when she is shot, and Cherry 2000 and RoboC.H.I.C. are far from immune to bullet wounds. The sexualized resonance of this cannot be missed when we consider that bullets cannot *penetrate* RoboCop when his adversaries yell "Fuck you!" at him, while Eve 8 is not only shot, but we see shots of her breasts when she tends to the injury in her motel room. There are other comparisons to be made here—such as that between the Terminator's dealing with his injuries at a sink and Eve 8's actions in a similar situation: they are both cyborgs, but the Terminator feels no pain as he pulls his eye out and gouges his arm open, while Eve 8 flinches—despite the fact that her biological system is, according to Eve, "entirely cosmetic." Also, while Sarah Connor is represented as a good fighter, she is constantly penetrated by both bullets and metal shards (parts of the Terminators) in both *Terminator* films; that is, her success in "battle" is always qualified or undermined by injury—the sexual resonance of which is hard to avoid, especially given the "obviously phallic" nature of the Schwarzenegger Terminator.[8]

Examples like these suggest that Tasker (1993, 19) is quite right to hold that:

> In crude terms, if images of men have often needed to compensate for the sexual presentation of the hero's body through emphasizing his activity, then images of women seem to need to compensate for the figure of the active heroine by emphasizing her sexuality, her availability within traditional feminine terms.[9]

Certainly, the male/masculine-coded cyborgs are decidedly *a*sexual: the Terminators have no conception of sexual desire, and RoboCop is on several occasions reminded that he can no longer be "a proper husband" to his/Murphy's wife. In contrast, while E. (Melanie Griffith, in *Cherry 2000*) asserts that "I am not a fucking machine," that is precisely what Cherry 2000 *is*. And the sexualization of Eve 8 could hardly be more blatant: McQuade even blames her violence on Eve the scientist's "teenage sex fantasies," and misogynistically yells: "So this device of yours is horny as well as psychopathic—that's quite a combination in a woman."

The Gendered Body of the Cyborg Film

In foregrounding the concept of pain and pointing to the relation between human bodies and manufactured bodies, the cyborg film displays a decidedly *un*Cartesian emphasis not only on the *body*, but on its *constructed* nature. A paradox is at play here: as Claudia Springer (1991, 303) puts it, "while disparaging the human body, the [cyborg] discourse simultaneously uses language and imagery associated with the body and bodily functions to represent its vision of human/technological perfection." This paradox is imbued with a number of gendered implications, too, which are unavoidable given the centrality of gendered body-imagery to the cyborg film. If cyborgs, in transgressing the boundaries between human and machine, are indeed "the consummate postmodern concept" (Springer, 1991, 306) it should follow that cyborg films are the consummate postmodern texts. However, despite the arguments of theorists such as Donna Haraway (1990) that cyborgs are androgynous entities that render gender boundaries meaningless, this is effectively irrelevant when we look at *actual* cyborg texts. In actual cyborg films, while boundary breakdowns between humans and technology are enthusiastically explored, "gender boundaries are

treated less flexibly," with cyborgs tending, in fact, "to appear masculine or feminine to an exaggerated degree" (Springer, 1991, 308,
309).

The mere titles of many cyborg films often imply that gender
is their primary concern. *Cherry 2000, RoboC.H.I.C.*, and *Eve of Destruction* all have sexual connotations and explicitly foreground
issues of the constructed nature of gender identity. And *Cyborg*,
despite its title, turns out to be little more than a Jean-Claude Van
Damme vehicle, where the assertion of a violent but ultimately
"good" masculinity is what is really at stake.

It is difficult to argue against reading the cyborg film as uphold-
ing often stereotypical and exaggerated gender differences at both a
narrative and visual level. The representation of cyborg (and other)
males in the cyborg film clearly fits with Steve Neale's theory that
violence displaces male sexuality (in our homophobic culture) by
undermining any notion of the male body as passive spectacle
through narrative intervention which justifies the camera's objectifying gaze by making him the object or perpetrator of violent action
(Neale, 1983). In light of this, with characters such as the Terminator
and RoboCop epitomizing filmic images of near-invincible soldiers,
Springer (1991, 317) claims that the cyborg film reveals "an intense
crisis in the construction of masculinity." That is, integrating men
(sic) with technology in the image of the hyper-masculine cyborg
operates to "shore up the masculine subject against the onslaught of
a femininity feared by patriarchy"—a femininity so feared, Springer
(1991, 318) suggests, that to avoid it the male body is transformed
into something which is no longer really human. This creates an
ambivalent relationship between masculinity and the male body—to
which patriarchy responds by suggesting that there is an essential
masculinity that *transcends* the body; and this, of course, is precisely what traditional philosophy has always insisted upon.
Descartes's own assertions, after all, rested purely on his mental
activity and did not *necessitate* his actual physical existence.

However, there are complexities surrounding the representation
of gender in the films: they are not simply stereotypical representations of masculine men and feminine women. Most notably, the
pumped-up hyper-masculine bodies of the male cyborgs can be read
either as straight reassertions of hegemonic masculinity, *or* as hys-
terical over-compensations for a masculinity in crisis (Tasker, 1993;
Creed, 1993). And the centrality of the figure of the bodybuilder

(male and female) in the cyborg film cycle often deconstructs the stabilities of gendered identity that the narratives work to ensure—with the result that an either/or reading of gender and its representation is completely inadequate. The constructedness of the cyborg itself implies the constructedness of gender, and Tasker (1993, 77) suggests that "[t]he combination of passivity and activity in the figure of the bodybuilder as action star, is central to the articulation of gendered identity in the films in which they appear," where such a figure combines "qualities associated with masculinity and femininity, qualities which gender theory maintains in a polarized binary. . . ."

There are similar problems in the *Terminator* films' representation of Sarah Connor and other women. While its "authors" (director James Cameron and producer Gale Ann Hurd) claim that the *Terminator* films are in fact feminist, Sarah's being a "strong" woman is hardly adequate grounds for such a claim. Her strength is anyway qualified by and contained within the patriarchal structures of the films, and other women characters are frequently coded as highly feminine "bimbos" (such as her roommate, Ginger). And even if Kyle is a physically small—and sexually innocent—man, he is still the one who teaches Sarah how to fight, and has epistemological superiority throughout most of the film. But most significant, I think, is that while Sarah is the one who eventually destroys the Terminator —supposedly a feminist statement in itself—it is Kyle who first blows it up (twice), removing its human-seeming shell and thus its "masculinity." The result is, as Margaret Goscilo (1987–1988, 49) so lucidly points out, that Sarah's destruction of the Terminator "has none of the sexualized, gender-specific charge of [its] own pursuit of her. What she destroys is no longer Schwarzenegger's recognizably male persona but a neuter machine run amok."

The central fear seems to be that in a possible cyborg future, biological gender would disappear, rendering patriarchy's centrally constituting hierarchy of masculine over feminine untenable. So, asserting an essential masculinity simultaneously with an essential humanity seems imperative, as the resulting masculine nature of the "purely" mental provides a "transcendental masculinity"—ensuring that even with no biological gender the hegemony of masculinity can be sustained. This of course runs into complications when we consider the cyborg film's implication that a cyborg with no biological mother is denied human status—or any real "self"-hood—while cyborgs who started out as human beings retain such a status. This in itself supports Mary Ann Doane's contention that the representations of cyborg films—or, in fact, science fiction films more generally—are concerned not so much with production as with *re*production (Doane, 1990, 164).

There is a clear history of (male) desire to create life without the mother—from Adam and Eve and *Metropolis* to contemporary films such as *Frankenhooker, Weird Science, Junior*, and the cyborg film. This "womb envy" (Doane, 1990, 169) is apparent in the cyborg film where narrative structures juxtapose the questions of biological and technological reproduction. Such structures are "provocative," Doane points out (1990, 169), because the technologies thus represented "threaten to put into crisis the very possibility of the question of origins, the Oedipal drama and the relation between subjectivity and knowledge that it supports." The suggestion is that *motherhood* is feared by (patriarchal) masculinity because it deconstructs conceptual boundaries between "self" and "other"—throwing into question traditional assumptions about "self"-hood and personal identity—and that technology is thus looked to to control, limit, and regulate the maternal. However, Doane also asserts that an ambivalence occurs because as well as being frightening, the concept of motherhood ensures a fair degree of epistemological *certainty*—it is the mother who guarantees at least the *possibility* of certain historical knowledge. The tension between envious fear of and epistemological reliance on the maternal is clearly at play in the cyborg film's representations of gender and human/machine interaction, with the insistent presence of cyber*bodies*—despite the simultaneous assertion of an essential "humanness" that transcends the body. Such tension is clearly a motivating factor in the appropriation of the maternal function represented by the "good" Terminator in *Terminator 2*, and in the "masculinization" of Eve the scientist in *Eve of Destruction*, as I will discuss below.

Fe/males, Re/production and the Primal Scene

The role of women as mothers is certainly a central theme in the cyborg film. Sarah Connor is the "mother of the future" in the *Terminator* films, and her representation centers around that role. Despite her other roles, Sarah's main function in the films is, it seems, to keep herself alive so that she can have her son and then ensure that he survives: her valuing of him over herself is made clear in *Terminator 2* when she reprimands him for coming to rescue her from the asylum, asserting that he is more important than her.[10] It seems that Sarah's sexuality and gender are subordinated to her reproductive function to a considerable extent. Even more alarming, though, is the way in which the "good" Terminator takes over Sarah's role in *Terminator 2*. As Susan Jeffords (1993, 248–49) illustrates, because the Terminator moves from being the source of humanity's annihilation to the "*single* guarantor of its continuation," it becomes "not only the protector of human life, but its generator. By 'giving' John Connor his life, the Terminator takes, in effect, Sarah Connor's place as his mother." As if to add insult to injury, Sarah herself describes the Terminator thus: "It would die to protect [John]. Of all the would-be fathers who came and went over the years, this machine, this thing, was the only one who measured up." And when Sarah *is* given a chance to speak out against masculine birth compensation, it is couched in near-hysterical terms ("Fucking men like you built the hydrogen bomb. . . . You think you're so creative"), and her own son stops her in her tracks, telling her that "We need to be a little more constructive here" (Jeffords, 1993, 252).

Eve of Destruction is especially alarming in its play with the concept of motherhood: it seems by the close of the narrative that Eve has *rejected* her role as (Timmy's) biological mother *and* as (Eve 8's) technological mother, because she both destroys Eve 8—and with it her own unconscious revolt—and does not seem to know or care where her son has gone: she is more intent on helping McQuade limp out of the subway(!). This ending is quite bizarre, in that it seems to have radically "masculinized" Eve; it is certainly unable to allow her to retain both creative *and* procreative abilities.

Constance Penley (1990, 119) investigates the operations and significance of the time-loop paradox in *The Terminator*, arguing that the film "is as much about time as it is about machines." Her consequent assertion that "[t]he idea of returning to the past to generate an event that has already made an impact on one's identity lies at the core of the time-loop paradox story" (Penley, 1990, 119) seems reasonable enough—especially considering that the paradox is frequently described as "the grandfather paradox" in scientific discussions of the concept. This gives further weight to her "feminist" reading of how the narrative serves as a masculine fantasy of omnipotence and self-creation for John Connor (whose primal scene is illustrated in *The Terminator*). Penley reads *The Terminator*'s use of the time-loop paradox as undermining any feminist potential of the film, as she sees it as representing John Connor's fantasy of orchestrating his own primal scene. This again limits Sarah Connor's role to being primarily that of John's mother—which is what Penley finds objectionable and regressive about the film. She holds that because *The Terminator* continues in the sci-fi tradition "to dissipate the fear of the same, to ensure that there is a difference" in gendered terms, it ultimately (re)presents "a conservative moral lesson about maternity, futuristic or otherwise: mothers will be mothers, and they will always be women" (Penley, 1990, 175).

However, Penley's reading comes under attack from Mark Jancovich (1992), who suggests that the narrative does not *necessitate* our reading it as John Connor's story—in fact, he claims that this is hard to do because he is never *seen* in the film. I find Jancovich's point interesting, but not entirely convincing: first, it immediately privileges *sight* by stating that John Connor is a less important character because he is not seen. Also, while it is true that Sarah Connor is "associated with the maternal while also performing activities usually restricted to men" (Jancovich, 1992:11), this alone does not make *The Terminator* a feminist film—especially when, as I have mentioned above, Sarah's "masculine" attributes are constantly undermined and made decidedly secondary to her role as John's mother. And, while I accept the argument that *The Terminator*'s primal scene is not *necessarily* orchestrated by John Connor, but could be read as *Sarah's* wish-fulfillment, I remain skeptical. First, the film's generally stereotypical and sexist representations undermine this reading, which does not fit in with the film as a whole. Second, "masculinizing" Sarah is anyway not a feminist move: as Luce Irigaray has written: "women merely 'equal' to men would be 'like them,' and therefore not women" (cited in Sellers, 1991, 71). Representing "masculine" women is far from being feminist, as it fails to adequately deconstruct the basic dualism of gender constructed and sustained by the patriarchal order.

The original *Terminator* film does not play havoc with the time-loop paradox in the way that the second film does in its attempt to represent a more "positive" ending (Jancovich, 1992, 14). While the first film merely violates the causality principle in the way that many scientists see as entirely plausible (Parker, 1992), the second film violates its *own* logic because, if the future has changed, its characters' own pasts cannot have existed. The strength that Jancovich (1992, 14) identifies as that of the first film, then—"that its presentation of time as a cycle does not imply a subjectless determinism"—is lost in *Terminator 2*: the later film fails to assert that the past and future are dependent on each other. Jancovich likens *The Terminator* to John Wyndham's short story, "Chronoclasm." Both narratives, he points out, challenge the very idea of a chronoclasm by illustrating the *interdependence* of past and future, rather than suggesting that events would *change* with the advent of time-travel (Jancovich, 1992, 13). Also, both stories point to the importance of human *desire*, which exists precisely because the "self" is unrealizable without continual interaction with others: this is what differentiates the Terminators from humans, and is what motivates Kyle to come back through time to rescue Sarah and her (their) unborn son.

Maurice Merleau-Ponty (1992, 415) asserts a necessary connection between subjectivity and temporality, arguing that time is "not an object of our knowledge, but a dimension of our being." The Terminators—who last just as long as their batteries do—have no conscious relation to time, just as they have no *conscious* motivations, or consciousness at all. The emphasis on memories (whether conscious or unconscious) and relations with others, then, are obvious marks of humanness in the cyborg film. And both these concepts require a "self" that interacts with other people *in time*. The primal scene narrative enacted in and by *The Terminator* suggests the human desire to control time; and, while it shows that human beings cannot *change* events, it shows how important their (our) decisions are to events in the world. The cyborg film—along with other "dystopic future" films—is clearly revealed as critiquing not only possible futures, but also the present. These films clearly cite present human actions and decisions as heavily responsible for our future, and especially for our dystopic visions of that future.

Conclusions

I would firmly agree with Telotte (1988) that the cyborg film embodies a reaction against the increasingly popular acceptance of the mind-brain identity theory, both because of worries at the thought of strong AI and because of resistance to collapsing such traditionally distinct conceptual categories as human and machine—especially with all their gendered implications. The films

I have looked at certainly try to (re)assert fairly radical forms of dualisms, shoring up both humanness and masculinity against the postmodern fears of encroaching technology and femininity (a strange pairing!). However, despite resting on distinctly Cartesian assumptions, they come up with no advance on Descartes's *Meditations* as to how or where the mysterious "link" is between the "mind" and the "body."

As David Porush (1985, 85) has pointed out in regard to "cybernetic fiction," "[t]he most primitive response to the threat of cybernetics is paranoia." The same appears to be true of the cyborg film and other cyborg texts in the postmodern age. Porush makes the link between cybernetics and paranoia very clear—suggesting that it is essentially because cybernetics *threatens* to, and paranoia is *threatened by*, "control through the forces beyond the power of the individual" (Porush, 1985, 85). In the gendered context of the cyborg film, this paranoia is perhaps more understandable than if we take it as "just" a response to the purely technophobic threats posed by AI, postmodern medicine, and technological advances in general. After all, a rejection of AI in favor of some kind of unique *human* being tends to privilege the body and women more than has traditionally been the case. And if the fear of losing the human "self" is closely linked to that of losing the masculine nature of the philosophical/cultural subject, then paranoia is to be expected. The cyborg film *narrative* operates as a *myth* to reassert the "mind-body" dualism and those of sex and gender that parallel it, where its ideological aims are achieved by first illustrating the materialist position, and then showing it to be inadequate, naive, and in some sense "morally wrong." The patriarchal bias of the narrative comes into play because Cartesian dualism is held up as the (only) viable alternative to materialism, and this belies the cyborg film's visual suggestions that the "self" is in fact a unified "body-subject."

The cyborg film, in accepting and therefore worrying about the computer/mind analogy (and thus the machine/human analogy), extends already considerable concerns about "our ambivalent feelings about technology, our increasing anxieties about our own nature in a technological environment," to include its own "kind of evolutionary fear that these artificial selves may presage our disappearance or *termination*" (Telotte, 1992, 26). This creates complex problems and contradictions for the cyborg film and its response to the perceived threat from the cyborg and all that it represents.

So, despite an apparent narrative concern to (re)assert dualisms of mind/body, male/female, and masculine/feminine, I conclude that such a project is often undermined by several visual elements and devices of the cyborg film. At the level of representation, the cyborg film suggests that the gendered human body is as central to constituting "self"-hood and personal identity as is the individual "mind," making the distinction between "mind" and "body" a virtually impossible one. In the end, though, it is difficult to make assertions regarding *unspoken* implications about the body-subject in the cyborg film. The endings of these films, while often unconvincing, still make it hard to avoid the recuperative functions of their stories and narrative structure.

Clearly, the "mind-body problem" is a central issue in the cyborg film, whose narrative tends to reassert an essentially mental, Cartesian "self" over any materialist conception of selfhood. And while various devices operate to align the audience with the Cartesian rather than materialist position, the centrality of the *body* in these films tends to undermine the narrative emphasis on the disembodied "self," rendering the films' own position riddled with ambiguity and uncertainty. Such confusion is often mirrored in the cyborg film's gender representations, which, in an attempt to reassert a hegemonic masculinity, raise questions about the stability of that very concept and its traditional justifications. So, despite the fact that it is ironic that "a debate over gender and sexuality finds expression in the context of the cyborg, an entity that makes sexuality, gender, even humankind itself, anachronistic" (Springer, 1991, 322), it is clear that issues of gender *do* in fact underlie and inform the narrative concerns and visual representations of the cyborg film, and by implication underlie many of our contemporary fears about the future.

NOTES

1. The term "cyborg"—standing for cybernetic organism—is not really the proper name for what popular culture refers to as cyborgs: a human being *is* a cybernetic organism, after all. The cyborgs in these films, then, "should" rather be called *symbiotes* to denote the human/machine hybrids represented by Terminators, RoboCops, etc. However, having noted this technical "inaccuracy," I will continue to refer to symbiotes as cyborgs, accepting the popular use of the term (which, arguably, is now correct anyway, given that most people regard "cyborg" as denoting a human/machine hybrid).
2. I am not implying here that such concerns are exclusively contemporary. Indeed, such concerns have been central to a wide variety of genres—

literary as well as cinematic—for a very long time (Doane, 1990; Franklin, 1990; Geduld, 1975; Porush, 1985; Telotte, 1988). However, as my discussion is of a group of very recent films (1980s and 1990s), I *am* suggesting that many of the particular concerns represented in and through them are in some sense exclusively contemporary—primarily when they deal explicitly with *new* advances in technology.

3. "He" is the appropriate subject here, as the films which deal explicitly with this issue are the *RoboCop* trilogy, which of course involve a(n originally human) male protagonist.

4. Here I am referring to a wide range of dualisms, from radical Cartesian rationalist forms to the more body-oriented dualisms espoused by philosophers such as Henri Bergson. Effectively, many of my references to Descartes refer to the range of appropriations and inflations of his views that have occurred in the history of western philosophy, rather than to only his views per se.

5. Despite my assumptions here, it *could* perhaps be argued that *Terminator 2* does in fact suggest that the "good" Terminator does in some sense acquire a "soul" of sorts. For instance, it takes on the role of John Connor's "father"; it learns how to use colloquialisms (and therefore not be "such a dork all the time," as John Connor puts it); and could be said to "die" rather than merely be "terminated," because, as Forest Pyle writes (1993, 240), "the Schwarzenegger terminator sacrifices himself in order to prevent the possibility that any prototypes or computer chips from this deadly technology would remain," going against John Connor's wishes for the first time—thus committing its most "human" act of all. However, I remain skeptical: first, it seems that its humanity is more of a projection (by John Connor) than an actuality. Second, when the Terminator tells John that "I understand now why you cry, but it is something I can never do," there seems to me to be a hint that he cannot ever cry precisely because he does not really, fully understand human emotions. Either way, Pyle is certainly right to observe that this illustrates how far the film's "knotting of human and cyborg is inextricable," and that it responds to the original film by making "the triumph of humans and humanism . . . dependent on the humanizing of cyborgs" (1993, 240).

6. The area of memories and emotions is an area in which a discussion of the cyborg film overlaps most obviously with discussions about *Blade Runner*. Some people regard *Blade Runner* as a cyborg film, in fact, and have suggested that I might include it in my discussion. However, there are two (main) reasons for my decision to avoid its inclusion. First, the replicants of *Blade Runner* are, it seems, *not* cyborgs: they are effectively, human beings, and *not* in any real sense hybrids of human and technological "parts." The whole point is that the only way in which their "inhumanity" can be detected is by revealing their lack of a (genuine) childhood (and the genuine memories that go along with it). It is not a question of their having mechanical parts! So, essentially, I feel that the central concerns examined by *Blade Runner* revolve more around genetic engineering than they do around cybernetics. Second, I feel that *Blade Runner* has already been written about to the point of exhausting the possibilities for further real insight! After all, not only numerous articles, but entire books have been published on the film (e.g. Kerman, 1991).

7. It is interesting that while RoboCop is seemingly inpenetrable so far as bullets are concerned (unlike "female" cyborgs), he *is* relatively more vulnerable than are the Terminators to "traditional," human types of attack. So, while there are many impressive sequences where bullets *do* in fact bounce off RoboCop, we also see him being beaten and ripped apart by better-equipped enemies. This serves to represent RoboCop both as an impressive, phallic fighting machine, *and* as an essentially human being who *is* capable of feeling pain (but only, like Rambo/Rocky-type characters, when the opposition is incredibly intense).
8. The phallic coding and representation of the Terminators and RoboCops is frequently remarked on and/or discussed by critics who have written about the films (Codell, 1989; Springer, 1991; Jancovich, 1992; Tasker, 1993).
9. Here she makes reference to the work of both Richard Dyer (1982) and Steve Neale (1983).
10. I am not suggesting that in "real life" a mother cannot simultaneously value her child's life more than her own and be a feminist. What I am questioning here is whether Sarah Connor's representation is regressive or not.

REFERENCES

Best, S. (1989) "Robocop: The Recuperation of the Subject," *Canadian Journal of Political and Social Philosophy* 13 (1–2): 44–54.

Codell, J. (1989) "Murphy's Law, Robocop's Body, and Capitalism's Work," *Jump Cut* 34: 12–19.

Creed, B. (1993) *The Monstrous-Feminine: Film Feminism, Psychoanalysis.* London & New York: Routledge.

Doane, M. A. (1990) "Technophilia: Technology, Representation, and the Feminine," in M. Jacobus et al. (eds.) *Body/Politics: Women and the Discourse of Science.* New York: Routledge.

Dyer, R. (1982) "Don't Look Now," *Screen 23* (3–4): 61–73.

Franklin, S. (1990) "Postmodern Mutant Cyborg Cinema," *New Scientist* 22/29 December: 70–1.

Geduld, H. M. (1975) "Celluandroid: The Robot in Cinema," *The Humanist* 35: 40.

Goscilo, M. (1987–88) "Deconstructing *The Terminator*," *Film Criticism* 12(2): 37–52.

Haraway, D. (1990) "A Manifesto For Cyborgs: Science, Technology, and Socialist Feminism in the 1980s," in L. J. Nicholson (ed.) *Feminism/Postmodernism.* New York: Routledge.

Jancovich, M. (1992) "Modernity and Subjectivity in *The Terminator*: The Machine as Monster in Contemporary American Culture," *The Velvet Light Trap* 30: 3–17.

Jeffords, S. (1993) "Can Masculinity Be Terminated?" in S. Coohan and I. R. Hark (eds.) *Screening the Male: Exploring Masculinities in Hollywood Cinema.* London: Routledge.

Kerman, J. B. (1991) *Retrofitting Blade Runner.* Bowling Green: BGSU Popular Press.

Merleau-Ponty, M. (1992) *The Phenomenology of Perception*, trans. Colin Smith. London: Routledge.

Neale, S. (1983) "Masculinity as Spectacle," *Screen* 24(6): 2–16.

Parker, B. (1992) "Tunnels Through Time: Relativity and Time Travel," *Astronomy* June: 28–35.

Penley, C. (1990) "Time Travel, Primal Scene and the Critical Dystopia," in A. Kuhn (ed.) *Alien Zone: Cultural Theory & Contemporary Science Fiction Cinema*. London and New York: Verso.

Porush, D. (1985) *The Soft Machine: Cybernetic Fiction*. Cambridge: Methuen.

Pyle, Forest (1993) "Making Cyborgs, Making Humans: Of Terminators and Blade Runners," in J. Collins et al. (eds.) *Film Theory Goes to the Movies*. London: Routledge.

Sardar, Z. (1990) "Surviving the Terminator: The Postmodern Mental Condition," *Futures* 22: 203–10.

Sellers, S. (1991) *Language & Sexual Difference: Feminist Writing in France*. London: Macmillan.

Springer, C. (1991) "The Pleasure of the Interface," *Screen* 32(3): 303–23.

Tasker, Y. (1993) *Spectacular Bodies: Gender, Genre and the Action Cinema*. London: Routledge.

Telotte, J. P. (1988) "The Ghost in the Machine: Consciousness and the Science Fiction Film," *Western Humanities Review* 42(3): 249–57.

Telotte, J. P. (1991) "The Tremulous Public Body: Robots, Change and the Science Fiction Film," *Journal of Popular Film and Television* 19(1): 14–23.

Telotte, J. P. (1992) "*The Terminator, Terminator 2*, and the Exposed Body," *Journal of Popular Film and Television* 20(2): 26–34.

S. KAY TOOMBS

2

The Lived Experience of Disability

Maurice Merleau-Ponty rejects the Cartesian dualism that elevates the mind, and relegates the body to a passive supporting role. Instead, he emphasizes that bodies are the active, mediating link to the world. Kay Toombs applies Merleau-Ponty's challenge to the Cartesian dualism in her analysis of her own body. Her experiences living with progressive multiple sclerosis are explored as disruptions in her perceptions of distance, time, and space. Toombs shows how the body is the focal point of measurement of distance between the self and objects, of the time it takes the individual to get to objects, and of the space between the body and other objects. But with progressive multiple sclerosis, changes in these perceptions are transformed as her body both deteriorates and goes through remissions. These changes in the perceptions of concrete time, space, and distance illustrate how even though they seem "real" and solid, time, space, and distance are changeable and transformed relative to her bodily location.

Following Merleau-Ponty, Toombs uses a phenomenological approach in her analysis of the body. Phenomenology is both a methodology and a philosophy that views the individual as active in constructing meaning in and through experience. Phenomenology challenges the assumption of an objective, detached observer as being able to get outside of social experience. Instead, it is an approach

From S. Kay Toombs, "The Lived Experience of Disability," *Human Studies* 18, no. 1 (January 1995): 9–23. Reprinted by permission of Kluwer Academic Publishers and the author.

that focuses on the individual's experience as the primary evidence of reality. Using the approach, Toombs highlights how her bodily experiences come to determine her perception of reality.

My interest in the phenomenology of illness and disability has grown out of my own experience as a person living with multiple sclerosis—an incurable, progressively disabling disease of the central nervous system. Over the past twenty years (since the age of thirty) my physical capacities have altered in a startling number of ways. At one time or another my illness has affected my ability to see, to feel, to move, to hear, to stand up, to sit up, to walk, to control my bowels and my bladder, and to maintain my balance. Some abilities, such as sensing the position of a limb, I have lost abruptly and then slowly regained. Some, such as clear-sighted vision in one or the other eye, I have lost and regained numerous times. Other physical capacities have disappeared and never returned. I can, for example, no longer walk because I am quite unable to lift my legs. This latter change has, however, been gradual. For a number of years, although the muscles in my legs became weaker and weaker, I was able to get around "on my own two feet" using first a cane, then crutches, and finally a walker for support. Now I use a wheelchair or battery operated scooter for mobility.

All these physical changes can, of course, be described in terms of central nervous system dysfunction and explicated with respect to a demyelinating disorder. Indeed, it may even be possible, through the use of sophisticated medical technology, to visualize lesions in the brain to account for specific physical incapacities. Yet, such a mechanistic description (based as it is on a biomedical model of disease) captures little, if anything, of my actual experience of bodily disorder. I do not experience the lesion(s) in my brain. Indeed, for me and others with similar disorders, illness is not even experienced as a matter of abnormal reflexes. Rather, my illness is the impossibility of taking a walk around the block or of carrying a cup of coffee from the kitchen to the den.

In this essay I suggest that phenomenology provides a powerful means to illuminate the human experience of loss of mobility—a bodily dysfunction that is common in neurological and other degenerative diseases. In particular, in rendering explicit the dynamic relation between body and world, the phenomenological notion of *lived body* provides important insights into the disruption of space and time that are an integral element of physical disability. Furthermore, a phenomenological account of bodily disorder discloses the emotional dimension of physical dysfunction. In providing a window into lived experience, phenomenology gives invaluable information about the everyday world of those who live with disabilities. Such information is of enormous practical significance when devising effective therapies in the clinical setting and in determining how best to address the personal, social, and emotional challenges posed by chronic disabling diseases.

In considering the meaning of disability it is helpful to recall the phenomenological notion of *lived body* (Sartre, 1956; Merleau-Ponty, 1962). As an embodied subject, I do not experience my body primarily as an object among other objects *of* the world. Rather than being an object for me-as-subject, my body *as I live it* represents my particular point of view *on* the world (Merleau-Ponty, 1962, 70). I am embodied not in the sense that I *have* a body—as I have an automobile, a house, or a pet—but in the sense that I *exist* or *live* my body (Toombs, 1992). In this respect the lived body is not the objective, physiological body that can be seen by others (or examined by means of various medical technologies) but, rather, the body that is the vehicle for seeing.

Furthermore, the *lived body* is the basic scheme of orientation, the center of one's system of coordinates. I experience myself as the Here over against which everything else is There. As orientational locus in the world, my body both orients me to the world around by means of my senses and positions the world in accord with my bodily placement and actions (Husserl, 1982, 116–17; Husserl, 1989, 165–66; Schutz, 1962, 222–26).

Additionally, the *lived body* is the locus of my intentions. I actively engage the world through the medium of my body. I not only find myself within the world but continually move towards it and organize it in terms of my projects. Objects present themselves as invitations to my body's possible actions. For instance, the piece of chalk presents itself as "an instrument for writing" or "an item to be replaced in the drawer"; the desk inside the office is encountered as "a location for working" or, perhaps, as "something to walk around in order to get to the door." The surrounding world is always grasped in terms of a concrete situation. Contained in the action of reaching for the cup is the intention to bring it to one's lips. One reaches for the cup *in order* to drink from it.

Physical space is thus for my body an oriented space. Points in space do not represent merely objective positions but rather they mark the varying range of my aims and gestures. For example, the narrow passageway through which I must pass represents a "restrictive potentiality" for my body, requiring a modification of my actions. I must perhaps turn sideways in order to make my way through it (Merleau-Ponty, 1962, 143). Surrounding space is experienced as functional space—that environment within which I carry out my various projects. From my center outwards the world around me arranges itself in terms of near and far goals.

Motor disorders resulting in loss of mobility engender a profound disruption in the *lived body*. For instance, such disorders transform the experience of the body as orientational and intentional locus—thus transforming the experience of space. In the normal course of events locomotion opens up space, allowing one freely to change position and move towards objects in the world. Loss of mobility anchors one in the *Here*, engendering a heightened sense of distance between oneself and surrounding things. A location that was formerly regarded as "near" is now experienced as "far." For example, when I could walk, the distance from my office to the classroom (about thirty yards) was unremarkable—as were the stairs I climbed to reach the third floor of the building. As my mobility decreased, the office appeared near to the classroom on the way to the lecture, but far from it on the return journey; the stairs became an obstacle to be avoided, as much as possible, by using the elevator. Today, if I were to be without my battery operated scooter, the distance from the office to the classroom would appear immense—absolutely beyond my capacity to reach it. And the third floor is unattainable when the elevator malfunctions, leaving me stranded waiting for the repairman. (If an elevator repairman is not readily available, then my inability to climb stairs necessitates rescheduling my classes on the first floor, exchanging rooms with a professor from another department, having to send someone to carry my books and papers down to me from my office.)

Loss of mobility illustrates in a concrete way how the subjective experience of space is intimately related both to one's bodily capacities and to the design of the surrounding world. The answer to the question, "Is it too far to go?" has little to do with the distance that can be measured in feet or yards. For the person in a wheelchair, the answer depends in large part on what is *between* here and there. Are there obstacles that prevent the use of a scooter, is the terrain suitable for a wheelchair?

With the loss of various bodily capacities, physical space assumes an unusually restrictive character. Sidewalks may be too uneven to walk on, carpets too thick to wheel over, doorways too narrow to navigate with a wheelchair, slopes too steep to climb. When I could walk, a local shopping mall seemed relatively "flat." Now, as I propel myself around it in my wheelchair, it appears positively mountainous! (A cyclist friend gave me an interesting analogy. He said that before he tries a new cycling route he no longer asks a noncyclist to describe the terrain. Since noncyclists have usually only navigated the route in cars, they will assure him there are no hills. However, once he rides his bicycle, he discovers long, steep inclines of which the automobile riders were totally unaware.)

The dimensions of high and low also vary according to the position of one's body and the range of possible movements. From a wheelchair the top three shelves in the grocery store are too high to reach since they have been designed for shoppers who are standing up. (Consequently, the wheelchair user must either be accompanied by an upright person or find a store employee to take items off the shelf. Either option is inconvenient and renders one dependent on others for the simplest of tasks.) Similarly, regardless of its dimensions in inches, a curb is as high as a wall if one is on a motorized scooter (and cannot get off or onto the sidewalk). The floor is infuriatingly distant and impossibly low, if one is unable to bend to retrieve the car keys that have slipped out of one's hand (especially if there is no one around who can pick them up!).

With respect to the changed character of physical space, it is important to recognize that those of us who negotiate space in a wheelchair live in a world that is in many respects designed for those who can stand upright. Until recently all of our architecture, every avenue of public access, was designed for people with working legs. Hence, people with disabilities (and those who regularly accompany them) necessarily come to view the world through the medium of the limits and possibilities of their own bodies. One is always aware that one is "sizing up" the environment to see whether it is accommodating for the changed body. For instance, I well remember that my first impression of the Lincoln Memorial was not one of awe at its architectural beauty but rather dismay at the number of steps to be climbed. This bodily perception is, of course, not limited to those with disabilities. (Recall the example of the narrowed passageway that is encountered as a "restrictive potentiality" for the body because of the necessity to make certain adjustments in bodily bearing in order to pass through it.) What is peculiar about this "seeing through the body" in the event of changed bodily function is that it renders explicit one's being as a being-in-the-world. A problem with the body is a problem with the body/environment.

The disruption of this unified body/world system also includes the disruption of the body as intentional locus. Surrounding objects that were formerly used unthinkingly are now encountered as overt problems to the body. (Recall how my experience of the stairs to my office changed as my ability to climb them declined.) For the person with a tremor, a bowl of soup is not simply "something to be eaten." It is a concrete problem to be solved. How does one get the liquid on to the spoon and then the spoon to one's lips without spilling the contents? For those with gait disturbance swinging doors are not just "a device to be opened" but "an obstacle to be negotiated with care" from a wheelchair or with crutches. Ordinary things assume a maddeningly resistant quality. For instance, attempting to put panty hose on immobile legs requires the most elaborate contortions and exceptional patience! As bodily capacities change it is necessary to develop alternative ways of interacting with objects, to formulate rules of action other than those used when one had other abilities. The necessity for continually finding new ways to solve the challenges posed by objects differentiates the experience of someone who has had abilities and then lost them from the experience of a person who has never had those abilities. Indeed, some of the uncertainty experienced in degenerative diseases relates to the fact that one has to learn *and relearn* how to negotiate the surrounding world on an ongoing basis. The "I can do it again" can never be taken-for-granted.

To give some idea of the changed interaction with the surrounding world that occurs with loss of mobility, let me recount a *typical* experience. On arriving at the regional airport to begin a professional trip, I look for a parking space that is wide enough to lower the wheelchair lift so that I can get out of my handicapped equipped van. (There is no handicapped parking space that is "van accessible" so I must find a space at the end of a row in order to put down the lift. If there is no space, then I must find a person who is willing to park my van for me and drop me off.) Once I am out of the van I look for a ramp to get into the terminus on my scooter. There is only one in the whole length of the sidewalk. However, the rental cars awaiting customers are routinely parked in front of the ramp, blocking access. (This means I must alert someone *inside* the terminus and wait for the cars to be moved before I can get into the building. Now that I have a cellular phone—as long as I have the appropriate phone number—I can alert someone in the building. Otherwise, I must wait for an upright person to arrive and request them to go inside and get assistance for me.)

Once in the terminus I go to the airline check-in counter. In my battery operated scooter I am approximately three and a half feet tall and the counter is on a level with my head. All my transactions with the person behind the counter take place at the level of my ear. The person behind the counter must stretch over it in order to take my tickets, and I must crane my neck and shout in order to be heard.

The small commuter plane arrives and there are steps leading into the cabin. Since I cannot walk, I must be carried on board—a process that requires a transfer from my scooter to a device that looks rather like a barstool on wheels. To transfer I turn the scooter seat, manually lifting my legs and putting my feet on the ground. I can then be pulled into a standing position and lowered onto the carry-on device that has been placed adjacent to my scooter. Someone then picks up my legs, places them on the footrest and I am strapped in and requested to fold my arms over my chest (in the manner of a corpse!). I am then wheeled out to the plane and two people lift the carry-on device—as one does a stretcher—and carry me up the steps. Once on board, I again transfer to get into my assigned seat. (This whole operation is, of course, performed in full view of all the people in the airport lobby. They also watch as I am lifted into the plane.)

At the first destination, when all other passengers have alighted, I am carried off the plane (necessitating a repeat of the transfer procedure from airplane seat, to carry-on device, and then to scooter or wheelchair). We arrive at the terminal building to find that the only entrance is up two flights of stairs and the elevator has been broken for two days! Once again I must transfer so that I can be carried up the stairs into the terminal. (The necessity to repeat this procedure numerous times is not only difficult and frustrating for me but, judging from their words and actions, it is obviously irritating to those who are carrying me.)

In the terminal building I am outside the security checkpoint. However, it is not possible to go through the security gate in a wheelchair or scooter. Consequently, I am taken to the side (once again in full view of everyone who happens to be in the area) and my whole body—from armpits to fingertips, from the top of my head to the base of my spine, from groin to ankle, from under my chin and over my breasts and abdomen—is "patted down" ("frisked") by an airport employee.

I leave and go to the restroom. Although the door is wide enough, the "handicapped accessible" stall is too short to accommodate the length of my scooter. I must, therefore, sit in it with the door open. (Obviously, if that particular stall is occupied—whether by a person with a disability or by an "able bodied" individual—I must wait until it is vacant since I cannot get through the door of the "normal" sized stalls with a wheelchair or scooter.)

I leave on the second "leg" of my trip. Although I do not have to negotiate steps to board the larger plane that will take me to my destination I must still be carried to my seat (and off the plane) since the aisle between the seats on an airplane is not wide enough to accommodate a wheelchair. This also means that, in the event of a long trip, I must request an "aisle chair" (a smaller narrower version of the "barstool on wheels") to get to the restroom during the flight. Not only is it extremely undignified having to request this assistance but I must wait until it is "convenient" for the personnel servicing the flight to attend to my needs. (In practical terms I have learned that this means I should request assistance about thirty minutes before I think I will need it—and never at a time when the meal/drink carts are out of the galley.) I am then wheeled to the restroom in full view of most of the passengers who watch as I transfer from aisle chair to toilet!

After arriving at my destination, de-planing, and getting to the hotel—a trip that necessitates taking a taxi since the airport limousine cannot accommodate a person in a scooter or wheelchair—I find that (the *Americans with Disabilities Act* notwithstanding) not one of the four hotel restaurants is accessible from *inside* the building. Each one can only be reached by going up steps from the hotel lobby. Limited access is available from *outside* the building but this necessitates going two blocks in the pouring rain. Later, I discover that a colleague and I are unable to walk from the hotel to a nearby place of interest since we can go no farther than a block *in any direction*—

there are no curb cuts that would enable me to ride my scooter off one sidewalk and onto another.[1]

This *routine* experience illustrates another aspect of the changed experience of space that occurs with loss of mobility. The surrounding world appears (feels) different than it did prior to bodily dysfunction. In particular, the world is experienced as overtly obstructive, surprisingly nonaccommodating. Actions are sensed as *effortful*, where hitherto they had been *effortless*. On occasion the world threatens even. And often it presents itself as questionable. The "knowing how" of one's engagement in the world is rendered circumspect. The effortful nature of worldly involvement that is characteristic of incapacitating disorders can engender a sense of fatigue that I shall call "existential fatigue." To organize and carry out projects requires not only physical ability but, as importantly, an exercise of will. When ceaseless and ongoing effort is required to perform the simplest of tasks (getting out of bed, dressing, taking a shower, going on a trip), there is a powerful impulse to withdraw, to cease doing what is required. Consequently, physical incapacity exerts a centripetal force in another sense. The person with a disability is tempted severely to curtail involvements in the world.

Surrounding space also changes in the sense that objects assume a different meaning. The bookcase outside my bedroom was once intended by my body as "a repository for books," then as "that which is to be grasped for support on the way to the bathroom," and is now intended as "an obstacle to get around with my wheelchair." Additionally, space changes in the sense that permanent loss of function requires the reorganization of functional space. I must remove the beautiful, glass topped coffee table from my study if I am to get my wheelchair in there. This reinterpretation and reorganization of space is not without emotional import. Removing the coffee table not only alters the aesthetics of my study—and thus changes the "feeling" of the room (a "feeling" that is very meaningful to me)—but it symbolizes a *permanent* change in my mode of being-in-the-world. In this regard it is important to recognize the *lived body* as possibility, potentiality for action in the world. At the pre-reflective level my leg is not an object but, rather, the *possibility which I am* of walking, running, playing tennis (Sartre, 1956, 402). Permanent loss of function represents a modification of the existential possibilities inherent in the *lived body*.

The *lived body* manifests one's being-in-the-world not only as orientational and intentional locus but in the sense that distinct bodily patterns (walking, talking, gesturing) express a unique corporeal style, a certain bodily bearing that identifies the *lived body* as peculiarly me (Merleau-Ponty, 1962, 150). Motor disorders transform corporeal style. New patterns of movement are experienced as unfamiliar, unrecognizable. Even after a number of years, I still have difficulty recognizing my increasingly peculiar way of moving as my own. When I catch sight of myself in a mirror, I feel a sense of puzzlement. Is that person reflected in the glass really me? At the same time I now perceive "normal" movement to be an extraordinary accomplishment. I catch myself watching students running across the campus, or colleagues taking the stairs two-at-a-time, and I marvel at their effortless ability to do so. Try as I might, I can no longer remember how it was to move like that. It is not simply that I cannot recall the last occasion when I walked upright. It is that I cannot recollect, or re-imagine, the felt bodily sense of "walking."

Merleau-Ponty would argue that my inability to recall or re-imagine "walking" can be understood in terms of bodily intentionality. For instance, he notes that the phenomenon of "phantom limb" is best explained in terms of the body's involvement with the environment. The person who feels the phantom limb does so for as long as the body remains open to the types of actions for which the limb would be the center if it were still operative (Merleau-Ponty, 1962, 76). Thus, my inability to re-imagine "walking" might be understood in terms of a permanent change in bodily intentionality. My limbs are no longer open to the possibility of moving in a certain manner (i.e., in the mode of "walking").

The transformation of corporeal style is particularly profound when it involves the loss of uprightness. The significance of this loss is not confined to technical problems of locomotion. We assign value to upright posture. We applaud the man who can "stand on his own two feet." We praise those who are "upstanding." We look askance at those who are "unstable" or "weak kneed." I am most aware of the diminishing effect of loss of uprightness whenever I attend stand-up gatherings such as receptions. In my wheelchair I am approximately three-and-a-half feet tall and the conversation takes place above my head. When speaking to a standing person, I must look up at them and they down to me. This gives me the ridiculous sense of being a child again surrounded by very tall adults.

Loss of upright posture not only concretely diminishes one's own autonomy (as a person who routinely uses a wheelchair I have no choice but to request assistance in a world designed for upright bodies) but it causes others—those who are still upright—to treat one as dependent. Whenever I am accompanied by an upright person, in my presence strangers invariably address themselves to my companion and refer to me in the third person. "Can *SHE* transfer from her wheelchair to a seat? Would *SHE* like to sit at this table?" "What would *SHE* like us to do?" This almost always happens at airports. The person at the security barrier looks directly at me, then turns to my husband and says, "Can *SHE* walk at all?" We now have a standard reply. My husband says, "No, but *SHE can* talk!" (When I am unaccompanied people often act as if my inability to walk has affected not only my intelligence but also my hearing. When forced to address me directly they articulate their words in an abnormally slow and unusually loud fashion—in the manner that one might use to address a profoundly deaf person who was in the process of learning to lip read.)

In addition, normal social conventions with regard to the absolute control one exercises over one's bodily bearing are disregarded with loss of upright posture. For example when I am wheeling myself around the shopping mall, strangers will (without my permission) start pushing my wheelchair, explaining they are "helping" me. On one occasion, in order to get me from the cab to the curb, a taxi driver simply picked me up (with no warning or no inquiry as to whether I would like him to do so!).[2]

With respect to the discomfort I feel when people push my wheelchair without my permission, it might be helpful to refer to Merleau-Ponty's insight that, through the performance of habitual tasks, we incorporate objects into bodily space (Merleau-Ponty, 1962, 143). For example, the woman who routinely wears a hat with a long feather on it intuitively allows for the extension of the feather when she goes through a doorway—just as a 6'7" man unthinkingly allows for his height. Similarly, when one is proficient at typing, one no longer experiences the keys of the computer as objective locations at which one must aim. To get used to a computer keyboard is to incorporate it into one's bodily space. For the person who routinely uses a wheelchair the device becomes a part of the body. One intuitively allows for the width of the wheels when going through a doorway; one performs the necessary hand/arm movements to move forwards and backwards without thinking about it. With habitual use the wheelchair becomes an extension of one's bodily range. Thus, when a stranger pushes my wheelchair without my permission, it is invading my personal bodily space.

Shame is an integral element of disordered body style, a nonrational response to the change in the body. Shame manifests itself in several ways that can be understood in terms of *lived body* disruption. At one level, to use Sartre's terminology, shame is the experience of being-for-the-Other (Sartre, 1956, 445–60). One sees one's disordered body style through the eyes of the Other and thus constitutes it in a negative fashion. This is not a culture that celebrates physical difference or dependence. There is great emphasis on health, physical fitness, productivity, sexuality, and youth. The person who staggers, uses crutches, a cane, or a wheelchair is far from the ideal (Goffman, 1963; Asch and Fine, 1988; Murphy, 1987). Although to feel shame it is not necessary that one actually be observed by another person (Goffman, 1963, 7–8), more often than not the "gaze" of the Other *is* concrete (recall my experience at airports). It is important to emphasize the *felt* dimension of interaction with others. I directly experience your responses (facial expressions, gestures, averted eyes, words directed away from me to my companion, irritation). It is not merely a matter of what I *think* you feel about me. In this regard I continue to be astonished at the insensitivity of those who can walk. As I write this paper, I have just returned from wheeling myself around a local shopping mall. The place is a favorite "haunt" of "walkers" who go there to exercise. In the space of thirty minutes two complete strangers made the following remarks to me: "Why don't you change places and let *me* ride in your wheelchair for a while and *you* walk. My legs are tired!" and "If you want to exercise, you should get out of that wheelchair and walk around like the rest of us." The sad truth is that these kinds of remarks are commonplace. So much so that I no longer pay much attention to them. On almost every occasion when I use my scooter in a store, someone will say to me, "Oh, I wish I had one of those scooters to do my shopping. It would make things a lot easier!" And, insensitive as they are, these remarks are less hurtful than the overtly negative comments and actions that are also a common part of my everyday experience.[3]

With regard to the interrelation between emotion and bodily being, as Sartre (1956, 455) and others have noted, "psychical qualities" are ways in which the body is *lived*. The "voices of aggressive people are hard, their muscles bunched, their blood pulses more fiercely through the vessels" (Van den Berg, 1955, 42). In neurological disorder shame manifests itself as an increase in the severity of symptoms. In the experience of the "gaze" of the Other an already existing tremor invariably intensifies, spastic limbs become more rigid, difficulty controlling movement is more pronounced. (I remember the occasion of receiving my doctoral degree. I could still walk a few steps if supported, and I could climb stairs with assistance. The day before the ceremony, a colleague and I went over to the auditorium to practice climbing the few steps onto the stage where I was to be seated. I negotiated the steps without too much difficulty. However, on the following day—in the concrete experience of about sixteen thousand eyes watching me—I was completely unable to lift my right leg. It was not just that I was conscious of the fact that my body moved in a peculiar fashion. Rather, I was temporarily paralyzed. No amount of willing resulted in a corresponding contraction of the muscles. I did eventually "drag" my leg up the steps but my incapacity was much more pronounced than it had been the previous day when no one was present in the auditorium.)

Shame is also present in the frustration of intentionality. The "inability to" interact with the world is not only the experience of loss, "I can no longer do," but diminishment, "I must depend on others to do for me" and, further, "I should be able to do for myself." Once again this is a nonrational response to the change in body and perhaps reflects the strong emphasis in our culture on the importance of independence and autonomy, of "being able to look after oneself," of being capable of "running one's own life."

The transformation in being-in-the-world that occurs with disability incorporates not only a change in surrounding space and a disruption of corporeal identity, but also a change in temporal experiencing (Toombs, 1992; Toombs, 1990.) Just as lived spatiality is characterized by an outward directedness, purposiveness, and intention, so time is ordinarily experienced as a gearing towards the future. Normally we act in the present in light of anticipations of what is to come, more or less specific goals relating to future possibilities. With bodily dysfunction this gearing into the future is disrupted in a number of ways.

For instance, temporal experiencing changes in the sense that the sheer physical demands of impaired embodiment ground one in the present moment, requiring a disproportionate attention to the *here* and *now*. One is forced to concentrate on the present moment and the present activity rather than focusing on the next moment. Mundane tasks take much longer than they did prior to the change in abilities. For instance, when habitual movements are disrupted, the most ordinary activities such as getting out of bed, rising from a chair, getting in and out of the shower, knotting a tie, undoing a button, demand unusual exertion, intense concentration, and an untoward amount of time. (Think, for example, of the difference between the time and effort required to tie one's shoelaces using one, as opposed to both, hands—especially if one is right handed and only able to use the left hand to perform the task.) In this respect persons with disabilities find themselves "out of synch" with those whose physical capacities have not changed. This temporal disparity is not insignificant in terms of relations with others. "What's taking so long?" others ask impatiently.[4]

In the case of progressive disability time may be disturbed in the sense that the future, rather than the present, assumes overriding significance. The uncertainty associated with diseases such as multiple sclerosis may cause one to project into the future rather than living in the present moment. For instance, a newly diagnosed patient may start living *as if* already severely incapacitated, or as if the threat is imminent. Indeed, a study carried out at the large multiple sclerosis clinic at the University of Western Ontario showed that receiving a diagnosis of M.S. was, for many patients, equivalent to "moderate disability," regardless of physical status.[5] In this event the actual present is forfeited and transposed into an imagined future.

In progressively degenerative diseases time may also be disrupted in another way. Given the nature of such disorders, the future assumes an inherently problematic quality. In thinking of goals and projects, one can never be sure what one's physical status will be at some future point in time. As was noted earlier, the assumption "I can do it again" can no longer be taken-for-granted by a person whose physical abilities are constantly diminishing. This uncertainty can be extremely debilitating in the sense that it makes it difficult to continue to strive towards future goals. Are such goals unrealistic in light of the probability of decreased and decreasing abilities? Moreover, the future is not only problematic but overtly threatening. The truism, "Things could be worse" takes on a whole new meaning for those living with progressively incapacitating disorders. This change in the relation to the future contributes to personal meanings, in particular one's sense of what is possible in one's life (Toombs, 1995). In sum, then, phenomenology provides important insights into the lived body disruption that is intrinsic to the human experience of disability. For instance, as I have noted in this paper, phenomenology discloses how loss of mobility necessarily changes one's experience of surrounding space, alters one's taken-for-granted awareness of (and interaction with) objects, disrupts corporeal identity, affects one's relations with others, and causes a change in the character of temporal experience.

Such insights have practical application in the clinical context. Indeed, if therapy is to be successful, it is essential to address the global sense of disorder that permeates the patient's everyday life. Let me give a couple of examples to illustrate this point. Technical solutions, such as the adoption of a cane or crutches to enhance mobility, are less likely to be effective if explicit attention is not given to the affective responses, such as shame and embarrassment, that inevitably accompany such solutions. (Patients will not use these devices if they are ashamed to be seen doing so.)[6] Patients must learn to accept such objects as extensions of bodily space, rather than as symbols of disability, before they can effectively incorporate them into the lived body.

In this regard (and recalling Merleau-Ponty's discussion on incorporating objects into the body) it is important to note that different modes of extending bodily space have varying psychological effects. Before I purchased a lightweight wheelchair I was unable to wheel myself around because a standard model was too heavy for me to operate. Consequently, I had to be pushed. I hated "being in" a wheelchair. It made me feel utterly dependent on others. It was a symbol of limitation. I used it as little as possible (even though that meant sometimes cutting back on social engagements). Then I obtained a lightweight wheelchair that I could operate myself. I no longer needed to be pushed (except up slopes!) "*Using*" rather than "*being in*" a wheelchair is an affirming, rather than a demeaning, experience. (This phraseology is not just a matter of semantics.) When I manipulate the chair myself, I am in control, I can go where I want to go "under my own steam." Thus, wheeling represents freedom rather than limitation. My wheelchair has become, in effect, my legs—an integral part of my body. So much so, that I prefer wheeling myself in the manual wheelchair to riding on my battery operated scooter. (It is, of course, the case that devices such as battery operated scooters do allow the person operating them to be in control and thus to feel less dependent than if they are being "pushed around.")

In terms of effective therapy, it is also important to pay explicit attention to such factors as the change in temporal experience occasioned by various physical incapacities. For instance, therapists can assist those with degenerative disorders to address future fears in a realistic fashion, thus enabling them to live more effectively in the present. Fears for the future are almost always concrete—Will I be able to continue working at my job? Will I have enough physical strength to care for my children? Will I embarrass myself in a public setting? Will I be able to walk from my office to the classroom? Once these fears have been explicitly articulated, then strategies can be developed to deal with them in the present. This allows the person facing the challenges to remain in control of his or her situation. If, however, the change in temporal experiencing is not addressed, a person living with chronic, debilitating disease may feel (and probably does feel) that his or her situation is totally out of control. This makes it difficult, if not impossible, to deal in a positive fashion with the bodily changes that are occurring.

A phenomenological account of loss of mobility also has practical implications in the social context. For instance, in detailing the types of lived body disruption that accompany loss of uprightness, phenomenology provides important information for those engaged in activities such as developing ways to re-constitute public space (both physical and social) so that it is accommodating to differing modes of being-in-the-world. Such an account also forcefully reminds us of the overt barriers (including commonplace attitudes and prejudices) that prevent those with disabilities from flourishing in our society.

NOTES

1. I should note that these examples represent just the "tip of the iceberg." I am no longer able to travel alone because, more often than not, so-called "handicapped accessible" rooms in hotels do *not* have wheelchair accessible bathrooms, let alone accessible showers or commodes. Consequently, my traveling companion has to be able to manually assist/lift me/hold me up if I am to be able to use the bathroom. It is simply a fact of life that the majority of bathrooms/restrooms in modern buildings (including private houses) are constructed in such a way that the doorways are not wide enough for wheelchairs to pass through them.

A routine invitation to a restaurant, a theater, someone's house for dinner, a business meeting, a friend's apartment, or a shopping excursion requires that I ascertain if I can get into and out of buildings, if there is adequate parking, if there are ramps and elevators, if I am blocked by stairs (either into the house or inside it), if rooms/hallways/bedrooms are so arranged in private houses that it will be possible to negotiate around furniture in my wheelchair, if I can get in and out of automobiles, if I can transfer from my wheelchair to the toilet. As bodily capacities decrease, the challenges posed in the negotiation of space obviously become more numerous.

2. While I have no doubt that these actions are taken with the best of intentions, imagine how you would feel if a taxi driver simply picked you up, lifted you out of the cab, and set you down on the curb.

3. In this respect it has been my experience that, in spite of the passage of the *Americans with Disabilities Act*, negative attitudes towards persons with disabilities remain unchanged. As an example, on a recent professional trip to New Orleans, a friend went to check whether a certain very well-known restaurant was accessible for a wheelchair. The building was accessible. However, the employee at the restaurant made it very clear that people in wheelchairs were not welcome in the restaurant and insisted we would be more comfortable at another establishment.

4. For a detailed account of the disruption in communication that occurs with such a change in temporality, see Robillard (1993).

5. This information was given to me by Dr. George C. Ebers, Department of Clinical Neurological Sciences, University of Western Ontario, London, Ontario.

6. It is important to re-emphasize that shame is a nonrational response to the change in corporeal style. I have experienced shame each time I have had to adopt a new mode of locomotion (cane, crutches, walker, wheelchair, scooter). I recall that when I first used my scooter I would ride it from the office to the classroom, park it *outside* the door, and stagger into the classroom on my own two feet—hoping that I would not lose my balance altogether before I reached the podium. I thought the students would think less of me if I came into the classroom on a scooter. This was ridiculous, of course. I should have known better but it was part of my sense of changed and changing embodiment.

REFERENCES

Asch, A. and Fine, M. (Eds.) (1988). *Women with Disabilities*. Philadelphia: Temple University Press.

Goffman, E. (1963). *Stigma: Notes on the Management of Spoiled Identity*. Englewood Cliffs, NJ: Prentice Hall.

Husserl, E. (1982). *Cartesian Meditations: An Introduction to Phenomenology*. Trans. D. Cairns. The Hague: Martinus Nijhoff.

Husserl, E. (1989). *Ideas Pertaining to a Pure Phenomenology and to a Phenomenological Philosophy: Studies in the Phenomenology of Constitution*. Trans. Rojcewicz and A. Schuwer. Dordrecht: Kluwer Academic Publishers.

Merleau-Ponty, M. (1962). *Phenomenology of Perception*. Trans. C. Smith. London: Routledge and Kegan Paul.

Murphy, R. (1987). *The Body Silent*. New York: Henry Holt.

Robillard, A. B. (1993). Intensive Care Unit (ICU): Exteriorization of the Self AKA Communication Problems. Paper presented at the annual meeting of the Society for Phenomenology and Human Sciences, New Orleans, LA.

Sartre, J. P. (1956). *Being and Nothingness: A Phenomenological Essay on Ontology.* Trans. H. Barnes. New York: Pocket Books.

Schutz, A. (1962). On Multiple Realities. In M. Natanson (Ed.), *The Problem of Social Reality.* Volume 1 of *Alfred Schutz: Collected papers.* The Hague: Martinus Nijhoff.

Toombs, S. K. (1990). The Temporality of Illness: Four Levels of Experience. *Theoretical Medicine* 11:227–41.

Toombs, S. K. (1992). *The Meaning of Illness: A Phenomenological Account of the Different Perspectives of Physician and Patient.* Dordrecht: Kluwer Academic Publishers.

Toombs, S. K. (1995). Sufficient unto the Day: A Life with Multiple Sclerosis. In S. K. Toombs, D. Barnard and R. A. Carson (Eds.), *Chronic Illness: From Experience to Policy.* Bloomington: Indiana University Press.

Van den Berg, J. H. (1955). *The Phenomenological Approach to Psychiatry.* Springfield, IL: Charles C. Thomas.

FREDERIK POHL

HANS MORAVEC

3

Souls in Silicon

While mind transplants into a computer are not
within range of today's medical and technical reality, medicine has attempted a total head transplant
of a chimpanzee. In the late 1990s, the head of one
ape was grafted onto the body of another, "success"
determined by the new "full-bodied" chimp opening
its eyes, watching movement within the room, and
responding to pain in its attached body.

1. Considering this article by Frederik Pohl and
   Hans Moravec is about a form of immortality,
   how do they continue the "I think, therefore I
   am" aspects of the mind/body dualism? In what
   other ways is Cartesianism as discussed in the
   article by Holland reproduced?
2. Keeping in mind Toombs's wheelchair, in what
   way does the computer become an extension of
   the person? Can you find examples of the body-
   as-machine metaphor being reproduced and/or
   challenged?
3. If available, would you consider this type of
   mind/body transfer? Why or why not? Would
   this be really "you"? Why or why not? How is
   your answer grounded in, or a challenge to, traditional Western conceptualizations?

It is the year 20-something—we don't know the
exact date yet, but figure twenty to fifty years
from today—and your doctor has just given you some really bad
news. That nasty little pain in your lower abdomen turns out to be
serious. The doctor explains to you with great tact and kindness that,
although medicine can now fix almost everything that can go wrong
with the human body, there remain one or two really ferocious

From Frederik Pohl and Hans P. Moravec, "Souls in Silicon," *Omni* 16 (November
1993): 68, 70, 72, 74, 76. ©1993 by Omni Publications International, Ltd.
Reprinted by permission of Omni Publications International, Ltd.

ailments that cannot be cured. You won't be in pain, he says. You won't even be bedridden, except at the very end—but the fact is that you have just six months left to live.

Naturally, you don't enjoy hearing that. It comes at a particularly bad time, you think, because now that you're approaching ninety, you've just begun thinking seriously about how you're going to enjoy your retirement years. Then the doctor clears his throat and says, "Of course, there is an alternative."

That gets your attention right away. "Alternative?" you say. "You mean I don't have to die in six months after all?"

The doctor purses his lips, professionally precise. "That isn't exactly what I mean," he says. "Your body is certainly going to die. There's nothing we can do about that; but that death doesn't have to be, well, *fatal*. You're a possible candidate for a mind transplant."

So a couple of weeks later you're undergoing tests in the best surgical hospital in your area. You're surprised to find out that most of the tests aren't medical. They're psychological, and they test things like your memory retention, your reflex speed, even your IQ. The CEO of your company comes by your hospital room with a dozen roses. There is a small flask of her best 1990 Scotch hidden among the flowers, and when the nurses aren't looking, she shares a last drink with you. "You'll be back in the office in two weeks," she predicts. And then one morning they wake you up, give you a tranquilizer, slide you onto a gurney, and wheel you down to the operating room.

They don't put you to sleep, only make you a little drowsy so you can drift off to sleep if you want to. They do anesthetize your entire scalp, because the skin of your head is sensitive to pain, but the real cutting-and-splicing operation is going to be done on your brain, which has no nerve endings to feel pain. They've fixed it so that you can watch the whole thing on a TV monitor if you want to. (You're not at all sure you want to, but every once in a while you sneak a look.) You already have a good idea of what they're going to do, because the surgeons and the computer people have gone over it with you, with a model of the brain. You're a little impressed with the number of people in that operating room, all concentrated on you—two brain surgeons, an anesthesiologist, four nurses . . . and five computer experts. That's a lot of highly trained specialists to be working on you, you think . . . but you can't help feeling a little lonely in that crowd.

What they do to you doesn't hurt. You feel a kind of gently pushing this way and that as they lift a flap of scalp to expose the skull, and you definitely feel the vibration as they cut the bone and lift it away. You stop looking into the monitor at that point. You close your eyes and try to concentrate on thinking about your wife and kids all waiting in one of the hospital's lounges, along with a couple of people from your company. Maybe you even do drift off to sleep. . . .

And while you're doing that you know the surgeons are exposing that tough lump of meat in the midsection of the brain that is called the "corpus callosum." You even know what the corpus callosum is, because they've told you that its half a billion fibers operate as conduits, passing information back and forth between the two halves of your brain.

Then the surgeons step back, and the computer people take over. They don't touch any scalpels themselves. They operate micromanipulators which gently slide a *very* dense and fine comb into the corpus callosum. The comb has some hundred thousand tines, and each tine has a hundred thousand connections. The tines slip elastically into the space between the fibers, until each fiber has made a contact with one or more of the connections. It's a mammoth job, but it is done nondestructively. The whole thing takes only about eight hours.

And then they bandage you up and wheel you back to your own room, and you really do go to sleep.

When you wake, you don't even have a headache—you're full of selective analgesics—and the doctor's there grinning at you. "Congratulations," he says. "Welcome to immortality."

Of course, that's science fiction—today. (But nuclear power, spaceships, television, and robots were also science fiction—once— and now they're all over the place.)

The idea of storing human intelligence in some kind of machine is pretty old stuff in science fiction, almost as old as science-fiction magazines themselves. One of the earliest writers to use the notion was Neil R. Jones, who published his short story "The Jameson Satellite" in 1931. It told of a college professor named Jameson who, learning that he was soon to die, decided he would like something better than the usual funeral and burial. Like all college professors, Jameson was of course very rich. (When college professors read this story this is generally the point at which they start laughing uncontrollably.) So he took some of his money and built a spaceship in his backyard. When the professor did at last die, his executor loaded his corpse into the spaceship and fired it off into low Earth orbit. There Jameson remained, frozen solid, for a long time—forty million years—until some wandering aliens called Zoromes discovered it and decided to recruit the professor into their band. So they surgically removed the brain from the frozen corpse, thawed it out and implanted it in a robot machine that resembled a breadbox with tentacular metal arms and legs. Then, renamed 21MM392 by his new Zorome friends, the professor went on to have endless adventures in space.

There were plenty of other such stories, but almost all of them assumed you would have to store the physical, organic human brain in some kind of machine. That seems pretty unlikely as a really long-range solution to the problem of immortality, since, sadly, the human brain is by its organic nature subject to rather rapid decay (as well as being afflicted with the steady deterioration that costs each one of us a few thousand brain cells dead or decrepit each day). When computers came along, they offered a more hopeful place to store intelligence.

We don't have any computers today that can come anywhere close to the capacities of the human brain—a typical late twentieth-century computer has roughly the "brainpower" of a housefly—but the things keep getting better, and they do it very fast. Between the early days of this century, when the first mechanical adding machines began to be useful, and the arrival of electric calculators during the World War II era, machine computation increased a thousandfold in speed and capacity. Then electronic machines came along, so that between 1940 and 1980 there was an additional millionfold improvement as vacuum tubes and then transistors took over. Since then, with accelerating miniaturization and the use of advanced integrated circuits, the curve continues to steepen, while future computers—using such techniques as quantum devices, diamond semiconductors, increasing miniaturization down to the atomic scale—suggest that computing power will continue to grow at its historical rate or better for an indefinite time into the future.

The human brain, with its 100 billion neurons and roughly 100 trillion connections, requires a lot of computing power, to be sure . . . but not more than computers early in the next century should provide.

Given the probable existence of such hypercomputers within the lifetimes of many of us now alive, how do we go about getting all the memory, speed, and flexibility of a human mind into the machine?

That's where the corpus callosum comes in. Suppose that a neural comb like the one we have described is slipped into it and connected to an external computer. At first that computer does nothing but pass the brain's traffic from one hemisphere to the other and eavesdrop on it. It retains what it learns. Over time, it constructs a model of what goes on in your brain. More than that, the computer can put enough signal on each connection point to overwhelm the normal traffic if it needs to so that, when the model is nearly complete, the computer begins to insert its own messages into the flow. The computer becomes an auxiliary brain; then, when the original, organic brain begins to deteriorate, the computer smoothly assumes its functions.

And when the brain at last dies, as all organic things must, your mind is complete and functioning—in the computer. Optical, auditory, chemotactic, and other sensors let you know what is happening in your environment; speech synthesizers and graphics programs let you communicate with others in the "real" world . . . and you live on, though your body has died.

So here you are, a couple of months after you've had your operation.

It's now the Labor Day weekend. You've spent most of the summer "convalescing"—not really convalescing in the usual sense, because the operation didn't leave you particularly damaged, but getting used to this new companion in your mind.

You have to wear this portable computer all the time, of course. By 20-something the thing is made with quantum-effect devices, a hundredth the size of the microchips of the 1990s, so it isn't particularly large or heavy. Still, it's got to be able to hold a lot of information in its data file, so it's as big as, say, a 1990s' laptop.

That doesn't mean it has to *look* like a laptop. The engineers have built the whole thing into a sort of helmet, which covers your entire head. Although your children are now in their fifties and sixties, they still remember the old movies they saw in their kindergarten days; their affectionate name for you is "Darth Vader." The helmet does cramp your style a little. You can't swim while you're wearing the helmet, and it's not a good idea to ski or play football—but at your age you've pretty nearly decided to give up the more violent sports anyway. Apart from that, you can do anything you ever did.

No, that's not true. Actually, you can do a great deal *more* than you ever did—with your mind, at least—because the companion in the helmet is actually helping out your memory. Baseball? When you and your great-granddaughter watch the Tokyo Mets playing the Vladivostok Dodgers you astonish her by remembering the batting averages of every Mets catcher since 1960. It's all in the data file. Cooking? If your wife thinks of making the chicken-and-wine dish you once had in Paris for dinner, she doesn't have to look up the recipe. You could recite it for her, if you chose—actually, you probably just go ahead and make the dish, though eating any of it when it's done is a little trickier. Business? When you go back to work, your entire corporate financial dossier for the last fifty years is right there in your memory, and you can tell, off the top of your head, which divisions pulled their weight and which have generally underperformed . . . and even why.

Remember that, all this time, the computer that sits on your head isn't only teaching you, it's also *learning* you. It learns who your friends are, and what experiences you shared together, and what they mean to you. It learns what music you like to hear, and what sorts of books you like to read, and what plays and films you enjoy. It learns everything you know about your own life, from the first three-year-old birthday party (when you didn't, after all, get the Super Nintendo you had your heart set on) to the last disagreement you had with your wife . . . and how pleasingly you made up afterward. It remembers everything you remember, likes everything you like, worries about everything that worries you. . . .

It *is* you. And when that demon in your belly at last makes the body you have occupied all these years useless, and the couple of pounds of wetware in your skull has to die . . . *you* live on in the machine.

Do you really call that living, you ask?

Well, what *do* you call living? Is Stephen Hawking alive, for instance?

Hawking is generally acknowledged to be the world's greatest living theoretical physicist, but his body has been all but dead for many years. He is a victim of the disease called ALS—Lou Gehrig's disease—and he cannot even feed himself; worse, a complication a few years ago cost him his voice. But that does not keep Hawking from being a great scientist and a loved human being. It does not prevent him from traveling, or even from lecturing in public, though to be sure he must use a speech synthesizer for the purpose. Since the synthesizer is American made and Hawking is very English, he apologizes for its American accent—but it is still Stephen Hawking speaking. And you, with your advanced hardware and sophisticated software of the next century, can certainly do better than that. You will be able to speak in your own voice or to sing—sing as well as you ever did, and, if you like, much better than ever, with the voice of any opera star who ever lived.

But at least Hawking does have a body, you argue, although admittedly one in bad repair. When he is speaking through his voice synthesizer people can *see* him, anyway. You won't have even that much, right? Wrong! The mere lack of a body won't keep your friends from seeing you—just as you were, or as much handsomer as you wish. (Push back that receding hairline, smooth out those wrinkles—why not?) All you need for the purpose is a TV monitor. You can be the one who controls the image it shows, and that image can be you, made up out of the data bits your computer mind will generate for you. By then, the image will probably be in 3-D as well. Possibly it could be even physically present as a sort of puppet operated by your computer mind so that it can be touched and embraced.

Well, that's all well enough for your friends, you say, but what about yourself? Can you *feel?* you ask. Can you hear and see and smell? Can you perceive heat and cold? Can you feel the sensation of pain, or the touch of a lover's gentle caress?

Of course you can. It is not your brain that feels or sees any of those things, you know. Your brain can't. It doesn't have the necessary equipment. The brain is blind, deaf, and without sensation. All the brain knows is what the sensory organs of the body tell it, and your machine-stored mind can have all the sensory organs you like: video eyes, microphone ears, transducer sensory to convey the physical sensation of touching. Indeed, that could be only the beginning for you. The machine brain can be equipped with far better sensors than the standard accessory package that comes with the human body, for there are better designs on the market. The human eye, for example, cannot see infrared or ultraviolet (but video cameras can); the ear misses the bat's shrill squeak and the low-frequency sounds of nature (but microphones do not); there is no human sense that can pick up radio waves direct, but machines do it all the time—why not be in yourself your own TV set, pocket radio, or even radar?

It's possible, though, that adding new senses might not be a good idea. The brain you were born with had to work hard in order to learn how to interpret all those sensory inputs. There is some evidence that, after a certain point, new kinds of sensory inputs can be emotionally damaging. Young people who have their sight restored at maturity, after having been blind from birth, find the experience disorienting; Dr. Jerome Lettvin of MIT has found that many such people commit suicide.

Of course, your machine brain isn't bound by the same rules as your old organic one. Very possibly a few extra programs could be written in, or a little extra hardware added to your system, and you could then easily enough deal with senses that would allow you to "see" and "feel" anything that any instrument can detect.

All right, you say at last, but that's still not *living*. What about eating? What about the taste of a fine wine? For that matter, what about the buzz you get from a six-pack? And then you get right down to the question that's really on your mind: What about *sex*?

The answer: Don't worry. No problem at all.

Well, no *theoretical* problem, anyway. Remember the main point: Everything you experience is experienced in the brain. It is the brain that interprets all those sensory inputs, including the pleasures of love-making. Once the eavesdropper in your corpus callosum learns how your brain works, it is only a step or two to reach the point where it can create for you any array of sensual inputs you like, not just sex. Not even just very good sex. *Incredible* sex, without such penalties as AIDS or unwanted pregnancy or even the wrath of a jealous lover, since all of it takes place in your mind.

You don't even have to give up your present mate, either. The technical problems of love-making between some collection of data bits stored in a Cray-100 (or whatever) and your flesh-and-blood nearest and dearest are daunting, but that's only temporary. If you are determined to be monogamous you can arrange with your nearest and dearest to join you in machine storage when the times comes. That may not be quick. Your devotion may require a good deal of patience . . . but then you've got all of eternity.

At least, you have eternity as long as you go on paying your utility bills.

Well, how much "science" is in this particular piece of science fiction?

Quite a lot, actually. That isn't to say that this is something you can count on by the year 2001. It may take longer. It may take *much* longer, because some pretty daunting technical problems are involved. Brain anatomists will tell you that there are important sections of the brain—for instance, the brainstem and the cerebellum—not directly reached by the corpus callosum; perhaps more connections must be made than we have outlined. Then there is the tricky question of hooking nerves to wires. Nerve impulses are at least partly electrical in nature, but they are also at least partly chemical. It isn't just a matter of taking a soldering iron to the nerve endings in the brain and joining them to an equal number of copper wires. Some sort of interface will be needed, and no one can now say what form it will have to take.

So the mind-transplant procedure has a long way to go to become a mature technology. How long, exactly? Perhaps about as long, say, as computers themselves had to wait in 1945, at the time of the huge, clumsy vacuum-tube things like ENIAC; or as nuclear energy had in 1938, when Hahn and Strassmann first split the uranium atom. But science goes faster these days—largely because of the computer itself, which makes scientists effectively a good deal smarter than their unaided native brains would allow. If the mind-transplant procedure can be done at all, as seems at least theoretically plausible, it is at least a good gambling bet that something like it will be real within the next few computer generations.

By the time you've been back on the job for a few years, you've become fully accustomed to your new existence. You find it's pretty neat: you even wonder why your flesh-and-blood friends put off joining you.

For one thing, you will have a lot more spare time than you ever had before. Your mental life won't be held to the 55-mph speed limit of an organic brain any more. Computer functions go far faster than organic synapses; you can do in seconds what it takes your meat friends hours to accomplish.

Fortunately, you're not alone in machine storage. You have machine-stored colleagues and friends to talk with, and relate to, and do things with; they move as fast as you do, and actually you find your "living" colleagues just a little slow and dull.

And the things you do with peers are really a lot of fun. Travel? Why, you can enjoy a simulated Campari on the synthesized Champs

Élysées or experience the thrills of skin diving on what your senses tell you is the Great Barrier Reef whenever you like.

You know how this works in advance. When you were a child, you remember, you saw Hollywood films filled with such spectacles as the great spaceships of the Empire and the collapse of cities in earthquakes and nuclear wars. You were aware even then that things had never really happened, but were computer-generated images put together by special-effects firms like George Lucas's Industrial Light & Magic. The same techniques, now brought to perfection, can provide you with any "surround" you like for your adventures, as real to you as any weekend on the Jersey shore was when you were still in your body of flesh. For that matter, you're not limited to dull reality. You can choose to invent your own fantasy world (Barsoom, or Middle Earth, or the *Arabian Nights*, or the Heechee Universe), and the computer will build it around you, complete with food, drink, and companionship. And you have plenty of time for all this sort of fun. Not only do you do things fast, but you never have to waste any time in sleep.

And, of course, you are better at your job than even your best ever was—better than any flesh-and-blood person ever could be.

For that reason, you're not really surprised when your CEO calls you in just before your one hundredth birthday. She tells you that the compulsory retirement rule has been repealed for machine-stored intelligences.

You knew that was coming. When you look at her with your video eyes you feel a little compassion. She's definitely beginning to show her age, and you wish you had been able to persuade her to take the next step to join you.

But, although you like her and sympathize with her, you turn her down.

You've had other offers, you explain. The most interesting has come from NASA. They have a great need for someone like you— several someones like you—for some of the exciting, new long-range space missions they're planning.

After all, living human beings make a lot of trouble for spaceship designers: flesh-and-blood people need food and air and water; they need to be kept warm (but not too hot!) and shielded from the radiation of solar flares; worst of all, they sometimes get sick, and it just isn't feasible to include physicians and dentists on a normal space mission. On the other hand, it is certainly worthwhile to try to have the presence of a human being to make the on-the-spot decisions, take care of the unexpected glitches, interpret what is discovered. And in you and your kind they have the perfect astronauts.

So, with regret, you tell your CEO that you'll be leaving the company to start training for your new job, which will be investigating the frozen surface of the planet Pluto. And there you are, with a whole new career, and a whole new life . . . and you're still a youth hardly out of your first century!

JESSICA R. JOHNSTON

II Social Bodies

When someone is the "head" of a corporation, or the "butt" of a joke, what does that mean? Most cultures tend to describe their world in "bodily metaphors." For Americans the "head" of something is usually the top or beginning. The "heart" of something is usually the center; the "foot" suggests the end or bottom; there is the "blood" of grapes and the "bowels" of the earth; and rocks have "veins," computers have "viruses" (O'Neill, 1985, p. 26).

Social theorists have analyzed the social significance of metaphors. In one of the classic books, entitled *The Social Uses of Metaphor*, J. Sapir and J. C. Crocker (1977) suggest that metaphors are important sources of evidence for how cultures think about and construct the world. John Kirkpatrick and Geoffrey White suggest that metaphors serve two functions. First, they can be models of reality, providing descriptions of what a person can expect of social life. Second, and often simultaneously, they provide guidelines for thinking, moralizing, and problem solving within that described social reality (Kirkpatrick & White, 1985, p. 21).

The body-as-machine metaphor discussed in the first section is a good example of the social significance of metaphors. This metaphor is not just a philosophical image, but has become a powerful and influential way of viewing both the body and the world within which it operates. The body-as-machine metaphor has been efficiently integrated within, and contributed to, the evolution of the

Western industrialized economic order. Taylorism and scientific management at the turn of the twentieth century are examples of the application of this metaphor to the real world. Bodily movements and gestures were explored, broken down, and rearranged into simple machinelike movements in the hope of increasing the efficiency of man's labor. And in current usage, the body-as-machine metaphor is applied when children today are taught that food is "fuel," and that the heart is a "pump." The machine has become the standard against which the body is appraised.

The "body-as-machine" develops into an aesthetic, fusing the body and the machine into one compelling metaphor, generating values towards which we are told to aspire. The machine metaphor has defined "good" in the twentieth century, constructing what a healthy or "fine-tuned" or "well-run" body, family, group, and society ought to be. The body-as-machine metaphor is used to describe somatic and psychological states in mechanistic terms: we can be worn out, wound up, or burned out. And reflecting the transformation of the culture from a mechanistic to electronic orientation, we can now be turned off, tuned in, charged, or energized (Scheper-Hughes & Lock, 1986, p. 23). Brains can be "hard-wired," "programmed," or "reprogrammed."

Significantly, the body-as-machine metaphor is a reversal of the metaphors identified in the opening paragraphs of this section. Instead of machines being described in human terms, the body is compared to a machine. For example, human minds are like computers, and the body is an "engineered specimen of machinery." "Wetware" now refers to the human being that uses computer software. This process of changing the image of humans to fit the world they designed has been labeled "negative anthropomorphism" (Scheper-Hughes & Lock, 1986, p. 21).

Negative anthropomorphism has been cited as a source of alienation within society (Scheper-Hughes & Lock, 1986, p. 22). Distinct from how machines and computers actually work, or what they enable us to do, they have become the cultural authority and aesthetic. "Function" is valued over other assessments, highlighting only what "works." But to esteem only what works makes function itself a value above all else. Bodies in this conceptualization then become pared down to their functions and malfunctions, primed for both the medical profession and consumer industry to fix (Stein, 1985, p. 8).

Gendered Bodies

Traditional Western interpretations of the body construct just two, mutually exclusive, biological sexes based on their reproductive functions. The differences between male and female are innately grounded in reproduction metaphors, with explanations proceeding from a seemingly scientific biologically functional foundation.

However, the two-sex model of the human body has been in fashion only for the last few hundred years. Before that, there was a one-sex model. The female body was considered just an inferior version of the male. The utilization of a one-gender model, supposedly without attributing inherent female inferiority, is still available for many contemporary social processes, as in the case of unisex fashion and gender-neutral labor. On the other hand, several Native American cultures envision a three-gender model. In general, when it comes to determining the categories of sexual beings, there is a whole spectrum of fragments, variations, and projections.

Feminist analyses of both the body and gender constructions of the body focus on how power relations within social systems affect the "reality" of the body. Initially, those interpretations of the body were a political issue as feminists struggled to gain control over women's fertility and their right to abortion. Their analysis of gender and power also investigated how scientific discourse conceptualized both women's and men's bodies.

As has been discussed in section one, the Cartesian mind/body dualism divides human experience into a bodily realm and a consciousness realm. Feminist critiques of the Cartesian dualism illuminate how the female body is used exclusively as the metaphor for the corporeal pole of the dualism. The female body represents nature (Mother Nature), emotionality, irrationality, and sensuality. The dangerous, appetitive female body is seen as ruled by emotions, standing in contrast to the masterful, masculine will, the locus of social power, rationality, and self-control (Gowaty, 1997). In this comparison, the female body is always "other," mysterious and unruly.

The topics of feminist social theory of the body are as diverse as are the disciplines and methodologies with which they are analyzed. From hysteria and "rest cures" in the nineteenth century to the recent focus on PMS, anorexia nervosa, and menopause, feminist analysis explores how and why women's bodies have been constructed as more susceptible to pathologies than their male counterparts.

Feminist scholars have explored women's sexual desire and experiences, focusing specifically on how heterosexual norms have constrained understandings of the body. Women's experiences with the appearance of their bodies have been investigated, analyses ranging from the more routine beauty practices, fitness regimes, and fashion to dieting, female eating disorders, and cosmetic surgery. Representations of the female body in film and on television have been examined, showing how cultural images in the media set standards for women by presenting images of "desirable" female bodies as seductive, white, affluent, and thin.

Overall, feminist scholarship is critical of the two-sexed biological foundation underlying much of Western thought. Simone de Beauvoir's famous statement in the 1950s that "Women are made, not born," launched a whole generation of feminist scholars focused on challenging the doctrine of "natural difference" (de Beauvoir, 1989). Feminists have sought to demonstrate how gender is socially, not biologically, constructed. Contesting women as "natural mothers," "naturally less aggressive," "naturally weaker," feminist interpretations of the female body focus on the power of cultural mandates to legitimate gendered relations of domination and subordination.

Recently, feminist scholarship has begun to analyze the suppositions behind even this sex/gender distinction. While challenging the assumed basic nature of the two-sexed body guiding much of contemporary research, current analyses also illuminate how heterosexuality has been another hidden assumption of past research. This current scholarship shows how, even in academic research, the taken-for-granted nature of heterosexuality has bolstered both the foundations and the distinctions between male and female.

Judith Butler has been highly influential in breaking the boundaries of interpretation around notions of differences between a biologically sexed and socially constructed gender. She challenges the assumption that genitals define the boundary between two sexes and two genders. Instead, she suggests each individual body enacts and can be read as a "gender performance" (Butler, 1990). How do you know if a person is female or male? The daily performances supported through appropriate costumes, hairstyles, and bodily actions such as ways of sitting, standing, and talking all generate easily read binary distinctions between men and women. Attacking the binary thought process inherent in the two-sexed model, theorists like

Butler are now celebrating the transgressive nature of performance and display inherent in bodybuilding, the male transvestite, and the early performances of Madonna. Bulter suggests that looking at the performances inherent in these "gender-troubled" arenas illuminates the daily performances we all act out to display Western assumptions of appropriate gender roles.

Body image within a system of patriarchy has traditionally been perceived as a woman's issue. While women's concern for appearance is linked to female sex-role stereotypes, until recently, the role that physical appearance and body image play for men has been ignored. From the flapper of the Roaring Twenties to the buxom Marilyn Monroe in the 1950s to the waiflike thinness of Twiggy in the 1960s, images of women's bodies have been symbolic icons and markers of decades. Yet, an examination of women's bodies which excludes men's relationship to their bodies tends to support and reproduce the Cartesian dualism of mind/man, body/women. Assuming men are above or beyond having a relationship with their bodies assumes men are just minds without bodies.

A review of current magazines and the media, however, suggests a celebration and focus on a young, lean, and muscular male body (Mishkind, 1987, p. 37). Men now serve as marketing targets for diet sodas, light beers, health spas, and reconstructive surgery. In his article in this section, Marc Mishkind suggests that with the collapse of other historical social values there has been a shift in emphasis towards men and their consumption habits, with an increased focus on their commodified appearance. Men may focus on different aspects of their bodies and discuss their bodies with a different vocabulary, but their various body parts are now being made into objects of commodification.

The increased attention to men's physical appearance, clothing, and "beautification" does not imply any relaxation of the pressure on women to conform. Viewed in combination, this trend seems to suggest there might develop an "equal objectification" of males. If women increasingly were to see and respond to men as men have traditionally responded to women, the change, while it might represent a kind of equalization, would not be a very satisfactory one. Males would then have to share the burden of coercion imposed by appearance norms. But it is by no means clear that the similar burden on women would thereby be removed or even reduced (Schur, 1987, p. 61).

Men's Studies is concerned with many of these issues, and like its counterpart in Women's Studies, focuses on gender/sex as a problematic body construct. In conjunction with Women's Studies, Men's Studies also demonstrates that the differences between the sexes are small in comparison to the variations within them, and between cultural and historical situations. For example, there are cultural situations where rape is nonexistent or extremely rare, where the male is not aggressive, where homosexuality is expected within the life cycle, where mothers are not the primary caregivers.

One concept explored in Men's Studies is the social construction of masculinity. As with femininity, masculinity is traditionally thought to emerge from the body. It is supposedly inherent in a male body or is supposed to express the drives of a male body. And as half of the binary gender concept, masculinity is also defined by what it is not. It is a relational concept such that boys learn to be men through learning not to be women (Kimmel, 1987, p. 15). Men are to avoid all "sissy" stuff and all feminine behaviors. To be masculine is to act and look differently from women.

The body of the athlete is considered the ideal masculine body type. The athletic male body epitomizes competition and hierarchy among men, and the domination of women. Yet, this construction of gender becomes contested and questionable when the performance cannot be sustained, when for example, female athletes surpass a man's performance, when a man is injured or becomes chronically ill, or if a man is inept or never plays sports.

It is suggested that the increased cultural attention given to the male body and the increased demand placed on men to achieve a mesomorphic or muscular build is pushing men further along the continuum of bodily concern, with more joining the population of women with eating disorders (Mishkind, 1987, p. 44). Men feel ashamed when they focus on their bodies, presumably because this has been associated traditionally with the female sex-role stereotype (Mishkind, 1987, p. 44). Living within the male/female dualism, a masculine man should not be concerned with body image issues.

Interestingly, the new information technology industry and the sedentary work necessary for proficient computer use undercuts the traditional construction of masculinity and the body-as-machine connection. Indeed, the image of the computer nerd's body is invariably male, white, late adolescent, and physically unattractive. Portrayed as pale with pimply skin and thick, unflattering spectacles, skinny, with poor fashion sense, and "soft" from too much physical inactivity and junk food, they are feminized as "wimps" but maintain some power through their technological prowess.

And these "wimps" become targets for advertisers. Marketing has attempted to redefine keyboard work as an arena for competition and power, an area of technical mastery over challenges. Computer games are constructed with hyper-masculine and hyper-feminine bodies conquering and subduing opponents. For more on this aspect of metaphors and the vicarious pleasures of playing with stereotypically gendered bodies, see Anne Balsamo's (1996) *Technologies of the Gendered Body*.

The Body as a Commodity

Advertisements are not merely ways of communicating information about products. They are message systems designed to organize perceptions and "create structures of meaning" (Williams, 1968, p. 12). They comprise frameworks through which a world of objects is translated into a world of social relationships with other people. Advertisers draw upon sociocultural meanings from both the viewers' life-worlds and the mass media. They then entwine these meanings into images that are returned to viewers—now framed in relation to products and services. This process is known as commodification, where advertisers turn a value, such as freedom, femininity, excitement, into a product or commodity that can purchased.

Commodification of the body turns the individual into an object composed of product-mediated parts—lips, eyes, waist, hips, hair, odors, and even clothes. Individuals become a means to display a collection of body parts, each serviced by appropriate products. The popular media and commercial interests have found that a body that both "looks good and feels great" is a very marketable commodity. Yet the portrayal of looking healthy collapses the experience of health with the mere presentation of health, suggesting that the attainment and/or the spectacle of a healthy body is available to be purchased across a wide variety of products.

A "healthy lifestyle" entails an entire category of consumer goods, binding together a set of consumption priorities with individual responsibility for that consumption. In a consumer culture, the commodification of health, of body maintenance, develops into corresponding industries that are intimately connected to the whole political and economic system. More than 12 percent of the entire

US gross national product is devoted to health care (Burnham, 1989, p. 357), entangling themes of health with clothing size, cardiovascular conditioning with the waistline, endurance with body shape. Thus, however much "health" appeals to the rationality of self-preservation and offers the incentives of longevity and lowered risk of disease, messages of "health" are strongly entwined with the consumer culture idealizing appearance and the youthful body.

Connected to commodification is the process of reification, where images of abstracted body parts are styled and endowed with a life of their own, so that desirable social relationships—successful parenthood, intimate partnership, etc.—are positively influenced by purchase of the advertised objects. Reification refers to the trick through which relationships are restructured by commodities to seem "natural." Lace is merely a type of material, but is reified or coded to suggest femininity and sensuousness. What happens when a man wears lace? The seeming naturalness of the association of lace with femininity ignores the learned knowledge and the production values that have structured the arbitrary relationship in the first place. Coloring hair to cover gray, while making sure it looks "natural," ignores other social relationships: the valuing of youth over maturity, the economic structure that results, the financial ability and desire of individuals to purchase the color, and the entire infrastructure dependent upon a person, male or female, believing in the need to transform their look.

The commodified and reified body becomes the body beautiful and is geared to the narcissistic ends of personal health, happiness, social success, and social acceptability. Mike Featherstone, in the article in this section titled "The Body in Consumer Culture," explores the details and theoretical underpinnings of general consumer lifestyles and bodily presentation. He suggests that attractive bodies, both male and female, are portrayed as living at the level of sheer appearance. At this level, social power is translated into economic power, with "correct" purchases displayed through focused accentuation of idealized body parts. Bodies in their natural state are interpreted by advertising as flawed body parts, exposed for the consumer industry to transform through individual efforts and self-maintenance. The time and money needed to restructure one's body into the commodified ideal ultimately reflects and can affect a person's social locations. (For a sophisticated theoretical analysis of the interaction between class and taste, see Bourdieu, 1984 and 1986.)

Female Commodified Bodies

Advertisements traditionally have structured a woman's view of herself from a man's (real or absent) perspective. This type of advertising is evident as early as a 1920s ad for Pompeian Night Cream. In the text of the ad, two women, one a spokesperson for the night cream, have an intimate discussion about husband and wife relationships. The other is a worried wife afraid she is losing her husband's affection. In the words of the night cream advocate, the advertisement states:

> From an unusually attractive woman my friend had developed into a chronic complainer—and it offended even *me* to see the way she appeared in the mornings at the breakfast table. . . . So after one of her confidences I said,
> "Now, frankly, my dear, I believe your husband is interested in another woman. *He is interested in the woman you used to be.*" I emphasized the necessity of taking care of her complexion. I told her how bad hers looked, and how it ruined her beauty. And I was glad to tell her what almost magical results she could get by using *Pompeian Night Cream.*
> (Emphasis in original.)

The spokesperson for Pompeian Night Cream does not take the complaints of her friend/wife as real, but seeing her friend through the husband's eyes, invalidates her complaints and ignores her position and voice. Why the friend/wife is complaining is not the issue. The problem is constructed as threefold: the ability to keep the man's attention; to be worthy of his gaze; and the competition between women for the man's attention. The solution to "the problem" is a commodity: Pompeian Night Cream will keep her attractive to her man. Women are not "naturally" acceptable, but must work at changing themselves in order to be available, receptive, and attractive to men.

Robert Goldman (1992) suggests the term "commodity feminism" to describe how the political discourse inherent in feminism has, in the 1990s, been turned into a commodity style and product to be purchased. Advertisements for women today suggest that emancipation is attainable through the consumption of a product. Within this conceptualization, the female body is reframed as the location of freedom and sexual pleasure through voluntarily, knowingly, and self-reflectively becoming an object of the male gaze. In an advertisement for Triumph undergarments, a woman stands viewing her body in a full-length mirror. Her arms are over her head, holding her full head of hair, as she poses in her black bra, underwear, garter belt, and black nylons. The caption says, "I wear it. He pays attention. It's a control thing."

This advertisement demonstrates how women are now being portrayed as choosing to be sexual objects because it suits their liberated interests. Power imbalances are redressed in terms of commodity consumption, in this case, in terms of underwear and personal appearance choices. Freedom and choice are conjoined with images of sexuality and commodities. Traditionally, the idealized female slim figure allows a woman to be available to a man's attention. In this ad, she is empowered by and takes control through a traditionally commodified feminine form. Femininity as defined by the commodity leads to the control of a man. The male gaze is absent, but the style of performance is suggestive of his future perspective, internalized as part of the woman's enjoyment of herself. She actually increases her power through her ability to make herself an object, to make herself available to his gaze. Feminism is no longer focused on equal treatment or opportunity, but becomes a whole commodity consumption lifestyle displayed through the female body.

To stay continually competitive, advertisers adapted feminist mandates and its rejection of ads that continuously positioned women as envying the body or the look conveyed by model images. Today's advertisements continue to use the male gaze, but are also now combining the ideals of ultrafeminine romance with an ahistorical and fictional portrayal of independence. So, while current ads still continue to address women as malleable surfaces and as resolving problems through the purchase of commodities, those commodities are positioned to exhibit tenets of feminism. These new ads juxtapose and connect the unconventional with the conventional, frequently representing women taking control and power over their lives and relationships through a commodity that determines their attractiveness to men. Advertisers may be addressing women in terms of new gender roles embracing newfound "freedoms" and life chances, but those new roles are still being structured on the same old scenarios for gaining power—using the body and appearance to simulate and stimulate desire. Through mastering the currency of "the look" whether for an assumed self-pleasure or self-determination, women are shown to acquire power over men. The commodification of different body parts is endorsed as the route to control, power, success, and strength through being attractive. Susan Bordo, in her chapter in this section titled "Material Girl," examines in depth the importance of gendered, classed, and racialized body parts as features of modern advertising. She explores how the ideals of advertising have come to shape people's experience of their bodies. The power of commodified images is shown to even structure resistance strategies to the power of advertising. Bordo comes to question Madonna's assertions of independence and resistance through her transformed appearances and constructions of "the look."

Racialized Bodies

Scholarship has traced the interconnections between racism and the body, showing how the body has been central to the actual construction of the concept of race. The race of a person is usually initially identified from the visible body; the lips, eyes, hair, and skin color. Yet, many bodies share these visible traits outside the narrowed category of "race." The distribution of physical characteristics is scattered across the spectrum of humanity, revealing again the arbitrary nature of classifications and categorizations. The racialized body is interpreted as visibly exposing the essential relationship between a region, or a continent, or a history, collapsing these seeming distinctions into an "epidermal hierarchy" of culture and identity (Wiegman, 1995, p. 9). Race becomes embodied as a visual marker, translating seemingly observable physical differences, geographies, politics, and ideology into the "naturalness" of the body (Wiegman, 1995, p. 22).

That "naturalness" usually has an assumed foundation in biology. The eugenics movement and the study of cranial capacity at the turn of the nineteenth century, the Jensen report of the late 1960s, and *The Bell Curve* in the mid-1990s are all examples of the promotion of this naturalized racial biology. This view objectifies race, dividing people into categories that combine entwined biological, sociological, and cultural types. As was discussed in the first section, when biological and cultural explanations are juxtaposed, biological explanations tend to dominate. Race constructed as a biological category becomes "scientifically" interpreted as a neutral and natural genetic category.

In the nineteenth century, "scientific" measurement of the brain and skull was used to explain the differences between individuals and groups. In the 1820s, phrenology claimed a direct comparison between women and "lower races" based on their skull formation. "In short, lower races represented the 'female' type of the human species, and females the 'lower races' of gender" (Stepan, 1990, pp. 39–40). Through these measurements, the African male was aligned with "the feminine." Whether it was brain weight, cranial capacity, the facial angle, or the brain volume, an "objective" measure was found to substantiate the differences between social superiorities and inferiorities.

These types of physical and social categorizations, while being an arbitrary grouping of traits, have real consequences in people's lived experiences. "Race" cannot be abstracted from the social and political environment within which it is defined and lived. The entwined commingling of biological, historical, and cultural categorizations affects social and political stratification.

Recently, scholars have explored how these social conceptualizations of racial differences have displayed divisions similar to the mind/body split inherent in Cartesian dualism. Naturalists in the seventeenth century presumed man was "mind" while woman was confined to the sensuous and physical "body." These naturalists also assumed the African body, both male and female, embodied a seemingly degenerated racial sexuality. Africans were seen as sexually uninhibited "creatures" with unlimited appetites and satisfactions. And while it was accepted that women in general were lower than men, comparisons of African and European female bodies revealed they were biologically different from one another. The "nonwhite" woman was thought to be endowed with an uncontrolled animalistic sexuality—a myth that justified the use of black women for slave breeding and exempted them from the possibility of being raped. By linking the body with both femininity and "animality," "women of color" entwined both sexuality and race.

The construction of difference between white men and African men was based on the perception of both the African's seemingly smaller brain capacities along with his "perversely developed" sexuality. In patriarchal relations, men's dominance over women is the primary sign of power. White men were the defenders of white female sexuality. In the slave economy, black men were "scientifically" feminized as inferior through phrenological measurements. This feminization is represented in the bumbling black Sambo, Uncle Remus, and Jim Crow.

During Reconstruction, though, the Freedman's Bureau gave the black male theoretical equality in political and economic spheres. In theory, he became part of the patriarchy—head of the household, able to enter into contractual labor agreements for the entire family, taking on the gender codes of the white bourgeois ideology. Theorists suggest that this legal enfranchisement of the black male slave during Reconstruction heightened the threat to white masculine supremacy. Black males were now to enter the public arena with all the rights and privileges of men. The black man's threat to white masculine power arose from the frightening possibility of cross-race masculine sameness.

This threat of masculine sameness combines with the fear that slaves, freed from the restraining influences of slavery, were "retrogressing" toward their "natural state" of bestiality. Older slaves were susceptible to the fall, but more threatening were the young men who, born free, had never felt the "civilizing" effects of slavery. The essential nature of the newly matured black man was seen as bestial and unsupported by the enforced moral behavior of slavery. The "new Negro" was reverting to a native savagery, a "reversion" that became most conspicuous in fabricated reports of black men raping white women. The black man was reduced to the body, and to the penis itself. The black freed man was "man" without mind, hyper-masculinized as the black-beast-rapist.

This hyper-masculinized construction has extended into the twentieth century in the Black Power movement. Even the *Shaft* and *Superfly* figures from the 1970s suggest images of the powerfully masculine black male. The image of black man is one of physical prowess and a "natural masculinity." This natural masculinity is translated into a "natural athleticism," and is discussed in detail in this section by Mary G. McDonald, in "Michael Jordan's Family Values: Marketing, Meaning, and Post-Reagan America." McDonald explores how Jordan is able to counter the attributed white fears of black men, exploiting normative male values of athletic success and fatherhood. He consciously constructs his black body into a symbol of masculinity and white corporate achievement, commodifying black athleticism as freedom and economic prosperity.

Cybernetic Bodies

As metaphors, cyborgs are fictional and symbolic representations of cultural experience, and as such, they can highlight many of the issues surrounding the body discussed in this section. Examining the constructions of different cyborg body types will illuminate the body-as-machine metaphor, and how gender and racial distinctions are (re)produced. For example, why are cyborgs usually male and white? And why, if a cyborg is represented as female, is the body always white, hyper-feminized with rounded breasts, and the personality portrayed as cold and yet seductive?

Cyborgs represent both utopian hopes and dystopian fears of what life is like and what can be expected of life in the next century. As the epitome of the body-as-machine metaphor, cyborg bodies call into question, and force comparisons with, the human and machine, the real and the artificial. The cyborg body is all-powerful, is the model of strength, self-sufficiency, functionality, and rationality. Yet, these values are contested when stories involving cyborgs construct a deep and dangerous loss as the body is penetrated by technology.

In the utopian interpretation of the future, technology generates a perpetual self-rebirth and transcendence from the mortality and limitations of flesh. With hip replacements, artificial hearts, contact lenses, plastic surgery, and mind-altering drugs, what it means to be human is being redefined. A more dystopian interpretation however reveals a future where the body is constantly violated by technological interventions. In this dystopian view, humans become homogenized and unable to resist or negotiate the enforced discipline of technology.

Cyborgs, as portrayed in movies such as *Terminator, Star Trek*, and *RoboCop*, represent a more dystopian future by displaying the collapse of medical, technical, and political boundaries. The cyborg "personality" is unemotional and invincible, embodying a post-national hybrid of profit-minded government and business organizations and a military-industrial complex that has grown to international proportions.

There are four types of cyborgs found in film and literature, each displaying a different slippage between machine/human/gender anxieties (Springer, 1993). The first is the macho cyborg most often identified with Arnold Schwarzenegger's *Terminator*. This cyborg has a hypermasculine white male body with aggressive, bulging "muscles," and a heightened physical strength. Its large size and physical power distinguish the macho-cyborg. Its armor-like body protects it from assaults that would destroy an ordinary human, attacks such as fire that burns off skin, bullet wounds, and car or motorcycle crashes. Significantly, this type of cyborg also maintains the conventional male gender role.

The second type is labeled the androgynous cyborg and is identified with the more advanced hybrid in *Terminator 2*. While Schwarzenegger's cyborg body represented an industrial age of large power machines, the androgynous cyborg body is a metaphor for the "information age." It is faster, sleeker, and more compact compared to old power machines. It evokes a comparison of computer and microelectronics with steam or bulky rocket engines. The electronic technology of the androgynous cyborg does not display an externally visible musculature like the macho Schwarzenegger cyborg. Instead, the more advanced body musculature is concealed and fluid, in some ways feminized by being smaller, internalized, more refined, and more dangerous.

In comparison with the androgynous cyborg, the macho cyborg represents a form of outdated, rigid masculinity (Springer, 1993). Indeed, instead of maintaining conventional sex roles, the androgynous cyborg is "polygendered," meaning that it has the ability to take on the role of male or female. In *Terminator 2*, the androgynous cyborg became a male L.A. cop, a male asylum guard, the heroine, and a foster mother. Theorists suggest this type of gender switching, inherent in the androgynous cyborg, subverts conventional notions of gender, and represents transformations and fears about sexual difference and gender performance. While the technological, enhanced body of the macho cyborg is a departure from the unadorned body/fortress of the Rambo icon, the advanced nature of the androgynous cyborg suggests a continued weakening of an unaltered masculine omnipotence. Thus, while leaving intact the conceptualization of the increasing power of technology, the metaphor of the androgynous cyborg body suggests a fear between the ever-advancing power of technology and the undermining of gender distinctiveness.

The competition between the two types of cyborgs in *Terminator 2* expresses a form of nostalgia for a time when masculine superiority was taken for granted. This nostalgia is expressed in the *Terminator 2* story line by giving allegiance to the macho cyborg as the benevolent father figure. In the end, Schwarzenegger's cyborg is victorious over the androgynous cyborg, proving the superiority of a solid masculinity. Even in its "dying" moments, the Schwarzenegger cyborg is triumphal—while the androgynous cyborg squirms, shimmies, and screams as it melts, Schwarzenegger dies with a chivalric wave of the hand and a "thumbs up" (Springer, 1993).

The third type of cyborg is the post-organic, as displayed by the Picard/Locutus transformation in *Star Trek: First Contact*, and Murphy in *RoboCop*. This type of cyborg began as an organic human, a person who preexisted before the body was implanted with technological prostheses. The transformed body presents the individual as taken over or rewired, a type of individual-to-electronic reassembly. The rewiring is usually performed by a ruthless and deceptive corporate paternalism. The body is reproduced as a corporate product, with an attempt to erase the individuality and discrete identity of the human. The human becomes a being without agency, without gender, penetrated and desexed. The transformation is a form of high-tech rebirth, representing fears of the loss of choice, morality, individuality, and identity inherent in embracing technology.

All three of the cyborgs discussed above represent a contradiction in biological reproduction and the "gender trouble" inherent within self-reproduction. Conventional biological reproduction is irrelevant for cyborgs. The cyborg threatens the heterosexual matrix by having a successful body that is self-reproducing but not biologically reproductive. As masculine bodies, the cyborgs have no genitals, and thus challenge the organic notions of sex and sex roles, maternity and paternity. The cyborg can be disassembled, and reassembled, without reference to gender. The memories of the cyborg can be reprogrammed and its body (re)produced, making birth, death, and gender inapplicable, insignificant.

Less frequently seen is the fourth type, the female cyborg (Springer, 1993). The female identity is used when technology must be seductive. By associating technology with the female body, the female cyborg represents the threat of unleashed female sexuality. An excellent example is the "queen" Borg in *Star Trek: First Contact*. Here, the female body and machine are merged to produce the terrifying prospect of female intelligence and power. The queen Borg is a highly sensuous female, who attempts to seduce both Data and Picard with her femininity, her intellect, her superiority, and her power.

Comparison of the female and male cyborgs raises several questions. Why are Locutus, RoboCop, and both Terminators asexual and the queen Borg highly sexualized? Does the female cyborg role display a Cartesian dualism, that women are constructed as bodies, and as such are seductively disruptive? Does using the cyborg as female undermine or confirm the gendered Cartesian split of body/feminine and mind/masculine? Or does the use of the female body as a metaphor for power and control ultimately challenge the seemingly "natural" correspondence between maternity and femininity, female and emotions? Are the female cyborgs a feminist revenge fantasy? Or does the death of the female cyborg ultimately reestablish the patriarchal order by containing women's position? Does the female cyborg assert the invincibility of patriarchal power, or does she demonstrate that patriarchal power can be manipulated, is weak and predictable?

The seemingly contradictory answers to these questions confirm the utility of using the cyborg body as a metaphor to explore many of the tensions within American culture. As a metaphor, the cyborg body highlights the seeming invisibility of whiteness, while illuminating the disruptions of the distinctions between male and female, between nature and culture, between artificial and real, between produced and reproduced. Cyborg bodies call into question and force comparisons of the individual within a collective and the distinction between animal and human, human and machine. The cyborg displays a "failed distinction" between organic and implanted hardware, highlighting the impotency of normal flesh. Cyborgs, as the ultimate body-as-machine metaphor, are symbolic representations of our combined historical experience with technology and machines, highlighting both the hopes and fears of white male interactions with technology.

MIKE FEATHERSTONE

4 | The Body in Consumer Culture

Mike Featherstone examines the historical and contemporary effects of consumer ideals on the body. In
a consumer culture, the body becomes a vehicle for
both the display of pleasure and the experience
of pleasure. Advertising continually suggests that
people must spend time, money, and effort to construct "the look," both looking like they have the
potential for fun, and that they are simultaneously
enjoying themselves to the fullest. This construction
of body parts around youth and appearance, however, demands increasing personal investment as
individuals consciously attempt to transform their
bodies to fit culturally mediated appearance ideals.
Featherstone's exploration of body-maintenance techniques highlights how contemporary advertising
utilizes body-as-machine metaphors. His in-depth
analysis provides the basic groundwork for other
social theorists in this section that focuses on gendered and racial constructions of the body in consumer culture.

The vast range of dietary, slimming, exercise, and
cosmetic body maintenance products which are
currently produced, marketed, and sold point to the significance of
appearance and bodily presentation within late capitalist society.
Consumer culture latches onto the prevalent self-preservationist conception of the body, which encourages the individual to adopt
instrumental strategies to combat deterioration and decay (applauded

From Mike Featherstone, "The Body in Consumer Culture," *Theory, Culture, and
Society* 1 (1982): 18–33. Reprinted by permission of Sage Publications.

too by state bureaucracies who seek to reduce health costs by edu-
cating the public against bodily neglect) and combines it with the
notion that the body is a vehicle of pleasure and self-expression.
Images of the body beautiful, openly sexual and associated with
hedonism, leisure, and display, emphasize the importance of appearance and "the look."

Within consumer culture, advertisements, the popular press, television, and motion pictures provide a proliferation of stylized
images of the body. In addition, the popular media constantly
emphasize the cosmetic benefits of body maintenance. The reward
for ascetic body work ceases to be spiritual salvation or even
improved health, but becomes an enhanced appearance and more
marketable self. . . . Today, it can be ventured, diet and body maintenance are increasingly regarded as vehicles to release the temptations of the flesh. Discipline and hedonism are no longer seen as
incompatible, indeed the subjugation of the body through body
maintenance routines is presented within consumer culture as a precondition for the achievement of an acceptable appearance and the
release of the body's expressive capacity. Consumer culture does not
involve the complete replacement of asceticism by hedonism, this
shift occurs primarily on the level of the cultural imagery; in reality,
it demands a good deal of "calculating hedonism" from the individual (Jacoby, 1980, p. 63).

The emphasis upon body maintenance and appearance within
consumer culture suggests two basic categories: the inner and the
outer body. The inner body refers to the concern with the health and
optimum functioning of the body which demands maintenance and
repair in the face of disease, abuse, and the deterioration accompanying the aging process. The outer body refers to appearance as well
as the movement and control of the body within social space. . . . For
our purposes it is the appearance and management of impressions of
the outer body that is of particular interest. Within consumer culture, the inner and the outer body became conjoined: the prime purpose of the maintenance of the inner body becomes the enhancement
of the appearance of the outer body.

Consumer Culture

Today's popular heroes are no longer the mighty, the builders of
empires, the inventors and achievers. Our celebrities are movie

stars and singers, "beautiful" people of leisure who profess a philosophy of enjoyment rather than discipline and toil. (Pachter, 1975, p. 330)

Traditional values and mores gradually gave way as more and more aspects of life were brought under the influence of the expanding market with its propaganda for commodities. As free time and leisure activities also became drawn into the orbit of the market, hobbies, pastimes, and experiences come to increasingly depend upon the purchase of commodities. Hence, free time demands systematic planning and the time spent in maintenance activities does not necessarily diminish. It has been suggested that women spend as much time occupied in housework in the post–World War Two era as they did in the early decades of the twentieth century. The decisive change has been in the nature of the tasks performed with the creation of an ever-expanding range of new "essential" tasks and appliances for home maintenance by the domestic science experts and manufacturers of household goods (Ehrenreich & English, 1979, p. 163). Consumer goods themselves need maintenance, as commodities voraciously demand other commodities, and looking after a house, car, and an expanding array of consumer goods makes inroads into free time. Body maintenance, too, provides an expanding market for the sale of commodities as we shall see below. . . .

Certain themes, infinitely revisable, infinitely combinable, recur within advertising and consumer culture imagery: youth, beauty, energy, fitness, movement, freedom, romance, exotica, luxury, enjoyment, fun. Yet whatever the promise in the imagery, consumer culture demands from its recipients a wide-awake, energetic, calculating, maximizing approach to life—it has no place for the settled, the habitual, or the humdrum.

Writing about the role of advertising in the creation of consumer culture, Stuart Ewen (1976, p. 33) charts the process whereby business leaders in the United States in the 1920s, aware of the need for new markets to absorb the increased capacity for mass production, aggressively rose to the task by stimulating new needs, desires, and buying habits: "Advertising offered itself as a means of efficiently creating consumers," he remarks.[1] It helped to break down traditional values by discrediting puritan notions of thrift, patience, steadfastness, abstinence, and moderation. Individuals had to be persuaded to adopt a critical attitude towards body, self, and lifestyle.

Robert and Helen Lynd (1929, p. 82; Ewen, 1976, p. 37) in their study of *Middletown* suggest that modern advertising differed from that of the pre–First World War era by:

> concentrating increasingly on a type of copy aiming to make the reader emotionally uneasy, to bludgeon him with the fact that decent people don't live the way he does . . . This copy points an accusing finger at the stenographer as she read her motion picture magazine and makes her acutely conscious of her unpolished finger nails . . . and sends the housewife peering anxiously into the mirror to see if her wrinkles look like those that made Mrs. X in the advertisement "old at thirty-five" because she did not have a Leisure Hour electric washer.

Advertising thus helped to create a world in which individuals are made to become emotionally vulnerable, constantly monitoring themselves for bodily imperfections which could no longer be regarded as natural.

Consumerism, according to Ewen (1976, p. 54), did not emerge in the 1920s as a smooth progression from earlier patterns of consumption but rather represents "an aggressive device of corporate survival." Ewen quotes many sources from amongst the business community to illustrate the conscious effort to "educate" and manipulate the masses to accept the new "fanciful needs" and consumer values. Yet, however much business leaders like Edward Filene emphasized the need to teach "the masses not what to think but *how to think*" (Ewen, 1976, p. 55), this should not be taken as evidence that the masses were so easily duped. Elements of the new value complex were welcomed by individuals as genuinely progressive. The traditional values challenged by advertising and consumer culture did not surrender to false needs merely through a process of mass deception. Rather, however much advertising persuaded individuals to adopt instrumental strategies through a welter of scientific and pseudoscientific justifications for new products, it also involved a genuinely critical element. The discrediting of traditional values should not, therefore, be seen negatively as resulting in the loss of community and brotherhood—the romantic side of *Gemeinschaft*—but as involving a reasonable critique of dogmatic authority, arbitrary structures of prejudice, and patriarchal domination. For individual family members to earn an independent income and be accorded the equality of independent consumers in the marketplace offered tangible freedoms, however limited and restricted they might turn out to be. . . .

Images of the Body

> Ours is an age obsessed with youth, health, and physical beauty. Television and motion pictures, the dominant visual media, churn out persistent reminders that the lithe and graceful body, the dimpled smile set in an attractive face, are the keys to happiness, perhaps even its essence. (Kern, 1975, p. ix)

Within consumer culture the body is proclaimed as a vehicle of pleasure: it is desirable and desiring, and the closer the actual body approximates to the idealized images of youth, health, fitness, and beauty, the higher its exchange-value. Consumer culture permits the unashamed display of the human body. Clothing is designed to celebrate the "natural" human form, a marked contrast to the nineteenth century in which clothes were designed to conceal the body. Victorian male attire reflected the concern for respectability with the male body regarded as a clothes-horse for loose fitting conservative clothes in subdued colors. The female form had to be crammed into corsets to achieve the hourglass figure despite the vigorous propaganda against tight-lacing and the resulting disablement of internal organs (Colmer, 1979). In the bedroom the naked body was not regarded as a thing of beauty and joy; sex should take place in the dark. Even in the "gay" "naughty" 1890s, sex manuals like S. Stall's *What a Young Man Ought to Know* (1897) cautioned that sex should only take place once a week and partners should never undress in front of each other (Kern, 1975, p. 111). Within consumer culture the body ceases to be a vessel of sin and the secularized body has found more and more contexts for display both inside and outside the bedroom. The popularity of the outdoor Californian lifestyle and centrally heated living areas have helped to make more acceptable leisure clothing which makes visible the form of the human body.

While the body incorporates fixed capacities such as height and bone structure, the tendency within consumer culture is for ascribed bodily qualities to become regarded as plastic—with effort and "body work" individuals are persuaded that they can achieve a certain desired appearance. Advertising, feature articles, and advice columns in magazines and newspapers ask individuals to assume self-responsibility for the way they look. This becomes important not just in the first flush of adolescence and early adulthood, for notions of "natural" bodily deterioration and the bodily betrayals that accompany aging become interpreted as signs of moral laxitude (Hepworth & Featherstone 1982). The wrinkles, sagging flesh, tendency towards middle age spread, hair loss etc, which accompany aging should be combated by energetic body maintenance on the part of the individual—with help from the cosmetic, beauty, fitness, and leisure industries.

The perception of the body within consumer culture is dominated by the existence of a vast array of visual images. Indeed the inner logic of consumer culture depends on the cultivation of an insatiable appetite to consume images. The production of images to stimulate sales on a societal level is echoed by the individual production of images through photography (Sontag, 1978). Christopher Lasch (1979a, p. 47) has noted the profound effect of photography on the perception of social life:

> Cameras and recording machines not only transcribe experience but alter its quality, giving to much of modern life the character of an enormous echo chamber, a hall of mirrors. Life presents itself as a succession of images, of electronic signals, of impressions recorded and reproduced by means of photography, motion pictures, television and sophisticated recording devices. Modern life is so thoroughly mediated by electronic images that we cannot help responding to others as if their actions—and our own—were being recorded and simultaneously transmitted to an unseen audience or stored up for close scrutiny at some later time.

Day-to-day awareness of the current state of one's appearance is sharpened by comparison with one's own past photographic images as well as with the idealized images of the human body which proliferate in advertising and the visual media. Images invite comparisons; they are constant reminders of what we are and might with effort yet become. The desire for one's own body also becomes catered for with one of the effects of the new camera technology (instant photographs, videotapes) being to further private narcissistic uses.[2] Women are of course most clearly trapped in the narcissistic, self-surveillance world of images, for apart from being accorded the major responsibility in organizing the purchase and consumption of commodities, their bodies are used symbolically in advertise-ments (Winship, 1980; Pollock, 1977). The cosmetic and fashion industries are eager to redress this imbalance and promote men alongside women to enjoy the dubious equality of consumers in the marketplace (Winter & Robert, 1980).

Images make individuals more conscious of external appearance, bodily presentation, and "the look." The motion picture industry has since the early days of consumer culture been one of the major cre-ators and purveyors of images. In this context it is interesting to note that Bela Balázs speculated in the early 1920s that film was trans-forming the emotional life of twentieth century man by directing him away from words towards movement and gesture. A culture domi-nated by words tends to be intangible and abstract, and reduces the human body to a basic biological organism, whereas the new empha-sis upon visual images drew attention to the appearance of the body, the clothing, demeanor, and gesture (Kern, 1975).The Hollywood cinema helped to create new standards of appearance and bodily presentation, bringing home to a mass audience the importance of "looking good." Hollywood publicized the new consumer culture values and projected images of the glamorous celebrity lifestyle to a worldwide audience. The major studios carefully disciplined and packaged film stars for audience consumption.[3] To ensure that the stars conformed with the ideals of physical perfection, new kinds of makeup, hair care, and techniques such as electrolysis, cosmetic sur-gery, and toupees were created to remove imperfections. Mary Pickford, who subjected herself to a rigorous daily cosmetic, exer-cise, and dietary regime in the early 1920s, later branched out into the cosmetic industry.

Helena Rubinstein, who amassed a fortune of over five hundred million dollars, capitalized on these trends by enthusiastically advo-cating beauty for the masses. She reassured women that there was nothing wrong with wanting to hold onto youth, and formulated the consumer culture equation of youth = beauty = health. "To preserve one's beauty is to preserve health and prolong life" (Rubinstein, 1930). The new female ideal (epitomized by the flapper) was not without its critics; Cynthia White (1970) remarks that editorials in British women's magazines in the early 1920s were firmly against the use of makeup and lipstick but by the late 1920s they had capitu-lated and were for cosmetics—a decision not unrelated to the increasing amount of cosmetic advertising they carried. The 1920s was a crucial decade in the formulation of the new bodily ideal. By the end of the decade women, under the combined impact of the cosmetic, fashion, and advertising industries, and Hollywood, had for the first time in large numbers put on rouge and lipstick, taken to short skirts, rayon stockings, and had abandoned the corset for rubber "weight-reducing" girdles (Allen, 1931). The new Hollywood styles threatened to carry all before them and iron out regional and local differences. J. B. Priestley (1977) on his *English Journey* of 1933, while taking tea in a rural cafe in Lincolnshire, noted that the girls of the nearby tables had carefully modeled their appearance on their favorite film stars:

> Even twenty years ago girls of this kind would have looked quite different even from girls in the nearest large town; they would have had an unmistakable small town rustic air; but now they are almost indistinguishable from girls in a dozen different capitals, for they all have the same models, from Hollywood.

The major impact of the cosmetic, fashion, and advertising industries in the interwar years was on women; only slow inroads were made in the field of male fashions and cosmetics (one of the most difficult taboos to break down), until the 1960s and 70s. Yet Hollywood did help to bring about changes in the male ideal in the 1920s: Douglas Fairbanks, the first international cinema superstar, famous for the feats of athleticism he performed in costume spectaculars, was marketed as a virility symbol and fitness fanatic. Like his wife, Mary Pickford, disciplined body maintenance and routines played a prominent role in his private life with his daily training schedule of wrestling, boxing, running, and swimming as strenuously publicized as his screen career (Walker, 1970).

Fairbanks, who celebrated the athletic, adventurous outdoor life in his films, also helped to popularize the suntan. Going against the established wisdom which held that the fashionable body must avoid the effects of the sun, lest it be associated with the tanned laboring body, he allowed his darkened face to appear in films and the popular press. Other celebrities followed suit, and sunbathing, which had emerged in the 1890s in Germany as a form of treatment of the tubercular, now gained a wider cosmetic appeal alongside its claims for health: "The skin of the average overclothed man is white, spotty and inelastic, the skin of a healthy man is brown, smooth and sleek," proclaimed an American article of 1929. The interwar years also saw the transformation of the beach into a place where one gained a suntan—the hallmark of a successful holiday. For the first time sunbathing on the beach brought together large numbers of people in varying degrees of undress, legitimating the public display of the body.

From its early days the publicity machine of Hollywood has catered for and generated a great deal of interest in the "backstage" areas, the private lives of the stars, their beauty tips, exercise, and diet regimens.[4] The Hollywood fan magazines of the 1920s and 1930s "indoctrinated their true believers with the notions that women were beautiful, men were manly, crime didn't pay, lovers lived happily ever after time after time, and Lana Turner was discovered eating a sundae at Schwab's Drug Store" (Levin, 1970, p. 7). Magazines such as *Photoplay, Silver Screen, Screen Book, Modern Screen,* and *Motion Picture* as well as publicizing the "secrets of the stars" also offered readers the chance of self-improvement with advertisements claiming to provide remedies for acne, oversized busts, undersized busts, fatness, etc. In the early days publicity stills of the stars were retouched to eliminate blemishes in the actor's or actress's appearance; increasingly this work became unnecessary through the effort stars put into maintaining and enhancing their appearance: in effect they were able to become what they seemed. Hollywood stars began to rely less on aids and supports to effect a given appearance; rather, they carefully achieved the appearance of the "body natural." Body supports such as the corset (later to reemerge as the naughty basque—a titillating body packaging aid for sexual fun and games) found fewer advocates in a culture which endorsed the exposure of the body on the beach and the wearing of casual leisure clothing. Increasingly exercise was presented as a healthy means of strengthening the body's natural support system (Hornibrook, 1924), a technique which would enable the body to pass muster under the close gaze of the camera.

Body Maintenance

Stay young, stay beautiful, live longer. These are the catch phrases of today's hard living society. . . . While the secret of longer life is still a long way off, many people are searching for a short cut—through health foods, yoga, gardening. Grab your survival kit and live longer. (The *Sun*)

Body maintenance cannot of course be claimed as a novel creation of consumer culture. In traditional societies, religious communities such as monasteries demanded ascetic routines with an emphasis upon exercise and dietary control (Turner, 1982). The adoption of ascetic regimes usually meant, however, that the body was subordinated to "higher" spiritual ends. The dominant ethos of Christianity was to denigrate and repress the human body. Jesuits were taught on entering the order to accept Ignatius Loyola's maxim *Perinde ac cadaver* (henceforth as a corpse) (Benthall, 1976, p. 69). The Christian tradition glorified an aesthetics of the soul, not the body. Ascetic regimes would release the spirit and subdue the sexual side of the body. Within consumer culture, on the other hand, sexual experts proclaim that dietary control and exercise will enhance sexual prowess; exercise and sexuality are blurred together through neologisms such as "sexercise" and "exersex." The shame in the naked body gradually gave way under the persistent critique of sexual experts and commercial interests. To enjoy heightened pleasure individuals have not only to consult the sexual manual and resort to a growing range of pills, aids, and devices, they must look good, too. Self-surveillance through taking instant pictures and videotapes celebrated sexual aesthetics: the naked body or the body packaged in erotic sexual leisurewear could be recorded as proof of the achievement of a desired effect (Hepworth & Featherstone, 1982).

The term "body maintenance" indicates the popularity of the machine metaphor for the body. Like cars and other consumer goods, bodies require servicing, regular care, and attention to preserve maximum efficiency.[5] As the consumption of goods increases, the time required for care and maintenance increases, and the same instrumental rational orientation adopted towards goods is turned inwards onto the body. The tendency to transform free time into maintenance work imposes even greater demands on the individual and makes the monitoring of the current state of bodily performance essential if individuals are to get the most out of life: the hectic life increases the need for "human servicing" (Linder, 1970, p. 40).

Preventive medicine offers a similar message and through its offshoot, health education, demands constant vigilance on the part of the individual who has to be persuaded to assume responsibility for his health. Introducing the category "self-inflicted illness," which results from body abuse (overeating, drinking, smoking, lack of exercise, etc.), health educationalists assert that individuals who conserve their bodies through dietary care and exercise will enjoy greater health and live longer. The calculation of the potential saving to state health services provides further grounds for castigating those who do not heed the new message as self-indulgent "slobs" (Featherstone & Hepworth, 1980, 1981; Hepworth & Featherstone, 1982). In effect, the health education movement is trying to bring about a change in the moral climate so that individuals assume increasing self-responsibility for their health, body shape, and appearance. To some extent, this can be seen as building on and accentuating self-help tendencies which were present within the Victorian middle class whose preoccupation with health matters led them to diet, take pills, take up athletics, etc. (Haly, 1979). Yet however much health educationalists appeal to the rationality of self-preservation and offer the incentives of longevity and lowered risk of disease, their body maintenance messages are strongly influenced by the consumer culture idealization of youth and the body beautiful. In the late 1970s, the British Health Education Council found that the most effective advertising message was to highlight the cosmetic rewards of fitness and dietary care. Health educationalists have little time for the health food crank or the fitness fanatic in their advertisements; these are discarded in favor of images of men and women who maximize, who get more out of life, who "look good and feel good," who are more attractive and therefore socially acceptable. Within this logic, fitness and slimness become associated not only with energy, drive, and vitality but worthiness as a person; likewise the body beautiful comes to be taken as a sign of prudence and prescience in health matters.

The popular media and commercial interests have found the "looking good and feeling great" health education message to be a saleable commodity. Eager to endorse body maintenance as a part of the consumer lifestyle, popular newspapers like the *Sun* and *Mirror* in Britain pass on the message to a wider audience with frequent articles on slimming, exercise, health foods, and appearance. Center-page spreads enable readers to calculate their degree of success or failure in meeting age/height/weight targets and how to complete questionnaires to work out their "survival power." Feature articles on the calorific value of different types of food complement center-page spreads on the calorie burning power of different types of activity (running, sitting, walking, sleeping, kissing, sex, etc.), enabling the enterprising reader to draw up a daily calorific balance sheet to see if he or she can meet their designated target. In the last decade, there has also been a noticeable growth in the number of specialist magazines on jogging, running, health foods, exercise, and especially slimming. Self-help books on body maintenance also sell well: In December 1981 four out of ten books on the US bestseller list were of the "how to lose weight" variety. Common to the popular media treatment of body maintenance, be it from the popular press, specialist magazines of the "Doctors' Answers" type, advertisements for vitamins, slimming products, or government health education propaganda, is the encouragement of self-surveillance of bodily health and appearance as well as the incentive of lifestyle benefits. Body maintenance is firmly established as a virtuous leisure time activity which will reap further lifestyle rewards resulting from an enhanced appearance: body maintenance in order to look good merges with the stylized images of looking good while maintaining the body. The images in the advertisements, popular press, and health education pamphlets are of lithe, bright-eyed, beautiful people, in varying states of nakedness, enjoying their body work. The fat are invariably portrayed as glum and downcast: joke figures, survivals from a bygone age.

One of the noticeable features of the twentieth century, according to Theodore Zeldin (1977, p. 440), has been the triumph of the thin woman over the fat woman. It can be added that in the second half of the twentieth century this ideal is becoming firmly established for men, too, with the last bastions of corpulence amongst the working class now under siege. As the slim form becomes mandatory, almost every conceivable consumer product is discovered to have slimming properties. In 1931, the manufacturers of Lucky Strike cigarettes spent nineteen million dollars on advertising and successfully convinced many women that smoking was a vital aid to dieting (Susman, 1973, p. 132). Today grapefruit juice, disco dancing, plankton, and sex are marketed with similar conviction. The beauty industry now offers "shapeovers" ("look ten pounds slimmer without dieting")[6] to accompany "makeovers" as an essential part of every woman's cosmetic repertoire.

Within consumer culture slimness has become associated with health, and the health educational message that being overweight is a health risk has become absorbed into the conventional wisdom. Yet a good deal of the "advice" that abounds in the media and advertisements is clearly of a pseudoscientific nature. Rubin Andres has recently conducted an extensive review of a number of slimming studies and concluded that the overweight actually live longer. The age/height/weight charts originally constructed by insurance companies, which hang in doctors' surgeries and are publicized in the popular media, are inaccurate—in some cases as much as fourteen pounds off. Andres' conclusion that slimness has little to do with health merely confirms those reached by earlier researchers such as Bruch (1957) and Beller (1977) and may be destined to have a similar lack of impact.

Women of course are well aware that the major reason for dieting is cosmetic and that "looking good" not only becomes necessary to achieve social acceptability but can become the key to a more exciting lifestyle. As one woman remarked in a slimming magazine article: "Being overweight was, for me, like living with the brakes on. And I *hated* being held back." The lifestyle benefits are played up in slimming magazines and the popular press: not only do successful slimmers get more admiring glances, they feel more attractive and are confident to go out more, take up new exciting hobbies, and live out their version of the Martini people lifestyle (Hepworth & Featherstone, 1982).

Like slimming, jogging provides further insight into the transvaluation of use within consumer culture: everything has to be good for something else and the range of alleged benefits multiplies endlessly. Apart from reducing the chance of coronary heart disease, it is claimed jogging helps to cure impotence, increase confidence, psychological well-being, and puts "you in control of your body." Jogging has also been claimed to result in prolonged cosmetic benefits—improving posture, reducing stomach sag, helping to burn off excessive fat (Hepworth & Featherstone, 1982, p. 107). The notion of running for running's sake, purposiveness without purpose, a sensuous experience in harmony with embodied and physical nature, is completely submerged amidst the welter of benefits called up by the market and health experts (Featherstone & Hepworth, 1982).

The instrumental strategies which body maintenance demands of the individual resonate with deep-seated features of consumer culture which encourage individuals to negotiate their social relationships and approach their free time activities with a calculating frame of mind. Self-preservation depends upon the preservation of the body within a culture in which the body is the passport to all that is good in life. Health, youth, beauty, sex, fitness are the positive attributes which body care can achieve and preserve. With appearance being taken as a reflex of the self, the penalties of bodily neglect are a lowering of one's acceptability as a person, as well as an indication of laziness, low self-esteem, and even moral failure. Within consumer culture it is hardly surprising that aging and death are viewed so negatively—they are unwelcome reminders of the inevitable decay and defeat that are in store, even for the most vigilant of individuals. The secularization of the body has resulted in the eclipse of the traditional religious purpose of the body in which it was regarded as a transitory vehicle, a means to higher spiritual ends. Today, pain, suffering, and death are seen as unwelcome intrusions in the midst of a happy life (Ariès, 1974) and the consumer culture imagery has decreed that life can and should be everlastingly happy. Amidst images of comfort, fulfillment, and cleanliness, the unpleasant odors and sights surrounding death become intolerable: "the dirty death" (Ariès, 1981, p. 568) has to be hidden away.

Within the limitations of its logic consumer culture is incapable of providing other than flawed solutions to the problems of aging and death. On the one hand it hides them away, suppresses them in the midst of illusions of endless hedonism, while flattering our vanity that we are enjoying the good life here and now. Yet it also needs to stimulate the fear of the decay and incapacities accompanying old age and death to jolt individuals out of complacency and persuade them to consume body maintenance strategies. In a feature article entitled "Have You the Looks That Last?" (day six of the *Sun's* "Staying Alive Week" in June 1978) readers were warned:

> You may look sexy and beautiful now, but will you still be attractive when you're 50? Or 60? Or even 70? To get the most out of life it makes sense to keep in tip-top shape in middle-age and beyond. Beauties like Joan Collins and Cyd Charisse believe that lasting good looks takes lots of hard work.

The illusion of technical mastery and even transcendence over the lifespan fits in well with the "calculating hedonism" (Jacoby, 1980, p. 63) demanded by consumer culture. Within the "live for yourself" calculus, children are seen as bad investments in terms of time, money, and affection and even resented as possible rivals. Cars, jogging, tourism, self-actualization, and the new therapies offer more predictable pleasures and a better return on the investment of time and money (Jacoby, 1980, p. 64). This suggests that within consumer culture a new relationship between the body and self has developed.

The Performing Self

> Today's modern society puts a premium on youth and good
> looks, in fact to look better, to look younger, to look more attrac-
> tive has become a basic need for most of us because people who
> look good, are made to feel good. (The Lasertone Beauty
> Therapy Treatment leaflet, 1982)

A number of commentators have suggested that a new personality
type has emerged in the course of the twentieth century. David
Reisman (1950), for example, refers to the replacement of the "inner-
directed" by the other-directed type and Daniel Bell (1976) mentions
the eclipse of the puritan by a more hedonistic type. Interest in this
new personality type has been sharpened recently by discussions of
narcissism (Lasch, 1976, 1977b, 1979a). This new narcissistic type of
individual, which it is argued has recently come into prominence, is
described as: "excessively self-conscious," "chronically uneasy
about his health, afraid of aging and death," "constantly searching
for flaws and signs of decay," "eager to get along with others yet
unable to make real friendships," "attempts to sell his self as if his
personality was a commodity," "hungry for emotional experiences,"
"haunted by fantasies of omnipotence and eternal youth." Lasch
(1979b, p. 201) argues that the culture of narcissism first took shape
in the 1920s, matured in the postwar era and is now rapidly disinte-
grating.[7] For our purposes the interesting feature of the narcissistic
type and the culture of narcissism which spawned it, is that it points
to a new relationship between body and self. Within consumer culture, which approximately coincides with the culture of narcissism,
the new conception of self which has emerged, which we shall refer
to as the "performing self," places greater emphasis upon appearance, display, and the management of impressions.

One indication of the movement towards the performing self can
be gleaned from the shift in the self ideal proclaimed in self help
manuals from the nineteenth century to the early twentieth century.
In the nineteenth century, self help books emphasized the Protestant
virtues—industry, thrift, temperance, not just as means but as valid
ends in their own right (Lasch, 1979a, p. 57). Achievement was
measured not against others but against abstract ideals of discipline
and self denial. With the bureaucratization of the corporate career,
these virtues gave way to an emphasis upon competition with one's

peers, salesmanship, "boosterism," and the development of "personal magnetism."

Warren Susman (1979) has characterized this shift as entailing the replacement of the nineteenth century concern with character by a new focus upon personality in the early twentieth century. The words most frequently associated with *character* were: citizenship, democracy, duty, work, honor, reputation, morals, integrity, and manhood. Locating the transition in the middle of the first decade of the twentieth century, Susman argues that subsequent advice manuals emphasized *personality*, and a new set of associated adjectives came into prominence: fascinating, stunning, attractive, magnetic, glowing, masterful, creative, dominant, forceful. In his book *Personality: How to Build It* (1915), H. Laurent remarked: "character is either good or bad, personality famous or infamous" (Susman, 1979, p. 217). A comparison of two books written by O. S. Marden, separated by twenty years at the turn of the century, further illustrates the transition. His *Character: The Greatest Thing in the World*, 1899, stressed the ideals of the Christian gentleman: integrity, courage, duty, as well as the virtues of hard work and thrift. In 1921 he published *Masterful Personality*, which emphasized a set of different virtues: now attention should be given to the "need to attract and hold friends," to "compel people to like you," "personal charm," and women should develop "fascination." Good conversation, energy, manners, proper clothes, and poise were also deemed necessary (Susman, 1979, p. 220).

The new personality handbooks stressed voice control, public speaking, exercise, sound catering habits, a good complexion, and grooming and beauty aids—they showed little interest in morals. Susman (1979, p. 221) remarks:

> The social role demanded of all in the new culture of personality was that of performer. Every American was to become a performing self . . . the new stress on enjoyment of life implied that true pleasure could be obtained by making oneself pleasant to others.

Individuals should attempt to develop the skills of actors, a message not just emphasized by self help manuals, but by advertising and the popular press in the 1920s. Hollywood provided many of the models for the new ideal with stars marketed as "personalities." Douglas Fairbanks, the archetype "personality star," even wrote his own kind of self-help book, *Make Life Worthwhile: Laugh and Live* (Susman, 1979, p. 233).

Richard Sennett's book *The Fall of Public Man* is interesting in this context because he examines the historical origins of the new belief that appearance and bodily presentation express the self. In the eighteenth century, he suggests, appearance was not regarded as a reflection of the inner-self but more playfully distanced from an individual's character which was regarded as fixed at birth. The replacement of this traditional holistic worldview by a more "existentialist" view in which each individual was responsible for the development of his own personality, occurred in the nineteenth century. Following Marx's fetishism of commodities argument, Sennett sees the development of the department store in the second half of the nineteenth century as crucial to the process. The department store sold the newly available, cheap, mass-produced clothing by using increasingly sophisticated techniques of advertising and display. Clothing which indicated a fixed social status came to be avoided and an individual's dress and demeanor came more and more to be taken as an expression of his personality: clothes in the words of Thomas Carlyle became "emblems of the soul." Individuals had now to decode both the appearance of others and take pains to manage the impressions they might give off while moving through the world of strangers. This encouraged greater bodily self-consciousness and self-scrutiny in public life.[8]

The "performing self" became more widely accepted in the interwar years with advertising, Hollywood, and the popular press legitimating the new ideal for a wider audience. Within consumer culture, individuals are asked to become role players and self-consciously monitor their own performance. Appearance, gesture, and bodily demeanor become taken as expressions of self, with bodily imperfections and lack of attention carrying penalties in everyday interactions. Individuals therefore become encouraged to search themselves for flaws and signs of decay: as Lasch (1979a, p. 92) remarks:

> All of us, actors and spectators alike, live surrounded by mirrors. In them, we seek reassurance of our capacity to captivate or impress others, anxiously searching out blemishes that might detract from the appearance we intend to project. The advertising industry deliberately encourages the pre-occupation with appearances.

If individuals are required to be "on stage" all the time, it can lead to what Goffman (1969) has termed as "bureaucratization of the spirit," for the performing self must produce an even performance every time. The demands here are no less stringent for professional actors: White (1981) recounts the story of a promising theater actor from New York who was interviewed for a film part in Hollywood, but was declared a nonstarter by the studio after his first interview, without being given a screen test, because he lacked the stylized, offstage actors' presentation of self which had become mandatory in Hollywood. It is not enough to have the capacity to perform within specific contexts, it becomes essential to be able to project constantly a "winning image."

Behind the emphasis upon performance, it can be argued, lies a deeper interest in manipulating the feelings of others. Anthropologists and ethnologists have long been interested in developing theories of nonverbal bodily communication. One offshoot in the postwar era has been the positivist study of body behavior: kinesics (Kristeva, 1978) which seeks to reconstruct the grammar of body language. Paul Ekman, a researcher in this field, has recently catalogued seven thousand facial expressions, which according to his experiments can be used to tell exactly what individuals are feeling. There has also been some interest in the practice of kinesics from the popular press and self-help literature: "keep a controlling hand in arguments and negotiations," "decide when the other person is lying," "interpret gestures of friendliness and flirtation," "detect boredom" runs the advertising blurb for a popular paperback entitled *How to Read a Person Like a Book*. Another, entitled *Kinesics: The Power of Silent Command*, tells the reader how to learn to "project unspoken orders that must be obeyed," "how Silent Command brings you the love and admiration of others." Arguing that we should try to break through this type of body manipulation by attempting to produce a widespread competence in body language, Benthall (1976, p. 92) writes:

> The body as a whole is still a repressed element in our culture; we tend to *believe* (or find it hard to disbelieve) the sincerity of the politician when he looks us straight in the eye over the TV screen, or that of the actress whose flashing teeth urge us to buy her brand of toothpaste. In both cases a verbal message is lent considerable persuasiveness by the controlled use of certain tricks of bodily deportment, which work largely at an uncon-

scious rather than a conscious level. Until we become more aware of the body's power and resourcefulness, we will not feel a sufficiently educated outrage against its manipulation and exploitation. Rather than campaigns for literacy or numeracy, we may need a campaign for corporacy.

The performing self has also gained impetus from the institutional changes which have brought about the rise of the managerial-professional middle class. One effect of the bureaucratization of industry and the growth of bureaucratic administrative organizations has been to undermine the bourgeois achievement ideology so that there are more and more areas of work in which the precise evaluation of an individual's achievement on universalistic criteria becomes impossible. Hence "extra-functional elements of professional roles become more and more important for conferring occupational status" (Habermas, 1976, p. 81). The difficulty of evaluating an individual's competence on strictly rational criteria opens up the space for the performing self, schooled in public relations techniques, who is aware that the secret of success lies in the projection of a successful image. In the dense interpersonal environment of modern bureaucracy, individuals depend upon their ability to negotiate interactions on the basis of "personality." Impression management, style, panache, and careful bodily presentation therefore become important.

It has also been argued that this type of individual has been furthered by the growth of the "helping professions" which have expanded by discrediting traditional mores and family centered remedies in favor of a new ideology of health, based upon therapy, human growth, and scientism (Lasch, 1977a). In education, social work, health education, marriage guidance, probation, the helping professionals have not only been able to develop careers based upon interpersonal skills but have also transferred and imposed the new modes of emotional and relational management onto their clients (de Swaan, 1981, p. 375). Social relations take on a veneer of informality and equality, but actually demand greater discipline and self control as management through command gives way to management by negotiation. The "negotiating self" is also granted legitimization outside the work sphere as the new styles of social interaction spread into family life not only through the direct intervention of experts but also through the feature articles, advice pages, and problems programs of the popular media (Hepworth & Featherstone, 1982; Ehrenreich & English, 1979). In effect the professional-managerial middle class, which expanded in the course of the twentieth century, is in the process of becoming "the arbiter of contemporary lifestyles and opinions" (de Swaan, 1981, p. 375).

The tendency towards narcissism, the negotiating, performing self is therefore most noticeable in the professional-managerial middle class who have both the time and money to engage in lifestyle activities and the cultivation of the persona. It is arguably spreading to sectors of the working class (Dreitzel, 1977) and up the age scale to the middle-aged (Hepworth & Featherstone, 1982; Featherstone & Hepworth, 1982). This is not to suggest that the implications of the consumer culture imagery of the body and the performing self do not encounter resistance: groups like the Gray Panthers and the women's movement have mounted a strong (if as yet ineffectual) critique of "ageism" and "sexism." While pockets of working-class culture clearly remain, it has been suggested that the working class increasingly draw upon the media as a source of identity models (Davis, 1979). Consumer culture imagery and advertising cannot be dismissed as merely "entertainment," something which individuals do not take seriously. In rejecting this position and its obverse, that individuals are somehow programmed to accept essentially false wants and needs, we can indicate two broad levels on which consumer culture operates: (a) it provides a multiplicity of images designed to stimulate needs and desires, (b) it is based on and helps to change the material arrangements of social space and hence the nature of social interactions. Taking the interactional level first, it can be argued that changes in the material fabric of everyday life have involved a restructuring of social space (e.g., new shopping centers, the beach, the modern pub) which provides an environment facilitating the display of the body. Individuals may of course choose to ignore or neglect their appearance and refuse to cultivate a performing self, yet if they do so they must be prepared to face the implications of this choice within social encounters.

Finally, with regard to the proliferation of images which daily assault the individual within consumer culture, it should be emphasized again that these images do not merely serve to stimulate false needs fostered onto the individual. Part of the strength of consumer culture comes from its ability to harness and channel genuine bodily needs and desires, albeit that it presents them within a form which makes their realization dubious. The desire for health, longevity, sexual fulfillment, youth, and beauty represents a reified entrapment of transhistorical human longings within distorted forms. Yet in a time of diminished economic growth, permanent inflation, and shortages of raw materials, the contradictions within the consumer culture values become more blatant, not only for those who are excluded—the old, unemployed, low paid—but also for those who participate most actively and experience more directly the gap between the promise of the imagery and the exigencies of everyday life.

NOTES

1. Here we follow Ewen's assumption that consumer culture arose in the interwar years, first in the United States in the 1920s (in Britain later, not until the 1930s). Advertising and other elements of consumer culture were of course present before this time. T. Peterson (1964, p. 19) for example notes a surge in the amount of money spent on advertising, an increasing dependence of magazines on advertising revenue, and the creation of new advertising agencies, around the turn of the century. Nevertheless, Ewen argues for the distinctiveness of the "break" at the start of the interwar era.

2. One British daily newspaper in 1981 referred to a firm which specialized in a home videotape service for couples. They would devise a plot and photograph the couple engaged in sex. The tape could then be played back at their leisure and would serve as a memento in old age of how they had once performed.

3. The star system was not the invention of Hollywood. Hess and Nochlin (1973) remark that it originated in the 1890s with the theatrical publicity picture (e.g., Toulouse-Lautrec). The image of the star was reduced to a salient gesture on property (e.g., Sarah Bernhardt's tresses). The more these attributes became fixed in the public's mind, the more the star's actual appearance tended to become stylized and rigid.

4. Today it is not only the secrets of the stars but those of politicians too which cause interest. Public relations experts take the media on tours of politicians' backstage areas to divulge the body maintenance routines which produce the energy, vitality, health, and zest-for-life of politician-celebrities such as Ford, Carter, Reagan, and Thatcher.

5. See for example O. Gillie (1978), *The Sunday Times Book of Body Maintenance*, Diagram Group (1977), *Man's Body: An Owner's Manual.*

6. The headline of a double-page spread in the *News of the World* magazine, *Sunday*, in January 1982. The text, surrounding a picture of a young woman in a leotard smiling as she exercised, referred to exercises devised by Adrian Arpel, "America's queen of self-improvement," the "boss of her own international cosmetics business" who claimed "anyone can shed ten pounds and ten years without a diet or facelift."

7. A number of commentators have criticized Lasch's periodization. Oestereicher (1979) sees the narcissistic as merely a continuation of the inner-directed individualistic self. Wrong (1979, p. 310) and Narr (1980, p. 68) criticize the vagueness of Lasch's periodization. Lasch (1979b) has

since replied to his critics and attempted to clarify this issue. It is worth adding that Lasch (1977b, 1979a) has referred to the writings of Stuart Ewen (1976) linking together the rise of consumer culture in the 1920s with the growth of narcissism.

8. While Sennett traces the origins of the new personality structure back to the 1860s he argues that it became more noticeable in the 1890s revolt against Victorian sobriety and prudery. This brought into prominence tighter fitting, more colorful clothes for women with a more widespread use of makeup—discreetly advertised in women's magazines (Sennett, 1976, p. 190). Lasch and Susman both locate the transition from character to personality as occurring around the turn of the century.

REFERENCES

Allen PL (1931), *Only Yesterday*, Volume 1, Harmondsworth: Penguin

Alt J (1976), Beyond Class: The Decline of Labor and Leisure, *Telos*

Ariès P (1974) *Western Attitudes Toward Death*, Baltimore: Johns Hopkins UP

Ariès P (1981) *The Hour of Our Death*, New York: Knopf

Baudrillard J (1975) *The Mirror of Production*, St. Louis: Telos P

Bell D (1976) *Cultural Contradictions of Capitalism*, London: Heinemann

Beller AS (1977), *Fat and Thin: A Natural History of Obesity*, New York: Farrar, Strauss & Giroux

Benthall J (1976), *The Body Electric: Patterns of Western Industrial Culture*, London: Thames and Hudson

Berger P & Kellner D (1964), Marriage and the Construction of Reality, *Diogenes*

Bruch H (1957) *The Importance of Overweight*, New York: W Norton

Clarke J, Critcher C & Johnson R (eds) (1979), *Working Class Culture*, London: Heinemann

Colmer M (1979), *Whalebone to See-Through: A History of Body Packaging*, London: Johnson & Bacon

Cowley M (1951), *Exiles Return*, New York: Viking

Davis H (1979), *Beyond Class Images*, London: Croom Helm

Diagram Group (1977), *Man's Body: An Owner's Manual*, London: Corgi

Dreitzel P (1977), The Politics of Culture, in N Birnbaum (ed) *Beyond the Crisis*, New York: OUP

Ehrenreich B & English D (1979), *For Her Own Good: 150 Years of Experts' Advice to Women*, London: Pluto Press

Ewen S (1976), *Captains of Consciousness: Advertising and the Social Roots of the Consumer Culture*, New York: McGraw-Hill

Featherstone M & Hepworth M (1980), Changing Images of Middle Age, in M Johnson (ed) *Transitions in Middle and Later Life*, London: British Society of Gerontology

Featherstone M & Hepworth M (1981), Images de la maturité, *Gerontologie*

Featherstone M & Hepworth M (1982), Ageing and Inequality: Consumer Culture and the New Middle Age in D Robbins et al. (eds), *Rethinking Social Inequality*, Aldershot: Gower P

Foucault M (1977), *Discipline and Punish*, Harmondsworth: Penguin

Giddens A (1981), *A Contemporary Critique of Historical Materialism*, London: Macmillan

Gillie O (1978), *The Sunday Times Book of Body Maintenance*, London: Joseph

Goffman E (1969), *The Presentation of Self in Everyday Life*, London: Allen Lane

Goffman E (1972), *Relations in Public*, Harmondsworth: Penguin

Habermas J (1976), *Legitimation Crisis*, London: Heinemann

Haly B (1979), *The Healthy Body and Victorian Culture*, Cambridge, MA: Harvard UP

Hepworth M & Featherstone M (1982). *Surviving Middle Age*, Oxford: B Blackwell

Hess TB & Nochila N (1973), *Woman as Sex Object*. London: Allen Lane

Hornibrook FA (1924), *The Cult of the Abdomen: The Cure of Obesity and Constipation*, London: Heinemann

Jacoby R (1980), Narcissism and the Crisis of Capitalism, *Telos*

Kern S (1975), *Anatomy and Destiny: A Cultural History of the Human Body*, Bobbs-Merrill

Kline S & Leiss W (1978), Advertising, Needs and Commodity Fetishism, *Canadian Journal of Political and Social Theory*

Kristeva J (1978), Gesture: Practice or Communication, in T Polhemus (ed), *Social Aspects of the Human Body*, Harmondsworth: Penguin

Lasch C (1976), The Narcissistic Society, *New York Review of Books*

Lasch C (1977a), *Haven in a Heartless World: The Family Besieged*, New York: Basic Books

Lasch C (1977b), The Narcissistic Personality of Our Time, *Partisan Review*

Lasch C. (1979a), *The Culture of Narcissism*, New York: Norton

Lasch C (1979b), Politics and Social Theory: A Reply to the Critics. *Salmagundi*

Lefebvre H (1971), *Everyday Life in the Modern World*, London: Allen Lane

Levin M (1970), *Hollywood and the Great Fan Magazines*, London: Ian Allen

Linder SB (1970), *The Harried Leisure Class*, New York: Columbia UP

Lukács G (1971), *History and Class Consciousness*, trans R Livingstone, London: Merlin P

Lynd R & Lynd H (1929), *Middletown: A Study in Contemporary American Culture*, London: Constable

Mandel (1970), *Late Capitalism*, London: New Left Books

Miller MB (1981), *The Bon Marché: Bourgeois Culture and the Department Store*, London: Allen & Unwin

Narr WD (1980), The Selling of Narcissism, *Dialectical Anthropology*

Oestereicher E (1979), The Privatization of the Self in Modern Society, *Social Research*

Park R, Burgess EW & McKenzie R (1925), *The City*, Chicago: Chicago UP

Park R (1952), *Human Communities*, New York: Free Press

Peterson T (1964), *Magazines in the Twentieth Century*, Urbana: Illinois UP

Pollack G (1977), What's Wrong With Images of Women? *Screen Education*

Priestly JB (1977), *English Journey*, (orig. 1934) Harmondsworth: Penguin

Reisman D (1950), *The Lonely Crowd: A Study of the Changing American Character*, New Haven: Yale UP

Rose G (1978), *The Melancholy Science: An Introduction to Adorno*, London: Macmillan

Rubinstein H (1930), *The Art of Feminine Beauty*, New York: Liveright

Sennett R (1976), *The Fall of Public Man*, Cambridge: Cambridge UP

Sontag S (1978), *On Photography*, London: Allen Lane

Stein M (1960), *The Eclipse of Community*, New York: Harper

Susman W (1973), *Culture and Commitment 1929–1945*, New York: Braziller

Susman W (1979), Personality and the Making of Twentieth Century Culture, in J Higham and PK Conkin (eds), *New Directions in American Intellectual History*, Baltimore: Johns Hopkins UP

de Swaan A (1981), The Politics of Agoraphobia, *Theory and Society*

Turner BS (1982), The Discourse of Diet, *Theory, Culture and Society*

Walker A (1970), *Stardom: The Hollywood Phenomenon*, New York: Stein and Day

White CL (1970), *Women's Magazines 1693–1968*, London: Joseph

White E (1981), *States of Desire*, New York: Bantam

Williams R (1960), The Magic System, *New Left Review*

Williamson J (1978), *Decoding Advertisements*, London: Boyars

Willis E (1970), Consumerism and Women, *Socialist Revolution*

Winship J (1980), Sexuality for Sale, in S Hall, D Hobson, A Lowe and P Willis (eds), *Culture, Media, Language*, London: Hutchinson

Winter MF & Robert ER (1980), Male Domination, Late Capitalism and the Growth of Instrumental Reason, *Berkeley Journal of Sociology*

Wrong D (1979), Bourgeois Values, No Bourgeoisie: The Cultural Criticism of Christopher Lasch, *Dissent*

Zeldin T (1977), *France 1848–1945, Volume 2: Intellect, Taste and Anxiety*, Oxford: Oxford UP

MARC E. MISHKIND
JUDITH RODIN
LISA R. SILBERSTEIN
RUTH H. STRIEGEL-MOORE

5

The Embodiment of Masculinity

Cultural, Psychological, and Behavioral Dimensions

Men talk about their bodies, but they do so with a different vocabulary and orientation than do women. Mishkind et al. document the male focus and language, suggesting there is an increasing focus on male body parts in advertisements and the media. The effect on men is complicated. Since, traditionally, body image issues have been perceived as a woman's problem, and masculinity has been defined in opposition to all things feminine, the tensions surrounding male body maintenance ideals have become more complex and intense. The male athletic body has become a visible icon toward which many men strive, but they must do so through body maintenance rituals that display non-feminine appearance norms. This article complements Mike Featherstone's analysis in "The Body in Consumer Culture" by exploring the specifics of the male orientation toward the body, highlighting again the power and influence of consumer culture on the individual's body.

From Marc E. Mishkind, Judith Rodin, Lisa R. Silberstein, and Ruth H. Striegel-Moore, "The Embodiment of Masculinity: Cultural, Psychological, and Behavioral Dimensions," in *Changing Men: New Directions in Research on Men and Masculinity*, ed. Michael S. Kimmel (Thousand Oaks, CA: Sage Publications, 1987), 37–52. Reprinted by permission of Sage Publications.

Women have been traditionally concerned with their appearance. Indeed, the pursuit of and preoccupation with beauty are central features of the female sex-role stereotype (Rodin, Silberstein, & Striegel-Moore, 1985). Perhaps because of this, we have ignored the significant role that physical appearance and body image play for men. Certainly, an examination of current magazines and other media strongly suggests that bodily concern is strong for men. Advertisements celebrate the young, lean, muscular male body, and men's fashions have undergone significant changes in style both to accommodate and to accentuate changes in men's physiques toward a more muscular and trim body (Gross, 1985). Today men serve as marketing targets for products such as diet sodas and cosmetics that would have been considered too feminine only a few years ago.

The changes in society's attitudes toward men's bodies, along with the changes in men's behaviors regarding their appearance, have prompted us to examine the role of body image in men's lives. How does body image figure into men's sense of masculinity in particular and their self-concept in general? We suggest that men arrange themselves along a continuum, from unconcerned with body at one end to extremely concerned at the other. This conceptualization may help predict the type and degree of behavior in which individuals engage to change their physical appearance and come closer to the masculine ideal.

This article addresses several issues. First, how do men feel about their bodies? Given that these feelings often are assessed in comparison to some ideal body type, we consider what this ideal is and what benefits accrue to someone who more closely represents the ideal body type. We then ask how this ideal body type relates to current conceptions of masculinity and the male sex role. We next examine various efforts that men undertake to achieve the ideal, and we evaluate the positive and negative consequences of these efforts. Following this, we try to identify behaviors associated with increased levels of concern. Finally, we ask why at this historical moment men are paying increased attention to their appearance and are striving in growing numbers to achieve the male body ideal. Our thesis is that the male body ideal, and various pressures for men to conform to it, may be producing psychological and physical ill effects at the present time, effects that will increase because they reflect a historical trend.

How Men Feel about Their Bodies

One index of men's bodily concern is their degree of satisfaction with their physical appearance. Of college-age men we surveyed, 95 percent expressed dissatisfaction with some aspect of their bodies. Studies suggest that men carry with them images of both their own body and also their ideal body, and that these two images are nonidentical. For example, when shown line drawings depicting seven body types, more than 70 percent of undergraduate men saw a discrepancy between their own body and their ideal body type (see also Tucker, 1982b).[1]

This dissatisfaction is not general and diffuse but highly specific and differentiated. Men consistently express their greatest dissatisfaction toward chest, weight, and waist. Other areas have also elicited dissatisfaction, most notably arms, hips, nose, stomach, shoulders, and height (Berscheid, Walster, & Bohrnstedt, 1973; Calden, Lundy, & Schlafer, 1959; Clifford, 1971; Miller, Coffman, & Linke, 1980; Secord & Jourard, 1953).

Given that men experience significant body dissatisfaction because they see themselves as deviating from the ideal, it becomes crucial to determine the ideal male body type. When asked about physique preferences, the overwhelming majority of males report that they would prefer to be mesomorphic (i.e., of well-proportioned, average build) as opposed to ectomorphic (thin) or endomorphic (fat). This preference is expressed by boys as young as five and six (Lerner & Gellert, 1969; Lerner & Schroeder, 1971) and also by college-age men (Dibiase & Hjelle, 1968; Tucker, 1982b). Within the mesomorphic category, a majority select what we shall refer to as the hypermesomorphic or muscular mesomorphic body as preferred (Deno, 1953; Tucker, 1982b). This physique is the "muscle man"-type body characterized by well-developed chest and arm muscles and wide shoulders tapering down to a narrow waist. Men indicate greater body satisfaction to the extent that their self-reported (Tucker, 1982b) or actual (Jourard & Secord, 1954; Sugerman & Haronian, 1964) body shape resembles this ideal.

That many men feel bodily dissatisfaction because they do not resemble the mesomorphic or hypermesomorphic ideal might not in itself be particularly distressing. The discrepancy between self and ideal is problematic only if men believe that those closest to the ideal reap certain benefits not available to those farther away. Research strongly suggests that this is true, both because physical appearance is so important generally in our society and because of the specific benefits that accrue to mesomorphic men.

It is axiomatic in Western culture that "what is beautiful is good" (Dion, Berscheid, & Walster, 1972; Hatfield & Sprecher, in press). This stereotype is already evident in preschoolers, who view attractive peers as friendlier and smarter than unattractive peers (Dion, 1973) and for whom physical attractiveness is correlated significantly with popularity (Vaughn & Langlois, 1983). Teachers treat attractive children more favorably and perceive them as more intelligent than less attractive children (Adams & Cohen, 1976a, 1976b; Clifford, 1975; Clifford & Walster, 1973; Felson, 1980; Martinek, 1981).

Attractive adults are believed to live happier and more successful lives (Berscheid & Walster, 1974). There is surely some truth to this; attractive people enjoy distinct advantages in interpersonal situations (see Hatfield & Sprecher, in press). For example, an attractive person is more likely to receive help (Benson, Karabenick, & Lerner, 1976; West & Brown, 1975), to elicit cooperation in conflict situations (Sigall, Page, & Brown, 1971), and to experience more satisfying interpersonal relationships (Blumstein & Schwartz, 1983; Reis, Nezle, & Wheels, 1980). Attractive applicants have a better chance of getting jobs and receive higher starting salaries (Cann, Siegfried, & Pearce, 1981; Dipboye, Fromkin, & Wibach, 1975).

By contrast, obese people are stigmatized and punished by adults and children alike (see Rodin et al., 1985). Children have more negative attitudes toward obese children than toward children with a wide range of handicaps, such as being in a wheelchair, missing a hand, or having a facial disfigurement (Goodman, Richardson, Dornbusch, & Hastorf, 1963; Richardson, Hastorf, Goodman, & Dornbusch, 1961). Adults expect obese individuals to have more negative personality traits and lead less happy lives than lean individuals (Hiller, 1981), and negative attitudes are expressed particularly strongly when obese persons are perceived as being personally responsible for their condition (DeJong, 1980).

Because physical appearance is so important in our culture, we want to ask if the mesomorphic male body is considered the most attractive body type, and if there is any evidence to suggest that the mesomorphic individual gains the various benefits that accrue to attractive individuals. Mesomorphic physiques are considered better looking and more attractive than nonmesomorphic physiques

(Horvath, 1981; Kirkpatrick & Sanders, 1978; Staffieri, 1967), and mesomorphic males do receive numerous social benefits. Studies demonstrate that people assign overwhelmingly positive personality traits to drawings or photographs of mesomorphic males and mostly negative traits to ectomorphic and endomorphic males (Brodsky, 1954; Kirkpatrick & Sanders, 1978; Lerner, 1969; Staffieri, 1967; Wells & Siegel, 1961; Wright & Bradbard, 1980). For example, Kirkpatrick and Sanders found that the positive traits ascribed to mesomorphs by young adults were strong, best friend, has lots of friends, polite, happy, helps others, brave, healthy, smart, and neat. By contrast, the endomorph was characterized by a preponderance of negative traits, including sloppy, dirty, worries, lies, tired, stupid, lonely, and lazy. The ectomorph was also described negatively, though not to the extent of the endomorph: quiet, nervous, sneaky, afraid, sad, weak, and sick.

These stereotypes exist in both middle and lower classes (Wells & Siegel, 1961), in blacks as well as whites (Brodsky, 1954; Wright & Bradbard, 1980), and they gain increasing strength with age until young adulthood (Lerner, 1972; Lerner & Korn, 1972) but may decrease thereafter (Kirkpatrick & Sanders, 1978). Personality descriptions consistent with these stereotypes have been elicited when boys of varying physiques are given personality ratings by peers (Hanley, 1951), parents (Washburn, 1962), teachers (Hendry & Gillies, 1978), and "objective" judges (Walker, 1963).

Males may behave in accord with these stereotypes. Early research sought to demonstrate an inborn relationship between body build and personality (e.g., Sheldon, 1942); however, it is now generally agreed that such relationships are learned (McCandless, 1960) and have no or minimal genetic determinants (see Montemayor, 1978). The research we reviewed reveals deeply entrenched cultural preferences toward mesomorphic males and aversions to endomorphic and ectomorphic males. Given this preference and the demonstrated importance of physical appearance in our society, it is no wonder that men aspire to resemble the mesomorphic ideal and feel dissatisfied to the extent that they do not.

Mesomorphy and Masculinity

We have seen that men care a great deal about their body build and that they aspire to a widely held ideal of physical attractiveness, the muscular mesomorph. The muscular male probably enjoys social advantages that are yet undocumented. But why has it become so? We believe that the muscular mesomorph is the ideal because it is intimately tied to cultural views of masculinity and the male sex role, which prescribes that men be powerful, strong, efficacious—even domineering and destructive. For example, Rosenkrantz et al. (1968) found strong agreement that the masculine stereotype included items such as aggressive, independent, dominant, self-confident, and unemotional. Masculinity on the Spence and Helmreich (1978) Personal Attributes Questionnaire is represented by high scores on items such as independent, active, competitive, persistent, self-confident, and feels superior. A muscular physique may serve as a symbolic embodiment of these personal characteristics.

Writers who have made a connection between muscles and these "ideal" masculine qualities describe men as making their bodies an "instrument of their power" (Reynaud, 1983), "armoring" themselves (Nichols, 1975), or adopting the "soldier archetype" of masculinity (Gerzon, 1982). These assertions are substantiated empirically by Darden (1972), who found that people rate mesomorphically proportioned bodies as the most masculine. The embodiment of masculinity, the muscular mesomorph, is seen as more efficacious, experiencing greater mastery and control over the environment, and feeling more invulnerable. Indeed, research suggests that people apply such stereotypically masculine traits as "active," "daring," and "a fighter" to mesomorphic boys but not to endomorphic or ectomorphic boys (Hanley, 1951; Hendry & Gillies, 1978). Males also view their own bodies primarily along these active and functional dimensions, in contrast to women, who evaluate themselves primarily along an aesthetic dimension (Kurtz, 1969; Lerner, Orlos, & Knapp, 1976; Story, 1979), and men consider physical attractiveness virtually equivalent to physical potency (Lerner at al., 1976). Hence they experience an intimate relationship between body image and potency—that is, masculinity—with the muscular mesomorph representing the masculine ideal. A man who fails to resemble the body ideal is, by implication, failing to live up to sex-role norms, and may thus experience the consequences of violating such norms.

A Man's Body and His Sense of Self

How important is a man's body to his sense of self? How connected to a man's self-worth are his feelings about his body? Studies have revealed consistently a significant correlation between men's body satisfaction and self-esteem, the average correlation of these studies being around 0.5. Although some studies have found a stronger relationship between body-esteem and self-esteem for women than for men (Lerner, Karabenick, & Stuart, 1973; Martin & Walter, 1982; Secord & Jourard, 1953), others have found comparable or even greater relationships between body satisfaction and measures of self-esteem, anxiety, and depression for men than for women (Franzoi & Shields, 1984; Goldberg & Folkins, 1974; Lerner et al., 1976; Mahoney, 1974). How a man feels about himself is thus tied closely to how he feels about his body. It remains for researchers to examine the relative importance of body image to a man's sense of self when compared with other variables such as career achievement, but the data already available suggest that feelings about body play a significant role in self-esteem.

Efforts to Decrease the Gap between Actual and Ideal Body Shape

We have seen that a great number of men acknowledge a gap between their actual and ideal body types, and that the greater this gap, the lower their self-esteem. As a result, men feel motivated to close this gap. This often depends upon which parts of the body are the foci of dissatisfaction.

In a large-scale factor-analytic study, Franzoi and Shields (1984) found three primary dimensions along which men's bodily satisfaction and dissatisfaction occur. The first factor, "physical attractiveness," includes the face and its constituent features, such as cheekbones, chin, ears, and eyes. These features contribute to making a man appear "handsome" or "good-looking." The second factor, dubbed "upper-body strength," contains muscle groups that men typically want to build up in order to improve their physique: biceps, shoulder width, arms, and chest. The third factor, "physical conditioning," contains items that reflect a man's concern with being physically "fit" or in "good shape," such as physical stamina, energy level, physical condition, stomach, and weight.

Each of these three dimensions—facial attractiveness, upper-body strength, and physical conditioning—suggests specific ways in which men could attempt to narrow the distance between their real and ideal selves. A man who wishes to improve his facial attractiveness may perhaps modify his hairstyle or undertake cosmetic surgery.

However, we believe that men pursue this kind of self-improvement less frequently. First, facial appearance is viewed typically as less malleable than one's body: "Good looks" are seen as something with which one is or is not endowed. Second, this dimension seems more closely tied to aesthetic dimensions of attractiveness than functional dimensions, and the latter are more central to masculine physical attractiveness.

A man who desires to increase his muscle size and strength—that is, to embody the muscular mesomorphic ideal—may engage in weight lifting or use weight-training machines. Physical conditioning is most likely to be achieved through long workouts of running, swimming, aerobic exercising, or other activities that build stamina and endurance while decreasing body fat. Given that the physical effects of endurance workouts may be less readily visible than the effects of body building, we surmise that men who want to be widely recognized for their physical masculinity are more likely to opt for muscle building as their form of physical exercise. There is evidence that weight-lifting men, compared with those who engage in other athletic activities, are more likely attempting to compensate for a lowered sense of masculinity (Harlow, 1951; Thune, 1949), but replications with current samples are needed.

A different route to altering one's body shape involves dieting. Although women continue to be the largest consumers of diet books and diet products, men constitute a rapidly increasing market. Light beers and diet sodas are promoted by male athletes in order to establish a masculine association to products with formerly feminine connotations. The "drinking-man's diet" was an effort to capture a relatively untapped male market, and the businessman's lunch is being replaced now by salad bars and lighter fare. Our clinical experience suggests that men are entering diet programs in increasing numbers for both appearance and health.

Increased efforts expended on exercise and dieting are reinforced by a societal attitude that everyone can improve himself or herself through sufficient effort. People believe that body size and shape are almost totally under volitional control (Bennett, 1984). In fact, this is largely a myth. Individual differences in body build have a large genetic component. Identical twins, for example, even when reared apart, are significantly more similar in weight than fraternal twins or siblings (see Stunkard, Foch, & Hrubec, 1985). Adopted children resemble their biological parents in weight, far more than their adoptive parents (Stunkard et al., 1985). For those men who are genetically disposed to deviate from the muscular mesomorphic ideal, the costs of attempting to achieve this ideal may be considerable.

A man who strives to bridge the self-denial gap will experience a heightened attentiveness to and focus on his body. This may render his standards more perfectionistic (and hence perhaps more out of reach) and enhance his perceptions of his shortcomings. Both his limitations and the gap itself can become increasingly salient. To the extent that he feels that he falls short, he will experience the shame of failure. He also may feel ashamed at being so focused on his body, presumably because this has been associated traditionally with the female sex-role stereotype.

There may also be physical costs of trying to bridge the gap between self and ideal. Studies investigating the physiological changes that result from dieting suggest that dieting is an ineffective way to attain long-term weight loss; it may, in fact, contribute to subsequent weight gain and binge eating (Herman & Polivy, 1975; Rodin et al., 1985; Wooley & Wooley, 1984). A substantial decrease in daily caloric intake will result in a reduced metabolic rate, which thus impedes weight loss (Apfelbaum, 1975; Garrow, 1978). Upon resuming normal caloric intake, a person's metabolic rate does not rebound immediately to its original pace; in fact, a longer period of dieting will prolong the time it takes for the metabolic rate to regain its original level (Evan & Nicolaidis, 1981). Thus even normal eating after a period of dieting may promote weight gain. Food restriction produces other physiological changes that contribute to maladaptations in food utilization and an increased proportion of fat in body composition (Bjorntorp & Yang, 1982; Fried, Hill, Nickel, & DiGirolamo, 1983; Miller, Faust, Goldberger, & Hirsch, 1983). Dieting may ultimately produce effects the opposite of those intended. In addition to these biological ramifications, dieting also produces psychological results that are self-defeating. Typically, a dieter feels deprived of favorite foods and when "off" the diet, is likely to overeat (Polivy & Herman, 1985).

Bodybuilding attempts may also carry hazards. Men tend to see an overdeveloped muscular body as the most masculine physique (Darden, 1972), and many bodybuilders ingest male hormones and steroids in their efforts to attain this exaggerated hypermesomorphic look (Todd, 1983). These represent only a minority of body-conscious men, but the health ramifications for them may be significant.

Thus far we have focused only on the negative consequences of trying to attain the masculine body ideal. There are potentially powerful positive consequences. The more a man experiences himself as closing the self-ideal gap—for example, through exercising—the more positive he will feel toward body and self. Higher frequencies of exercise have been associated with greater body satisfaction (Joesting, 1981; Joesting & Clance, 1979), and programs of physical activity have led to more positive feelings toward one's body (McGlenn, 1980; Tucker, 1982a). The more a man works toward attaining his body ideal and the closer he perceives himself as approximating it, the greater his sense of self-efficacy.

Some men opt not to involve themselves in the deliberate pursuit of the mesomorphic ideal, which can also have both positive and negative effects. Lack of concern with changing one's physical appearance may protect a man from intense bodily preoccupation and its ramifications, but those who experience dissatisfaction but do not strive to change their physiques are likely to suffer from guilt and self-criticism. A recent Gallup survey reports that many people who refrain from exercising feel that their lives would be better if they were to do so (Harris & Gurin, 1985).

Subcultures of High Bodily Concern

The increased cultural attention given to the male body and the increasing demands placed on men to achieve the mesomorphic build push men further along the continuum of bodily concern. Men are likely experiencing more body dissatisfaction, preoccupation with weight, and concern with their physical attractiveness and body shape now than they did even two decades ago. Fashion designers currently are broadening the chest and tapering the waist of men's clothing lines in order to fit their male customers (Gross, 1985). However, research is needed to document these current trends.

At the extreme, such concerns could lead to excessive attention to one's body and to an obsessive preoccupation with body-altering behavior such as weight lifting, exercising, and dieting. With women, extreme bodily concern, coupled with difficulties in achieving the ideal body type, portends disregulated eating patterns such as bulimia—frequent and compulsive binge eating, sometimes followed by purging (Striegel-Moore, Silberstein, & Rodin, 1986). Those subcultures of women that amplify the sociocultural emphasis on appearance and weight (e.g., dancers, models) manifest higher rates of eating disorders (Crago, Yates, Beutler, & Arizmendi, 1985; Druss & Silverman, 1979; Garner & Garfinkel, 1978). Similarly, we might expect that subgroups of men that place relatively greater emphasis on physical appearance would be at greater risk for excessive weight control behaviors and even eating disorders.

An illustrative group is the gay male subculture, which places an elevated importance on all aspects of a man's physical self—body build, grooming, dress, handsomeness (Kleinberg, 1980; Lakoff & Scherr, 1984). We predicted that gay men would be at heightened risk for body dissatisfaction and for eating disorders. In a sample of heterosexual and homosexual college men, gay men expressed greater dissatisfaction with body build, waist, biceps, arms, and stomach. Gay men also indicated a greater discrepancy between their actual and ideal body shapes than did "straight" men and showed higher scores on measures of eating disregulation and food and weight preoccupation.[2] If the increased focus on appearance continues for men in general, such concerns and eating disorders may begin to increase among all men.

Why Now?

We have argued that men are moving further along the continuum of bodily concern. But why do men at this time in history appear to be pursuing the muscular mesomorphic ideal to a greater extent than ever before? Western society currently places an unprecedented emphasis on life-style change and self-management as the major health-promoting activities (Surgeon General's Report, 1984). The burden of illness has shifted from infectious diseases to cardiovascular disorders, automobile accidents, and cancers, many of which are considered preventable through behavior change (Hamburg, Solomon, & Parron, 1983). Looking healthy is the external manifestation of the desired healthy state, so the body symbolizes the extent of one's self-corrective behavior. Further, what were once considered exclusively male abilities and domains are decreasingly so. Whereas once a man could be assured of his masculinity by virtue of his occupation, interests, or certain personality characteristics, many women now opt for the same roles. Gerzon (1982) writes that the five traditional archetypes of masculinity—soldier, frontiersman, expert, breadwinner, and lord—are now archaic artifacts, although the images remain. The soldier archetype conveys the image of the strong, muscle-armored body. The frontiersman and lord are no longer viable roles for anyone, and the expert and bread-winner are no longer exclusively male. Thus men may be grasping for the soldier archetype—that is, building up their bodies—in an exaggerated attempt to incorporate what possible options remain of the male images they have held since youth. One of the only remaining ways men can express and preserve traditional male characteristics may be by literally embodying them.

It is worth considering whether this ubiquitous interest in achieving the maleness-as-soldier ideal is a reflection of the conservative militaristic trends in our society. Is it a coincidence that men are opting for muscle building at a time of greater U.S. military intervention in foreign governments, and increased xenophobic patriotic media events such as *Rambo*, which features an overly muscled mesomorph who returns to Vietnam to avenge American pride and honor for a war we "lost"? Perhaps, also, the current ideal of thinness for women represents the flip side of this phenomenon. The thin female body connotes such stereotypically feminine traits as smallness, weakness, and fragility, which are the mirror opposite of the strength and power represented by the muscular male body. The current female body ideal may be considered the "last bastion of femininity."

We therefore propose a second, "polarization" hypothesis: The male and female body ideals, which are physically and symbolically opposite extremes, may be a reaction against sexual equality, an expression of a wish to preserve some semblance of traditional male-female differences. Lippa (1983) found that what people considered the "ideal" male and "ideal" female body shapes were more different from each other than what people believed to be the "typical" male and female body shapes. Even these typical body shapes were more differentiated than men's and women's actual body shapes.

Conclusions

The body plays a central role in men's self-esteem, and men are striving in growing numbers to achieve the male body ideal. This may have a profound impact on their psychological and physical health. We suspect that the causes and consequences of bodily concern reviewed here represent a growing cultural trend, attributable to increased emphasis on self-determination of health and the ambiguity of current male and female sex roles. Surprisingly little research of any type has addressed these issues, and developmental studies in particular are greatly needed. Perhaps we have failed to focus more scholarly attention on body and bodily esteem because, as Blumstein and Schwartz (1983) have noted, "since most scholars overvalue the power of the mind, they tend to denigrate or even ignore the power of the body." It is also possible that society's effort to relegate bodily concern exclusively to the female sex-role stereotype had deflected attention from the major role it plays for men and may contribute to men's conflicts in acknowledging concern with their appearance. Answers to these and other scientific questions regarding the role of the body in men's lives will be fundamental to our understanding of the male experience.

NOTES

1. A recent study may appear to contradict this assertion that a large percentage of men experience a discrepancy between their actual and ideal body shapes. Fallon and Rozin (1985) report no such discrepancy. However, these researchers averaged their data, not taking into account that some men wish to increase their body size and other men wish to decrease their body size, and that both are expressions of bodily dissatisfaction. If we were to average our own data we would be led to the same erroneous conclusion.

2. Subjects were 47 undergraduate males recruited from introductory psychology classes (assumed to be predominantly heterosexual) and 71 homosexual male undergraduates and graduate students recruited from gay student organizations. Compared with the heterosexual men, the homosexual men showed a greater self-ideal discrepancy on both the Fallon and Rozin (1985) figures (1.3 versus .9, t = 2.9, p < .01) and Tucker (1982b) figures (1.4 versus .9, t = 3.1, p < .01). The homosexual men scored higher on the Dieting subscale of the Garner, Olmsted, Bohr, and Garfinkel (1982) Eating Attitudes Test (5.0 versus 2.4, t = 3.6, p < 001), the Drive for Thinness subscale of the Garner, Olmsted, and Polivy (1982) Eating Disorders Inventory (3.4 versus 1.1, t = 3.36, p < .01), and the Bulimia subscale of the Eating Disorders Inventory (.7 versus .2, t = 2.8, p < .01).

REFERENCES

Adams, G. R., & Cohen, A. S. (1976a). An examination of cumulative folder information used by teachers in making differential judgments of children's abilities. *Alberta Journal of Educational Research, 22*, 216–25.

Adams, G. R., & Cohen, A. S. (1976b). Characteristics of children and teacher expectancy: An extension to the child's social and family life. *Journal of Educational Research, 70*, 87–90.

Apfelbaum, M. (1975). Influence of level of energy intake on energy expenditure in man: Effects of spontaneous intake, experimental starvation and experimental overeating. In G. A. Brey (Ed.), *Obesity in perspective* (Vol. 2) (OBHEW Publication No. NIH 75–708). Washington, DC: Government Printing Office.

Bennett, W. I. (1984). Dieting: Ideology versus physiology. *Psychiatric Clinics of North America, 7*, 321–34.

Benson, P. L., Karabenick, S. A., & Lerner, R. M. (1976). Pretty pleases: The effects of physical attractiveness, race, and sex on receiving help. *Journal of Experimental Social Psychology, 12*, 409–15.

Berscheid, E., & Walster, E. (1974). Physical attractiveness. In L. Berkowitz (Ed.), *Advances in experimental social psychology* (Vol. 7). New York: Academic Press.

Berscheid, E., Walster, E., & Bohrnstedt, G. (1973). The happy American body—survey report. *Psychology Today, 7*, 119–23, 126, 128–31.

Bjorntorp, P., & Yang, M. U. (1982). Refeeding after tasting in the rat: Effects on body composition and food efficiency. *American Journal of Clinical Nutrition, 36*, 444–49.

Blumstein, P. W., & Schwartz, P. (1983). *American couples.* New York: William Morrow.

Brodsky, C. M. (1954). A study of norms for body form-behavior relationships. *Anthropological Quarterly, 27*, 91–101.

Calden, G., Lundy, R. M., & Schlafer, R. J. (1959). Sex differences in body concepts. *Journal of Consulting Psychology, 23*, 378.

Cann, A., Siegfried, W. D., & Pearce, L. (1981). Forced attention to specific applicant qualifications: Impact on physical attractiveness and sex of applicant biases. *Personnel Psychology, 34*, 65–75.

Clifford, E. (1971). Body satisfaction in adolescence. *Perceptual and Motor Skills, 33*, 119–25.

Clifford, M. M. (1975). Physical attractiveness and academic performance. *Child Study Journal, 5*, 201–309.

Clifford, M. M., & Walster, E. (1973). The effect of physical attractiveness on teacher expectations. *Sociology of Education, 46*, 248–58.

Crago, M., Yates, A., Beutler, L. E., & Arizmendi, T. G. (1985). Height-weight ratios among female athletes: Are collegiate athletics the precursors to an anorexic syndrome? *International Journal of Eating Disorders, 4*, 79–87.

Darden, E. (1972). Masculinity-femininity body rankings by males and females. *Journal of Psychology, 80*, 205–12.

DeJong, W. (1980). The stigma of obesity: The consequences of name assumption concerning the causes of peripheral deviance. *Journal of Health and Social Behavior, 21*, 75–87.

Deno, E. (1953). Self-identification among adolescent boys. *Child Development, 24*, 269–73.

Dibiase, W. J., & Hjelle, L. A. (1968). Body image stereotypes and body type preferences among male college students. *Perceptual and Motor Skills, 27*, 1143–46.

Dion, K. K. (1973). Young children's stereotyping of facial attractiveness. *Developmental Psychology, 9*, 183–88.

Dion, K. K., Berscheid, E., & Walster, E. (1972). What is beautiful is good. *Journal of Personality and Social Psychology, 24*, 285–90.

Dipboye, R. L., Fromkin, H. L., & Wibach, K. (1975). Relative importance of applicant sex, attractiveness and scholastic standing in evaluations of job applicant resumes. *Journal of Applied Psychology, 60*, 39–43.

Druss, R. G., & Silverman, J. A. (1979). Body image and perfectionism of ballerinas: Comparison and contrast with anorexia nervosa. *General Hospital Psychiatry, 1*, 115–21.

Evan, P., & Nicolaidis, S. (1981). Changes in efficiency of ingestants are a major factor of regulation of energy balance. In L. A. Cioffi, W. P. T. James & T. B. Van Itallie (Eds.), *The body weight regulatory system: Normal and disturbed mechanisms*. New York: Raven.

Fallon, A. E., & Rozin, P. (1985). Sex differences in perceptions of desirable body shape. *Journal of Abnormal Psychology, 94*, 102–5.

Felson, R. B. (1980). Physical attractiveness, grades and teachers' attributions of ability. *Representative Research in Social Psychology, 11*, 64–71.

Franzoi, S. L., & Shields, S. A. (1984). The body esteem scale: Multi-dimensional structure and sex differences in a college population. *Journal of Personality Assessment, 48*, 173–78.

Fried, S. K., Hill, J. O., Nickel, M., & DiGirolamo, M. (1983). Prolonged effects of fasting-refeeding on rat adipose tissue lipoprotein lipaseactivity: Influence of caloric restriction during refeeding. *Journal of Nutrition, 113*, 1861–69.

Garner, D. M., & Garfinkel, P. E. (1978). Sociocultural factors in anorexia nervosa. *Lancet, 2*, 674.

Garner, D. M., Olmsted, M. P., & Polivy, J. (1982). The eating disorder inventory: A measure of cognitive/behavioral dimensions of anorexia nervosa and bulimia. In P. L. Darby, P. E. Garfinkel, D. M. Garner & D. V. Coscina (Eds.), *Anorexia nervosa*. New York: Allan R. Liss.

Garner, D. M. Olmsted, M. P., Bohr, Y., & Garfinkel, P. E. (1982). The eating attitudes test: Psychometric features and clinical correlates. *Psychological Medicine, 48*, 173–78.

Garrow, J. (1978). The regulation of energy expenditure. In G. A. Bray (Ed.), *Recent advances in obesity research* (Vol. 2). London: Newman.

Gerzon, M. (1982). *A choice of heroes: The changing faces of American manhood*. Boston: Houghton Mifflin.

Goldberg, B., & Folkins, C. (1974). Relationship of body-image to negative emotional attitudes. *Perceptual and Motor Skills, 39*, 1053–54.

Goodman, N., Richardson, S. A., Dornbusch, S. M., & Hastorf, A. H. (1963). Variant reactions to physical disabilities. *American Sociological Review, 28*, 429–35.

Gross, M. (1985, September 8). The impact of fitness on the cut of clothes: Men's fashions of the Times. *New York Times*.

Hamburg, D., Solomon, F., & Parron, D. (1983). *Health and behavior*. Washington, DC: National Academy Press.

Hanley, C. (1951). Physique and reputation of junior high school boys. *Child Development, 22*, 247–60.

Harlow, R. (1951). Masculine inadequacy and the compensatory development of physique. *Journal of Personality, 19*, 312–33.

Harris, T. G., & Gurin, J. (1985, March). The new eighties lifestyle: Look who's getting it all together. *American Health*, pp. 42–47.

Hatfield, E., & Sprecher, S. (in press). *Mirror, mirror: The importance of looks in everyday life*. New York: SUNY Press.

Hendry, L. B., & Gillies, P. (1978). Body type, body esteem, school, and leisure: A study of overweight, average, and underweight adolescents. *Journal of Youth and Adolescence, 7*, 181–95.

Herman, C. P., & Polivy, J. (1975). Anxiety, restraint, and eating behavior. *Journal of Abnormal Psychology, 84*, 666–72.

Hiller, D. V. (1981). The salience of overweight in personality characterization. *Journal of Psychology, 108*, 233–40.

Horvath, T. (1981). Physical attractiveness: The influence of selected torso parameters. *Archives of Sexual Behavior, 10*, 21–24.

Joesting, J. (1981). Comparisons of students who exercise with those who do not. *Perceptual and Motor Skills, 53*, 426–66.

Joesting, J., & Clance, P. R. (1979). Comparison of runners and nonrunners on the body-cathexis and self-cathexis scales. *Perceptual and Motor Skills, 48*, 1046.

Jourard, S. M., & Secord, P. F. (1954). Body size and body-cathexis. *Journal of Consulting Psychology, 18*, 184.

Kirkpatrick, S. W., & Sanders, D. M. (1978). Body image stereotypes: A developmental comparison. *Journal of Genetic Psychology, 132*, 87–95.

Kleinberg, S. (1980). *Alienated affections: Being gay in America*. New York: St. Martin's.

Kurtz, R. M. (1969). Sex differences and variations in body attitudes. *Journal of Consulting and Clinical Psychology, 33*, 625–29.

Lakoff, R. T., & Scherr, R. L. (1984). *Face value, the politics of beauty*. Boston: Routledge & Kegan Paul.

Lerner, R. M. (1969). The development of stereotyped expectancies of body-build relations. *Child Development, 40*, 137–41.

Lerner, R. M. (1972). "Richness" analysis of body build stereotype developments. *Developmental Psychology, 7*, 219.

Lerner, R. M., & Gellert, E. (1969). Body build identifications, preference, and aversion in children. *Developmental Psychology, 1*, 456–62.

Lerner, R. M., & Korn, S. J. (1972). The development of body build stereotypes in males. *Child Development, 43*, 912–20.

Lerner, R. M., & Schroeder, C. (1971). Physique identification, preference, and aversion in kindergarten children. *Developmental Psychology. 5*, 538.

Lerner, R. M., Karabenick, S. A., & Stuart, J. L. (1973). Relations among physical attractiveness, body attitudes, and self concept in male and female college students. *Journal of Psychology, 85*, 119–29.

Lerner, R. M., Orlos, J. B., & Knapp, J. R. (1976). Physical attractiveness, physical effectiveness, and self-concept in late adolescents. *Adolescence, 11*, 313–26.

Lippa, R. (1983). Sex typing and the perception of body outlines. *Journal of Personality, 51*, 667–82.

Mahoney, E. R. (1974). Body-cathexis and self-esteem: The importance of subjective importance. *Journal of Psychology, 88*, 27–30.

Martin, M., & Walter, R. (1982) Korperselbstbild und neurotizismus bei Kindern und Jugendichen. *Praxis der Kinderpsychologie und Kinderpsychiatrie, 31*, 213–18.

Martinek, T. J. (1981). Physical attractiveness: Effects on teacher expectations and dyadic interactions in elementary age children. *Journal of Sports Psychology, 3*, 196–205.

McCandless, B. R. (1960). Rate of development, body build and personality. *Psychiatry Research Reports, 13*, 42–57.

McGlenn, R. L. (1980). Relationship of personality and self image change of high and low fitness adolescent males to selected activity programs (Doctoral dissertation, United States International University, 1976). *Dissertation Abstracts International, 40*, 1410B–11B.

Miller, T. M., Coffman, J. G., & Linke, R. A. (1980). Survey on body image, weight, and diet of college students. *Journal of the American Dietetic Association, 77*, 561–66.

Miller, W. H., Faust, I. M., Goldberger, A. C., & Hirsch, J. (1983). Effects of severe long-term food deprivation and refeeding on adipose tissue cells in the rat. *American Journal of Physiology, 245*, E74–E80.

Montemayor, R. (1978). Men and their bodies: The relationship between body type and behavior. *Journal of Social Issues, 34*, 48–64.

Nichols, J. (1975). *Men's liberation: A new definition of masculinity.* New York: Penguin.

Polivy, J., & Herman, C. P. (1985). Dieting and binging: A causal analysis. *American Psychologist, 40*, 193–201.

Reis, H. T., Nezle, K. J., & Wheels, L. (1980). Physical attractiveness in social interaction. *Journal of Personality and Social Psychology, 38*, 604–17.

Reynaud, E. (1983). *Holy virility: The social construction of masculinity.* London: Pluto.

Richardson, S. A., Hastorf, A. H., Goodman, N., & Dornbusch, S. M. (1961). Cultural uniformity in reaction to physical disabilities. *American Sociological Review, 26*, 241–47.

Rodin, J., Silberstein, L. R., & Striegel-Moore, R. (1985). Women and weight: A normative discontent. In T. B. Sonderegger (Ed.), Nebraska Symposium on Motivation, 1984: Psychology and gender. Lincoln: University of Nebraska Press.

Rosenkrantz, P., Vogel, S., Bee, H., Broverman, I., & Broverman, D. (1968). Sex-role stereotypes and self-concepts in college students. *Journal of Consulting and Clinical Psychology. 32*, 287–95.

Secord, P. F., & Jourard, S. M. (1953). The appraisal of body-cathexis: Body cathexis and the self. *Journal of Consulting Psychology, 17*, 343–47.

Sheldon, W. H. (1942). *The varieties of temperament.* New York: Harper & Row.

Sigall, H., Page, R., & Brown, A. C. (1971). Effort expenditure as a function of evaluation and evaluator attractiveness. *Representative Research in Social Psychology. 2*, 19–25.

Spence, J. T., & Helmreich, R. L. (1978). *Masculinity and femininity.* Austin: University of Texas Press.

Staffieri, J. (1967). A study of social stereotypes of body image in children. *Journal of Personality and Social Psychology, 7*, 101–4.

Story, M. D. (1979). Factors associated with more positive body self-concepts in preschool children. *Journal of Social Psychology, 108*, 49–56.

Striegel-Moore, R., Silberstein, L. R., & Rodin, J. (1986). Toward an understanding of risk factors for bulimia. *American Psychologist, 41*, 246–63.

Stunkard, A. J., Foch, T. T., & Hrubec, Z. (1985). *A twin study of human obesity.* Unpublished manuscript, University of Pennsylvania.

Stunkard, A. J., Sorenson, T. I. A., Hanis, C., Teasdale, T. W., Chakraborty, R., Schull, W. J., & Schulsinger, F. (1985). *An adoption study of human obesity.* Unpublished manuscript, University of Pennsylvania.

Sugerman, A. A., & Haronian, F. (1964). Body type and sophistication of body concept. *Journal of Personality, 32*, 380–94.

Surgeon General's Report. (1984). *The health of the nation.* Washington, DC: U.S. Department of Health and Human Services.

Thune, J. (1949). Personality of weight lifters. *Research Quarterly of the American Physical Education Association, 20*, 296–306.

Todd, T. (1983, August 1). The steroid predicament. *Sports Illustrated, 39*, 62–78.

Tucker, L. A. (1982a). Effect of a weight-training program on the self-concepts of college males. *Perceptual and Motor Skills, 54*, 1055–61.

Tucker, L. A. (1982b). Relationship between perceived somatotype and body cathexis of college males. *Psychological Reports, 50*, 983–89.

Vaughn, B. E., & Langlois, J. H. (1983). Physical attractiveness as a correlate of peer status and social competence in preschool children. *Developmental Psychology, 19*, 561–67.

Walker, R. N. (1963). Body build and behavior in young children, II: Body build and parents' ratings. *Child Development, 34*, 1–23.

Washburn, W. C. (1962). The effects of physique and intrafamily tensions on self-concept in adolescent males. *Journal of Consulting Psychology, 27*, 460–66.

Wells, W. D., & Siegel, B. (1961). Stereotyped somatotypes. *Psychological Reports, 8*, 77–78.

West, S. C., & Brown, T. J. (1975). Physical attractiveness, severity of emergency and helping: Field experiment and interpersonal stimulation. *Journal of Experimental Social Psychology, 11*, 531–38.

Wooley, S. C., & Wooley, O. W. (1984). Should obesity be treated at all? In A. J. Stunkard & E. Stellar (Eds.), *Eating and its disorders.* New York: Raven.

Wright, D. C. & Bradbard, M. R. (1980). Body build-behavioral stereotypes, self-identification, preference and aversion to black preschool children. *Perceptual and Motor Skills, 51*, 1047–50.

SUSAN BORDO

6

"Material Girl"

The Effacements of Postmodern Culture

Susan Bordo begins her examination of the malleable, "plastic" nature attributed to contemporary
women's bodies with an exploration of the body-
as-machine metaphor. Beginning with God as the
ultimate watchmaker and the body as His time-
piece, she explores the logic of this metaphor and
its effect on contemporary appearance norms.
Reflecting dominant cultural values inherent in the
mechanized conceptualization of the body, she
shows how commodified appearance norms have
utilized contemporary scientific efforts to redefine
"malfunction," further expanding the body's "im-
provements." This definition of improvement contributes to the perception of the surface of the
body as plastic, malleable, and in need of transformation. Bordo also explores women's ability to
resist dominant discourses about bodily transformations. Focusing on pop singer Madonna as the
ultimate example of resistant transformation, Bordo
suggests that many resistant readings are limited
to a narrow focus on transformative discourses,
rather than on the results or consequences of the
acts themselves. Her investigation of media images
serves as a good foundation from which to read the
selection later in this book on the aerobicizing
female body, titled, "Firm but Shapely, Fit but Sexy,
Strong but Thin." Comparison of these two authors'
views will provide an understanding of the current
culture studies debates on the power of discourses

From Susan Bordo, "Material Girl: The Effacements of Postmodern Culture," in
Unbearable Weight: Feminism, Western Culture, and the Body (Berkeley: Uni-
versity of California Press, 1993), 245–48, 250–51, 253–65, 267–75, 340–41.
Reprinted by permission of the University of California Press and the author.

to determine individuals' acts of accommodation and resistance to larger cultural mandates.

Plasticity as Postmodern Paradigm

In a culture in which organ transplants, life-extension machinery, microsurgery, and artificial organs have entered everyday medicine, we seem on the verge of practical realization of the seventeenth-century imagination of body as machine. But if we have technically and technologically realized that conception, it can also be argued that metaphysically we have deconstructed it. In the early modern era, machine imagery helped to articulate a totally determined human body whose basic functionings the human being was helpless to alter. The then-dominant metaphors for this body—clocks, watches, collections of springs—imagined a system that is set, wound up, whether by nature or by God the watchmaker, ticking away in a predictable, orderly manner, regulated by laws over which the human being has no control. Understanding the system, we can help it to perform efficiently, and we can intervene when it malfunctions. But we cannot radically alter its configuration.

Pursuing this modern, determinist fantasy to its limits, fed by the currents of consumer capitalism, modern ideologies of the self, and their crystallization in the dominance of United States mass culture, Western science and technology have now arrived, paradoxically but predictably (for it was an element, though submerged and illicit, in the mechanist conception all along), at a new, postmodern imagination of human freedom from bodily determination. Gradually and surely, a technology that was first aimed at the replacement of malfunctioning parts has generated an industry and an ideology fueled by fantasies of rearranging, transforming, and correcting, an ideology of limitless improvement and change, defying the historicity, the mortality, and, indeed, the very materiality of the body. In place of that materiality, we now have what I will call cultural plastic. In place of God the watchmaker, we now have ourselves, the master sculptors of that plastic. This disdain for material limits and the concomitant intoxication with freedom, change, and self-determination are enacted not only on the level of the contemporary technology of the body but in a wide range of contexts, including much of the contemporary discourse on the body, both popular and academic. In this essay, looking at a variety of these discursive con-

---

texts, I attempt to describe key elements of this paradigm of plasticity and expose some of its effacements—the material and social realities it denies or renders invisible.

Plastic Bodies

"Create a masterpiece, sculpt your body into a work of art," urges *Fit* magazine. "You visualize what you want to look like, and then you create that form." "The challenge presents itself: to rearrange things."[1] The precision technology of body-sculpting, once the secret of the Arnold Schwarzeneggers and Rachel McLishes of the professional bodybuilding world, has now become available to anyone who can afford the price of membership in a gym. "I now look at bodies," says John Travolta, after training for the movie *Staying Alive*, "almost like pieces of clay that can be molded."[2] On the medical front, plastic surgery, whose repeated and purely cosmetic employment has been legitimated by Michael Jackson, Cher, and others, has become à fabulously expanding industry, extending its domain from nose jobs, face-lifts, tummy tucks, and breast augmentations to collagen-plumped lips and liposuction-shaped ankles, calves, and buttocks. In 1989, 681,000 procedures were done, up 80 percent over 1981; over half of these were performed on patients between the ages of eighteen and thirty-five.[3] The trendy *Details* magazine describes "surgical stretching, tucking and sucking" as "another fabulous [fashion] accessory" and invites readers to share their cosmetic-surgery experiences in their monthly column "Knife-styles of the Rich and Famous." In that column, the transportation of fat from one part of the body to another is described as breezily as changing hats might be:

> Dr. Brown is an artist. He doesn't just pull and tuck and forget about you. . . . He did liposuction on my neck, did the nose job and tightened up my forehead to give it a better line. Then he took some fat from the side of my waist and injected it into my hands. It goes in as a lump, and then he smooths it out with his hands to where it looks good. I'll tell you something, the nose and neck made a big change, but nothing in comparison to how fabulous my hands look. The fat just smoothed out all the lines, the veins don't stick up anymore, the skin actually looks soft and great. [But] you have to be careful not to bang your hands.[4]

Popular culture does not apply any brake to these fantasies of re-arrangement and self-transformation. Rather, we are constantly told that we can "choose" our own bodies. "The proper diet, the right amount of exercise and you can have, pretty much, any body you desire," claims Evian. Of course, the rhetoric of choice and self-determination and the breezy analogies comparing cosmetic surgery to fashion accessorizing are deeply mystifying. They efface, not only the inequalities of privilege, money, and time that prohibit most people from indulging in these practices, but the desperation that character-izes the lives of those who do. "I will do anything, *anything*, to make myself look and feel better," says Tina Lizardi (whose "Knife-styles" experience I quoted from above). Medical science has now designated a new category of "polysurgical addicts" (or, in more casual refer-ences, "scalpel slaves") who return for operation after operation, in perpetual quest of the elusive yet ruthlessly normalizing goal, the "per-fect" body.[5] The dark underside of the practices of body transformation and rearrangement reveals botched and sometimes fatal operations, exercise addictions, eating disorders. And of course, despite the claims of the Evian ad, one cannot have *any* body that one wants—for not every body will *do*. The very advertisements whose copy speaks of choice and self-determination visually legislate the effacement of indi-vidual and cultural difference and circumscribe our choices.

That we are surrounded by homogenizing and normalizing images —images whose content is far from arbitrary, but is instead suffused with the dominance of gendered, racial, class, and other cultural iconography—seems so obvious as to be almost embarrassing to be arguing here. Yet contemporary understandings of the behaviors I have been describing not only construct the situation very differently but do so in terms that preempt precisely such a critique of cultural imagery. Moreover, they reproduce, on the level of discourse and interpretation, the same conditions that postmodern bodies enact on the level of cultural practice: a construction of life as plastic possi-bility and weightless choice, undetermined by history, social loca-tion, or even individual biography. A 1988 *Donahue* show offers my first illustration.

The show's focus was a series of television commercials for DuraSoft colored contact lenses. In these commercials as they were originally aired, a woman was shown in a dreamlike, romantic fan-tasy—for example, parachuting slowly and gracefully from the heav-ens. The male voiceover then described the woman in soft, lush terms: "If I believed in angels, I'd say that's what she was—an angel, dropped from the sky like an answer to a prayer, with eyes as brown as bark." [Significant pause] "No . . . *I don't think so.*" [At this point, the tape would be rewound to return us to:] "With eyes as violet as the colors of a child's imagination." The commercial concludes: "DuraSoft colored contact lenses. Get brown eyes a second look."

The question posed by Phil Donahue: Is this ad racist? Donahue clearly thought there was controversy to be stirred up here, for he stocked his audience full of women of color and white women to discuss the implications of the ad. But Donahue was apparently living in a different decade from most of his audience, who repeatedly declared that there was nothing "wrong" with the ad, and everything "wrong" with any inclinations to "make it a political question." Here are some comments taken from the transcript of the show:

> "Why does it have to be a political question? I mean, people perm their hair. It's just because they like the way it looks. It's not something sociological. Maybe black women like the way they look with green contacts. It's to be more attractive. It's not something that makes them—I mean, why do punk rockers have purple hair? Because they feel it makes them feel better." [white woman]

> "What's the fuss? When I put on my blue lenses, it makes me feel good. It makes me feel sexy, different, the other woman, so to speak, which is like fun." [black woman]

> "I perm my hair, you're wearing make-up, what's the difference?" [white woman]

> "I want to be versatile . . . having different looks, being able to change from one look to the other." [black female model]

> "We all do the same thing, when we're feeling good we wear new makeup, hairstyles, we buy new clothes. So now it's contact lenses. What difference does it make?" [white woman]

> "It goes both ways . . . Bo Derek puts her hair in cornstalks, or corn . . . or whatever that thing is called. White women try to get tan." [white woman]

> "She's not trying to be white, she's trying to be different." [about a black woman with blue contact lenses]

"It's fashion, women are never happy with themselves."

"I put them in as toys, just for fun, change. Nothing too serious, and I really enjoy them." [black woman][6]

Some points to note here: first, putting on makeup, styling hair, and so forth are conceived of only as free *play*, fun, a matter of creative expression. This they surely are. But they are also experienced by many women as necessary before they will show themselves to the world, even on a quick trip to the corner mailbox. The one comment that hints at women's (by now depressingly well documented) dissatisfaction with their appearance trivializes that dissatisfaction and puts it beyond the pale of cultural critique: "It's fashion." What she means is, "It's *only* fashion," whose whimsical and politically neutral vicissitudes supply endless amusement for women's eternally superficial values. ("Women are never happy with themselves.") If we are never happy with ourselves, it is implied, that is due to our female nature, not to be taken too seriously or made into a political question. Second, the content of fashion, the specific ideals that women are drawn to embody (ideals that vary historically, racially, and along class and other lines) are seen as arbitrary, without meaning; interpretation is neither required nor even appropriate. Rather, all motivation and value come from the interest and allure—the "sexiness"—of change and difference itself. Blue contact lenses for a black woman, it is admitted, make her "other" ("the other woman"). But that "other" is not a racial or cultural "other"; she is sexy because of the piquancy, the novelty, the erotics of putting on a different self. *Any* different self would do, it is implied.

Closely connected to this is the construction of *all* cosmetic change as the same: perms for the white women, corn rows on Bo Derek, tanning, makeup, changing hairstyles, blue contacts for black women—all are seen as having equal political valance (which is to say, *no* political valance) and the same cultural meaning (which is to say, *no* cultural meaning) in the heterogeneous yet undifferentiated context of the things "all" women do "to be more attractive." The one woman in the audience who offered a different construction of this behavior, who insisted that the styles we aspire to do not simply reflect the free play of fashion or female nature—who went so far indeed, as to claim that we "are brainwashed to think blond hair and blue eyes is the most beautiful of all," was regarded with hostile silence. Then, a few moments later, someone challenged: "Is there anything *wrong* with blue eyes and blond hair?" The audience enthusiastically applauded this defender of democratic values.

This "conversation"—a paradigmatically postmodern conversation, as I will argue shortly—effaces the same general elements as the rhetoric of body transformation discussed earlier. First, it effaces the inequalities of social position and the historical origins which for example, render Bo Derek's cornrows and black women's hair-straightening utterly noncommensurate. On the one hand, we have Bo Derek's privilege, not only as so unimpeachably white as to permit an exotic touch of "otherness" with no danger of racial contamination, but her trendsetting position as a famous movie star. Contrasting to this, and mediating a black woman's "choice" to straighten her hair, is a cultural history of racist body-discriminations such as the nineteenth-century comb test, which allowed admission to churches and clubs only to those blacks who could pass through their hair without snagging a fine-tooth comb hanging outside the door. (A variety of comparable tests—the pine-slab test, the brown bag test—determined whether one's skin was adequately light to pass muster.)[7]

Second, and following from these historical practices, there is a disciplinary reality that is effaced in the construction of all self-transformation as equally arbitrary, all variants of the same trivial game, without differing cultural valance. I use the term *disciplinary* here in the Foucauldian sense, as pointing to practices that do not merely transform but *normalize* the subject. That is, to repeat a point made earlier, not every body will do. A 1989 poll of E*ssence* magazine readers revealed that 68 percent of those who responded wear their hair straightened chemically or by hot comb.[8] "Just for fun"? For the kick of being "different"? When we look at the pursuit of beauty as a normalizing discipline, it becomes clear that not all body transformations are the same. The general tyranny of fashion—perpetual, elusive, and instructing the female body in a pedagogy of personal inadequacy and lack—is a powerful discipline for the normalization of *all* women in this culture. But even as we are all normalized to the requirements of appropriate feminine insecurity and preoccupation with appearance, more specific requirements emerge in different cultural and historical contexts, and for different groups. When Bo Derek put her hair in cornrows, she was engaging in normalizing feminine practice. But when Oprah Winfrey admitted on her show that all her life she has desperately longed to have "hair that swings from side to side" when she shakes her head, she revealed the power of racial as well as gender normalization, normalization not only to "femininity," but to the Caucasian standards of beauty that still dominate on television, in movies, in popular magazines. (When I was a child, I felt the same way about my thick, then curly, "Jewish" hair as Oprah did about hers.) Neither Oprah nor the *Essence* readers nor the many Jewish women (myself included) who ironed their hair in the 1960s have creatively or playfully invented themselves here.

DuraSoft knows this, even if Donahue's audience does not. Since the campaign first began, the company has replaced the original, up front magazine advertisement with a more euphemistic variant, from which the word *brown* has been tastefully effaced (In case it has become too subtle for the average reader, the model now is black—although it should be noted that DuraSoft's failure to appreciate brown eyes also renders the eyes of most of the world not worth "a second look." In the television commercial, a comparable "brownwash" was effected; here "eyes as brown as . . ." was retained, but the derogatory nouns—"brown as boots," "brown as bark"—were eliminated. The announcer simply was left speechless: "eyes as brown as . . . brown as . . . ," and then, presumably having been unable to come up with an enticing simile, shifted to "violet." As in the expurgated magazine ad, the television commercial ended: "Get *your* eyes a second look."

When I showed my students these ads, many of them were as dismissive as the *Donahue* audience, convinced that I was once again turning innocent images and practices into political issues. I persisted: If racial standards of beauty are not at work here, then why no brown contacts for blue-eyed people? A month later, two of my students triumphantly produced a DuraSoft ad for brown contacts, appearing in *Essence* magazine, and with an advertising campaign directed solely at *already* brown-eyed consumers, offering the promise *not* of "getting blue eyes a second look" by becoming excitingly darker, but of "subtly enhancing" dark eyes, by making them *lighter* brown. The creators of the DuraSoft campaign clearly know that not all differences are the same in our culture, and they continue, albeit in ever more mystified form, to exploit and perpetuate that fact.[9]

Plastic Discourse

The *Donahue* Durasoft show (indeed, any talk show) provides a perfect example of what we might call a postmodern conversation. All sense of history and all ability (or inclination) to sustain cultural criticism, to make the distinctions and discriminations that would permit such criticism, have disappeared. Rather, in this conversation, "anything goes"—and any positioned social critique (for example, the woman who, speaking clearly from consciousness of racial oppression, insisted that the attraction of blond hair and blue eyes has a cultural meaning significantly different from that of purple hair) is immediately destabilized. Instead of distinctions, endless *differences* reign—an undifferentiated pastiche of differences, a grab bag in which no items are assigned any more importance or centrality than any others. Television is, of course, the great teacher here, our prime modeler of plastic pluralism: if one "Donahue" show features a feminist talking about battered wives, the next show will feature mistreated husbands. Women who love too much, the sex habits of priests, disturbed children of psychiatrists, daughters who have no manners, male strippers, relatives who haven't spoken in ten years all have their day alongside incest, rape, and U.S. foreign policy. All are given equal weight by the great leveler—the frame of the television screen.

This spectacle of difference defeats the ability to sustain coherent political critique. Everything is the same in its unvalanced difference. ("I perm my hair, you're wearing makeup, what's the difference?") Particulars reign, and generality—which collects, organizes, and prioritizes, suspending attention to particularity in the interests of connection, emphasis, and criticism—is suspect. So, whenever some critically charged generalization was suggested on *Donahue*'s DuraSoft show, someone else would invariably offer a counterexample—I have blue eyes, and I'm a black woman; Bo Derek wears cornrows—to fragment the critique. What is remarkable is that people accept these examples as *refutations* of social critique. They almost invariably back down, utterly confused as to how to maintain their critical generalization in the face of the destabilizing example. Sometimes they qualify, claiming they meant some people, not all. But of course they meant neither all nor some. They meant *most*—that is, they were trying to make a claim about social or cultural *patterns*—and that is a stance that is increasingly difficult to sustain in a postmodern context, where we are surrounded by endlessly displaced images and are given no orienting context in which to make discriminations.

Those who insist on an orienting context (and who therefore do not permit particulars to reign in all their absolute "difference") are seen as "totalizing," that is, as constructing a falsely coherent and morally coercive universe that marginalizes and effaces the experiences and values of others. ("Is there anything *wrong* with blue eyes and blond hair?") As someone who is frequently interviewed by local television and newspaper reporters, I have often found my feminist arguments framed in this way, as they were in an article on breast-augmentation surgery. After several pages of "expert" recommendations from plastic surgeons, my cautions about the politics of female body transformation (none of them critical of individuals contemplating plastic surgery, all of them of a cultural nature) were briefly quoted by the reporter, who then went on to end the piece with a comment on *my* critique—from the director of communications for the American Society of Plastic and Reconstructive Surgery:

> Those not considering plastic surgery shouldn't be too critical of those who do. It's the hardest thing for people to understand. What's important is if it's a problem to that person. We're all different, but we all want to look better. We're just different in what extent we'll go to. But none of us can say we don't want to look the best we can.[10]

With this tolerant, egalitarian stroke, the media liaison of the most powerful plastic surgery lobby in the country presents herself as the protector of "difference" against the homogenizing and stifling regime of the feminist dictator.

Academics do not usually like to think of themselves as embodying the values and preoccupations of popular culture on the plane of high theory or intellectual discourse. We prefer to see ourselves as the demystifyers of popular discourse, bringers-to-consciousness-and-clarity rather than unconscious reproducers of culture. Despite what we would *like* to believe of ourselves, however, we are always within the society that we criticize, and never so strikingly as at the present postmodern moment. All the elements of what I have here called postmodern conversation—intoxication with individual choice and creative *jouissance*, delight with the piquancy of particularity and mistrust of pattern and seeming coherence, celebration of "difference" along with an absence of critical perspective differentiating and weighing "differences," suspicion of the totalitarian nature of generalization along with a rush to protect difference from its homogenizing abuses—have become recognizable and familiar in much of contemporary intellectual discourse. Within this theoretically self-conscious universe, moreover, these elements are not merely embodied (as in the *Donahue* show's DuraSoft conversation) but explicitly thematized and *celebrated*, as inaugurating new constructions of the self, no longer caught in the mythology of the unified subject, embracing of multiplicity, challenging the dreary and moralizing generalizations about gender, race, and so forth that have so preoccupied liberal and left humanism.

For this celebratory, academic postmodernism, it has become highly unfashionable—and "totalizing"—to talk about the grip of culture on the body. Such a perspective, it is argued, casts active and creative subjects as passive dupes of ideology; it gives too much to dominant ideology, imagining it as seamless and univocal, overlooking both the gaps which are continually allowing for the eruption of "difference" and the polysemous, unstable, open nature of all cultural texts. To talk about the grip of culture on the body (as, for example, in "old" feminist discourse about the objectification and sexualization of the female body) is to fail to acknowledge, as one theorist put it, "the cultural work by which nomadic, fragmented, active subjects confound dominant discourse."[11]

So, for example, contemporary culture critic John Fiske is harshly critical of what he describes as the view of television as a "dominating monster" with "homogenizing power" over the perceptions of viewers. Such a view, he argues, imagines the audience as "powerless and undiscriminating" and overlooks the fact that:

> Pleasure results from a particular relationship between meanings and power. . . . There is no pleasure in being a "cultural dope." . . . Pleasure results from the production of meanings of the world and of self that are felt to serve the interests of the reader rather than those of the dominant. The subordinate may be disempowered, but they are not powerless. There is a power in resisting power, there is a power in maintaining one's social identity in opposition to that proposed by the dominant ideology, there is a power in asserting one's own subcultural values against the dominant ones. There is, in short, a power in being different.[12]

Fiske then goes on to produce numerous examples of how *Dallas, Hart to Hart,* and so forth have been read (or so he argues) by various subcultures to make their own "socially pertinent" and empowering meanings out of "the semiotic resources provided by television."

Note, in Fiske's insistent, repetitive invocation of the category of power, a characteristically postmodern flattening of the terrain of power relations, a lack of differentiation between, for example, the power involved in creative *reading* in the isolation of one's own home and the power held by those who control the material production of television shows, or the power involved in public protest and action against the conditions of that production and the power of the dominant meanings—for instance, racist and sexist images and messages—therein produced. For Fiske, of course, there *are* no such dominant meanings, that is, no element whose ability to grip the imagination of the viewer is greater than the viewer's ability to "just say no" through resistant reading of the text. That ethnic and subcultural meaning *may* be wrested from *Dallas* and *Hart to Hart* becomes for Fiske proof that dominating images and messages are only in the minds of those totalitarian critics who would condescendingly "rescue" the disempowered from those forces that are in fact the very medium of their creative freedom and resistance ("the semiotic resources of television").

Fiske's conception of power—a terrain without hills and valleys, where all forces have become "resources"—reflects a very common postmodern misappropriation of Foucault. Fiske conceives of power as in the *possession* of individuals or groups, something they "have" —a conception Foucault takes great pains to criticize—rather than (as in Foucault's reconstruction) a dynamic of noncentralized forces, its dominant historical forms attaining their hegemony, not from magisterial design or decree, but through multiple "processes, of different origin and scattered location," regulating and normalizing the most intimate and minute elements of the construction of time, space, desire, embodiment.[13] This conception of power does *not* entail that there are no dominant positions, social structures, or ideologies emerging from the play of forces; the fact that power is not held by any *one* does not mean that it is equally held by *all*. It is in fact not "held" at all; rather, people and groups are positioned differentially within it. This model is particularly useful for the analysis of male dominance and female subordination, so much of which is reproduced "voluntarily," through our self-normalization to everyday habits of masculinity and femininity. Within such a model, one can acknowledge that women may indeed contribute to the perpetuation of female subordination (for example, by embracing, taking pleasure in, and even feeling empowered by the cultural objectification and sexualization of the female body) without this entailing that they have power in the production and reproduction of sexist culture.

Foucault does insist on the *instability* of modern power relations—that is, he emphasizes that resistance is perpetual and unpredictable, and hegemony precarious. This notion is transformed by Fiske (perhaps under the influence of a more deconstructionist brand of postmodernism) into a notion of resistance as *jouissance*, a creative and pleasurable eruption of cultural "difference" through the "seams" of the text. What this celebration of creative reading as resistance effaces is the arduous and frequently frustrated historical struggle that is required for the subordinated to articulate and assert the value of their "difference" in the face of dominant meanings— meanings which often offer a pedagogy directed at the reinforcement of feelings of inferiority, marginality, ugliness. During the early fifties, when *Brown v. the Board of Education* was wending its way through the courts, as a demonstration of the destructive psychological effects of segregation, black children were asked to look at two baby dolls, identical in all respects except color. The children were asked a series of questions: which is the nice doll? which is the bad doll? which doll would you like to play with? The majority of black children, Kenneth Clark reports, attributed the positive characteristics to the white doll, the negative characteristics to the black. When Clark asked one final question, "Which doll is like you?" they looked at him, he says, "as though he were the devil himself" for putting them in that predicament, for forcing them to face the inexorable and hideous logical implications of their situation. Northern children often ran out of the room; southern children tended to answer the question in shamed embarrassment. Clark recalls one little boy who laughed, "Who am I like? That doll! It's a nigger and I'm a nigger!"[14]

Failing to acknowledge the psychological and cultural potency of normalizing imagery can be just as effective in effacing people's experiences of racial oppression as lack of attentiveness to cultural and ethnic differences—a fact postmodern critics sometimes seem to forget. This is not to deny what Fiske calls "the power of being different"; it is, rather, to insist that it is won through ongoing political *struggle* rather than through an act of creative interpretation. Here, once again, although many postmodern academics may claim Foucault as their guiding light, they differ from him in significant and revealing ways. For Foucault, the metaphorical terrain of resistance is explicitly that of the "battle"; the "points of confrontation" may be "innumerable" and "instable," but they involve a serious, often deadly struggle of embodied (that is, historically situated and shaped) forces.[15] Some progressive developers of children's toys have self-consciously entered into struggle with racial and other forms of normalization. The Kenya Doll comes in three different skin tones ("so your girl is bound to feel pretty and proud") and attempts to create a future in which hair-straightening *will* be merely one decorative option among others. Such products, to my mind, are potentially effective "sites of resistance" precisely because they recognize that the body is a battleground whose self-determination has to be fought for.

The metaphor of the body as battleground, rather than postmodern playground, captures, as well, the *practical* difficulties involved in the political struggle to empower "difference." *Essence* magazine has consciously and strenuously tried to promote diverse images of black strength, beauty, and self-acceptance. Beauty features celebrate the glory of black skin and lush lips; other departments feature interviews with accomplished black women writers, activists, teachers, many of whom display styles of body and dress that challenge the hegemony of white Anglo-Saxon standards. The magazine's advertisers, however, continually play upon and perpetuate consumers' feelings of inadequacy and insecurity over the racial characteristics of their bodies. They insist that, in order to be beautiful, hair must be straightened and eyes lightened; they almost always employ models with fair skin, Anglo-Saxon features, and "hair that moves," insuring association of their products with fantasies of becoming what the white culture most prizes and rewards.

This ongoing battle over the black woman's body and the power of its "differences" ("differences" which actual black women embody to widely varying degrees, of course) is made manifest in the twentieth-anniversary issue, where a feature celebrating "The Beauty of Black" faced an advertisement visually legislating virtually the opposite (and offering, significantly, "escape"). This invitation to cognitive dissonance reveals what *Essence* must grapple with, in every issue, as it tries to keep its message of African-American self-acceptance clear and dominant, while submitting to economic necessities on which its survival depends. Let me make it clear here that such self-acceptance, not the reverse tyranny that constructs light-skinned and Anglo-featured African-Americans as "not black enough," is the message *Essence* is trying to convey, against a culture that *denies* "the Beauty of Black" at every turn. This terrain, clearly, is not a playground but a minefield that constantly threatens to deconstruct "difference" *literally* and not merely literarily.

"Material Girl": Madonna as Postmodern Heroine

John Fiske's conception of "difference," in the section quoted above, at least imagines resistance as challenging specifiable historical forms of dominance. Women, he argues, connect with subversive "feminine" values leaking through the patriarchal plot of soap operas; blacks laugh to themselves at the glossy, materialist-cowboy culture of *Dallas*. Such examples suggest a resistance directed against *particular* historical forms of power and subjectivity. For some postmodern theorists, however, resistance is imagined as the refusal to embody *any* positioned subjectivity at all; what is celebrated is continual creative escape from location, containment, and definition. So, as Susan Rubin Suleiman advises, we must move beyond the valorization of historically suppressed values (for example, those values that have been culturally constructed as belonging to an inferior, female domain and generally expunged from Western science, philosophy, and religion) and toward "endless complication" and a "dizzying accumulation of narratives."[16] She appreciatively (and perhaps misleadingly) invokes Derrida's metaphor of "incalculable choreographies"[17] to capture the dancing, elusive, continually changing subjectivity that she envisions, a subjectivity without gender, without history, without location. From this perspective, the truly resistant female body is, not the body that wages war on feminine sexualization and objectification, but the body that, as Cathy Schwichtenberg has put it, "uses simulation strategically in ways that challenge the stable notion of gender as the edifice of sexual difference . . . [in] an erotic politics in which the female body can be refashioned in the flux of identities that speak in plural styles."[18] For this erotic politics, the new postmodern heroine is Madonna.

This celebration of Madonna as postmodern heroine does not mark the first time Madonna has been portrayed as a subversive culture-figure. Until the early 1990s, however, Madonna's resistance has been interpreted along "body as battleground" lines, as deriving from her refusal to allow herself to be constructed as a passive object of patriarchal desire. John Fiske, for example, argues that this was a large part of Madonna's original appeal to her "wanna-bes"—those hordes of middle-class pre-teeners who mimicked Madonna's moves and costumes. For the "wanna-bes," Madonna demonstrated the possibility of a female heterosexuality that was independent of patriarchal control, a sexuality that defied rather than rejected the male gaze, teasing it with her own gaze, deliberately trashy and vulgar, challenging anyone to call her a whore, and ultimately not giving a damn how she might be judged. Madonna's rebellious sexuality, in this reading, offered itself, not as coming into being through the look of the "other," but as self-defining and in love with, happy with itself—an attitude that is rather difficult for women to achieve in this culture and that helps to explain, as Fiske argues, her enormous appeal for pre-teen girls.[19] "I like the way she handles herself, sort of take it or leave it; she's sexy but she doesn't need men . . . she's kind of there all by herself," says one. "She gives us ideas. It's really women's lib, not being afraid of what guys think," says another.[20]

Madonna herself, significantly and unlike most sex symbols, has never advertised herself as disdainful of feminism or constructed feminists as man-haters. Rather, in a 1985 *Time* interview, she suggests that her lack of inhibition in "being herself" and her "luxuriant" expression of "strong" sexuality constitute her brand of feminist celebration.[21] Some feminist theorists would agree. Molly Hite, for example, argues that "asserting female desire in a culture in which female sexuality is viewed as so inextricably conjoined with passivity" is "transgressive":

> Implied in this strategy is the old paradox of the speaking statue, the created thing that magically begins to create, for when a woman writes—self-consciously from her muted position as a woman and not as an honorary man—about female desire, female sexuality, female sensuous experience generally, her performance has the effect of giving voice to pure corporeality, of turning a product of the dominant meaning-system into a producer of meanings. A woman, conventionally identified with her body, writes about that identification, and as a conse-

quence, femininity—silent and inert by definition—erupts into patriarchy as an impossible discourse.[22]

Not all feminists would agree with this, of course. For the sake of the contrast I want to draw here, however, let us grant it, and note, as well, that an argument similar to Fiske's can be made concerning Madonna's refusal to be obedient to dominant and normalizing standards of female *beauty*. I am now talking, of course, about Madonna in her more fleshy days. In those days, Madonna saw herself as willfully out of step with the times. "Back in the fifties," she says in the *Time* interview, "women weren't ashamed of their bodies." (The fact that she is dead wrong is not relevant here.) Identifying herself with her construction of that time and what she calls its lack of "suppression" of femininity, she looks down her nose at the "androgynous" clothes of our own time and speaks warmly of her own stomach, "not really flat" but "round and the skin is smooth and I like it." Contrasting herself to anorectics, whom she sees as self-denying and self-hating, completely in the thrall of externally imposed standards of worthiness, Madonna (as she saw herself) stood for self-definition through the assertion of her own (traditionally "female" and now anachronistic) body-type.

Of course, this is no longer Madonna's body type. Shortly after her 1987 marriage to Sean Penn she began a strenuous reducing and exercise program, now runs several miles a day, lifts weights, and has developed, in obedience to dominant contemporary norms, a tight, slender, muscular body. Why did she decide to shape up? "I didn't have a flat stomach anymore," she has said. "I had become well-rounded." Please note the sharp about-face here, from pride to embarrassment. My goal here, however, is not to suggest that Madonna's formerly voluptuous body was a non-alienated, freely expressive body, a "natural" body. While the slender body is the current cultural ideal, the voluptuous female body is a cultural form, too (as are all bodies), and was a coercive ideal in the fifties. My point is that in terms of Madonna's own former lexicon of meanings—in which feminine voluptuousness and the choice to be round in a culture of the lean were clearly connected to spontaneity, self-definition, and defiance of the cultural gaze—the terms set by that gaze have now triumphed. Madonna has been normalized; more precisely, she has self-normalized. Her "wanna-bes" are following suit. Studies suggest that as many as 80 percent of nine-year-old suburban girls (the majority of whom are far from overweight) are making rigorous dieting and exercise the organizing discipline of their lives.[23] They do not require Madonna's example, of course, to believe that they must be thin to be acceptable. But Madonna clearly no longer provides a model of resistance or "difference" for them.

None of this "materiality"—that is, the obsessive body-praxis that regulates and disciplines Madonna's life and the lives of the young (and not so young) women who emulate her—makes its way into the representation of Madonna as postmodern heroine. In the terms of this representation (in both its popular and scholarly instantiations) Madonna is "in control of her image, not trapped by it"; the proof lies in her ironic and chameleon-like approach to the construction of her identity, her ability to "slip in and out of character at will," to defy definition, to keep them guessing.[24] In this coding of things, as in the fantasies of the polysurgical addict (and, as I argue elsewhere in this volume, the eating-disordered woman), *control* and *power*, words that are invoked over and over in discussions of Madonna, have become equivalent to *self-creating*. Madonna's new body has no material history; it conceals its continual struggle to maintain itself, it does not reveal its pain. (Significantly, Madonna's "self-exposé," the documentary *Truth or Dare*, does not include any scenes of Madonna's daily workouts.) It is merely another creative transformation of an ever-elusive subjectivity. "More Dazzling and Determined Not to Stop Changing," as *Cosmopolitan* describes Madonna: ". . . whether in looks or career, this multitalented dazzler will never be trapped in *any* mold!"[25] The plasticity of Madonna's subjectivity is emphasized again and again in the popular press, particularly by Madonna herself. It is how she tells the story of her "power" in the industry: "In pop music, generally, people have one image. You get pigeonholed. I'm lucky enough to be able to change and still be accepted . . . play a part, change characters, looks, attitudes."[26]

Madonna claims that her creative work, too, is meant to escape definition. "Everything I do is meant to have several meanings, to be ambiguous," she says. She resists, however (in true postmodern fashion), the attribution of serious artistic intent; rather (as she told *Cosmo*), she favors irony and ambiguity, "to entertain myself" and (as she told *Vanity Fair*) out of "rebelliousness and a desire to fuck with people."[27] It is the postmodern nature of her music and videos

that has most entranced academic critics, whose accolades reproduce in highly theoretical language the notions emphasized in the
popular press. Susan McClary writes:

> Madonna's art itself repeatedly deconstructs the traditional
> notion of the unified subject with finite ego boundaries. Her
> pieces explore . . . various ways of constituting identities that
> refuse stability, that remain fluid, that resist definition. This
> tendency in her work has become increasingly pronounced; for
> instance, in her recent controversial video "Express Yourself"
> . . . she slips in and out of every subject position offered within
> the video's narrative context . . . refusing more than ever to
> deliver the security of a clear, unambiguous message or an
> "authentic" self.[28]

Later in the same piece, McClary describes "Open Your Heart to
Me," which features Madonna as a porn star in a peep show, as creating "an image of open-ended *jouissance*—an erotic energy that
continually escapes containment."[29] Now, many feminist viewers
may find this particular video quite disturbing, for a number of reasons. First, unlike many of Madonna's older videos, "Open Your
Heart to Me" does not visually emphasize Madonna's subjectivity or
desire—as "Lucky Star," for example, did through frequent shots of
Madonna's face and eyes, flirting with and controlling the reactions
of the viewer. Rather, "Open Your Heart to Me" places the viewer in
the position of the voyeur by presenting Madonna's body as object,
now perfectly taut and tightly managed for display. To be sure, we do
not identify with the slimy men, drooling over Madonna's performance, who are depicted in the video; but, as E. Ann Kaplan has
pointed out, the way men view women *in* the filmic world is only
one species of objectifying gaze. There is also the viewer's gaze,
which may be encouraged by the director to be either more or less
objectifying.[30] In "Open Your Heart to Me," as in virtually all rock
videos, the female body is offered to the viewer purely as a spectacle,
an object of sight, a visual commodity to be consumed. Madonna's
weight loss and dazzling shaping-up job make the spectacle of her
body all the more compelling; we are riveted to her body, fascinated
by it. Many men and women may experience the primary reality of
the video as the elicitation of desire *for* that perfect body; women,
however, may also be gripped by the desire (very likely impossible
to achieve) to *become* that perfect body.

These elements can be effaced, of course, by a deliberate abstraction of the video from the cultural context in which it is historically embedded—the continuing containment, sexualization, and objectification of the female body—and in which the viewer is implicated as well and instead treating the video as a purely formal text. Taken as such, "Open Your Heart to Me" presents itself as what E. Ann Kaplan calls a "postmodern video": it refuses to "take a clear position vis-á-vis its images" and similarly refuses a "clear position for the spectator within the filmic world . . . leaving him/her decentered, confused."[31] McClary's reading of "Open Your Heart to Me" emphasizes precisely these postmodern elements, insisting on the ambiguous and unstable nature of the relationships depicted in the narrative of the video, and the frequent elements of parody and play. "The usual power relationship between the voyeuristic male gaze and object" is "destabilized," she claims, by the portrayal of the male patrons of the porno house as leering and pathetic. At the same time, the portrayal of Madonna as porno queen-object is deconstructed, McClary argues, by the end of the video, which has Madonna changing her clothes to those of a little boy and tripping off playfully, leaving the manager of the house sputtering behind her. McClary reads this as "escape to androgyny," which "refuses essentialist gender categories and turns sexual identity into a kind of play." As for the gaze of the viewer, she admits that it is "risky" to "invoke the image of porn queen in order to perform its deconstruction," but concludes that the deconstruction is successful: "In this video, Madonna confronts the most pernicious of her stereotypes and attempts to channel it into a very different realm: a realm where the feminine object need not be the object of the patriarchal gaze, where its energy can motivate play and nonsexual pleasure."[32]

I would argue, however, that despite the video's evasions of clear or fixed meaning there *is* a dominant position in this video: it is that of the objectifying gaze. One is not *really* decentered and confused by this video, despite the "ambiguities" it formally contains. Indeed, the video's postmodern conceits, I would suggest, facilitate rather than deconstruct the presentation of Madonna's body as an object on display. For in the absence of a coherent critical position telling us how to read the images, the individual images themselves become preeminent, hypnotic, fixating. Indeed, I would say that ultimately this video is entirely about Madonna's body, the narrative context virtually irrelevant, an excuse to showcase the physical achievements of the star, a video centerfold. On this level, any parodic or destabilizing element appears as cynically, mechanically tacked on, in bad faith, a way of claiming trendy status for what is really just cheesecake—or, perhaps, soft-core pornography.

Indeed, it may be worse than that. If the playful "tag" ending of "Open Your Heart to Me" is successful in deconstructing the notion that the objectification, the sexualization of women's bodies is a serious business, then Madonna's *jouissance* may be "fucking with" her youthful viewer's perceptions in a dangerous way. Judging from the proliferation of rock and rap lyrics celebrating the rape, abuse, and humiliation of women, the message—not Madonna's responsibility alone, of course, but hers among others, surely—is getting through. The artists who perform these misogynist songs also claim to be speaking playfully, tongue-in-cheek, and to be daring and resistant transgressors of cultural structures that contain and define. Ice T, whose rap lyrics gleefully describe the gang rape of a woman—with a flashlight, to "make her tits light up"—claims that he is only "telling it like it is" among black street youth (he compares himself to Richard Wright), and he scoffs at feminist humorlessness, implying, as well, that it is racist and repressive for white feminists to try to deny him his indigenous "style." The fact that Richard Wright embedded his depiction of Bigger Thomas within a critique of the racist culture that shaped him, and that *Native Son* is meant to be a *tragedy*, was not, apparently, noticed in Ice T's postmodern reading of the book, whose critical point of view he utterly ignores. Nor does he seem concerned about what appears to be a growing fad—not only among street gangs, but in fraternity houses as well—for gang rape, often with an unconscious woman, and surrounded by male spectators. (Some of the terms popularly used to describe these rapes include "beaching"—the woman being likened to a "beached whale" —and "spectoring," to emphasize how integral a role the onlookers play.)

My argument here is a plea, not for censorship, but for recognition of the social contexts and consequences of images from popular culture, consequences that are frequently effaced in postmodern and other celebrations of "resistant" elements in these images. To turn back to Madonna and the liberating postmodern subjectivity that McClary and others claim she is offering: the notion that one can play a porno house by night and regain one's androgynous innocence by day does not seem to me to be a refusal of essentialist categories about gender, but rather a new inscription of mind/body dualism. What the body does is immaterial, so long as the imagination is free. This abstract, unsituated, disembodied freedom, I have argued in this essay, glorifies itself only through the effacement of the material praxis of people's lives, the normalizing power of cultural images, and the continuing social realities of dominance and subordination.

NOTES

1. Quoted in Trix Rosen, *Strong and Sexy* (New York: Putnam, 1983), pp. 72, 61.
2. "Travolta: 'You Really Can Make Yourself Over,'" *Syracuse Herald-American*, Jan. 13, 1985.
3. "Popular Plastic Surgery," *Cosmopolitan* (May 1990): 96.
4. Tina Lizardi and Martha Frankel, "Hand Job," *Details* (Feb. 1990): 38.
5. Jennet Conant, Jeanne Gordon, and Jennifer Donovan, "Scalpel Slaves Just Can't Quit," *Newsweek* (Jan. 11, 1988): 58–59.
6. "Donahue" transcript 05257, n. d., Multimedia Entertainment, Cincinnati, Ohio.
7. Dahleen Glanton, "Racism Within a Race," *Syracuse Herald-American*, Sept. 19, 1989.
8. *Essense* reader opinion poll (June 1989): 71.
9. Since this essay first appeared, DuraSoft has altered its campaign once more, renaming the lenses "Complements" and emphasizing how "natural" and subtle they are. "No one will know you're wearing them," they assure. One ad for "Complements" features identical black twins, one with brown eyes and one wearing blue lenses, as if to show that Dura-Soft finds nothing "wrong" with brown eyes. The issue, rather, is self-determination: "Choosing your very own eye color is now the most natural thing in the world."
10. Linda Bien, "Building a Better Bust," *Syracuse Herald-American*, March 4, 1990.
11. This was said by Janice Radway in an oral presentation of her work, Duke University, Spring, 1989.
12. John Fiske, *Television Culture* (New York: Methuen, 1987), p. 19.
13. Michel Foucault, *Discipline and Punish* (New York: Vintage, 1979), p. 138.
14. Related in Bill Moyers, "A Walk Through the Twentieth Century: The Second American Revolution," P.B.S. Boston.
15. Foucault, *Discipline and Punish*, pp. 26–27.
16. Susan Rubin Suleiman, "(Re)Writing the Body: The Politics and Poetics of Female Eroticism," in Susan Rubin Suleiman, ed., *The Female Body in Western Culture* (Cambridge: Harvard University Press, 1986), p. 24.
17. Jacques Derrida and Christie V. McDonald, "Choreographies," *Diacritics* 12, no. 2 (1982): 76.
18. Cathy Schwichtenberg, "Postmodern Feminism and Madonna: Toward an Erotic Politics of the Female Body," paper presented at the University of Utah Humanities Center, National Conference on Rewriting the (Post)Modern: (Post)Colonialism/Feminism/late Capitalism, March 30–31, 1990.

19. John Fiske, "British Cultural Studies and Television," in Robert C. Allen, ed., *Channels of Discourse* (Chapel Hill: University of North Carolina Press, 1987), pp. 254–90.
20. Quoted in John Skow, "Madonna Rocks the Land," *Time* (May 27, 1985): 77.
21. Skow, "Madonna Rocks the Land," p. 81.
22. Molly Hite, "Writing—and Reading—the Body: Female Sexuality and Recent Feminist Fiction," in *Feminist Studies* 14, no. 1 (Spring 1988): 121–22.
23. "Fat or Not, 4th Grade Girls Diet Lest They Be Teased or Unloved," *Wall Street Journal*, Feb. 11, 1986.
24. Catherine Texier, "Have Women Surrendered in MTV's Battle of the Sexes?" *New York Times*, April 22, 1990, p. 31.
25. *Cosmopolitan* (July 1987): cover.
26. David Ansen, "Magnificent Maverick," *Cosmopolitan* (May 1990): 311.
27. Ansen, "Magnificent Maverick," p. 311; Kevin Sessums, "White Heat," *Vanity Fair* (April 1990): 208.
28. Susan McClary, "Living to Tell: Madonna's Resurrection of the Fleshy," *Genders*, no. 7 (Spring 1990): 2.
29. McClary, "Living to Tell," p. 12.
30. E. Ann Kaplan, "Is the Gaze Male?" in Ann Snitow, Christine Stansell, and Sharon Thompson, eds., *Powers of Desire: The Politics of Sexuality* (New York: Monthly Review Press, 1983), pp. 309–27.
31. E. Ann Kaplan, *Rocking Around the Clock: Music Television, Postmodernism and Consumer Culture* (New York: Methuen, 1987), p. 63.
32. McClary, "Living to Tell," p. 13.

MARY G. McDONALD

7 Michael Jordan's Family Values

Marketing, Meaning, and Post-Reagan America

Mary McDonald explores both the man and the myth of Michael Jordan in the context of race, masculinity, and corporate values. The issues of hypersexuality and animality, historically attributed to black males, are self-consciously countered by advertising accounts of Jordan. Jordan's image highlights instead the sport icon and father as the ideal representation of masculinity. Jordan is (re)constructed displaying the envied social and cultural values of mainstream masculinity, associating the "natural body" with Disney, Nike, and corporate America's family values. This analysis of Jordan's body image both complements and contradicts the Mishkind et al. analysis of the male body in the selection, "The Embodiment of Masculinity." McDonald's interpretation of Jordan as the exceptional black athlete also provides an interesting contrast to Bordo's exploration of female resistant strategies.

Michael Jordan's body is one of the most visible and celebrated bodies of recent times. Thanks to the National Basketball Association's (NBA) clever promotion of appealing personalities, creative commercials produced by Nike and

From Mary G. McDonald, "Michael Jordan's Family Values: Marketing, Meaning, and Post-Reagan America," *Sociology of Sport Journal* 13, no. 4 (1996): 344–65. Reprinted by permission of Human Kinetics Publishers and the author.

other commercial sponsors, and his own marketing savvy, Jordan's fame has translated into 1995 endorsement earnings estimated to be $40 million (Lane & McHugh, 1995). As Michael Eric Dyson (1993) and David Andrews (1993, 1996) argue, Michael Jordan represents more than a successful marketing campaign that sells Nike sneakers, the NBA, Wheaties, Hanes underwear, Coca-Cola, Gatorade, Chevrolets, and McDonald's hamburgers: Jordan's body is a culturally significant site for the commodification and subsequent consumption of Black masculinity.

The marketing appeal of Michael Jordan is worth exploring given the historically complex representations of Black masculinity. Henry Louis Gates (1994) cites critic Barbara Johnson in suggesting that African-American men embody an "already read text." That is, images of African-American men carry historically forged racist and sexist meanings that associate African-Americans with nature, animality, hypersensuality, and eroticism. Once used to legitimate slavery and White supremacy, these representations persist in the visual media and hold particular significance within the conservative, backlash climate of post-Reagan America: the bodies of African-American men (and women) have been made to serve as "symbolic icons for the nation's ills" (Golden, 1994, p. 22). For example, Wilt Chamberlain stands for "perverse promiscuity," Clarence Thomas for sexual harassment, Mike Tyson for date rape, and O. J. Simpson for spousal abuse (Golden, 1994).

Given this historical legacy and current hysteria, how and why is it that Michael Jordan manages to be marketable and extremely successful as a cultural symbol? On one level, exploring the popularity of Michael Jordan is a seemingly simple task. Jordan offers a fresh, more tolerant, and thus, a more marketable vision of Black masculinity because he has achieved an extraordinary level of success in a culture that celebrates masculine achievements like those romanticized in sport. Off the court and in commercial endorsements, Jordan appears as an engaging, thoughtful, private family man. This portrait of Jordan apparently counters and challenges the socially constructed representations of African-American men as dangerous, incompetent, and overtly hypersexualized. Still, given the unstable, contextual state of cultural meanings, Jordan's public persona as an exceptional athlete and private family man cannot be blithely celebrated as a positive portrayal of African-Americans nor for that matter, simply dismissed as reactionary Reaganism. Rather, making sense of Michael Jordan's ubiquitous presence within popular media necessitates exploring the historically specific, often contradictory economic rationales, social relations, and ideologies in which Jordan and his image are embedded.

Informed by cultural studies sensibilities, in this paper I explore the public persona of Michael Jordan in selected sporting and advertising accounts to critically interrogate the image(s) we are being offered to consume. What makes representations of Michael Jordan so complex and intriguing for cultural analysis is that they offer a unique opportunity to illuminate the complicated political status of popular culture and identity. To interrogate the ideologies of race, class, masculinity, and sexuality inscribed on Michael Jordan's commodified body is to acknowledge that relations of power are always multiple and contradictory. We cannot fully understand Michael Jordan if we focus only on the socially constructed representations of his identity as an African-American, or a heterosexual, or a man, or a member of the capitalist class. While that sort of analytical compartmentalization may be appealing, its simplicity fails to provide an accurate reflection of the complex, interrelated, and fluid character of cultural meanings and power relations (Birrell & McDonald, 1993).

This analysis of Michael Jordan benefits from the concept of articulation which suggests that cultural meaning does not inhere to texts, identities, or practices; rather it is produced through their interactions (Hall, 1985; Hall, 1986a; Hall, 1986b; Hall, 1991; Howell, 1991; Grossberg, 1992). An articulation is an association or a link between distinctive ideological elements that operate in a specific historical place and time with identifiable consequences. Methodologically, this suggests that cultural analysis is an interpretive act requiring the exploration of both text(s) and context(s). The cultural process is further complicated by the incessant generation of new meanings and fresh associations.

In this paper I trace the contradictory ways in which representations of gender, race, class, and sexuality are articulated through the phenomenon of Michael Jordan within the context of post-Reagan America. Specifically, I explore the ways media accounts of Jordan's basketball talents reinforce lingering stereotypes that equate natural athleticism with men—particularly African-American men—and suggest people of color have privileged access to bodily pleasures and expressions (see Harris, 1991; Birrell, 1989; Wiggins, 1989; hooks,

1992; West, 1993). Likewise, the off-court persona of Jordan as a private family man participates in contemporary popular discourses on the family, engaging a variety of racial, class, gender, sexual, and national ideologies. The definition of what constitutes the family continues to be reformulated from a variety of positions, while dominant cultural portrayals of the nuclear family proclaim it is "in crisis," "on the decline" or just plain "broken." The alleged decline of the traditional nuclear family—a heterosexual couple with children featuring a breadwinner father and housewife mother—has been successfully deployed by the conservative New Right as the commonsense explanation for social problems ranging from crime, poverty, and sexual "promiscuity," to drug abuse (Reeves & Campbell, 1994).

Jordan and his promoters play up his seemingly natural athleticism while down playing any suggestion of excessive sensuality. An apparent devotion to "traditional family values" serves to further distance Jordan from the stereotypical portrayal of Black masculinity as hypersexual, immoral, and irresponsible, the very demonic characteristics members of the New Right claim threaten the nuclear family and, by association, the very moral fiber of America itself. In post-Reagan America where traditional family values and the public hysteria surrounding AIDS suggest sexuality is both immoral and life-threatening, Jordan's commodified body is culturally coded as natural in ways that are socially sanctioned and culturally envied.

Here Comes Mr. Jordan: The Marketing of Black Masculinity

Understanding Michael Jordan's status as a cultural and marketing icon in post-Reagan America means acknowledging the tremendous significance of both sport and advertising in the national consciousness. Mark Dyreson (1989) traces the symbiotic relationship between consumerism and sport to the 1920s, where Americans increasingly understood sport "as a vehicle of entertainment—one of the many items available for amusement in a culture which glorified consumption" (p. 261). The form and content of sport as a commodity have varied and shifted over the years, just as the crafting of Jordan as an appealing persona to be marketed and consumed has its own unique history. Exploring the convergence of the historical with the economic and biographical suggests that much of Jordan's appeal can be attributable to his athletic status:

professional basketball offers a prominent site for African-American men such as Jordan to be visible, culturally lauded, and clearly successful.

Michael Eric Dyson (1993) notes that Jordan represents the hope of freedom and ultimate escape from the pernicious beliefs and social structures that stand between African-Americans and economic prosperity, as well as physical and psychological security. Jordan's commodified body is, therefore, the "symbolic carrier of racial and cultural desires to fly beyond limits and obstacles" . . . and thus the player's "achievements have furthered the cultural acceptance of at least the Black athletic body" (p. 71). While acknowledging Dyson's arguments about the resistant potential of the Black athletic body, cultural critic bell hooks (1994) suggests the selling of Michael Jordan is best understood as the signpost and reinforcement of overtly depoliticized times. Beginning in the late 1970s, market forces co-opted much of the subversive potential of Black masculinity while male athletes increasingly espoused politically neutral positions in an effort to secure financially lucrative endorsement deals.

Significantly, the increasing numbers of Black male athletes endorsing products parallels the ascent of the Reagan era, a unique historical epoch characterized by a shift in the national *Zeitgeist*. First emerging under the leadership of President Ronald Reagan, this shift in the national consciousness suggests movement away from the overt political activism of the 1960s toward an era of backlash politics that also served to justify economic policies favoring the wealthy. By the 1980s, conservative voices had positioned a pro-business agenda as tantamount to the emotionally cherished ideals of family, respectability, and nation (Hall, 1988; Reeves & Campbell, 1994). The underlying rationale was that corporate expansion and freedom strengthened not only the economy, but the nuclear family and, by association, the very moral fiber of America. According to key members of the New Right, economic problems, such as inflation or the budget deficit, could be traced to the "permissive" and "hedonistic" politics of big government. Bleeding heart liberalism, characterized by the expansion of the state's social entitlement programs like the New Deal, the Great Society, and the War on Poverty, merely undermine the values of hard work, family, and nation. Illegitimate birth rates, joblessness, and welfare dependency were all created and/or reinforced by "economic incentives to bear out-of-wedlock children and disincentives to work created by the Great Society" (Edsall & Edsall, 1991, p. 15).

While always contested, challenged, and resisted, increasingly socially conservative world views gained popularity among a broad segment of the American population. According to Grossberg (1992), these positions include the growing acceptance of social and economic inequalities for various subordinated groups, the attempt to impose a narrowly defined notion of morality on all of society, the justification of inequality in the name of economic competition, and the demonization of activist groups who challenge the political and conservative status quo. Distancing himself from potentially controversial issues and espousing benign views (see Cole & Andrews, 1996), Jordan fits neatly with the regressive political climate of post-Reagan America. Andrews (1996) argues that Jordan's successes on the basketball court and in the advertising world offer apparent "proof" of a racially tolerant and color-blind society. Read from this perspective, Jordan's popularity is both the product of, and reinforcement for, New Right strategies to maintain White interests by suggesting that racism has been eradicated (Andrews, 1996).

The commodification of Michael Jordan also signals the loss of political agency and the once-radical political potential of Black athletes. Michael Jordan as a spectacular athlete and willing corporate apologist stands in stark contrast to another powerful vision of yesteryear: that of African-American athletes as political activists and outspoken critics of the establishment (hooks, 1994). Perhaps no one individual athlete better embodied the civil rights era and mandate for social change of the 1960s and 1970s than boxer Muhammad Ali. Ali spoke out against the war in Vietnam and in support of Black power, willingly sacrificing fame for his convictions. Ali's conversion to the Nation of Islam and refusal to serve in the Vietnam war cost him the heavyweight boxing title and earned him a prison term (Harris, 1995). While Ali no doubt embodied the sexism of professional boxing (see Sammons, 1995) and earned a tremendous amount of money, at the prime of his athletic career Ali also offered a decidedly subversive persona as an outspoken critic of the racial status quo. Othello Harris (1995) suggests that Ali countered stereotypes of African-Americans while moving beyond "White limits of acceptability in his beliefs and behavior" (p. 66).

While I don't wish to oversimplify complex cultural meanings, especially in light of feminist critiques of both sport and history, suffice it to say these contrasts between Ali and Jordan exemplify distinctions between the two divergent eras: where Ali embodied the pride of Black resolve in the 1960s, the commodification of Michael Jordan in the 1980s and 1990s is a sign of increasingly reactionary times. While also commodified, Ali was among a group of African-American athletes who helped publicize issues like economic stratification and racial segregation (hooks, 1994). Contrast the image of "rebellious masculinity" (hooks, 1994, p. 133) embodied by Ali to that of the genial association created by Nike in pairing Michael Jordan with Bugs Bunny in the "Hare Jordan" campaign. As hooks (1994) sees it, in those commercials where Jordan:

> speaks to the cartoon figure of Bugs Bunny as though they are equals—peers—his elegance and grace of presence is ridiculed and mocked by a visual aesthetics which suggests that his body makes him larger than life, a fantasy character. This visual image, though presented as playful and comic, in fact dehumanizes. (p. 134)

Creating appealing fantasy characters also was a key strategy employed by the NBA in the 1980s in an effort to revive the once-floundering, financially strapped league of the 1970s. As Cheryl Cole and Harry Denny (1994) note, a key element of the league's resurgence lies in the ability of promoters to distance the NBA from previous racist associations conflating the predominately Black athletic labor force with an "undisciplined" style of play and the stigma of drug abuse. Cole and Denny suggest that during the 1980s marketers and an equally invested sport media promoted professional basketball as an appealing cultural event complete with stylized play and extraordinary larger-than-life personalities like those of Earvin "Magic" Johnson of the Los Angeles Lakers and Larry Bird of the Boston Celtics. With an assist from Nike, fresh meanings were associated with Black masculinity in an effort to court White middle-class audiences. New narratives suggested that NBA athletes possessed exceptional skill, hard work, dedication, and determination. The presentation of NBA players as idealized athletic heroes committed to competition and meritocracy also suggests the New Right's understanding of a racially harmonious country (Cole & Denny, 1994).

By the time Jordan entered the league in 1984, the NBA was well on its way toward transforming games into spectacular entertainment events. Just as this time period saw the explosion of special effects in *Raiders of the Lost Ark* (1981), *ET* (1982), *Ghostbusters* (1984), *Back to the Future* (1985), *Batman* (1989), and other top-grossing blockbuster Hollywood films of the era, so too did the NBA exploit the spectacular, employing laser shows, dramatic player introductions, energizing music, halftime contests, and sideshows. The NBA changed basketball games into a unique type of athletic escapism. In doing so, NBA commissioner David Stern makes it clear that the NBA is targeting the entire family:

> They have themes parks, . . . and we have theme parks, only we call them arenas. They have characters: Mickey Mouse, Goofy. Our characters are named Magic and Michael [Jordan]. Disney sells apparel; we sell apparel. They make home videos; we make home videos. (quoted in Swift, 1991, p. 84)

That Stern would choose to align the NBA with Disney, the corporate exemplar of wholesome entertainment, is particularly telling. Disney's wholesomeness, excitement, and eternal optimism are the antithesis of the racist characterizations of "undisciplined" Blackness associated with the NBA of the 1970s. The reference to Disney also helps identify the NBA's idealized, target audience—Disney productions "relentlessly define the United States as White, middle-class, and heterosexual" (Giroux, 1994, p. 31).

By the 1990s, the NBA had been successfully "Disneyfied." The complete reversal of financial fortunes included a complete line of commodities: NBA licensed caps, jerseys, t-shirts, basketballs, videos, etc. To this day, however, the most valuable commodities continue to be the players themselves; the now-global NBA has successfully created a sense of audience identification and name recognition. Thus, the NBA has followed the long-established capitalist logic of the film and television industries. As David Lusted (1991) argues in regard to television: "A stock of recognized names acts as an assurance that audiences will return again (and again) to their role as viewers, perpetuating—via advertising or license revenue—the flow of cash to maintain the institution" (p. 251).

Still, this remaking of the NBA did not displace the themes most commonly connected to professional basketball including those of masculine prowess and competitive capitalism. Henry Giroux's (1994) analysis of Disney's sanitized aura can be applied to the NBA's complicity in what Giroux terms the "politics of innocence."

Behind Disney's guise of naiveté rests a multinational conglomerate that wields enormous cultural and political power:

> Disney's power and its reach into popular culture combine an insouciant playfulness and the fantastic possibility of making childhood dreams come true—yet only through the reproduction of strict gender roles, an unexamined nationalism, and a choice that is attached to the proliferation of commodities. (p. 31)

Similarly, NBA promotional strategies entice fans in ways that appear benevolent, yet mask particular relations of power. Underlying the visible space of the game is a semipublic masculinized and heterosexualized culture displayed through "a 'politics of lifestyle' marked by the semipublic sexual exchange of a conspicuously displayed network of adoring, supportive female fans, girlfriends, and/or wives: it is a masculine lifestyle meant to be embraced, admired, envied, and consumed" (Cole & Denny, 1994, p. 128). This masculinist preserve of the NBA is further complicated by the stereotypical association that equates people of color with sensuality and physicality. Thus, perceptions of hypersexuality and eroticism persist as powerful racist undercurrents within the consumer culture and the commodified space of the NBA (Cole & Denny, 1994).

Cole and Denny's (1994) contention that these racist assumptions are constantly being managed through the marketing of particular player personalities is important for understanding the cultural appeal of Jordan. The very public depiction of Michael Jordan as a wholesome family figure helps stabilize the league's hoped-for clean-cut image just as it diffuses lingering impressions of Black hypersexuality. Indeed, one of the first snapshots of Jordan in the NBA features the nuclear family: parents James and Deloris attended the 1984 press conference to witness the announcement of the $6-million contract awarded by the professional Chicago Bulls to Michael. Over the course of the next several years, even after the tragic murder of James Jordan in 1993, the pair provided affirmation of Jordan's All-American persona.

In *Michael Jordan: Come Fly With Me* (Sperling, 1989), a video produced by NBA Entertainment, basketball game footage is juxtaposed against voice-over narratives outlining Jordan's personal virtues. Accompanied by piano music and film of his own aesthetically pleasing body running and leaping on the court, Jordan states assertively that his parents' influence continues: "I was always taught never to forget where you came from. My parents, if I change as a person, they would be the first to tell me that, and they have not told me that yet. So, I'm doing well" (Sperling, 1989). This persona is an enticing portrait of Black masculinity, highlighting "natural" athleticism, and family sentiment in ways designed to provoke "desire without evoking dread" (Jackson, 1994, p. 49).

Body Language: Cultivating Michael Jordan's "Natural" Physicality

One of the most enduring and seemingly endearing aspects of the Michael Jordan phenomenon are the words and phrases coined to describe his particular type of physically expressive basketball talent. The most popular and lasting nicknames connote flight for Jordan—"Air," "Air Jordan," "His Airness," a "Flyer" who operates in either "Air Time" or "Rare Air" or is perpetually "Talking to the Air." Of course, these phrases did not originate out of thin air. References to flight are testimony to the tremendous role of advertising discourses in generating Jordan's image. "Air Jordan" is part of Nike's clever plan to market an air-sole shoe to challenge Converse, long the leader in the gym shoe segment of the market (Raissman, 1984). In 1984, Nike transferred a lion's share of their advertising budget into one preeminent multimillion-dollar five-year deal, an agreement sealed before Jordan's rookie year in the National Basketball Association (NBA). David Falk, Jordan's agent then with ProServ, explained the cultural logic of this marriage:

> Because of Michael's style of play—we like to call him a flier— he fits in well with the whole line of the shoe [Air Shoe] which is high tech. That's where the upper end of Nike's marketing strategy is going. (quoted in Raissman, 1984, p. 1)

Two early Air Jordan TV commercials first "aired" in the spring of 1985 helped construct Jordan's public persona. One commercial was created as a response to the NBA's "uniformity of uniform" clause when commissioner David Stern banned the original red-and-black Technicolor Nike Air Jordan shoes. The voice-over states: "On October 18, the NBA banned Michael Jordan from wearing these shoes. But the NBA can't stop you from buying these shoes. Air Jordan. Basketball by Nike" (Murphy, 1985, p. 34). In this commercial, Jordan is presented as a menacing figure—even angry—with a scowl, presumably in response to the authoritarian stance taken by the league in banning the Nike shoes. This portrayal of Jordan plays on racist depictions of Black men as threatening and intimidating. Significantly, it also is the last time Jordan is presented as an intimidating figure in an advertisement (Murphy, 1985). In subsequent promotional campaigns, Jordan would be represented as approachable and likable, an everyday American with extraordinary athletic talents.

The archetype that Nike, the NBA, and subsequent advertisers seized upon appeared in another early Nike commercial from the spring of 1985 entitled "Jordan Flight." It features Jordan moving across a black-topped basketball court at twilight with the Chicago skyline in the background. The sound of jet engines revving to an increasingly higher pitch reaches its zenith when Jordan slam dunks the basketball. Jordan remains in the air with his legs apart for the final ten seconds of the commercial, an apparent testimonial to both his incredible athleticism and the power of the red-and-black Technicolor Nike athletic shoes he wears (Katz, 1994). The voice-over booms: "Who said man was not meant to fly" (Murphy, 1985, p. 34). This commercial presents an affable Jordan as the quintessential "natural athlete," for as the rather hyperbolic claim goes, he can literally fly through the air.

A quick read of this Nike commercial suggests Michael Jordan's celebrated and commodified physicality is dramatically embellished in basketball and advertising discourses through catchy narratives and phrases, slow-motion replay, and special effects. These commercials, along with video highlights and televised NBA games, use multiple camera angles, slow-motion replays, and personalized narratives to create the illusion of an intimate, revealing, and pleasurable encounter with Michael "Air" Jordan. The ways in which Jordan is represented also assist in the reconstruction, legitimation, and embellishment of larger cultural associations between natural athleticism and masculinity (especially Black masculinity) which play a significant role in the area of contemporary gender relations. "Symbolic representations of the male body as a symbol of strength, virility, and power have become increasingly important in popular culture as actual inequalities between the sexes are contested in all areas of public life" (Messner, 1988, p. 212).

Images of masculinity as powerful and "natural" on televised sporting spectacles offer men of all socioeconomic backgrounds one of the most powerful sites to collectively identify with masculinity and an ideology of male physical and cultural superiority (Messner, 1988; Theberge, 1991). Still these representations offer contradictory meanings when connected with commonsense perceptions of African-American men. Traits, such as aggression and brute strength, have been historically associated with both African-American men and athleticism (Sabo & Jansen, 1992). Television sports commentary, for example, more often credits White basketball players with exhibiting "intelligence" while explaining the success of African-Americans in terms of their "innate" physicality (Jackson, 1989; Harris, 1991). This seemed to be the implicit message of the 1989 NBC television special *Black Athletes: Fact and Fiction,* according to Laurel Davis (1990). Relying heavily on questionable bioscientific discourses, NBC focused an entire show exploring the presumed link between racial difference and athletic performance. This quest downplayed human agency and dismissed sociopolitical issues, including the very racist preoccupation with the alleged "naturalness" of African-Americans (Davis, 1990). As Andrews (1996) has recently demonstrated, the media reinforce this type of pseudoscientific, essentialist logic with repeated references to Jordan as someone who was seemingly "born to dunk."

Media images, such as Nike commercials, have a powerful effect, subtly influencing our perceptions of the body. Here technology merges with ideology to reify notions of African-Americans as naturally athletic. For example, slow-motion replay offers a particularly compelling dramatic aesthetic. Margaret Morse (1983) argues that the conventions of slow-motion replay allow for an analysis of "body movements which are normally inaccessible to view; this capacity has justifiably lent slow motion an aura of scientificity" (p. 49). The video *Come Fly With Me* (Sperling, 1989) offers many examples of how slow-motion replay creates the dramatic, aesthetic athleticism of Jordan's athletic body. A scene near the end of the video features four different examples of Jordan dunking the basketball in slow motion, each from a dramatically different camera angle.

Slow motion's aura of scientific legitimacy helps to strengthen the illusion that Jordan can defy the laws of gravity. This presentation has proven to be persuasive. On June 13, 1991, for example, the ABC television show *Primetime Live* aired a segment narrated by Diane Sawyer, in which several people were asked, "Why does Michael Jordan seem to fly?" The broadcasted responses:

First Fan: Michael Jordan hangs in the air for at least 8 to 10 seconds.

Second Fan: Six seconds.

Third Fan: Ten seconds.

Fourth Fan: 4.56 seconds.

Fifth Fan: Oh, his hang time's got to be at least 8 seconds.

Sawyer: Eight seconds? Is it possible Michael Jordan is airborne that long? Is he exempt from gravity? In other words, if Michael Jordan had fallen from that apple tree, would Sir Isaac Newton still be waiting for a bop on the head? (*Primetime Live*, 1991)

The scene shifts to Peter Brancazio, a professor in the Department of Physics at Brooklyn College, who assures the audience that the "laws of physics apply to everyone, even Michael Jordan." Using basic physics, Brancazio concludes that a three-foot leap leaves Jordan in "flight" not for the three to ten seconds believed by the audience, but for about nine-tenths of a second.

By the time of Jordan's October 6, 1993, initial retirement from professional basketball, this reputation for flight had long been well-established: basketball and advertising discourses drawing on commonsense assumptions about athleticism repeatedly constructed Jordan as the ultimate natural athlete. Even the nickname "air" suggests an aura of naturalness and reinforces the rather hyperbolic notion that Jordan could defy gravity via his uncanny "hang time,"[1] the seeming ability to remain suspended in space as if in flight.

Still, these characterizations of flight are far from innocent, communicating much more than Michael Jordan's great athleticism and symbolic worth. Historically, African-Americans have been linked with nature in racist ways that seemingly suggest extraordinary "sexuality, sensuality, and an alternately celebrated or denigrated propensity for physical ability" (Desmond, 1994, p. 43).

These associations are rooted in the racist assumptions that Black men are "closer to nature" than White men and from Victorian notions that Africans have a different genetic makeup from their more genteel and intellectual European counterparts. Rooted in allegedly natural differences, these ideologies have helped to restrict Black men to certain occupational niches such as sports, music, and entertainment. Crucially, these ideologies operate by making the connection between sporting and sexual prowess (Jackson, 1994, p. 54).

The Black athletic body is often referenced in terms of an extraordinary physicality. According to critic Peter Jackson (1994), the dominant perspective of White heterosexual masculinity still expects superior sexual performance from people of color. The marketing strategy applied to Jordan suggests an apparent awareness of these larger issues. Under the direction of his original marketing agency ProServ and agent David Falk, and thanks partially to the promotional apparatuses of the NBA and sport media, Jordan has played up the "natural" Black athletic body while simultaneously repudiating any suggestion of culturally inappropriate sexuality. This serves to undermine stereotypical associations of Black sexuality with destructive and predatory behavior (Jackson, 1994).

The cultural power of these depictions of Black sexuality derives from America's simultaneous obsession with sex and fear of Black sexuality (West, 1993). The "exotic" images of African-American sexuality thus also speak to the paradox of sexuality and race in America. According to Cornel West (1993), behind "closed doors the dirty, disgusting, and funky sex associated with Black people is often perceived to be more intriguing and interesting, while in public spaces talk about Black sexuality is virtually taboo" (p. 120). Sexual myths about African-Americans, invented during Reconstruction to maintain White cultural and financial privilege, present them as either oversexed, threatening personas or as desexed individuals committed to serving White interests. Although the former might be the most pernicious, all of these types of representations distort and dehumanize African-Americans.

These myths flourish in professional sport where African-American male athletes make disproportionate contributions, most notably in baseball, football, and basketball. The masculinist culture of professional sport also encourages men of all backgrounds to treat women as sexual conquests (Curry, 1991). Too often being a male athlete means that one has power over and entitlement to women's bodies. Still, the stereotypes of Black sexuality ensure that African-American men disproportionately bear the pejorative label of hypersexuality (Rowe, 1994). In sport, there is a long history in which gender, race, and sexuality have been articulated to suggest depravity. For example, Jack Johnson became the heavyweight boxing champion of the world in 1908 when the pseudoscience of eugenics seemed to "prove" the mental and physical inferiority of African-Americans. While Johnson gained a measure of material success from boxing and performing in vaudeville, he was perhaps as much a draw (and certainly more infamous) for his sexual relations with White women (Roberts, 1983).

Lest the Johnson story seem like old history, consider also that the Associated Press named boxer Mike Tyson's rape trial and conviction as its 1992 story of the year in sport, despite considerable debate over whether a rape trial even belonged on the sports pages. Tyson was convicted of raping Desiree Washington, after the failure of a defense strategy that presented him as pathologically incapable of sexual control. While undoubtedly a White defendant would never have to bear the burden of overcoming stereotypes of hypersexuality, the strategy used by Tyson's lawyers actually played into racist and sexist world views. Tyson's trial provided a convenient link between criminality, race, sexuality, and sport (Birrell & McDonald, 1993). Angela Davis (1984) maintains the myth of the Black rapist has been historically conjured up to maintain White privilege and justify White violence and terror against the Black community. Far more African American women were raped by White men than White women by Black men, yet this idea still persists. Who better represents the stereotype of the Black rapist than Mike Tyson (Birrell & McDonald, 1993)? Alongside Willie Horton, the convicted rapist whose parole was used during the Bush presidential campaign to portray opponent Michael Dukakis as soft on crime, the Mike Tyson case has become "evidence" to justify White America's commonsense perception of violence among Blacks. This concept is especially powerful during a time when many civil rights advances have stagnated or been reversed by Reaganite economic and social policies (Birrell & McDonald, 1993).

While the Tyson case represents the most glaring association of sexual deviance and sport, representations of sexual prowess echo throughout the culture. The linkage between African American's "innate" physicality and sexuality were perhaps most crudely articulated in 1988 in the words of sportscaster Jimmy "The Greek" Snyder:

> The Black is a better athlete to begin with because he's been bred to be that way because of his thigh size and big size. . . . [The

advantage] goes all the way back to the Civil War, when during the slave period the slave owner would breed his big Black buck with his big woman so that they could have a big Black kid. That's where it all started. (quoted in Harris, 1991, p. 25)

These words provoked national outrage, resulting in the sports-caster's dismissal from CBS television. Rather than reflecting the words of one misinformed individual, however, the sentiment expressed by Snyder crudely represents a lingering cultural com-monsense belief that African-Americans are more animalistic as the very terms "bred" and "buck" suggests. The underlying message is that African-Americans have privileged access to bodily expressions and pleasure (hooks, 1992).

Critic bell hooks (1992) explains the paradoxical implications of this image of Black masculinity.

It is the young Black male body that is seen as epitomizing this promise of wildness, of unlimited physical prowess and un-bridled eroticism. It was this Black body that was most "desired" for its labor in slavery, and it is this body that is most repre-sented in contemporary popular culture as the body to be watched, imitated, desired, possessed. (p. 34)

Indeed, sensuality and sexuality offer one of the few resources African-American men and women have been able to parlay into wider popularity in the entertainment industries (hooks, 1992; Rowe, 1994). African-American actors, musicians, and athletes often are impelled to walk a narrow and ambiguous line between the sug-gestion of threat and the allure of desire, particularly in attempting to appeal to a wide range of audiences (Rowe, 1994).

The salience of the Black body has, if possible magnified in an era where bodies have increasingly become available for inspection and comparison (see Foucault, 1978; Watney, 1989; Theberge, 1991; King, 1993). The fitness boom in the late 1970s and early 1980s, coupled with the AIDS crisis, have added to an overall obsession with the fit, healthy body and with reasserting the superiority of the heterosexual body. Male athletes, especially African-American athletes, stand for the commodification of the hard body and an active heterosexuality.

Peter Jackson's (1994) analyses of British athletes Daley Thompson and John Barnes help elucidate the ways Jordan's athletic body negotiates notions of sensuality, sexuality, and athleticism.

According to Jackson, both Thompson and Barnes are presented in advertising discourses as the "acceptable face" of Black masculinity, their presumed sensual energy coupled with impeccable moral reputations and pleasing personalities. The well-known athletes' personas defuse any perceived sexual threat and defy the "conventional mapping of the mind-body dualism onto White and Black men respectively" (p. 56). Described in various media accounts as "supple and muscular" (Norment, 1991), "sexy" (Naughton, 1992), and offering basketball audiences "pleasure, sheer delight, and wonderment" (Vancil, 1992), Jordan's body offers consumers a voyeuristic encounter (see hooks, 1994). His carefully cultivated persona as a devoted son, husband, and father is a key component of this process, serving to distance Jordan from any overt association of hypersexuality (see Jackson, 1994; Cole & Denny, 1994).

"Just Wait Until We Get Our Hanes on You"

Two commercials for Hanes underwear illustrate the ways Jordan is marketed to exploit the Black body as safely erotic. The Hanes campaign offers some of the most overtly risqué representations of Jordan. While other athletes have made a career out of revealing their bodies in underwear ads (witness the meteoric rise in popularity of baseball player Jim Palmer after he posed in scant briefs several years ago), Jordan is presented rather modestly in Hanes commercials. Maintaining Jordan's wholesome person in the Hanes campaign must have provided a bit of a challenge because sensuality and eroticism are closely aligned with advertising campaigns for underwear. Over the past fifteen years, Calvin Klein has parlayed America's uncomfortable titillation with youthful sexuality into a business empire (Ingrassia, 1995). Calvin Klein launched a controversial campaign in the mid-1980s featuring young men in their "Calvins" as the object of an erotic gaze. More recently, White rap star Marky Mark was featured in Calvin Klein ads on billboards across the country. Dressed only in a pair of Lycra boxer shorts that hugged his muscular thighs and bulged provocatively at his crotch, Mark stood laughing with his baggy pants twisted around the ankles as if someone had just pulled his trousers down (Harris, 1993). His muscular body and apparently delighted reaction suggest agency, power, and approval: Mark appears as a willing and wanton accomplice in the ad's scenario.

In sharp contrast to the provocative profiles of the White enter-
tainers Jim Palmer and Marky Mark, Jordan appears in Hanes television commercials fully clothed. Where Mark's image of phallic
power is representative of the larger cultural trend to position men
in (hetero)sexualized, yet assertive ways to sell products, Jordan's
modest attire is representative of the cultural anxiety around Black
masculinity and sexuality. Hanes advertisers have clearly decided to
play it safe, locking into already well-established images of Jordan's
athleticism and position in the nuclear family.

For example, a commercial produced in 1992, opens with a
voice-over: "Michael Jordan in Hanes briefs." The camera focuses on
a smiling Jordan clutching a basketball, dressed in suit coat, white
(presumably Hanes) undershirt, and slacks. This casual suit reveals
far less flesh than does the sleeveless jersey and long, modest baggy
shorts of the Chicago Bulls uniform. Both a voice-over and graphic
proclaim: "Michael Jordan in NEW IMPROVED Hanes briefs." Jordan
then leaps into the air as special effects technologies produce the
illusion of flight. With background noise of a jet engine, Jordan continues to "fly" through the rafters of a basketball gymnasium, which
resembles an airplane hangar complete with an indoor runway.
Jordan circles several times over the basket before slamming the ball
through the hoop and returning to the ground. The good-natured
parody of the ads implies that "New Improved" Hanes underwear
can somehow improve performance.

Another Hanes commercial with Jordan alludes to the subject of
sexual performance. The scene opens with the words: "Michael
Jordan for Hanes fashion briefs." Wearing loafers, long casual shorts,
a bright blue shirt, and a baseball cap, Jordan dribbles a basketball
into a tastefully, expensively decorated room, apparently his own
house. Jordan shoots the basketball into a laundry basket and sits
down next to his father. James Jordan puts down his newspaper,
reaches into the laundry basket, and picks up a pair of red bikini
briefs from a pile of blander underwear. The elder Jordan asks,
"Michael, are these your Hanes? Son, is there a reason why you wear
them?" At this point Michael's wife, Juanita, enters the room, embraces her husband, and with a firm kiss on Michael's cheek says,
"Definitely." Given this feminine approval, James Jordan asks his
son, "Do you think Mom would like me in these?" Michael replies
hesitantly, "Maybe," at which point the word "definitely" flashes
across the screen. The commercial concludes with slow-motion

footage of Jordan bashfully smiling as the familiar Hanes jingle rings the sexually suggestive words: "Just wait until we get our Hanes on you."

This father-and-son bonding episode, complete with Michael Jordan's shy, sheepish expressions and repeatedly raised eyebrows, distances Jordan from both the overtly sexist views of many professional athletes and the racist vision of hypersexuality. Rather, this commercial promotes the notion of sexual restraint and a stable family relationship with James Jordan as a strong, sensitive father figure. This sets Michael Jordan apart from the homogenized and simplistic media portrayal of African-American families in post-Reagan America which suggest that strong men and father figures are nowhere to be found, having "vanished," abdicating their responsibility and abandoning their own families.

In contrast, James and Michael's conversation about Hanes is reminiscent of father-son talks about responsible sexuality. The generational signs are carefully crafted and are readily displayed in the divergent ways in which the two men are dressed. Michael Jordan's attire suggests boyhood and innocence, especially the casual shorts, loafers, and a baseball cap without any professional team affiliation. This ensemble sharply contrasts with James Jordan's clothing, which evokes the adult business world: a button-down, lightly colored Oxford shirt and nicely creased slacks. Their short dialogue suggests awkwardness and modesty. The younger Jordan appears uncomfortable with this parental query into his underwear choice and the resulting unspoken association of his own sexuality and his father's sexuality.

However modest, this short discussion represents a twist on intergenerational male bonding over female sexuality. Each man is looking for ways to dress in order to please a woman. Juanita is portrayed as the most actively sexual of the three, with the embrace and approval of a boyish and innocent, albeit sexy, Michael Jordan. Yet, even this portrayal is tempered by the white, long-sleeved, high-necked blouse and white slacks she wears. The white color suggests virginal restraint, or perhaps even a sanitized presence. The affectionate embrace and brief kiss on the cheek are devoid of any obvious reference to unbridled passion. Rather, intimacy is suggested as both Michael and Juanita knowingly raise their eyebrows, give each other sideways glances and, thus, allude to excitement and heterosexual intimacy (apparently thanks to the racy red bikini Hanes underwear).

The unspoken suggestion is that sexual passion is a personal issue and, thus, any tantalizing detail beyond innuendo is not for public discussion; rather it is best expressed and experienced in private.

Placed within the nuclear family, Jordan offers quite a different aura than does Marky Mark and professional (male) sport. The presence of Michael Jordan's wife and father evoke the socially constructed sentimental images often associated with the family, including warmth, emotional support, respectability, love, and sexual restraint. This blissful restraint between Juanita and Michael Jordan promotes what has, in the age of AIDS, become the ideological bastion of safe sex: the presumably monogamous heterosexual marriage. Magic Johnson's revelation of his HIV status no doubt adds to the common sense of this connection (see Cole & Denny, 1994). Johnson's public announcement occurred in November 1991, ironically the very month in which *Ebony* magazine featured a cover shot of Michael and Juanita Jordan embracing happily under the headline: "Michael and Juanita Jordan on Marriage, Love, and Life after Basketball." In this piece, Juanita speaks at length about the loving support husband Michael gives to her and their children (Norment, 1991).

Still, the contrast between the two basketball players may be diminishing. After revealing that he acquired HIV through unprotected sex in the effort to "accommodate" many women, Johnson is now increasingly referenced from a position within the nuclear family (see King, 1993; Cole & Denny, 1994; Rowe, 1994). In an effort to deflect criticism away from queries about Johnson's sexual identity, his wife Cookie has become increasingly visible.

> Frequent images of Johnson and family in the media and statements like, "Cookie is a very strong woman. Marrying her is the smartest thing I've ever done," have cemented the public respectability, which was undermined by his HIV status. Anchoring Johnson inside the family immediately temporizes his promiscuity, with his "bachelor's life" safely consigned to the past. (Rowe, 1994, p. 16)

Jordan has been repeatedly referenced within the nuclear family and pictured off-the-court with children throughout his basketball career. Early in his career Deloris and James Jordan praised Michael as a loving, moral son, as the elder Jordan's wholesome appeal seems to explain their son's success. The Jordans embody the seemingly lost ideal of family values. Consider, for example, the words of sportswriter Curry Kirkpatrick (1991):

> Jordan takes his sense of humor from his dad, who used to work around the house with his tongue hanging out (sound familiar?), his sense of business from his mom, and his work ethic from both. "The Jordans are from the old school where education and teachers and administration meant something to parents," says Laney High principal Kenneth McLaurin. (p. 72)

It is not widely known that Jordan and his wife, Juanita Vanoy, transgressed one of American society's moral rules in 1989 by having their first child out of wedlock. Jordan suffered relatively little adverse media publicity in this matter; he was reportedly urged by several business associates to marry Vanoy in order to protect his carefully cultivated moral image (Naughton, 1992). Even the source of this cynical assessment assures us that, once married, Jordan matured thanks to wife Juanita's influence (Naughton, 1992). Once married, the Jordan familial bliss means partaking in the good life afforded by the consumer culture and in the promise of greater material rewards: In the *Ebony* piece there is discussion of a dream home to be constructed for Michael and Juanita Jordan and their children, with six bedrooms, a guest house, an indoor/outdoor swimming pool (with Jacuzzi and sauna), and ample parking space for the Jordans' dozen or so cars including Porsches, Mercedes-Benzes, Testarossas, and a Jeep or two (Norment, 1991).

The Black Family as Contested Terrain

Nowhere is an image of harmonious family life more obviously represented than in a recent advertisement for Ball Park Franks.[2] In that ad, a casually dressed Michael and Juanita Jordan stand with a small child (presumably one of their young sons), all smiling gleefully at the camera while clutching hot dogs. Reminiscent of a family portrait, Jordan has one arm draped over Juanita's shoulder; she similarly places a light touch on the shoulder of the child. The headline reads: Michael's Family Values. The scripted text proclaims: "Enjoy Ball Park Franks, Fat Free Classics, and kid-size fun Franks, all with the delicious Ball Park taste that your family values."

In this advertisement, the Jordans lend support to one of the most ubiquitous themes of post-Reagan America: a vocal rhetoric that calls for a return to "traditional" family values. While never explicitly defined, the word "values" suggests a link between morality and responsibility; the entire phrase advises Americans to hearken back to bygone eras when family life was presumably simpler, purer, and more enjoyable. This emphasis on "pro-family" issues and traditional values can be partially seen as conservative backlash aimed at advances of women and other political minorities, and the perceived challenge to hegemony of heterosexual love and marriage. Returning to the past means returning to the rigid gender role conformity and racial segregation reasserted in the wake of World War II (Reeves & Campbell, 1994). By aligning himself with the term "family values," Michael Jordan joins a whole host of individuals who have exploited a storybook fantasy of family, hearth, and home. Realizing the powerful emotions and sentiment that could be mobilized around appeals to a mythical nuclear family, Ronald Reagan coopted images of harmonious domesticity as the presumed ideal American way of life. Despite the recent numerical decline of the nuclear family and Reagan's tumultuous relationship with his own children, as well as his status as the only divorcee to serve as president, appeals to a nostalgic, conflict-free family life proliferated throughout the Reagan-Bush era (Jeffords, 1994; Fiske, 1994). The 1990s continued to be fraught with nostalgic depictions of the family as the ultimate refuge of the traditional American values of hard work, discipline, and self-denial.

The conservative political agenda of the New Right, developed under the tenure of presidents Reagan and Bush and continuing through the 1990s under the direction of Newt Gingrich, politicized notions of family in particular ways. The presumed breakdown of the seemingly stable family unit with the never-divorced breadwinner/husband and housewife/mother continues to be used by conservatives to explain many of the social ills exacerbated by a rapidly deindustrializing economy and conservative political policies which privilege a corporate world view (Fiske, 1994). Ironically, the profile of the ideal nuclear family celebrated by Reagan might best be described as representing "the way we never were" to borrow Stephanie Coontz's (1992) phrase. Until the nineteenth century in Western industrializing countries, both women and men worked inside or around the home. Only during the Industrial Revolution did "men's work" move outside the home while middle-class White women remained confined and enshrined within the domestic sphere.

By the early portion of the twentieth century, consumerism, a developing youth culture and women's suffrage all contributed to the contestation of the extended family as the dominant norm. According to Elaine Tyler May (1988), only in the wake of World War II did Cold War fears, increased prosperity, new technologies, and fears over women's emancipation help fuel conformity to the suburban family ideal. Thus, this much-debated nuclear unit has only recently come into existence and has almost never been experienced by the vast majority of poor and disenfranchised people at any time. Furthermore, the romanticized ideal of the nuclear family, with the breadwinner husband/father and the wife/mother who does not work outside the home, now accounts for only 7 percent of American families (Hoff & Farnham, 1992).

Despite these numbers, the nuclear family continues to serve as the beacon of presumed morality in an era fraught with all sorts of changes and challenges. Under the guise of morality, fairness, and a commitment to family values, a whole host of regressive social policies have been enacted. For example, women's access to legal abortions has been greatly curbed, civil rights legislation has been rolled back, and antipornography campaigns have been waged against artists, while corporate freedom and capital expand (Clarke, 1991; Reeves & Campbell, 1994; Faludi, 1991). The New Right's claim of declining family values can thus be seen as a way to legitimize a series of policy changes enacted to expand capital as well as a way to remain staunchly antiwelfare, antiabortion, antiaffirmative action, and antigay (Reeves & Campbell, 1994). The classic example of this type of reductive reasoning is found in the statements made after the Los Angeles riots in 1992 by then Vice President Dan Quayle, who noted that "the anarchy and lack of structure in our inner cities are testament to how quickly civilization falls apart when the family foundation cracks" (quoted in Hoff & Farnham, 1992). This isolated focus on the family renders invisible political, economic, and cultural issues, which all continue to have enormous impact on the poor, people of color, and White women.

Images of Jordan within the nuclear family contrast strikingly with the suggestion of the Black family's decline and destruction. The well-publicized "decline" of the African-American family is a notion that itself is class-based, a strategy used by conservatives and liberals alike to marginalize the increasingly large number of people of color who find themselves in poverty. Rather than blaming poverty on larger economic changes—such as deindustrialization, a rapidly globalizing economy, or continuing political issues, including institutional racism and the gendered division of labor—the rhetoric returned to a classic blame-the-victim scenario. In post-Reagan America, renewed attacks were launched against the Black family as pathologically weak, indicative of what then Vice President Dan Quayle would call "a poverty of values" (Fiske, 1994).

These politicized notions of the family reinforced the conservative moralism of Reaganism that operates on the assumption of a binary logic privileging those who espoused the "traditional" virtues of hard work, determination, and loyalty while demonizing those who need legal, social, or financial assistance. Susan Jeffords (1994) argues that this dialogical reasoning of Reaganism positions individual Americans in two fundamentally different camps, separating the privileged "hard bodies" from the errant bodies. These "soft" and undesirable bodies are those which are infected—containing sexually transmitted diseases, immorality, laziness, and illegal chemicals. In a culture marked by race and gender, the soft body usually belonged to a female or person of color, whereas the prototype hard body was invariably male and White. According to Jeffords (1994), the classic example of the Reaganite hard body can be seen in some of the most popular Hollywood films of the era. The action film hero Rambo is the quintessential success story of the period: a muscular hard body—White, male, heterosexual—committed to military strength while fighting against the ineptitude of excessive governmental regulation and other bureaucracies (Jeffords, 1994). Jordan's hard body masculinity is much more consistent with the "kinder, gentler" version which Jeffords (1994) argues attracted popular appeal during the Bush presidency and continues into the 1990s. This prototype offers a twist on the classic masculine "hard body" of Rambo, a shift not toward softness but toward an increased commitment to self-reflection, the nuclear family, and intimacy. This "gentler" version of masculinity is less intimidating and, thus, partially explains how an African-American man could gain mainstream support without much White uneasiness.

By contrast, the mythical profile of the welfare mother represents the iconic soft body of Reaganism, a site where pro-family discourses intersect with racism, sexism, and classism. This depiction rests on stereotypical racist and sexist images of the (assumed) Black matriarch, domineering, castigating, and lazy, who robs a husband or lover of his "rightful" role as head of the family while depending on welfare for sustenance (Reeves & Campbell, 1994). According to Black feminist Patricia Hill Collins (1989), gender plays an important role in the commonsense depiction of poverty. Poor African-American women, the quintessential soft bodies of post-Reagan America, are often portrayed as overly masculine, apparently "choosing" to head the household in domineeering ways. This inappropriate gender socialization is then passed on to their impressionable offspring who repeat the cycle by marginalizing the importance of the traditional male provider. The result, according to both conservative and many liberal voices, is a life of welfare dependency (Collins, 1989). Thus, by appealing to circular reasoning, the absence of patriarchal power relations in these families is offered as the apparent "proof" of Black cultural deficiency (Baca Zinn, 1989; Collins, 1989). Or in the words of then Vice President Dan Quayle, "for those concerned about the children growing up in poverty, marriage is probably the best anti-poverty program of all" (quoted in Hoff & Farnham, 1992, p. 8).

The Jordan family serves as the moral obverse of this stereotypical vision of the Black family. This portrait is readily apparent in one *Newsweek* account published in March of 1995 just as Jordan was contemplating a return to professional basketball after a brief sabbatical/retirement. A picture of Jordan holding his daughter Jasmine as he raises his retired jersey to the rafters is juxtaposed against a text that records reactions of young Jordan fans from "the beleaguered" Houston projects where teens stand around "drinking malt liquor from brown paper sacks" (Leland, 1995, p. 54). In addressing the issue of what Jordan meant to them,

> a few of the players cited Jordan's game. But all talked about his life off the court: about his character, his family, and especially about his relationship with his father, James Jordan, who was murdered in 1993. "He's got a good attitude, he don't smoke, he don't drink," says Robert Taylor, 11, who considers Jordan his hero. "He's got two kids—*and* a wife." (p. 54)

As this passage suggests, the ideological salience of the Jordan familial bliss lies in the enticing depictions of harmony built on the traditional gender roles that middle-class men and women have been encouraged to follow when married. Juanita raises the children with love while Michael takes his role as the family's provider very seriously: "I've got to do more for her, because this is what she expects of her husband—to be taken out to dinner, to movies, on vacations. . . . From a husband's point of view, I've got to improve" (quoted in Norment, 1991, p. 70).

While Jordan's position within the nuclear family represents an ideal that only a tiny minority of Americans can achieve, the image of Jordan as a private family man articulates a conservative moral agenda. The visibility of the African-American family, such as the Jordans, reinforces the desirability of consumer comfort, patriarchal privilege, and familial bliss—all hallmarks of America, especially post-Reagan America (McDonald, 1995). The Jordans offer a particularly powerful image masking what Reeves and Campbell (1994) identify as the perils of "reverse Robin Hoodism." Despite significant challenges, post-Reagan America has seen budget cuts, program changes, and reorganizations in social programs, coupled with increased public opposition to welfare, affirmative action, and civil rights laws. These changes and challenges have disproportionately and adversely affected people of color (Shull, 1993). As Andrews (1993, 1996) also has argued in an era increasingly committed to corporate freedom and individualism, the happiness of the Jordan family seemingly offers "proof" that the American Dream is available to those people of color who are apparently committed enough to pull themselves up by their bootstraps.

Concluding Remarks: Family Matters

In discussing representations of Michael Jordan, I have attempted to highlight some of the historically specific economic rationales and dominant cultural beliefs that constitute and are reciprocally reinforced through these depictions. Michael Jordan is popular precisely because his commodified persona negotiates historically specific and complex gendered, racialized, and sexualized meanings in ways that are socially accepted and culturally envied by mainstream audiences. The appealing persona of Jordan suggests that Black masculinity, which historically has been viewed as inappropriate to White and middle-class America, is represented in an attractive, albeit still highly ideologically charged, way. Given the intense focus on Jordan's "natural body," representations of the nuclear family serve a key role in this process. Jordan's status as a family man assists in suppressing the socially constructed portrait of a threatening Black sexuality. This idealized vision of Jordan within the nuclear family also reinforces the pro-family discourses of the New Right.

Cultural analysis suggests that particular popular figures are linked to a variety of discourses, suggesting multiple, often contradictory meanings, and the need to explore representations within a variety of contexts. Given this insight, it is possible to acknowledge both politically progressive and regressive elements within the phenomenon of Michael Jordan. Indeed, representations of Jordan defy racist sexual stereotypes just as these depictions assist in furthering a reactionary agenda in regard to U.S. families. Still, because cultural processes are fluid, there is no guarantee a specific version and vision of Michael Jordan will remain etched in history forever. Meanings are never essential for all time; rather they have to be constantly renewed and remade. Fresh associations will be forged as the "text" of Jordan is a boundless one, subject to rearticulation in accordance with a variety of historically specific needs and individual circumstances, including Jordan's own human agency. To locate representations within the realm of the historical and political also is to locate the commonsense meanings circulating in the wider culture within the realm of construction, contestation, and change. From this critical perspective, to interrogate representations of Michael Jordan is to offer cultural criticism as a strategy of intervention in the politicized terrain of commodified popular culture. This conceptualization alerts us to the contested character of social relations, so that we can envision alternative forms of cultural practices as well as the insight necessary to engage critically in the practice of social change.

NOTES

1. It is interesting to note the ironic rearticulation of "hang time" to describe Michael Jordan's athletic talents. In this country's sordid history of race relations to speak of hanging, especially in relationship to African-American men, is to suggest lynching. That an African-American man is marketed for his "hang time" complete with a protruding tongue is ironic given the historical lethal power of lynching to reinforce ideologies of White dominance.
2. I would like to thank Laurel Davis for bringing this ad to my attention.

REFERENCES

Andrews, D. (1993). *Deconstructing Michael Jordan: Popular culture, politics, and postmodern America.* Unpublished doctoral dissertation, University of Illinois, Urbana-Champaign.

Andrews, D. (1996). The fact(s) of Michael Jordan's Blackness: Excavating a floating racial signifier. *Sociology of Sport Journal,* 13(2), 125–58.

Baca Zinn, M. (1989). Family, race, and poverty in the eighties. *Signs: Journal of Women in Culture and Society,* 14(41), 856–74.

Birrell, S. (1989). Racial relations theories and sport: Suggestions for a more critical analysis. *Sociology of Sport Journal*, 6(3), 212–27.

Birrell, S., & McDonald, M. (1993. February). *Privileged assault: The representation of violence and the inadequacy of segmented category analysis.* Paper presented at the meeting of the National Girls and Women in Sport Symposium, Slippery Rock, PA.

Calo, B. (Segment Producer). *Primetime Live.* (1991, June 13). *The puzzle of Michael Jordan: Why does he seem to fly?* [Transcript #197]. Journal Graphics, Denver, CO.

Clarke, J. (1991). *New times and old enemies: Essays on cultural studies and America.* London: Harper Collins Academic.

Cole, C., & Andrews, D. (1996). Look—it's NBA's *Show Time!*: Visions of race in the popular imaginary. *Cultural Studies: A Research Annual*, 1(1), 141–81.

Cole, C., & Denny, D. (1994). Visualizing deviance in post-Reagan America: Magic Johnson, AIDS, and the promiscuous world of professional sport. *Critical Sociology*, 20(3), 123–47.

Collins, P. H. (1989). A comparison of two works on Black family life. *Signs: The Journal of Women in Culture and Society*, 14(41), 875–79.

Coontz, S. (1992). *The way we never were: American families and the nostalgia trap.* New York: Basic.

Curry, T. J. (1991). Fraternal bonding in the locker room: A profeminist analysis of talk about competition and women. *Sociology of Sport Journal*, 8, 119–35.

Davis, A. (1984). Rape, racism, and the myth of the Black rapist. In A. Jaggar & P. Rothenberg, (Eds.), *Feminist frameworks: Alternative accounts of the relations between women and men* (2nd ed., pp. 428–31). New York: McGraw-Hill.

Davis, L. (1990). The articulation of difference: White preoccupation with the question of racially linked genetic differences among athletes. *Sociology of Sport Journal*, 7(2), 179–87.

Desmond, J. (1994). Embodying difference: Issues in dance and cultural studies. *Cultural Critique*, 26, 33–62.

Dyreson, M. (1989). The emergence of consumer culture and the transformation of physical culture: American sport in the 1920s. *Journal of Sport History*, 16(3), 261–81.

Dyson, M. (1993). Be like Mike? : Michael Jordan and the pedagogy of desire. *Cultural Studies*, 7(1), 64–72.

Edsall, T., & Edsall, M. (1991). *Chain reaction: The impact of race, rights, and taxes on the American public.* New York: W. W. Norton.

Faludi, S. (1991). *Backlash: The undeclared war against American women.* New York: Anchor.

Fiske, J. (1994). *Media matters: Everyday culture and political change.* Minneapolis, MN: University of Minnesota.

Foucault, M. (1978). *History of sexuality: An introduction.* New York: Vintage Books.

Gates, H. L. (1994). Preface. In T. Golden (Ed.) *Black male: Representations of masculinity in contemporary art* (pp. 11–14). New York: Whitney Museum of American Art.

Giroux, H. (1994). *Disturbing pleasures.* New York: Routledge.

Golden, T. (1994). My brother. In T. Golden (ed.), *Black male: Representations of masculinity in contemporary art* (pp. 19–43). New York: Whitney Museum of American Art.

Grossberg, L. (1992). *We gotta get out of this place: Popular conservatism and postmodern culture.* New York: Routledge.

Hall, S. (1985). Signification, representation, and ideology: Althusser and the post-structuralist debates. *Critical Studies in Mass Communication,* 2, 91–114.

Hall, S. (1986a). The problem of ideology: Marxism without guarantees. *Journal of Communication Inquiry,* 10(2), 28–44.

Hall, S. (1986b). On postmodernism and articulation: An interview. *Journal of Communication Inquiry.* 10(2), 45–60.

Hall, S. (1988). *The hard road to renewal: Thatcherism and the crisis of the left.* London: Verso.

Hall, S. (1991). Signification, representation and ideology: Althusser and the post-structuralist debates. In R. Avery & D. Eason (Eds.), *Critical perspectives on media and society* (pp. 88–113). New York: Guilford.

Harris, D. (1993). The current crisis in men's lingerie: Notes on the belated commercialization of a noncommercial product. *Salmagundi,* 100, 131–39.

Harris, O. (1991). The image of the African American in psychological journals, 1825–1923. *The Black Scholar,* 21(4), 25–29.

Harris, O. (1995). Muhammad Ali and the revolt of the Black athlete. In E. Gorn (Ed.), *Muhammad Ali: The people's champ* (pp. 54–69). Urbana, IL: The University of Illinois.

Hoff, J., & Farnham, C. (1992). Sexist and racist: The postcold war world's emphasis on family values. *Journal of Women's History,* 4(2), 6–9.

hooks, b. (1992). *Black looks: Race and representation.* Boston: South End.

hooks, b. (1994). Feminism inside: Toward a Black body politic. In T. Golden (Ed.), *Black male: Representations of masculinity in contemporary art* (pp. 127–40). New York: Whitney Museum of American Art.

Howell, J. (1991). A revolution in motion: Advertising and the politics of nostalgia. *Sociology of Sport Journal,* 8(3), 258–71.

Ingrassia, M. (1995). Calvin's world. *Newsweek,* 126(11), 60–66.

Jackson, D. (1989, January 22). Calling the plays in black and white. *The Boston Globe,* pp. A30–A33.

Jackson, P. (1994). Black male: Advertising and the cultural politics of masculinity. *Gender, Place, and Culture,* 1(1), 49–59.

Jeffords, S. (1994). *Hard bodies: Hollywood masculinity in the Reagan era.* New Brunswick, NJ: Rutgers University.

Katz, D. (1994). *Just do it: The Nike spirit in the corporate world.* New York: Random House.

King, S. (1993). The politics of the body and the body politic: Magic Johnson and the ideology of AIDS. *Sociology of Sport Journal,* 10, 270–85.

Kirkpatrick, C. (1991, December 23). The unlikeliest homeboy. *Sports Illustrated,* 75(27), 70–75.

Lane, R., & McHugh, J. (1995, December 18). A very green 1995. *Forbes,* 156(14), 212–32.

Leland, J. (1995, March 20). Hoop dreams: Will Michael Jordan return to basketball? *Newsweek,* 125(12), 48–55.

Lusted, D. (1991). The glut of personality. In C. Gledhill (Ed.), *Stardom: The industry of desire* (pp. 251–58). London: Associated University.

May, E. T. (1988). *Homeward bound: American families in the cold war era.* New York: Basic Books.

McDonald, M. (1995). *Clean "air": Representing Michael Jordan in the Reagan-Bush era.* Unpublished doctoral dissertation, University of Iowa, Iowa City.

Messner, M. (1988). Sport and male domination: The female athlete as contested terrain. *Sociology of Sport Journal*, 5, 197–211.

Morse, M. (1983). Sport on television: Replay and display. In A. Kaplan (Ed.), *Regarding television: Critical approaches—an anthology* (pp. 44–66). Los Angeles: American Film Institute.

Murphy, T. (1985, June). On the rebound. *Madison Avenue*, 27, 28–34.

Naughton, J. (1992), *Talking to the air: The rise of Michael Jordan.* New York: Warner.

Norment, L. (1991, November). Michael and Juanita Jordan talk about love, marriage, and life after basketball. *Ebony*, 47, 68–76.

Raissman, R. (1984, October 18). Jordan soars for Nike deal: New strategy seen. *Advertising Age*, 1, 58.

Reeves, J., & Campbell, R. (1994). *Cracked coverage: Television news, the anticocaine crusade, and the Reagan legacy.* Durham, NC: Duke University.

Roberts, R. (1983). *Papa Jack: Jack Johnson and the era of white hopes.* New York: Free Press.

Rowe, D., (1994). Accommodating bodies: Celebrity, sexuality, and "tragic Magic." *Journal of Sport and Social Issues*, 18(2), 6–26.

Sabo, D., & Jansen, S. (1992). Images of men in the sport media: The social reproduction of the gender order. In S. Craig (Ed.), *Men, masculinity, and the media: Research on men and masculinities* (pp. 169–84). Newbury Park, CA: Sage.

Sammons, J. (1995). Rebel with a cause: Muhammad Ali as sixties protest symbol. In E. Gorn (Ed.), *Muhammad Ali: The people's champ* (pp. 154–80. Champaign: University of Illinois Press.

Shull, S. (1993). *A kinder, gentler racism? The Reagan-Bush civil rights legacy.* Armonk, NY: M. E. Sharpe.

Sperling, D. (Executive Producer). (1989). *Michael Jordan: Come fly with me.* New York: CBS/Fox.

Swift, E. M. (1991, June 3). From corned beef to caviar. *Sports Illustrated*, 74(27), 54–58.

Theberge, N. (1991). Reflections on the body in the sociology of sport. *Quest.* 43, 123–34.

Vancil, M. (1992, May). Playboy interview: Michael Jordan. *Playboy*, 51–64.

Watney, S. (1989). *Policing desire: Pornography, AIDS, and the media* (2nd ed.) Minneapolis, MN: University of Minnesota.

West, C. (1993). *Race matters.* Boston: Beacon Press.

Wiggins, D. (1989). Great speed but little stamina: The historical debate over Black athletic superiority. *Journal of Sport History*, 16(2), 158–85.

8 Concord Watch Advertisement

Mike Featherstone suggests, in his selection "The Body in Consumer Culture," that the closer the actual body approximates the idealized images of youth, health, fitness, and beauty, the higher its exchange value. Connected with exchange value, the body is proclaimed to be a vehicle of pleasure. Keeping these two perspectives in mind, think about this ad.

1. How do you recognize this as an advertisement? If you take out the text, what else could it be? Besides a watch, what other product could this picture be advertising? Why is that significant?

2. How are race, age, class, and gender constructed and/or made invisible? To help answer that question, try reversing the male and female roles. How would this ad be different if one/ both of the people were overweight? Homosexual? Different races? Different ages? Disabled? How would the disabled or homosexual be identified? How would different classes be identified?

3. In what sense has a style of life been turned into a commodity? Discuss the symbols of the "style of life" represented in this ad. How do these bodies display class? What class does this ad target? How could this ad display other class experiences? In what way is the man taking power and control through traditional masculine performance(s)? In what way is the woman enacting traditional female performances? In what way are they challenging traditional roles? How could the ad be constructed to resist traditional roles?

4. How is masculinity as "style" connected to sexuality? How does this ad both acknowledge and disguise the social change inherent in feminism?
5. How does this ad display a sense of Featherstone's "calculating hedonism"?

JESSICA R. JOHNSTON

III | Disciplined Bodies

How are inmates within a prison controlled? The ratio of guards to inmates favors the inmates, yet the guards have the power. Exercising authority over inmates, or people in general, depends upon a multitude of factors. This section explores how bodies are controlled, disciplined, and transformed. Prisons are an obvious example of how human bodies can be regulated. What is significant about prison regulation, though, is the similarity in regulatory practices used by the helping professions of medicine and psychotherapy. The parallels between mechanisms of control used by these three institutions will be highlighted, demonstrating how subjects in prisons, medicine, and therapy come to voluntarily discipline themselves and their bodies to meet institutional standards. Further, this section explores how "bio-power" inherent in social control (or the techniques used by society to discipline bodies) is internalized and idealized as a form of self-control.

Contemporary analyses of control mechanisms can be divided into two distinct but interrelated disciplinary orientations. One orientation focuses on the larger macro aspect of the human species, looking at population demographics, fertility, birth and death rates, with the "power" of bio-power focused on monitoring and controlling society in general. The other orientation of bio-power examines the human body itself; not approached directly in its biological dimension, but as an object to be manipulated and controlled. Together these two orientations or knowledge structures form the "disciplinary technology" that Michel Foucault analyzes in detail in *Discipline and Punish* (1979).

According to Foucault, the aim of disciplinary technologies is to generate a docile body that may be subjected, used, transformed, and improved (Foucault, 1979). The technologies are applied through drills, training regimes, standardization of actions, and the control of space. Today, disciplinary technologies are used in a variety of institutional settings such as prisons, workshops, schools, and hospitals. Barbara Kamler reviews the power of indirect coercion in her analysis of schoolchildren in this section. Teachers need students who are docile and receptive, so that these pupils can be improved through education. Through songs, drills, and learning to sit still, Kamler highlights the real world structures that discipline children for their own good, preparing them for a future within the entwined world of regulation and order.

Hegemony

The body in the era of feudalism was a vehicle through which the sovereign or monarch symbolically displayed his or her power (Turner, 1984, p. 73). Public torture, execution, and mutilation physically stamped the body with the signature of authoritarian control and power. Control of individuals today, under capitalism, is less visible and less direct, working on the individual's psyche and therefore much more subtly on his or her body. Direct physical coercion is applied now only when the primary systems of control have been ineffective. The power to discipline though is not only performed through punishment. Power relationships are also enacted through gratifications, accomplished with rewards and privileges for good conduct. The effects of these disciplines are internalized within the individual as "common sense" or "respect," or "good habits." The invisibility and the indirectness of this type of social control are part of the concept of hegemony.

Hegemony is defined as a power relationship in which one group is able to establish a pattern of domination that is perceived as natural and inevitable. The subordinated seemingly give their consent to this domination. This power relationship is composed of three interrelated ideas. First, the forms of social control are indirect. They are negotiated, legitimated, and reproduced through "micropowers" inherent in social roles, such as parents, preachers, teachers, journalists, literati, experts of all sorts, as well as advertising executives, entertainment promoters, pop musicians, sports figures, celebrities, all of whom are involved in shaping the values and attitudes of a society. Even an individual's internal dialogue, that is talking and negotiating with oneself, is considered to be an intimate relationship permeated by power dynamics. Micro-powers permeate every relationship, every dialogue, and every thought process.

Second, hegemonic power does not operate through codes of law but through self-consciousness; not through direct physical punishment, but through the control that is internalized as part of the self. Hegemonic power is realized when the internalized community standards operate through and within the individual. Significantly, these community standards may not function in the best interest of the individual.

And third, social control measures that are self-initiated maintain a relatively smooth-functioning social order, an order that supports and upholds the hierarchically arranged social structure (Lears, 1985, p. 80). Society rules us then by having us rule ourselves. Discipline and surveillance become self-imposed, as we attempt to conform to the requirements of the social system. The effect of the naturalness and indirectness of hegemonic control can be experienced in the first article in this section—Norbert Elias's account of the social etiquette guiding the regulations of nose-blowing. Elias documents the transformation of bodily control, and the code of discipline inherent in the treatment of "snot" that has become taken for granted on today's public scene. People control their runny noses through elaborate rituals around sneezing, coughing, tissues, and handkerchiefs, rituals that have a long history entwined with hierarchy and power. The sense of revulsion some might feel reading Elias's examples points to the internalization of hegemonic codes.

Prison

Prison is an obvious form of oppressive power relation with its authoritarian control over the inmates' bodies. Foucault's analysis of penology and criminology has provided insight into the evolution of a precise, detailed, and rigorous control over the criminal body, a body that is "scientifically" managed within the social space of the penitentiary. Foucault examined the "technology of discipline" in his most famous example, the panopticon. The importance of this one site of disciplinary technology is that it becomes the foundation of a generalized form of social control over bodies throughout other seemingly less restrictive institutions like the army, factories, hospitals, and schools.

The basic layout of the panoptic prison was circular with a guard tower in the center. The tower windows were shuttered, allowing the guards full visibility of the prisoners but preventing the prisoners' awareness of when and by whom they were being observed. The inmates did not have knowledge of the actual presence of guards in the tower, yet the inmates behaved as if the surveillance was perpetual and total. Because the inmates were unsure of when they were being watched, they became their own guardians. Power and control over the body of individuals and groups were brought together through techniques of surveillance and spatial ordering.

Indeed, the panopticon is a particular visual structuring of space and human beings. The unified yet disembodied "gaze" of the prison tower combines hierarchy with surveillance, observation with regulation. For the guards in the tower, the gaze allows easy and ready access to the monitoring of all aspects of prisoners' lives. For the prisoner, the disembodied gaze provides the basis of a self-imposed discipline. As these strictures become taken for granted and effectively internalized within the prisoners, they also become less visible as a form of control. To the extent that these strictures become self-imposed, external authority does not have to be used. Panoptic discipline increases subordination by self control and self mastery of the body, not through direct coercion, but indirectly, through the prisoners, actions on their own bodies. The prisoner becomes a docile subject under an authoritarian yet disembodied gaze.

Medicine

The disciplinary technology of the panoptic prison can be seen as a model for social relationships in everyday life. The need to control bodies and the indirect coercion that accomplishes that control can be recognized today as an identifiable feature in medical encounters.

Medicine forms a hinge between the regulating of the population and the disciplining of the individual body. The medical profession's monitoring, supervision, and evaluation of individual bodies produces information which, when gathered and collated, can be used to establish knowledge structures to guide and control the population. Through the minute surveillance of the microscope, through medical and psychological examinations, through unceasing regimes of health, and through meticulous spatial divisions and arrangements of the "diseased" and the "well," medicine constructs a whole micro-power of control over the body. The knowledge structures produced from this monitoring ensure bodily details and gestures are broken down into their seemingly component parts, analyzed and reconstituted to produce coordinated and disciplined bodies within the population. But these two interconnected axes of the medical matrix need to be explored separately, each in more depth.

Regulation of the Population

Different communities will have different interpretations of well and unwell, and thus different norms of "healthy" behavior. The medical knowledge of the community then does not simply describe the body. Cultural knowledge usually includes a certain utopian conception of health for the individual and styles of living that are directed toward achieving that state, generating guidelines of "preventive medicine" for its members (Scheper-Hughes & Lock, 1986, p. 20). Today in American society, if anything can be shown to have an impact on the body, it is usually labeled a "medical problem." Pregnancy and aging were once regarded as natural processes. Drug addiction and alcoholism were once human weaknesses or moral deficiencies. Body size was seen as immutable. Today, drug addiction, alcoholism, and obesity are all at "epidemic proportions" and simultaneously specialties of the medical profession.

The organization of this medical knowledge is entwined with other institutions. Think about the last time that you needed a doctor's slip to legitimate an absence from work or school. "Health" and "illness" involve issues of deviance, conformity, and social control. "Health" and "illness" are then not neutral, value-free, scientific "facts." Their definitions are intimately connected to the needs and values of the social system.

The regulation of the population is one axis of the disciplinary technologies of the body. This axis is centered on the human body as a species, as living organisms with birth and death rates, health levels, and life expectancies. This medical gaze moves from analyzing microscopic details of the individual body to the relationships between people. On this axis, pathology is not an essentially static phenomenon to be localized to a specific point in the individual body, but becomes a collection of symptoms that advances throughout and between the relationships of people. For example, when there is an epidemic, there is a need to find an organizational structure which can both survey and constantly monitor the whole community, contrasting and categorizing the criteria of individual diseased bodies and the spread of the disease throughout the population (Armstrong, 1983, p. 255).

The concept of public health evolved to monitor both individual and community health. Public health emerged from the surveillance of individual patients, geographically locating those patients and the network of relationships between them within the community. The effect was a focus on the ill and the potentially ill, the unwell, and the healthy around a continuous distribution curve of health. The distribution curve both constructs categories of healthy and unhealthy, and simultaneously locates individuals within those categories.

The significance of this monitoring aspect of public health is its extension to the "normal" person. All individuals are subjected to its power. Public health enabled the "unwell" to be adequately known, supervised, and regulated. But also, "normal" was now conceptualized as an individual who was potentially ill. A person who might appear and feel healthy, but is defined by the category of "potentially ill," becomes a person who needs and seeks early detection and advice on appropriate behaviors and relationships.

The disembodied nature of public health thus further refines the gaze of the panopticon. It constructs a community organized by medical hierarchies, surveillance, and observations. Its gaze makes visible the interaction between people, normal and abnormal, and thereby transforms the physical space between bodies into a social space that can be regulated. Public health has developed into a symbolic guard tower with a disembodied gaze; the information provided becomes the point of potential surveillance with which individuals come to regulate their behavior in order to maintain "good health." Information gathered by public health agencies infiltrates many spheres of life, and is then used by individuals as they medically manage themselves. Individuals conforming to regimes in order to acquire and maintain healthy bodies are ruling themselves, molding their bodies to fit the medical profession's prescribed explanatory framework. The techniques are a significant resource with which individuals learn how to control themselves through institutionally sanctioned methods.

Regulation of the Individual

On the individual axis of medicine's political technology, most individuals would acknowledge the power and authority of medical knowledge over the health of their bodies. Physicians are the authorities, having dominion over the body and its performance, interpreting and explaining health to the patient/ client in seemingly value-neutral scientific terms. Laypeople, lacking direct access to this privileged knowledge, are willing "subjects" to the medical profession's interpretations of their body and definitions of "health." The hierarchical structure is constructed through the layperson's acquiescence to the doctor's "superior" understanding of the body.

For Foucault, the medical encounter is the supreme example of surveillance. The clinical examination involves an invasion of the "private" body space, analyzing and dissecting a previously unseen body. Clinical examinations subject the whole body—its surface, its crevices, its insides, its workings—to a medical gaze, which established the body, and thus the patient, as a discrete, and passive object of study. Further, the disparate power relationship between the doctor and patient is maintained as the doctor investigates, questions, touches the exposed flesh of the patient, while the patient acquiesces and confesses, with little knowledge of why the procedures are carried out. In the doctor's office, the body is rendered an object to be prodded, tested, and examined (Lupton, 1994, p. 24).

Medicine before the eighteenth century was a classificatory science concerned with sorting and cataloging diseases. During the eighteenth and nineteenth centuries, medical knowledge was transformed, with one of the key elements in this transformation the development of the clinical physical examination. The techniques and conclusions of the clinical exam gave the medical profession an authority over the body. The exam also simultaneously constructed the body as passive and docile (Armstrong, 1983, p. 2). The knowledge derived from the exam outlined a particular and detailed anatomy that was seen as the exclusive domain of the medical profession.

This categorization of the body produced an "anatomical atlas." Maps and atlases make the world they construct intelligible. Like all maps, the anatomical atlas directs attention to certain structures, certain similarities, certain systems and not others. In identifying certain structures as noteworthy and important, they form a set of rules for reading the territory. Consider a map of the American Southwest. The desert is seen differently by nuclear scientists and traditional Native Americans (see Kuletz, 1998). The anatomical atlas enables the anatomy student, when faced with the undifferentiated amorphous mass of the body, to see certain things and ignore others. The non-Western medical practitioner, viewing the body as a balance of harmonious forces, would have a quite different anatomical atlas from the Western perception of the body-as-machine (Armstrong, 1983, p. 3). The Western medical profession's anatomical atlas is one among many human interpretations of the body, just one way of seeing the body's forms and establishing its reality.

Thus, the doctor-patient relationship is based on certain mechanisms of power which, since the eighteenth century, have guided the perception of the body as "something docile that could be subjected, used, transformed, and improved" (Lupton, 1994, p. 24). The body has been examined with various techniques that analyze and monitor it from a position outside and above, as an object that could be understood, manipulated, and remade. The gentle use of a stethoscope or the experienced technician's gaze through a microscope are examples of the detached observer's efforts to judge a body's status, to analyze and identify its deficits, or to monitor and evaluate its functioning.

Based on the body-as-machine metaphor, scientific medicine has extended the body/machine's capacities, improved its performance, and extracted its power, thus increasing the body's utility. The body is treated not as a whole unit unto itself, but as a mechanism made up of separately usable parts, parts that can be transformed and more efficiently utilized.

This mechanistic view of the human body, though, deflects attention from other origins of physical distress, especially causes of disease derived from the environment, work processes, or social stress. Illness of the body/machine is equivalent to the breakdowns of machines, with cures defined increasingly as technical solutions focused on body parts. Social origins of disease and illness tend to become less visible and obvious, in effect depoliticizing social issues by removing them from critical scrutiny.

The disappearance of traditional cultural expressions of individual and collective discontent such as witchcraft, sorcery, and rituals of reversal such as Mardi Gras, have been connected to changes in the organization of social and public life in advanced industrial society. Today instead, medicine and psychiatry shape and respond to human distress. Negative and hostile feelings can be shaped and transformed by doctors and psychiatrists into symptoms of new "diseases" such as premenstrual syndrome, attention deficit disorder, and urban survival syndrome. Scholars now suggest that rather than viewing these syndromes as socially significant "signs," the identification of these types of syndromes recasts legitimate rage into individual pathologies and isolated "symptoms." Problems at the level of social structure, such as sexism, poverty, stressful work demands, or unsafe working conditions are transformed into problems of the individual that can be medically supervised. Irving Zola, in his article in this section, analyzes the power of medicine to structure how individuals transform themselves from agents of protest into docile bodies needing help from doctors. Patients come to think of themselves as "the problem," holding themselves responsible for any type of physiological breakdown. While bacteria may be sighted as an underlying cause, people still assume responsibility for being susceptible. AIDS, colds, acne, obesity are all seen as ultimately the individual's fault.

The result is that more and more human unrest, dissatisfaction, longing, and protest is filtered into the idiom of sickness and is safely managed by doctors as society's designated control agents. Within this theoretical framework, the bodily articulation of social distress is negated and the role of doctors becomes one of producing social consensus through the generation of docile bodies.

Psychotherapy

As has been discussed in previous sections, our Western metaphysical tradition divides "mind" and "body" into two quite distinct, if inseparable, entities. The human body is the lowly, subordinate carrier of the mind, which is the basis of rational thought and judgment. The body is a mere instrument, and the adequacy of its performance is continually subject to analysis, measurement, and discipline by the rational mind.

But how is the distinction between "rationality" and "irrationality" defined and more importantly by whom? Forms of irrationality are seemingly distinct and easily separated from the realm of reason. Those who display irrationality and are thought to be a threat to themselves or others are physically removed from society to be reeducated through therapy for their own good. According to Foucault "the asylum no longer punished the madman's guilt, it is true; but it did more. It organized that guilt, it organized it for the madman as a consciousness of himself. . . . From the acknowledgment of his status as object, from the awareness of his guilt, the madman was to return to his awareness of himself as a free and responsible subject, and consequently to reason" (Foucault, 1973, p. 247).

The organization of a "normal" person's consciousness is structured through a culture's system of rationality. The "free and responsible subject" who follows his/her culture's system is considered "rational." Freedom, though, is allowed only to those displaying rationality. The therapist attempts to reorganize the madman's consciousness through "reasoning," helping the mad see their irrationality. The juxtaposition of rationality and irrationality supposedly clarifies the distinctions between them, while the power of reason "corrects" misguided and erroneous assumptions. To be cured, madmen must acknowledge their mistaken "irrational" assumptions, and their "freedom" to display agreed-upon rationalities. Their bodies are then released from the asylums.

In this way Foucault highlights the indirect coercion inherent within the helping professions. When people permit—even welcome—therapists to enter their minds, and when individuals internalize the criteria of normality and thus become their own judge, then the power of surveillance becomes invisible. The disembodied gaze of the panoptic guard tower is internalized.

Indeed, a profession that gazes into the smallest crevices of human lives helps to maintain an orderly, rational society. A constant surveillance over mental functioning, conducted by the subjects themselves, keeps in check the stresses and the precarious contradictions that make up the social order (Armstrong, 1983, p. 26). Human beings actively (re)create themselves through a variety of techniques they apply to their own bodies, to their own thoughts, to their own conduct. These operations characteristically entail a process of self-understanding but one that is mediated by external authority (Rabinow, 1984, p. 8). Thus, while torture addressed the mind through the vehicle of the body, contemporary psychiatric and medical "gentle corrections" address the body through the mind. Both forms serve the goal of producing "normal" docile bodies.

Weight loss organizations are a good example of this type of behavior modification applied to the body. The goal of any type of behavior modification is the individual's voluntary conformity to institutional requirements. Weight loss organizations, through lectures, advice, supervision, and reading material, provide the codes and the social scripts for the transformation of the individual body into a conforming ideal. Weight loss organizations generate concepts and vocabulary which, if successful, come to dominate the ways in which their members come to perceive their bodies and themselves. Power, as defined by Foucault, is realized as people internalize the need to discipline and monitor their behavior in accordance with cultural mandates. The power of knowledge is demonstrated as weight loss organization members voluntarily attempt and really desire to control their bodies through their actions, attitudes, consciousness, and a "self-understanding" mediated by the institution. This type of self-understanding directs the person's behavior into safe, acceptable, and nondisruptive channels. By focusing on themselves as dysfunctional, as the problem, rather than exploring unrealistic social standards of weight ideals, members reinforce that social order. Individuals attempt to transform their bodies rather than the social system.

Another method to voluntarily transform one's body in order to fit the social structure is to chemically alter the body with medication. Cosmetic pharmacology is the use of drugs to transform personalities in order to meet cultural ideals. The culture constructs a psychological ideal of the mind and then manufactures additional substances for those who have trouble attaining those standards. Individuals then medicate themselves as the troubled entity, as if they are the problem. Drugs can be supplied to alter the body to be calm while in crisis, "in control" while it is not, alert when it is tired, full when it is hungry, sleepy when it is awake. Xenical, Viagra, and Prozac are current examples of how the body can be chemically altered to better meet socially constructed ideals. If there were a drug to increase your memory that didn't have side effects, would you take it? In what way would you then be transforming your body to meet a social standard? Instead of questioning the standard itself, chemical substances are supplied so individuals can attain those standards.

These chemical substances, whether physician prescribed or self-medicated, collapse a complex series of political and social questions about the body. Medicine and psychotherapy, as hegemonic forms of social control, depoliticize the social structural issues involved and mute the potential for action by people to change the conditions that are troubling them. The medicalization of social problems aims toward personal adjustment and mutes potential resistance, as people voluntarily medicate themselves to fix the problem. These micro-level processes tend to reinforce macro-level patterns of domination and subordination in society. Biochemical and psychological readjustment of individuals tends to create passivity, docility, and acceptance of power relationships.

While conventional interpretations of the health profession regard prisons, medicine, and psychotherapy as rational and progressive, Foucault, by contrast, claims that these "advances" do not liberate the body from external control, but rather intensify the means of social regulation. From the prison institutions to weight loss organizations, to teachers in the school, to the doctor in the community, mechanisms of social control monitor the physical and mental well-being of both the community and the individual within the community. It is these micro-mechanisms of power that, since the late eighteenth century, have played an increasing part in the management of people's lives through direct action on their bodies. They operate not through a code of law but through a technology of discipline, not by punishment but by internalization. Social control is not a static set of mechanisms with which we are forced to comply but a dynamic social practice, constantly in process, constantly reproducing itself in the ordinary workings of these institutions. But social control works at this macro-institutional level only because it works similarly at the micro level of the individual, working "automatically" on and through the individual's body and mind.

NORBERT ELIAS

9 | On Blowing One's Nose

Why is it that people are rarely seen picking their nose in public? How has it come about that when people blow their nose they are to use a tissue or handkerchief instead of the tablecloth or their fingers? Norbert Elias documents the historical transformation and increasing discipline of "polite" social behavior practiced in Western society. Elias discusses the hierarchical relationships between those who have the power to set the standards and the behaviors that become taken for granted as inappropriate. The seeming naturalness of regulations that guide the simple act of blowing the nose suggest there are many other behaviors that are regulated and deeply ingrained as the appropriate methods to control bodily functions in public life. The revulsion that is experienced when "snot" is seen highlights the power of the disciplinary technologies to deeply influence the core values that guide behavior. After reading Elias's account of transformations involved in nose blowing, think about which bodily functions are acceptable to display in public today, the rituals involved in displaying, hiding, or apologizing for a bodily function, how the display rituals are learned, who teaches them, and consequences of failing to display the appropriate "civilized" rituals surrounding bodily functions. The answers to these questions reveal the hegemonic powers surrounding the body within the structure of this social system.

From Norbert Elias, "On Blowing One's Nose," in *The Civilizing Process* (Oxford, UK: Blackwell Publishers, 1978), 143–52. Reprinted by permission of Blackwell Publishers.

Examples

A

Thirteenth century

From Bonvesin de la Riva (Bonvicino da Riva), *De la zinquanta cortexie da tavola* (Fifty table courtesies):

(a) Precept for gentlemen:

When you blow your nose or cough, turn round so that nothing falls on the table.

(b) Precept for pages or servants:

Pox la trentena è questa:
zaschun cortese donzello
Che se vore mondà lo naxo,
con li drapi se faza bello;
chi mangia, over chi menestra,
no de'sofià con le die;
Con li drapi da pey se monda
vostra cortexia.[1]

B

Fifteenth century

From *Ein spruch der ze tische kêrt*:

It is unseemly to blow your nose into the tablecloth.

C

From *S'ensuivent les contenances de la table*:

XXXIII. Do not blow your nose with the same hand that you use to hold the meat.[2]

D

From A. Cabanès, *Moeurs intimes du temps passé* (Paris, 1910), 1st series, p. 101:

In the fifteenth century people blew their noses into their fingers, and the sculptors of the age were not afraid to reproduce the gesture, in a passably realistic form, in their monuments.

Among the knights, the *plourans*, at the grave of Philip the

Bold at Dijon, one is seen blowing his nose into his coat, another into his fingers.

E

Sixteenth century
From *De civilitate morum puerilium*, by Erasmus, ch. 1:

To blow your nose on your hat or clothing is rustic, and to do so with the arm or elbow befits a tradesman; nor is it much more polite to use the hand, if you immediately smear the snot on your garment. It is proper to wipe the nostrils with a handkerchief, and to do this while turning away, *if more honorable people are present.*

If anything falls to the ground when blowing the nose with two fingers, it should immediately be trodden away.

[From the scholia on this passage:]

Between snot and spit there is little difference, except that the former fluid is to be interpreted as coarser and the latter more unclean. The Latin writers constantly confuse a breastband, a napkin, or any piece of linen with a handkerchief.

F

1558
From *Galateo*, by Della Casa, quoted from the five-language edition (Geneva, 1609), pp. 72, 44, 618:

You should not offer your handkerchief to anyone unless it has been freshly washed. . . .

Nor is it seemly, after wiping your nose, to spread out your handkerchief and peer into it as if pearls and rubies might have fallen out of your head.

. . . What, then, shall I say of those . . . who carry their handkerchiefs about in their mouths? . . .

G

From Cabanès, *Moeurs intimes*, pp. 103, 168, 102:

[From Martial d'Auvergne, "Love decrees"] . . . in order that she might remember him, he decided to have one of the most beautiful and sumptuous handkerchiefs made for her, in which his name was in letters entwined in the prettiest fashion, for it was joined to a fine golden heart bordered with tiny heartsease.[3]

[From Lestoil, *Journal d'Henri IV*] In 1594, Henri IV asked his valet how many shirts he had, and the latter replied: "A dozen, sire, and some torn ones." "And how many handkerchiefs?" asked the king. "Have I not eight?" "For the moment there are only five," he said.

In 1599, after her death, the inventory of Henri IV's mistress is found to contain "five handkerchiefs worked in gold, silver and silk, worth 100 crowns."

In the sixteenth century, Monteil tells us, in France as everywhere else, the common people blow their noses without a handkerchief, but among the bourgeoisie it is accepted practice to use the sleeve. As for the rich, they carry a handkerchief in their pockets; therefore, to say that a man has wealth, one says that he does not blow his nose on his sleeve.

H

Late seventeenth century
The Peak of Refinement
First High Point of Modeling and Restrictions
1672
From Courtin, *Nouveau traité de civilité*:

[At table] to blow your nose openly into your handkerchief, without concealing yourself with your serviette [napkin], and to wipe away your sweat with it . . . are filthy habits fit to make everyone's gorge rise. . . .

You should avoid yawning, blowing your nose, and spitting. If you are obliged to do so in places that are kept clean, do it in your handkerchief, while turning your face away and shielding yourself with your left hand, and do not look into your handkerchief afterward.

I

1694
From Ménage, *Dictionnaire étymologique de la langue française*:

Handkerchief for blowing the nose.

As this expression "blowing the nose" gives a very disagreeable impression, ladies ought to call this a pocket handkerchief, as one says neckerchief, rather than a handkerchief for blowing the nose. [N.B. *Mouchoir de poche, Taschentuch*, handkerchief as more polite expressions; the word for functions that have become distasteful is repressed.]

Eighteenth century

Note the increasing distance between adults and children. Only children are still allowed, at least in the middle classes, to behave as adults did in the Middle Ages.

J

1714

From an anonymous *Civilité française* (Liège, 1714), p. 141:

> Take good care not to blow your nose with your fingers or on your sleeve *like children*; use your handkerchief and do not look into it afterward.

K

1729

From La Salle, *Les Règles de la bienséance et de la civilité chrétienne* (Rouen, 1729), in a chapter called "On the Nose, and the Manner of Blowing the Nose and Sneezing," p. 23:

> It is very impolite to keep poking your finger into your nostrils, and still more insupportable to put what you have pulled from your nose into your mouth. . . .
>
> It is vile to wipe your nose with your bare hand, or to blow it on your sleeve or your clothes. It is very contrary to decency to blow your nose with two fingers and then to throw the filth onto the ground and wipe your fingers on your clothes. It is well known how improper it is to see such uncleanliness on clothes, which should always be very clean, no matter how poor they may be.
>
> There are some who put a finger on one nostril and by blowing through their nose cast onto the ground the filth inside; those who act thus are people who do not know what decency is.
>
> You should always use your handkerchief to blow your nose, and never anything else, and in doing so usually hide your face with your hat. [A particularly clear example of the dissemination of courtly customs through this work.]
>
> You should avoid making a noise when blowing your nose. . . . . Before blowing it, it is impolite to spend a long time taking out your handkerchief. *It shows a lack of respect toward the people you are with* to unfold it in different places to see

where you are to use it. You should take your handkerchief from your pocket and use it quickly in such a way that you are scarcely noticed by others.

After blowing your nose you should take care not to look into your handkerchief. It is correct to fold it immediately and replace it in your pocket.

L

1774

From La Salle, *Les Règles de la bienséance et de la civilité chrétienne* (1774 ed.), pp. 14f. The chapter is now called only "On the Nose" and is shortened:

> Every voluntary movement of the nose, whether caused by the hand or otherwise, is impolite and puerile. To put your fingers into your nose is a revolting impropriety, and from touching it too often *discomforts may arise which are felt for a long time.*[4] Children are sufficiently in the habit of committing this lapse; *parents should correct them carefully.*
>
> You should observe, in blowing your nose, all the rules of propriety and cleanliness.

All details are avoided. The "conspiracy of silence" is spreading. It is based on the presupposition—which evidently could not be made at the time of the earlier edition—that all the details are known to adults and can be controlled within the family.

M

1797

From La Mésangère, *Le voyageur de Paris* (1797), vol 2, p. 95. This is probably seen, to a greater extent than the preceding eighteenth-century examples, from the point of view of the younger members of "good society":

> Some years ago people made an art of blowing the nose. One imitated the sound of the trumpet, another the screech of a cat. Perfection lay in making neither too much noise nor too little.

Comments on the Quotations on Nose-Blowing

1. In medieval society people generally blew their noses into their hands, just as they ate with their hands. That

necessitated special precepts for nose-cleaning at table. Politeness, *courtoisie*, required that one blow one's nose with the left hand if one took meat with the right. But this precept was in fact restricted to the table. It arose solely out of consideration for others. The distasteful feeling frequently aroused today by the mere thought of soiling the fingers in this way was at first entirely absent.

Again the examples show very clearly how slowly the seemingly simplest instruments of civilization have developed. They also illustrate to a certain degree the particular social and psychological preconditions that were required to make the need for and use of so simple an instrument general. The use of the handkerchief—like that of the fork—first established itself in Italy, and was diffused on account of its prestige value. The ladies hang the precious, richly embroidered cloth from their girdles. The young "snobs" of the Renaissance offer it to others or carry it about in their mouths. And since it is precious and relatively expensive, at first there are not many of them even among the upper class. Henri IV, at the end of the sixteenth century, possessed (as we hear in Example G) five handkerchiefs. And it is generally taken as a sign of wealth not to blow one's nose into one's hand or sleeve but into a handkerchief. Louis XIV is the first to have an abundant supply of handkerchiefs, and under him the use of them becomes general, at least in courtly circles.

2. Here, as so often, the transitional situation is clearly visible in Erasmus. It is proper to use a handkerchief, he says, and if people of a higher social position are present, turn away when blowing your nose. But he also says: If you blow your nose with two fingers and something falls to the ground, tread on it. The use of the handkerchief is known but not yet widely disseminated, even in the upper class for which Erasmus primarily writes.

Two centuries later, the situation is almost reversed. The use of the handkerchief has become general, at least among people who lay claim to "good behavior." But the use of the hands has by no means disappeared. Seen from above, it has become "ill-mannered," or at any rate common and vulgar. One reads with amusement La Salle's gradations between *vilain*, for certain very coarse ways of blowing the nose with the hand, and *très contraire à la bienséance*, for the better manner of doing so with two fingers (Examples H, J, K, L).

Once the handkerchief begins to come into use, there constantly recurs a prohibition on a new form of "bad manners" that emerges at the same time as the new practice—the prohibition on looking into one's handkerchief when one has used it (Examples F, H, J, K, L). It almost seems as if inclinations which have been subjected to a certain control and restraint by the introduction of the handkerchief are seeking a new outlet in this way. At any rate, an instinctual tendency which today appears at most in the unconscious, in dreams, in the sphere of secrecy, or more consciously only behind the scenes, the interest in bodily secretions, here shows itself at an earlier stage of the historical process more clearly and openly, and so in a form in which today it is only "normally" visible in children.

In the later edition of La Salle, as in other cases, the major part of the very detailed precepts from the earlier one are omitted. The use of the handkerchief has become more general and self-evident. It is no longer necessary to be so explicit. Moreover, there is less and less inclination to speak about these details that La Salle originally discussed straightforwardly and at length without embarrassment. More stress, on the other hand, is laid on children's bad habit of putting the fingers in the nose. And, as with other childish habits, the medical warning now appears alongside or in place of the social one as an instrument of conditioning, in the reference to the injury that can be done by doing "such a thing" too often. This is an expression of a change in the manner of conditioning that has already been considered from other aspects. Up to this time, habits are almost always judged expressly in their relation to other people, and they are forbidden, at least in the secular upper class, because they may be troublesome or embarrassing to others, or because they betray a "lack of respect." Now habits are condemned more and more as such, not in regard to others. In this way, socially undesirable impulses or inclinations are more radically repressed. They are associated with embarrassment, fear, shame, or guilt, even when one is alone. Much of what we call "morality" or "moral" reasons has the same function as "hygiene" or "hygienic" reasons: to condition children to a certain social standard. Molding by such means aims at making socially desirable behavior automatic, a matter of self-control, causing it to appear in the consciousness of the individual as the result of his own free will, and in the interests of his own health or human dignity. And it is only with the advent of this way of consolidating habits, or conditioning, which gains predominance with the rise of the middle classes, that conflict between the socially inadmissible impulses and tendencies, on the one hand, and the pattern of social demands anchored in the individual, on the other, takes on the sharply defined form central to the psychological theories of modern times—above all, to psychoanalysis. It may be that there have always been "neuroses." But the "neuroses" we see about us today are a specific historical form of psychic conflict which needs psychogenetic and sociogenetic elucidation.

3. An indication of the mechanisms of repression may already be contained in the two verses quoted from Bonvicino da Riva (Example A). The difference between what is expected of knights and lords, on the one hand, and of the *donizelli*, pages or servants, on the other, calls to mind a much-documented social phenomenon. The masters find the sight of the bodily functions of their servants distasteful; they compel them, the social inferiors in their immediate surroundings, to control and restrain these functions in a way that they do not at first impose on themselves. The verse addressed to the masters says simply: If you blow your nose, turn round so that nothing falls on the table. There is no mention of using a cloth. Should we believe that the use of cloths for cleaning the nose was already taken so much for granted in this society that it was no longer thought necessary to mention it in a book on manners? That is highly improbable. The servants, on the other hand, are expressly instructed to use not their fingers but their foot bandages if they have to blow their noses. To be sure, this interpretation of the two verses cannot be considered absolutely certain. But the fact can be frequently demonstrated that functions are found distasteful and disrespectful in inferiors which superiors are not ashamed of in themselves. This fact takes on special significance with the transformation of society under absolutism, and therefore at absolutist courts, when the upper class, the aristocracy as a whole, has become, with degrees of hierarchy, a subservient and socially dependent class. This at first sight highly paradoxical phenomenon of an upper class that is socially extremely dependent will be discussed later in another context. Here we can only point out that this social dependence and its structure have decisive importance for the structure and pattern of affect restrictions. The examples contain numerous indications of how these restrictions are intensified with the growing dependence of the upper class. It is no accident that the first "peak of refinement" or "delicacy" in the manner of blowing the nose—and not only here—comes in the phase when the dependence and subservience of the aristocratic upper class is at its height, the period of Louis XIV (Examples H and I).

The dependence of the upper class also explains the dual aspect which the behavior patterns and instruments of civilization have at least in this formative stage. They express a certain measure of compulsion and renunciation, but they also immediately become a weapon against social inferiors, a means of distinction. Handkerchief, fork, plates, and all their related implements are at first luxury articles with a particular social prestige value (Example G).

The social dependence in which the succeeding upper class, the bourgeoisie, lives, is of a different kind, to be sure, from that of the court aristocracy, but tends to be greater and more compelling.

In general, we scarcely realize today what a unique and astonishing phenomenon a "working" upper class is. Why does it work? Why submit itself to this compulsion even though it is the "ruling" class and is therefore not commanded to do so? The question demands a more detailed answer than is possible in this context. What is clear, however, is the parallel to what has been said on the change in the instruments and forms of conditioning. During the stage of the court aristocracy, the restraint imposed on inclinations and emotions is based primarily on consideration and respect due to others and above all to social superiors. In the subsequent stage, renunciation and restraint of impulses is compelled far less by particular persons; expressed provisionally and approximately, it is now, more directly than before, the less visible and more impersonal compulsions of social interdependence, the division of labor, the market, and competition that impose restraint and control on the impulses and emotions. It is these pressures, and the corresponding manner of explanation and conditioning mentioned above, which make it appear that socially desirable behavior is voluntarily produced by the individual himself, on his own initiative. This applies to the regulation and restraint of drives necessary for "work"; it also applies to the whole pattern according to which drives are modeled in bourgeois industrial societies. The pattern of affect control, of what must and what must not be restrained, regulated, and transformed, is certainly not the same in this stage as in the preceding one of the court aristocracy. In keeping with its different interdependencies, bourgeois society applies stronger restrictions to certain impulses, while in the case of others aristocratic restrictions are simply continued and transformed to suit the changed situation. In addition, more clearly distinct national patterns of affect control are formed from the various elements. In both cases, in aristocratic court society as well as in the bourgeois societies of the nineteenth and twentieth centuries, the upper classes are socially constrained to a particularly high degree.

NOTES

1. The meaning of passage (b) is not entirely clear. What is apparent is that it is addressed especially to people who serve at table. A commentator, Uguccione Pisano, says: "Those are called *donizelli* who are handsome, young, and the servants of great lords. . . ." "These *donizelli* were not allowed to sit at the same table as the knights; or, if this was permitted, they had to sit on a lower chair. They, pages of a kind and at any rate social inferiors, are told: The thirty-first courtesy is this—every *courtois* "donzel" who wishes to blow his nose should beautify himself with a cloth. When he is eating or serving he should not blow (his nose?) through his fingers. It is *courtois* to use the foot bandage.

2. According to an editor's note (*The Babees Book*, vol. 2, p. 14), courtesy consisted in blowing the nose with the fingers of the left hand if one ate and took meat from the common dish with the right.

3. This cloth was intended to be hung from the lady's girdle, with her keys. Like the fork, night-commode, etc., the handkerchief is first an expensive luxury article.

4. This argument, absent in the earlier edition, shows clearly how the reference to damage to health is gradually beginning to emerge as an instrument of conditioning, often in place of the reminder about the respect due to social superiors.

IRVING KENNETH ZOLA

10 Medicine as an Institution of Social Control

Irving Zola documents the shift from religion and law as institutions of social control, to medicine and the corresponding values attributed to "health." He highlights how medicine is not a value-neutral science, but is bound together with other institutions of social control. As Norbert Elias demonstrated with the civilized behaviors attached to nose blowing, Zola similarly points out the power of authoritative institutions to determine appropriate interpretations of behaviors. Zola then takes the analysis of the power of institutions one step further by discussing how people, by holding themselves responsible for their illness, uphold and in effect reproduce the power of institutions. He suggests that as individuals interact with medical authorities, they come to assume responsibility for their own health, attempting to discipline themselves in line with the mandates dictated by medical experts. Surveying themselves for their lacks and faults, adopting the perspective of the medical gaze, they display the power of the panopticon as a form of social control. Zola's analysis thus displays Foucault's concept of micro-powers that are enacted upon and through individuals as they act upon themselves.

The theme of this essay is that medicine is becoming a major institution of social control,

From Irving Kenneth Zola, "Medicine as an Institution of Social Control," *Sociological Review* 20 (1972): 487–504. © 1972 by The Editors of the *Sociological Review*. Reprinted by permission of Blackwell Publishers.

nudging aside, if not incorporating, the more traditional institutions of religion and law. It is becoming the new repository of truth, the place where absolute and often final judgments are made by supposedly morally neutral and objective experts. And these judgments are made, not in the name of virtue or legitimacy, but in the name of health. Moreover, this is not occurring through the political power physicians hold or can influence, but is largely an insidious and often undramatic phenomenon accomplished by "medicalizing" much of daily living, by making medicine and the labels "healthy" and "ill" *relevant* to an ever-increasing part of human existence.

Although many have noted aspects of this process, by confining their concern to the field of psychiatry, these criticisms have been misplaced.[1] For psychiatry has by no means distorted the mandate of medicine, but indeed, though perhaps at a pace faster than other medical specialities, is following instead some of the basic claims and directions of that profession. Nor is this extension into society the result of any professional "imperialism," for this leads us to think of the issue in terms of misguided human efforts or motives. If we search for the "why" of this phenomenon, we will see instead that it is rooted in our increasingly complex technological and bureaucratic system—a system which has led us down the path of the reluctant reliance on the expert.[2]

Quite frankly, what is presented in the following pages is not a definitive argument but rather a case in progress. As such it draws heavily on observations made in the United States, though similar murmurings have long been echoed elsewhere.[3]

A Historical Perspective

The involvement of medicine in the management of society is not new. It did not appear full-blown one day in the mid-twentieth century. As Sigerist[4] has aptly claimed, medicine at base was always not only a social science but an occupation whose very practice was inextricably interwoven into society. This interdependence is perhaps best seen in two branches of medicine which have had a built-in social emphasis from the very start—psychiatry[5] and public health/preventive medicine.[6] Public health was always committed to changing social aspects of life—from sanitary to housing to working conditions—and often used the arm of the state (i.e., through laws and legal power) to gain its ends (e.g., quarantines, vaccinations). Psychiatry's involvement in society is a bit more difficult to trace, but taking the histories of psychiatry as data, then one notes the almost universal reference to one of the early pioneers, a physician named Johan Weyer. His, and thus psychiatry's involvement in social problems lay in the objection that witches ought not to be burned; for they were not possessed by the devil, but rather bedeviled by their problems—namely they were insane. From its early concern with the issue of insanity as a defense in criminal proceedings, psychiatry has grown to become the most dominant rehabilitative perspective in dealing with society's "legal" deviants. Psychiatry, like public health, has also used the legal powers of the state in the accomplishment of its goals (i.e., the cure of the patient) through the legal proceedings of involuntary commitment and its concomitant removal of certain rights and privileges.

This is not to say, however that the rest of medicine has been "socially" uninvolved. For a rereading of history makes it seem a matter of degree. Medicine has long had both a de jure and a de facto relation to institutions of social control. The de jure relationship is seen in the idea of reportable diseases, wherein, if certain phenomena occur in his practice, the physician is required to report them to the appropriate authorities. While this seems somewhat straightforward and even functional where certain highly contagious diseases are concerned, it is less clear where the possible spread of infection is not the primary issue (e.g., with gunshot wounds, attempted suicide, drug use and what is now called child abuse). The de facto relation to social control can be argued through a brief look at the disruptions of the last two or three American Medical Association conventions. For there the American Medical Association members—and really all ancillary health professions—were accused of practicing social control (the term used by the accusers was genocide) in first, *whom* they have traditionally treated with *what*—giving *better* treatment to more favored clientele; and secondly, *what* they have treated—a more subtle form of discrimination in that, with limited resources, by focusing on some diseases others are neglected. Here the accusation was that medicine has focused on the diseases of the rich and the established—cancer, heart disease, stroke—and ignored the diseases of the poor, such as malnutrition and still high infant mortality.

The Myth of Accountability

Even if we acknowledge such a growing medical involvement, it is easy to regard it as primarily a "good" one—which involves the steady destigmatization of many human and social problems. Thus Barbara Wootton was able to conclude:

> Without question . . . in the contemporary attitude toward antisocial behavior, psychiatry and humanitarianism have marched hand in hand. Just because it is so much in keeping with the mental atmosphere of a scientifically-minded age, the medical treatment of social deviants has been a most powerful, perhaps even the most powerful, reinforcement of humanitarian impulses; for today the prestige of humane proposals is immensely enhanced if these are expressed in the idiom of medical science.[7]

The assumption is thus readily made that such medical involvement in social problems leads to their removal from religious and legal scrutiny and thus from moral and punitive consequences. In turn the problems are placed under medical and scientific scrutiny and thus in objective and therapeutic circumstances.

The fact that we cling to such a hope is at least partly due to two cultural-historical blind spots—one regarding our notion of punishment and the other our notion of moral responsibility. Regarding the first, if there is one insight into human behavior that the twentieth century should have firmly implanted, it is that punishment cannot be seen in merely physical terms, nor only from the perspective of the giver. Granted that capital offenses are on the decrease, that whipping and torture seem to be disappearing, as is the use of chains and other physical restraints, yet our ability if not willingness to inflict human anguish on one another does not seem similarly on the wane. The most effective forms of brainwashing deny any physical contact and the concept of relativism tells much about the psychological costs of even relative deprivation of tangible and intangible wants. Thus, when an individual because of his "disease" and its treatment is forbidden to have intercourse with fellow human beings, is confined until cured, is forced to undergo certain medical procedures for his own good, perhaps deprived forever of the right to have sexual relations and/or produce children, *then* it is difficult for that patient *not* to view what is happening to him as punishment. This does not mean that medicine is the latest form of twentieth century torture, but merely that pain and suffering take many forms, and that the removal of a despicable inhumane procedure by current standards does not necessarily mean that its replacement will be all that beneficial. In part, the satisfaction in seeing the chains cast off by Pinel may have allowed us for far too long to neglect examining with what they had been replaced.

It is the second issue, that of responsibility, which requires more elaboration, for it is argued here that the medical model has had its greatest impact in the lifting of moral condemnation from the individual. While some skeptics note that while the individual is no longer condemned his disease still *is*, they do not go far enough. Most analysts have tried to make a distinction between illness and crime on the issue of personal responsibility.[8] The criminal is thought to be responsible and therefore accountable (or punishable) for his act, while the sick person is not. While the distinction does exist, it seems to be more a quantitative one rather than a qualitative one, with moral judgments but a pinprick below the surface. For instance, while it is probably true that individuals are no longer directly condemned for being sick, it does seem that much of this condemnation is merely displaced. Though his immoral character is not demonstrated in his having a disease, it becomes evident in what he does about it. Without seeming ludicrous, if one listed the traits of people who break appointments, fail to follow treatment regimen, or even delay in seeking medical aid, one finds a long list of "personal flaws." Such people seem to be ever ignorant of the consequences of certain diseases, inaccurate as to symptomatology, unable to plan ahead or find time, burdened with shame, guilt, neurotic tendencies, haunted with traumatic medical experiences, or members of some lower status minority group—religious, ethnic, racial or socioeconomic. In short, they appear to be a sorely troubled if not disreputable group of people.

The argument need not rest at this level of analysis, for it is not clear that the issues of morality and individual responsibility have been fully banished from the etiological scene itself. At the same time as the label "illness" is being used to attribute "diminished responsibility" to a whole host of phenomena, the issue of "personal responsibility" seems to be reemerging within medicine itself. Regardless of the truth and insights of the concepts of stress and the perspective of psychosomatics, whatever else they do, they bring man, *not* bacteria, to the center of the stage and lead thereby to a reexamination of the individual's role in his own demise, disability, and even recovery.

The case, however, need not be confined to professional concepts and their degree of acceptance, for we can look at the beliefs of the man in the street. As most surveys have reported, when an individual is asked what caused his diabetes, heart disease, upper respiratory infection, etc., we may be comforted by the scientific terminology if not the accuracy of his answers. Yet if we follow this questioning with the probe: "Why did you get X now?" or "Of all the people in your community, family etc. who were exposed to X, why did you get . . . ?" then the rational scientific veneer is pierced and the concern with personal and moral responsibility emerges quite strikingly. Indeed the issue "why me?" becomes of great concern and is generally expressed in quite moral terms of what they did wrong. It is possible to argue that here we are seeing a residue and that it will surely be different in the new generation. A recent experiment I conducted should cast some doubt on this. I asked a class of forty undergraduates, mostly aged seventeen, eighteen, and nineteen, to recall the last time they were sick, disabled, or hurt and then to record how they did or would have communicated this experience to a child under the age of five. The purpose of the assignment had nothing to do with the issue of responsibility, and it is worth noting that there was no difference in the nature of the response between those who had or had not actually encountered children during their "illness." The responses speak for themselves.

> The opening words of the sick, injured person to the query of the child were:
> "I feel bad"
> "I feel bad all over"
> "I have a bad leg"
> "I have a bad eye"
> "I have a bad stomachache"
> "I have a bad pain"
> "I have a bad cold"
> The reply of the child was inevitable:
> "What did you do wrong?"
> The "ill person" in no case corrected the child's perspective but rather joined it at that level.
> *On bacteria*
> "There are good germs and bad germs and sometimes the bad germs. . . ."

On catching a cold

"Well, you know sometimes when your mother says, 'Wrap up or be careful or you'll catch a cold', well, I. . . ."

On an eye sore

"When you use certain kinds of things (mascara) near your eye you must be very careful and I was not. . . ."

On a leg injury

"You've always got to watch where you're going and I. . . ."

Finally to the treatment phase:

On how drugs work

"You take this medicine and it attacks the bad parts. . . ."

On how wounds are healed

"Within our body there are good forces and bad ones and when there is an injury, all the good ones. . . ."

On pus

"That's the way the body gets rid of all its bad things. . . ."

On general recovery

"If you are good and do all the things the doctor and your mother tell you, you will get better."

In short, on nearly every level, from getting sick to recovering, a moral battle raged. This seems more than the mere anthropomorphizing of a phenomenon to communicate it more simply to children. Frankly, it seems hard to believe that the English language is so poor that a *moral* rhetoric is needed to describe a supposedly amoral phenomenon—illness.

In short, despite hopes to the contrary, the rhetoric of illness by itself seems to provide no absolution from individual responsibility, accountability, and moral judgment.

The Medicalizing of Society

Perhaps it is possible that medicine is not devoid of a potential for moralizing and social control. The first question becomes: "What means are available to exercise it?" Freidson has stated a major aspect of the process most succinctly:

> The medical profession has first claim to jurisdiction over the label of illness and *anything* to which it may be attached, irrespective of its capacity to deal with it effectively.[9]

For illustrative purposes this "attaching" process may be categorized in four concrete ways: first, through the expansion of what in life is deemed relevant to the good practice of medicine; secondly, through the retention of absolute control over certain technical procedures; thirdly, through the retention of near absolute access to certain "taboo" areas; and finally, through the expansion of what in medicine is deemed relevant to the good practice of life.

1. *The expansion of what in life is deemed relevant to the good practice of medicine*

The change of medicine's commitment from a specific etiological model of disease to a multicausal one and the greater acceptance of the concepts of comprehensive medicine, psychosomatics, etc., have enormously expanded that which is or can be relevant to the understanding, treatment, and even prevention of disease. Thus it is no longer necessary for the patient merely to divulge the symptoms of his body, but also the symptoms of daily living, his habits, and his worries. Part of this is greatly facilitated in the "age of the computer," for what might be too embarrassing, or take too long, or be inefficient in a face-to-face encounter can now be asked and analyzed impersonally by the machine, and moreover be done before the patient ever sees the physician. With the advent of the computer a certain guarantee of privacy is necessarily lost, for while many physicians might have probed similar issues, the only place where the data were stored was in the mind of the doctor, and only rarely in the medical record. The computer, on the other hand, has a retrievable, transmittable, and almost inexhaustible memory.

It is not merely, however, the nature of the data needed to make more accurate diagnoses and treatments, but the perspective which accompanies it—a perspective which pushes the physician far beyond his office and the exercise of technical skills. To rehabilitate or at least alleviate many of the ravages of chronic disease, it has become increasingly necessary to intervene to change permanently the habits of a patient's lifetime—be it of working, sleeping, playing, or eating. In prevention the "extension into life" becomes even deeper, since the very idea of primary prevention means getting there *before* the disease process starts. The physician must not only seek out his clientele but once found must often convince them that they must do something *now* and perhaps at a time when the potential patient feels well or not especially troubled. If this in itself does not get the prevention-oriented physician involved in the workings of society, then the nature of "effective" mechanisms for intervention surely does, as illustrated by the statement of a physician trying to deal with health problems in the ghetto:

> Any effort to improve the health of ghetto residents cannot be separated from equal and simultaneous efforts to remove the multiple social, political and economic restraints currently imposed on inner city residents.[10]

Certain forms of social intervention and control emerge even when medicine comes to grips with some of its more traditional problems like heart disease and cancer. An increasing number of physicians feel that a change in diet may be the most effective deterrent to a number of cardiovascular complications. They are, however, so perplexed as to how to get the general population to follow their recommendations that a leading article in a national magazine was entitled "To Save the Heart: Diet by Decree?"[11] It is obvious that there is an increasing pressure for more explicit sanctions against the tobacco companies and against high users to force both to desist. And what will be the implications of even stronger evidence which links age at parity, frequency of sexual intercourse, or the lack of male circumcision to the incidence of cervical cancer, can be left to our imagination!

2. *Through the retention of absolute control over certain technical procedures*

In particular this refers to skills which in certain jurisdictions are the very operational and legal definition of the practice of medicine—the right to do surgery and prescribe drugs. Both of these take medicine far beyond concern with ordinary organic disease.

In surgery this is seen in several different subspecialties. The plastic surgeon has at least participated in, of not helped perpetuate, certain aesthetic standards. What once was a practice confined to restoration has now expanded beyond the correction of certain traumatic or even congenital deformities to the creation of new physical properties, from size of nose to size of breast, as well as dealing with certain phenomena—wrinkles, sagging, etc.—formerly associated with the "natural" process of aging. Alterations in sexual and reproductive functioning have long been a medical concern. Yet today the frequency of hysterectomies seems not so highly correlated as one might think with the presence of organic disease. (What avenues the very possibility of sex change will open is anyone's guess.) Transplantations, despite their still relative infrequency, have had a tremendous effect on our very notions of death and dying. And at the other end of life's continuum, since abortion is still essentially a surgical procedure, it is to the physician-surgeon that society is turning (and the physician-surgeon accepting) for criteria and guidelines.

In the exclusive right to prescribe and thus pronounce on and regulate drugs, the power of the physician is even more awesome. Forgetting for the moment our obsession with youth's "illegal" use of drugs, any observer can see, judging by sales alone, that the greatest increase in drug use over the last ten years has not been in the realm of treating any organic disease but in treating a large number of psychosocial states. Thus we have drugs for nearly every mood:

> to help us sleep or keep us awake
> to enhance our appetite or decrease it
> to tone down our energy level or to increase it
> to relieve our depression or stimulate our interest.

Recently the newspapers and more popular magazines, including some medical and scientific ones, have carried articles about drugs which may be effective peace pills or anti-aggression tablets, enhance our memory, our perception, our intelligence, and our vision (spiritually or otherwise). This led to the easy prediction:

> We will see new drugs, more targeted, more specific and more
> potent than anything we have. . . . And many of these would be
> for people we would call healthy.[12]

This statement incidentally was made not by a visionary science fiction writer but by a former commissioner of the United States Food and Drug Administration.

3. *Through the retention of near absolute access to certain "taboo" areas*

These "taboo" areas refer to medicine's almost exclusive license to examine and treat that most personal of individual possessions—the inner workings of our bodies and minds. My contention is that if anything can be shown in some way to affect the workings of the body and to a lesser extent the mind, then it can be labeled an "illness" itself or jurisdictionally "a medical problem." In a sheer statistical sense the import of this is especially great if we look at only four such problems—aging, drug addiction, alcoholism, and pregnancy. The first and last were once regarded as normal natural processes and the middle two as human foibles and weaknesses. Now this has changed and to some extent medical specialties have emerged to meet these new needs. Numerically this expands medicine's involvement not only in a longer span of human existence, but it opens the possibility of medicine's services to millions if not billions of people. In the United States at least, the implication of declaring alcoholism a disease (the possible import of a pending Supreme Court decision as well as laws currently being introduced into several state legislatures) would reduce arrests in many jurisdictions by 10 to 50 percent and transfer such "offenders" when "discovered" directly to a medical facility. It is pregnancy, however, which produces the most illuminating illustration. For, again in the United States, it was barely seventy years ago that virtually all births and the concomitants of birth occurred outside the hospital as well as outside medical supervision. I do not frankly have a documentary history, but as this medical claim was solidified, so too was medicine's claim to a whole host of related processes: not only to birth but to prenatal, postnatal, and pediatric care; not only to conception but to infertility; not only to the process of reproduction but to the process and problems of sexual activity itself; not only when life begins (in the issue of abortion) but whether it should be allowed to begin at all (e.g., in genetic counseling).

Partly through this foothold in the "taboo" areas and partly through the simple reduction of other resources, the physician is increasingly becoming the choice for help for many with personal and social problems. Thus a recent British study reported that within a five year period there had been a notable increase (from 25 to 41 percent) in the proportion of the population willing to consult the physician with a personal problem.[13]

4. *Through the expansion of what in medicine is deemed relevant to the good practice of life*

Though in some ways this is the most powerful of all "the medicalizing of society" processes, the point can be made simply. Here we refer to the use of medical rhetoric and evidence in the arguments to advance any cause. For what Wootton attributed to psychiatry is no less true of medicine. To paraphrase her, today the prestige of *any* proposal is immensely enhanced, if not justified, when it is expressed in the idiom of medical science. To say that many who use such labels are not professionals only begs the issue, for the public is only taking its cues from professionals who increasingly have been extending their expertise into the social sphere or have called for such an extension.[14] In politics one hears of the healthy or unhealthy economy or state. More concretely, the physical and mental health of American presidential candidates has been an issue in the last four elections and a recent book claimed to link faulty political decisions with faulty health.[15] For years we knew that the environment was unattractive, polluted, noisy, and in certain ways dying, but now we learn that its death may not be unrelated to our own demise. To end with a rather mundane if depressing example, there has always been a constant battle between school authorities and their charges on the basis of dress and such habits as smoking, but recently the issue was happily resolved for a local school administration when they declared that such restrictions were necessary for reasons of health.

The Potential and Consequences of Medical Control

The list of daily activities to which health can be related is ever growing, and with the current operating perspective of medicine it seems infinitely expandable. The reasons are manifold. It is not merely that medicine has extended its jurisdiction to cover new problems,[16] or that doctors are professionally committed to finding disease,[17] nor even that society keeps creating disease.[18] For if none of these obtained today we would still find medicine exerting an enormous influence on society. The most powerful empirical stimulus for this is the realization of how much everyone has or believes he has something organically wrong with him, or put more positively, how much can be done to make one feel, look, or function better.

The rates of "clinical entities" found on surveys or by periodic health examinations range upwards from 50 to 80 percent of the population studied.[19] The Peckham study found that only 9 percent of their study group were free from clinical disorder. Moreover, they were even wary of this figure and noted in a footnote that, first, some of these 9 percent had subsequently died of a heart attack, and, secondly, that the majority of those without disorder were under the age of five.[20] We used to rationalize that this high level of prevalence did not, however, translate itself into action since not only are rates of medical utilization not astonishingly high but they also have not gone up appreciably. Some recent studies, however, indicate that we may have been looking in the wrong place for this medical action. It has been noted in the United States and the United Kingdom that within a given twenty-four to thirty-six-hour period, from 50 to 80 percent of the adult population have taken one or more "medical" drugs.[21]

The belief in the omnipresence of disorder is further enhanced by a reading of the scientific, pharmacological, and medical literature, for there one finds a growing litany of indictments of "unhealthy" life activities. From sex to food, from aspirins to clothes, from driving your car to riding the surf, it seems that under certain conditions, or in combination with certain other substances or activities or if done too much or too little, virtually anything can lead to certain medical problems. In short, I at least have finally been convinced that living is injurious to health. This remark is not meant as facetiously as it may sound. But rather every aspect of our daily life has in it elements of risk to health.

These facts take on particular importance not only when health becomes a paramount value in society, but also a phenomenon whose diagnosis and treatment has been restricted to a certain group. For this means that that group, perhaps unwittingly, is in a position to exercise great control and influence about what we should and should not do to attain that "paramount value."

Freidson in his recent book *Profession of Medicine* has very cogently analyzed why the expert in general and the medical expert in particular should be granted a certain autonomy in his researches, his diagnosis, and his recommended treatments.[22] On the other hand, when it comes to constraining or directing human behavior *because* of the data of his researches, diagnosis, and treatment, a different situation obtains. For in these kinds of decisions it seems that too often the physician is guided not by his technical knowledge but by his values, or values latent in his very techniques.

Perhaps this issue of values can be clarified by reference to some not so randomly chosen medical problems: drug safety, genetic counseling, and automated multiphasic testing.

The issue of drug safety should seem straightforward, but both words in that phrase apparently can have some interesting flexibility—namely what is a drug and what is safe. During Prohibition in the United States, alcohol was medically regarded as a drug and often prescribed as a medicine. Yet in recent years, when the issue of dangerous substances and drugs has come up for discussion in medical circles, alcohol has been officially excluded from the debate. As for safety, many have applauded the A.M.A.'s judicious position in declaring the need for much more extensive, longitudinal research on marijuana and their unwillingness to back legalization until much more data are in. This applause might be muted if the public read the 1970 Food and Drug Administration's Blue Ribbon Committee Report on the safety, quality, and efficacy of *all* medical drugs commercially and legally on the market since 1938.[23] Though appalled at the lack and quality of evidence of any sort, few recommendations were made for the withdrawal of drugs from the market. Moreover there are no recorded cases of anyone dying from an overdose or of extensive adverse side effects from marijuana use, but the literature on the adverse effects of a whole host of "medical drugs" on the market today is legion.

It would seem that the value positions of those on both sides of the abortion issue needs little documenting, but let us pause briefly at a field where "harder" scientists are at work—genetics. The issue of genetic counseling, or whether life should be allowed to begin at all, can only be an ever increasing one. As we learn more and more about congenital, inherited disorders or predispositions, and as the population size for whatever reason becomes more limited, then, inevitably, there will follow an attempt to improve the quality of the population which shall be produced. At a conference on the more limited concern of what to do when there is a documented probability of the offspring of certain unions being damaged, a position was taken that it was not necessary to pass laws or bar marriages that might produce such offspring. Recognizing the power and influence of medicine and the doctor, one of those present argued:

> There is no reason why sensible people could not be dissuaded from marrying if they know that one out of four of their children is likely to inherit a disease.[24]

There are in this statement certain values on marriage and what it is or could be that, while they may be popular, are not necessarily shared by all. Thus, in addition to presenting the argument against marriage, it would seem that the doctor should—if he were to engage in the issue at all—present at the same time some of the other alternatives:

> Some "parents" could be willing to live with the risk that out of four children, three may turn out fine.

Depending on the diagnostic procedures available they could take the risk and if indications were negative abort.

If this risk were too great but the desire to bear children was there, and depending on the type of problem, artificial insemination might be a possibility.

Barring all these and not wanting to take any risk, they could adopt children.

Finally, there is the option of being married without having any children.

It is perhaps appropriate to end with a seemingly innocuous and technical advance in medicine, automatic multiphasic testing. It has been a procedure hailed as a boon to aid the doctor if not replace him. While some have questioned the validity of all those test-results and still others fear that it will lead to second-class medicine for already underprivileged populations, it is apparent that its major use to date and in the future may not be in promoting health or detecting disease to prevent it. Thus three large institutions are now or are planning to make use of this method, not to treat people, but to "de-select" them. The armed services use it to weed out the physically and mentally unfit, insurance companies to reject "uninsurables" and large industrial firms to point out "high risks." At a recent conference, representatives of these same institutions were asked what responsibility they did or would recognize to those whom they have just informed that they have been "rejected" because of some physical or mental anomaly. They calmly and universally stated: none—neither to provide them with any appropriate aid nor even to ensure that they get or be put in touch with any help.

Conclusion

C. S. Lewis warned us more than a quarter of a century ago that "man's power over Nature is really the power of some men over other men, with Nature as their instrument." The same could be said regarding man's power over health and illness, for the labels health and illness are remarkable "depoliticizers" of an issue. By locating the source and the treatment of problems in an individual, other levels of intervention are effectively closed. By the very acceptance of a specific behavior as an "illness" and the definition of illness as an undesirable state, the issue becomes not whether to deal with a particular problem, but *how* and *when*.[25] Thus the debate over homosexuality, drugs, or abortion becomes focused on the degree of sickness attached to the phenomenon in question or the extent of the health risk involved. And the more principled, more perplexing, or even moral issue, of *what* freedom should an individual have over his or her own body is shunted aside.

As stated in the very beginning, this "medicalizing of society" is as much a result of medicine's potential as it is of society's wish for medicine to use that potential. Why then has the focus been more on the medical potential than on the social desire? In part it is a function of space, but also of political expediency. For the time rapidly may be approaching when recourse to the populace's wishes may be impossible. Let me illustrate this with the statements of two medical scientists who, if they read this essay, would probably dismiss all my fears as groundless. The first was commenting on the ethical, moral, and legal procedure of the sex change operation:

> Physicians generally consider it unethical to destroy or alter tissue except in the presence of disease or deformity. The interference with a person's natural procreative function entails definite moral tenets, by which not only physicians but also the general public are influenced. The administration of physical harm as treatment for mental or behavioral problems—as corporal punishment, lobotomy for unmanageable psychotics and sterilization of criminals—is abhorrent in our society.[26]

Here he states, as almost an absolute condition of human nature, something which is at best a recent phenomenon. He seems to forget that there were laws promulgating just such procedure through much of the twentieth century, that within the past few years at least one Californian jurist ordered the sterilization of an unwed mother as a condition of probation, and that such procedures were done by Nazi scientists and physicians as part of a series of medical experiments. More recently, there is the misguided patriotism of the cancer researchers under contract to the United States Department of Defense who allowed their dying patients to be exposed to massive doses of radiation to analyze the psychological and physical results of simulated nuclear fallout. True, the experiments were stopped, but not until they had been going on for *eleven* years.

The second statement is by Francis Crick at a conference on the implications of certain genetic findings:

> Some of the wild genetic proposals will never be adopted because the people will simply not stand for them.[27]

Note where his emphasis is: on the people, not the scientist. In order, however, for the people to be concerned, to act, and to protest, they must first be aware of what is going on. Yet in the very privatized nature of medical practice, plus the continued emphasis that certain expert judgments must be free from public scrutiny, there are certain processes which will prevent the public from ever knowing what has taken place and thus from doing something about it. Let me cite two examples.

> Recently, in a European country, I overheard the following conversation in a kidney dialysis unit. The chief was being questioned about whether or not there were self-help groups among his patients. "No," he almost shouted, "that is the last thing we want. Already the patients are sharing too much knowledge while they sit in the waiting room, thus making our task increasingly difficult. We are working now on a procedure to prevent them from ever meeting with one another."

The second example removes certain information even further from public view.

> The issue of fluoridation in the U.S. has been for many years a hot political one. It was in the political arena because, in order to fluoridate local water supplies, the decision in many jurisdictions had to be put to a popular referendum. And when it was, it was often defeated. A solution was found and a series of state laws were passed to make fluoridation a public health decision and to be treated, as all other public health decisions, by the medical officers best qualified to decide questions of such a technical, scientific and medical nature.

Thus the issue at base here is the question of what factors are actually of a solely technical, scientific, and medical nature!

To return to our opening caution, this paper is not an attack on medicine so much as on a situation in which we find ourselves in the latter part of the twentieth century; for the medical area is the arena or the example par excellence of today's identity crisis—what is or will become of man. It is the battleground, not because there are visible threats and oppressors, but because they are almost invisible; not because the perspective, tools, and practitioners of medicine and the other helping professions are evil, but because they are not. It is so frightening because there are elements here of the banality of evil so uncomfortably written about by Hannah Arendt.[28] But here the danger is greater, for not only is the process masked as a technical, scientific, objective one, but one done for our own good. A few years ago a physician speculated on what, based on current knowledge, would be the composite picture of an individual with a low risk of developing atherosclerosis or coronary-artery disease. He would be:

> . . . . an effeminate municipal worker or embalmer completely lacking in physical or mental alertness and without drive, ambition, or competitive spirit; who has never attempted to meet a deadline of any kind; a man with poor appetite, subsisting on fruits and vegetables laced with corn and whale oil, detesting tobacco, spurning ownership of radio, television, or motor car, with full head of hair but scrawny and unathletic appearance, yet constantly straining his puny muscles by exercise. Low in income, . . . blood pressure, . . . blood sugar, uric acid and cholesterol, he has been taking nicotinic acid, pyridoxine, and long term anti-coagulant therapy ever since his prophylactic castration.[29]

Thus I fear with Freidson:

> A profession and a society which are so concerned with physical and functional well-being as to sacrifice civil liberty and moral integrity must inevitably press for a "scientific" environment similar to that provided laying hens on progressive chicken farms—hens who produce eggs industriously and have no disease or other cares.[30]

Nor does it really matter that if, instead of the above depressing picture, we were guaranteed six more inches in height, thirty more years of life, or drugs to expand our potentialities and potencies; we should still be able to ask: what do six more inches matter, in what kind of environment will the thirty additional years be spent, or who will decide what potentialities and potencies will be expanded and what curbed?

I must confess that given the road down which so much expertise has taken us, I am willing to live with some of the frustrations and even mistakes that will follow when the authority for many decisions becomes shared with those whose lives and activities are involved. For I am convinced that patients have so much to teach to their doctors as do students their professors and children their parents.

NOTES

1. T. Szasz: *The Myth of Mental Illness*, Harper and Row, New York, 1961; and R. Leifer: *In the Name of Mental Health*, Science House, New York, 1969.
2. E.g. A. Toffler: *Future Shock*, Random House, New York, 1970; and P. E. Slater: *The Pursuit of Loneliness*, Beacon Press, Boston, 1970.
3. Such as B. Wootton: *Social Science and Social Pathology*, Allen and Unwin, London, 1959.
4. H. Sigerist: *Civilization and Disease*, Cornell University Press, New York, 1943.
5. M. Foucault: *Madness and Civilization*, Pantheon, New York, 1965; and Szasz, *op. cit.*
6. G. Rosen: *A History of Public Health*, MD Publications, New York, 1955; and G. Rosen: "The Evolution of Social Medicine," in H. E. Freeman, S. Levine, and L. G. Reeder (eds.), *Handbook of Medical Sociology*, Prentice-Hall, Englewood Cliffs, N.J., 1963, pp. 17–61.
7. Wootton, *op. cit.*, p. 206.
8. Two excellent discussions are found in V. Aubert and S. Messinger; "The Criminal and the Sick," *Inquiry*, Vol. 1, 1958, pp. 137–60; and E. Freidson: *Profession of Medicine*, Dodd-Mead, New York, 1970, pp. 205–77.
9. Freidson: *op. cit.*, p. 251.
10. J. C. Norman: "Medicine in the Ghetto," *New Engl. J. Med.*, Vol. 281, 1969, p. 1271.
11. "To Save the Heart; Diet by Decree?", *Time Magazine*, 10 January, 1968, p. 42.
12. J. L. Goddard quoted in the *Boston Globe*, August 7, 1966.
13. K. Dunnell and A. Cartwright: *Medicine Takers, Prescribers and Hoarders*, in press.
14. E. g. S. Alinsky: "The Poor and the Powerful," in *Poverty and Mental Health*, Psychiat. Res. Rep. No. 21 of the Amer. Psychiat. Ass., January 1967; and B. Wedge: "Psychiatry and International Affairs," *Science*, Vol. 157, 1961, pp. 281–85.
15. H. L'Etang: *The Pathology of Leadership*, Hawthorne Books, New York, 1970.
16. Szasz: *op. cit.*; and Leifer: *op. cit.*
17. Freidson: *op. cit.*; and T. Scheff: "Preferred Errors in Diagnoses," *Medical Care*, Vol. 2, 1964, pp. 166–72.
18. R. Dubos: *The Mirage of Health*, Doubleday, Garden City, N.Y., 1959; and R. Dubos: *Man Adapting*, Yale University Press, 1965.
19. E.g. the general summaries of J. W. Meigs: "Occupational Medicine," *New Engl. J. Med.*, Vol. 264, 1961, pp. 861–67; and G. S. Siegel: *Periodic Health Examinations—Abstracts from the Literature*, Publ. Hlth. Serv. Publ. No. 1010, U.S. Government Printing Office, Washington, D.C., 1963.

20. I. H. Pearse and L. H. Crocker: *Biologists in Search of Material*, Faber and Faber, London, 1938; and I. H. Pearse and L. H. Crocker: *The Peckham Experiment,* Allen and Unwin, London, 1949.
21. Dunnell and Cartwright: *op. cit.*; and K. White, A. Andjelkovic, R. J. C. Pearson, J. H. Mabry, A. Ross and O. K. Sagan: "International Comparisons of Medical Care Utilization," *New Engl. J. of Med.*, Vol. 277, 1967, pp. 516–22.
22. Freidson: *op. cit.*
23. *Drug Efficiency Study—Final Report to the Commissioner of Food and Drugs*, Food and Drug Adm. Med. Nat. Res. Council, Nat. Acad. Sci., Washington, D.C., 1969.
24. Reported in L. Eisenberg: "Genetics and the Survival of the Unfit," *Harper's Magazine*, Vol. 232, 1966, p. 57.
25. This general case is argued more specifically in I. K. Zola: *Medicine, Morality, and Social Problems—Some Implications of the Label Mental Illness*, Paper presented at the Amer. Ortho-Psychiat. Ass., March 20–23, 1968.
26. D. H. Russell: "The Sex Conversion Controversy," *New Engl. J. Med.*, Vol. 279, 1968, p. 536.
27. F. Crick reported in *Time Magazine*, April 19, 1971.
28. H. Arendt: *Eichmann in Jerusalem—A Report on the Banality of Evil*, Viking Press, New York, 1963.
29. G. S. Myers quoted in L. Lasagna: *Life, Death and the Doctor*, Alfred A. Knopf, New York, 1968, pp. 215–16.
30. Freidson: *op. cit.*, p. 354.

BARBARA KAMLER
ROD MACLEAN
JO-ANNE REID
ALYSON SIMPSON

11

Put Your Hands in Your Own Laps

Disciplining the Student Body

How do young girls or boys learn to be good students? Why would they want to be good students? Kamler et al. investigated how children are taught to control their bodies in the classroom and become, in Foucault's terminology, "docile bodies." Within the first month of school, teachers train their students, through rewards, punishments, games, songs, and verbal corrections, to discipline themselves and to keep their bodies under control, for their own good. As both Norbert Elias and Irving Zola illustrate in their articles, institutions no longer need to force people into conforming to social standards of bodily regulation. Individuals give their consent. But how is this consent achieved?

Kamler et al. suggest that through seemingly innocuous activities such as participating in songs or games, the indirectness of hegemonic power is highlighted, as most children learn to transform themselves into quiet, attentive, and receptive listeners. Docility is established in unruly children through their learning to discipline themselves and turn into students. Order, control, obedience, and the reproduction of the binary gender system are maintained and (re)produced. The bigger ideological questions connecting disciplined children with

From Barbara Kamler, Rod Maclean, Jo-Anne Reid, and Alyson Simpson, in "Put Your Hands in Your Own Laps: Disciplining the Student Body," in *Shaping Up Nicely: The Formation of Schoolgirls and Schoolboys in the First Month of School* (Canberra, Australia: Deakin University, Department of Employment Education and Training, 1994), 113–28. © 1994 by the Commonwealth of Australia. Reprinted by permission of the Commonwealth of Australia.

disciplined workers are hidden within the power relations that establish docility as good. The power of hegemonic relations is revealed, though, when the focus is turned to answering the question of what happens to children (or adults) who resist the indirect but omnipresent pressures to become docile.

Early childhood classrooms are filled with song. Songs such as "The Dingle Dangle Scarecrow," which encourage children to sing and move their bodies to the lyrics, are common fare in Mrs. T's prep [elementary] classroom.

Text 1 *"The Dingle Dangle Scarecrow"*

When all the cows were sleeping and the sun had gone to bed
Up jumped the scarecrow and this is what he said
"I'm a dingle dangle scarecrow with a flippy floppy hat,
I can shake my hands like this and shake my feet like that."

When all the hens were roosting and the moon behind the cloud
Up jumped the scarecrow and shouted very loud
"I'm a dingle dangle scarecrow with a flippy floppy hat,
I can shake my hands like this and shake my feet like that."

In this chapter we aim to make the commonplace strange, to disrupt our usual ways of viewing such classroom songs as innocent fun, and to analyze, rather, the multiple purposes they serve, the discourses they mobilize, and the gendered positionings they accomplish. In doing so, we wish to assert that a song of childhood is not necessarily a song of innocence. For after all, the "dingle dangle scarecrow" is the only figure in the song with agency and he is identified as male. His female defined counterparts, by contrast, are inactive; the cows are sleeping and the hens are exercising their biological imperative of roosting, but it is the scarecrow the children are asked to identify with. They become the scarecrow, they shake their hands and feet as he would and give voice to his words through the personal pronoun *I*, "I'm a dingle dangle scarecrow." This chapter argues that such songs are not a simple form of entertainment to keep children amused, but, read against other texts in the prep classroom, can be seen as doing important work in regulating children's bodies into the schoolgirls and schoolboys they become.

This chapter focuses on the regulation of the child body through regulatory practices associated with teacher discourse and action.

The data we examine come from 3 February, the fifth day of school, and analyzes selected instances of teacher talk, games, and songs, which demonstrate some of the surprisingly concrete ways in which Foucault's (1977) notion of the institutionally regulated docile body are inscribed in the discourses of the first month of school. Our analyses reveal that the discourses of power that perpetuate the symbolic binaries of gendered practice are not just to be found in language exchanges, but also in practices enacted on and through bodies. This chapter therefore foregrounds the centrality of the body to the process of gendering and engages the problems involved in analyses that rely too narrowly on linguistic representation for making sense of lived experience.

Texts of Body Regulation

At the conclusion of the first day of school, Mrs. T said of the children, "Oh, they'll shape up nicely," signifying to herself that as a group the new preps were mature physically, reasonably self-sufficient, and able to learn the routines and procedures of schooling. The use of the word *shape*, specifying the process as a physical rather than a mental one, seems significant in signaling discourses of body regulation. In our very first observations of Mrs T, the year before the study started, we noted striking instances of the use of regulatory language to control the student body, as field notes from that time indicate.

> I am overwhelmed and struck by the purpose of talk to regulate the child body. I always knew that children were regulated and their attention kept by rhymes and rhythms and songs but I have never seen the intense purpose being so overtly for control before. It was almost as though the purpose of the day was to ensure the obedience and that these orders were interspersed with a bit of curriculum activity here and there. The use of imperative was pervasive. The timing like clockwork. The teacher is skilled, warm, caring attentive to the children. She is master at Prep speak. It is a particular kind of discourse perhaps so intensive because it is seen to be the ground that paves the way for future obedience. Focus on the physical body so prevalent. Disciplining the child body. The order and movement controlled to avoid any disruption, breaking out of the prescribed order. (Field notes:, 23 October 1992)

Since that time the focus on the body has been of particular interest to us. Michel Foucault's work has been particularly helpful in offering a central emphasis on discourse as a form of power that both literally and metaphorically inscribes the collective and individual social body. We understand that discourse operates not as an abstract set of ideas but, as Elizabeth Grosz (1990, p. 63) suggests, as "a material series of processes," where power actively marks bodies as social, and inscribes them, as an effect of this, with differentiated "attributes of subjectivity."

This chapter will speculate on what is involved in that shaping, and the way in which a system of bodily discipline works in the production of prep subjectivities. We use the term "construction," to characterize the ongoing process by which the new schoolchild creates or puts together her attempts to present to herself and others a sense of a coherent subject in the face of the contradictory, oppositional, and changing subjectivities that she experiences as "self" within the practices of the classroom.

> Between the child and the world, the whole group intervenes . . . with a whole universe of ritual practices and utterances, which people it with meanings structured in accordance with the principles of the corresponding habitus. (Bourdieu, 1990, p. 76)

This chapter examines some of these ritual practices of schooling to allow us to better understand their power to inscribe arbitrary principles of classroom culture in the experiences of the body.

Songs of Discipline

To investigate song as one of the ritual practices of schooling, we return to "The Dingle Dangle Scarecrow" and contextualize it in the lived experience of Mrs. T's prep classroom. The song was sung during the first hour of school, and was one of eight songs sung during the first forty minutes of the day, as shown in Table 1. This segment of morning activity, typical of the start of many days during the first month of school, is bounded by song. When the children first gather on the rug, Mrs. T uses three songs to gather their attention, after a long session of morning news and "direction games" she again uses three songs to mark the end of the forty-minute segment, prior to the children moving to a new seat-

Table 1 3 February

NUMBER OF MINUTES	ACTIVITY/SONG
00.0	*Good morning. Gathering on the rug. Weather. Attendance.*
1.30	"Ciao buon giorno."
2.00	"Ciao buon giorno" (reprise)
3.20	"How many fingers on my hand?" (finish 5.07)
5.49	*Stand up. Move to circle for morning news.*
6.00	"I'm A Little Teapot."
7.32	*Sit down for morning news. Twelve students share news.*
18.10	"The Dingle Dangle Scarecrow."
	Thirteen students share news.
33.40	*Hands on heads.*
34.50	*Following directions at seats.*
39.50	*Return to Rug.*
40.30	"Incy Wincy Spider."
40.52	"Roll Over."
41.30	"Twinkle, Twinkle."

work activity in which they will identify their names and then trace over them.

"The Dingle Dangle Scarecrow" occurs in the midst of morning news and serves as an orchestrated interruption. This is the first formal news session of the year, where every child in the circle is given the chance to speak. With twenty-five children present this day it takes twenty-six minutes to move around all of them. The children grow restless, their bodies squirm, they are sprawled in a variety of positions on the rug. Mrs. T interrupts the news with the scarecrow song to refocus their attention.

The fact that the first forty minutes are spent organizing, regulating, and arranging the children's bodies on the rug and at their seats signals how intensely the first month of school is directed at regulating and disciplining the student body before children can get to the "real work of school." The songs play a significant role in this disciplining. If, following Frances Christie (1989), we classify songs as a curriculum genre, because they are social, members of the class interact with each other to achieve them, and they are goal oriented, it appears that in the prep classroom childhood songs undergo a shift in their generic purpose from pleasure to regulation.

Prior to the study, in October 1992, when we observed seventeen of the children in their kindergarten classroom across the street, the purpose of song was clearly pleasure. There was only one time when the whole group came together on the rug in the kindergarten and this was marked by song. The teacher began a song as the signal for the group to gather together, and the momentum and volume grew as children finished the activity in which they were engaged and joined the group. They then sang a series of well-known and, judging from the smiling and laughter, well-loved songs. This was a communal time in which the goals appeared to be pleasure, community, and pleasure in community.

In the prep classroom the children also engaged in song as a community, but the purpose shifted dramatically (although the linguistic form was the same) to collective regulation, a gathering of attention, an invitation to discontinue private conversation and move their mouths in unison. The singing is led by the teacher, who decides when and at what intervals the songs will occur and whose voice and gestures set the cadence, stress, and pitch. In the prep classroom a vehicle for pleasure is transformed into a technology of power, whereby the teacher can get the group to look at her and be subject to her disciplinary gaze.

The songs regulate the children by targeting their bodies. Most of the songs require them to perform actions on their own bodies and to do so in unison. Hands are often the target in the forty-minute segment. In "How Many Fingers On My Hand?" the children count 1, 2, 3, 4, 5 fingers, first on the left hand, then on the right; in "I'm A Little Teapot" the children form their hands and arms into the handle and spout of the teapot; in "Twinkle, Twinkle Little Star" the children raise their hands above their heads and make their fingers into twinkling stars. In each instance, children are required to move their hands not only for the fun of the movement, but also to keep them off other children.

"The Dingle Dangle Scarecrow" song regulates larger body movements. The children are told to get in their box at the start of the song and with one minor protest, which is ignored, they move down to the floor, forming their bodies into a small ball. Only a few of the children sing with the teacher until, at the signal "Up jumped the scarecrow," they jump up and join in the chorus "I can shake my hands like this, I can shake my feet like that." They move down again onto the floor and repeat the cycle for the second verse—a bodily contraction, a springing movement, and a shaking of the hands and feet—after which they are presumably ready to sit down and pay attention to the children who have yet to give their morning news.

The songs are a routinized practice. Following Foucault's explanation of institutional regulation, the songs appear to operate as one of a number of systems of surveillance and regulation that are "inscribed at the heart of the practice of teaching, not as an additional or adjacent part, but as a mechanism that is inherent to it and which increases its efficiency" (Foucault, 1977, p. 176). The efficiency argument finds some support in the fact that Mrs. T was observed teaching the children only a few new songs during the first month of school and relied rather on songs already familiar from television shows such as *Play School* and *Sesame Street*, and from kindergarten the year before. Because little energy had to be expended on remembering the words, the songs could function more directly as regulating mechanisms in the first month of school. In fact, to the dismay of one of our team who is a musician, Mrs. T sometimes used incorrect words to the songs. In "The Dingle Dangle Scarecrow," for example, the rhyme was sacrificed in two lines (see below). Parentheses indicate the original words:

- When all the cows *are* (were) sleeping and the sun *is in the sky* (had gone to bed)
- When all the hens *are* (were) roosting and the moon *is in the sky* (behind the cloud)

Mrs. T changes the verb tense from "were" to "are" and substitutes "is in the sky" for the more rhythmic "had gone to bed" and "behind the cloud" respectively. This did not seem to matter, however, because the central purpose was not so much the rhythmic pleasure of the song, as the bodily discipline it could achieve.

Body Parts

We now move our attention to the teacher injunctions about the body that surrounded the scarecrow song during the same first hour of school on 3 February. In focusing on one morning, we seek to provide specificity to our observations; our presence in the classroom throughout the month, however, allows us to present this period of time as representative of much that occurred on other days and at other hours. A common pattern that emerges here and elsewhere is that songs are most often preceded and followed by teacher talk that regulates the body and provides guidelines to students on how to produce the right body. In Text 2, we re-present

"The Dingle Dangle Scarecrow," this time within the context of the teacher talk surrounding it. In the transcript, the children are identified as "Student" rather than by name when it is not possible to specify from the videotape who is actually speaking.

Text 2 3 February

1	Mrs. T:	Everybody stand yourselves up for a little minute. Two feet
2		together, shhhhh, do this quietly. Nice big stretch up tall,
3		ohhh dear, Mrs T should be in bed I think and down again, give
4		your shoulders a wriggle, now your head, very slowly, oh
		slowly, that's it just to wake us up. Right down you get in your
		boxes.
5	Student:	What for?
6	Mrs. T:	Right down.
7	Mrs. T	When all the cows are sleeping and the sun is in the sky, up
8	& class:	jumped the scarecrow and this is what he said. "I'm a dingle
9		dangle scarecrow with a flippy floppy hat, I can shake my
		hands like this and shake my feet like that."
10	Mrs. T:	Down you go again, down you go.
11	Mrs. T	When all the hens are roosting and the moon is in the sky, up
12	& class:	jumped the scarecrow and shouted very loud "I'm a dingle
13		dangle scarecrow with a flippy floppy hat. I can shake my
		hands like this and shake my feet like that."
14	Mrs. T:	OK guys stand up nice and tall, come on Jodie stand up,
15		mustn't talk, tummies in, come on Con up you get, tummies
16		in, two feet together, shhhhhhhhh. I want your lips buttoned.
17	Student:	Ohhh.
18	Mrs. T:	Now sit down quietly, shh. You know I forgot something, I
		was going to give you people something, sit sweetie sit over
19		there. This morning I liked the way that you walked in so
20		quietly, I meant to go and give you another yellow star, so I'll
21		give it to you now and so far we've got three yellow stars on
22		the board, maybe when we get to five yellow stars there might
23		be something special, we'll have to think about that, Con could
24		you sit up nicely please and Tom you can sit there. But just sit
25		quietly, Con sit up nicely, that's it. Right, now, remember.
26		Some of you people have forgotten the rules, remember if
		someone is talking do you all talk at the same time?
27	Student:	No, no no no.
28	Mrs. T:	No, because why? Why don't you speak if someone else is
		speaking?

29 Student: Because.

30 Mrs. T: Because why?

31 Allan: (inaudible)

32 Mrs. T: Well that's one reason Allan, that's a good reason, does

33 anybody else have any other reasons why you might not talk,

34 Karen, Karen I like the way you're sitting up there beautifully
with your hand up.

35 Karen: 'cause it's wrong.

36 Mrs. T: Because yes because it's a bit wrong isn't it, why is it a bit

37 wrong do you think Thomas?

38 Thomas: Because it's rude.

39 Mrs. T: It is a bit rude, I find a little bit rude, if someone speaks

40 when I'm speaking I feel maybe it's just a little bit rude.

41 Student: (inaudible) and you just can't hear what you're saying.

42 Mrs. T: That's right, OK so where were we up too, sitting up

43 very nicely, we're going to get to all you people in a few minutes,
crossed legs.

Just prior to the song, Mrs. T gets the children to stand and stretch. The stated purpose is "just to wake us up" (turn 4), an innocent stretching time to move the body and help the children stay attentive to the morning news, which will continue in a few moments. The lexical naming of the children's body parts, their "feet," "shoulders," and "heads" (turns 1 to 3), occurs both here and at the conclusion of the song, where "tummies," "feet," and "lips" are named (turns 14 to 16) and Mrs. T attempts to get the children focused, straightened, and ready to return to the morning news.

These injunctions about the arrangement and rearrangement of student bodies, as in "tummies in, two feet together," "lips buttoned," regularly punctuate the first month of prep and are typically realized by lexically naming a variety of different body parts, including hands, lips, laps, eyes, noses, legs, arms, feet, rather than referring to the whole child body. The body parts are most often located linguistically within a teacher command, realized in the imperative mood, as is clear in the following body-targeting imperatives, which come from other portions of the morning of 3 February:

- hands to yourself please
- hands in your laps
- put up your hands
- crossed legs

- I want to see all these legs crossed
- I want your lips buttoned
- Listen with our ears not your mouths
- Look at me with your eyes so I know you are listening to me
- Can I have your eyes
- OK guys close the mouths

Posture, movement, and visual gaze are all monitored and directed through teacher imperatives. Mrs. T has the power to tell the children to move their bodies in particular ways, sometimes identifying herself as the source of the command through the pronominal *I* or *me*, other times not. The class is sometimes named as *everybody*, or *guys*, but more often not named. Their body parts, however, are named in the plural, through the pronominal *your*, although this shifts sometimes to a plural body part, *mouths*, belonging to the collective. It is less easy, however, to read where the imperatives are directed: the group or the individual? Are these the body parts belonging to one body or many? Which body is to respond? All? Some? What seems to be happening here is a discursive construction of a collective student body, for as Mary Willes (1981), points out, every year it is the job of the teacher to get children moving as one classroom body.

Individual child bodies, new to the régimes of formal schooling, are thus being shaped by Mrs. T into a student body, twenty-seven individual squirming bodies are being linguistically and bodily constituted as one, to move as if with one pair of hands, one pair of legs, one mouth that can tolerate only one voice at a time, one back that is erect and attentive, nice and straight. The body parts need to be well disciplined, they do not kick, they face the front, not the back, of the classroom, they raise their collective hand for permission to speak, to go to the toilet. They are quiet and speak softly, and they keep their hands in their collective lap.

The construction of the collective student body, however, is not accomplished through a simple imposition of power from the teacher at the top to the children at the bottom. The teacher discourse positions the body as object, as an accumulation of named parts that needs to be surveilled. Mrs. T acts upon those objects and begins simultaneously to provide the language in which to read those actions. As Valerie Walkerdine (1987) points out, actions on objects do not make any sense without a discourse through which to read them. These ways of classifying and categorizing the body, and referring to its various parts, are put to work so that "they generate self-surveillance, wherein the subject internalizes the disciplinary and cultural gaze as her or his own" (Luke, 1992, p. 111). What is of interest here, as Allan Luke points out, is how Foucault's (1988) notion of the technologies of power, which govern the conduct of individuals, interact with technologies of self, which permit individuals to act upon themselves and their own bodies.

Teacher evaluations attached to body postures certainly seem to play a role here, as exemplified by Mrs. T's talk to the children once they are seated again following the scarecrow song (turns 19 to 22). Here Mrs. T praises the group for walking. Her use of the pronominal you suggests the walking was accomplished as one body, and will now be rewarded. The action of walking is itself not an action worthy of praise, but when done quietly and collectively it is read by Mrs. T as worthy of yellow stars. Later in the year, presumably, stars will be awarded for academic work, but in the first month of school the serious work is constituted as body regulation. There is an interesting shift here as well from the pronominal *I* to *we*, which works to position the children discursively as colluding in Mrs. T's evaluations. She is clearly the dispenser of stars and praise—"I was going to give," "I liked the way," "I meant to go" "I'll give," but when it comes to stars, it is *we* who are *getting* them and *thinking* about an extra special reward. This linguistic slippage between student and teacher subjectivity works to help students engage in self-surveillance.

While many of Mrs. T's evaluations are directed at the collective student body, individuals are also singled out and named for either transgressing or complying (turns 23 to 25). It is through these naming practices that some of the more overt gendering work is accomplished. Con and Tom are named as boys who have transgressed, who have not internalized the attributes of "nicely" and "quietly." Although linguistically the teacher evaluations are not realized as negative evaluations, but as an interrogative ("could you sit up nicely?") and an imperative ("sit up nicely"), they position the boys negatively as having bodies that are hard to control. In Luke's words:

> Those who have not internalized the teacher's gaze, those who are not willing participants are singled out. . . . Where the technology of the self fails the technology of power steps in. Where the gaze has not been internalized by the children, it is externally asserted by the teacher. (Luke, 1992, p. 120)

The pattern of externally asserting the gaze however, is clearly gendered. Girls are more often named for being willing subjects, for bodily obedience and compliance, as in "Karen I like the way you're sitting up there beautifully with your hand up" (turns 33 to 34). While boys are seen for *not sitting*, girls are seen for *sitting*. This does not mean that there are not also girls transgressing or boys complying. It does mean that such actions are often not seen or named by the teacher. Michelle, for example, who is constituted through the teacher discourse as a good schoolgirl subject, engages in a great deal of aggressive body action, kicking Tom, hitting Con on the head. She is never singled out or named, however, for such transgressions. It is not clear whether Mrs. T even sees her behavior, because the teacher gaze itself is constituted within the male-female dualisms, and what is seen and named is always partial, both incomplete and interested.

To illustrate further how bodily practices such as sitting become tied to pupil selection in gendered ways, Text 3 presents an interactive sequence during a story reading later that morning. Mrs. T has set up a book on the easel and is looking for someone to help her, to move the pointer on the words as they are read aloud by her and the class.

Text 3 *February*

1	Mrs. T:	I'm looking for someone to help me, wonder who's sitting
2		up very nice. . . . Right now Ellen have you been sitting like
3		that all that time? How did you get to be so perfect? Have
4		you been practicing for years? You haven't it just comes
5		naturally to you? Come up here and be my helper, anybody
		who sits up like that guys has just got to help me.

As the lesson proceeds Rohan is named for not listening.

6	Mrs. T:	I'm sorry but we have to read it again. Rohan turn around
7		let's read it again because Rohan missed out on the story. "Look
		I'm at school."

Minutes later, however, Mrs. T chooses Rohan as a participant in the reading, ostensibly again on the basis of his body posture.

8	Mrs. T:	Now let's have a little look here, I wonder if I can ask
9		somebody and I'm only going to ask those people who are
10		sitting beautifully and I think perhaps, oh gee tricky tricky
11		tricky, Rohan you're sitting up pretty nice now actually,
12		how about coming up and seeing if you can find me the
		word that might say sssschoool. I wonder if he's clever.
13		Ellen do you think so?

Here posture is the criterion for choosing. Ellen is singled out from the collective body and praised for her sitting (lines 2 to 5). She is positioned by the teacher discourse within the male-female binaries. Sitting nicely is equated with being perfect (line 3), and this comes naturally to Ellen (lines 3 to 4), because she is a girl. She is defined as natural within the preconstructed binaries and is marked as working within the feminine. Anyone who sits like girls gets to help the teacher (lines 4 to 5). The good schoolgirl subjectivity thus becomes an extension of the female teacher subjectivity and gaze. Ellen is chosen to stand near the teacher, to hold the pointer and face the children. She is rewarded by being allowed to take on the gaze directly as teacher.

Her performance stands in direct contrast to Rohan's, which is clearly not perfect. He is "pretty nice" (line 10). His body still needs to be disciplined, the teacher gaze must stay firmly on him. Ellen the "perfect sitter" is asked to take on teacher subjectivity and maintain that gaze. Perfect sitting becomes invested with moral regulation and Ellen is invited to take on the teacher judgment and decide whether Rohan is clever, "I wonder if he's clever Ellen do you think so?" (lines 11 to 13). This type of gender regulation through posture, repeated many times during the first month in incidental, invisible ways, has real effects not only on children's bodies, but on their thoughts and ways of being. As Bourdieu (1990, p. 73) puts it, "What is 'learned by the body' is not something that one has, like knowledge that can be brandished, but something that one is."

Hands on Heads

It is dangerous to focus solely on teacher talk and select data to demonstrate how technologies of power play a part in the representation and reproduction of gendered subjectivities, because it constructs an overly neat and simple picture. It is not the case that teachers impose discipline and children comply; disciplinary power is not unitary any more than the subjectivities of the children who are in the process of becoming schoolgirls and schoolboys are unitary. Further, it is important to remember that transcripts of classroom events are themselves only constructions, and partial ones at that. The transcripts in Texts 1, 2, and 3 have been "found" and presented here as representative of the classroom action we observed. They are too incomplete a model to allow us to make any truth claims or pronouncements about what teachers should do. The ways in which we have presented transcripts thus far, in fact, privilege the linguistic over the visual representation. Although we have been discussing the student body and the ways in which it is regulated through teacher discourse, our transcripts have paid attention to words at the expense of the body and this omission constructs new fictions.

To counter this, we examine one final instance of body regulation discourse from a session of "Hands on Heads," which occurred towards the end of the first forty minutes on the morning of 3 February. In Text 4 we attempt to make more complex the analysis presented thus far by writing the body into the transcript. The procedure is to put the teacher imperatives in this facsimile of "Simon Says" in the left column and the corresponding actions of two children, Jodie and Tom, in the right column. This itself is a selection. Twenty-five children participated in this "game," yet we focus on the way in which two children responded to and resisted it, not only because we found their interaction fascinating, but because this was where the video camera was focused, yet another selection. In representing Text 4, the numbers in the left column divide the teacher talk into lines rather than turns, as has occurred elsewhere in this report. As the teacher is the only speaker, the left column constitutes one turn. The children's turns, by contrast, occur in the nonverbal domain and are represented in the right column. These are not numbered separately, but rather aligned with the teacher talk to highlight the relationship between what the teacher says and what some of the children do.

Text 4 3 February

1	Mrs. T:	Could we please have Amy, Nikola.	*Jodie crosses circle to move beside Tom.*
2		Could you just stick Amy over there for me please.	*Jodie pushes Tom away.*
3		That's it and then she can keep an eye on what	*Tom pushes Jodie.*
4		we're doing.	*Jodie moves to push Tom.*
5		Stand tall Jodie.	*Jodie moves away from Tom back across the circle where she began.*
6		Hands on heads, hands on shoulders.	*Jodie returns to Tom, hands out, tongue out.*

7	Hands ohh, hands behind backs,	
	hands on knees, gee some of you	
8	are very quick, but I'm quicker,	
9	I'll trick you, hands on feet.	*Tom pushes Jodie.*
10	Hands on elbows.	*Tom pushes Ayse who*
		returns from toilet.
11	Are you right there Ayse?	*Mrs. T pulls Ayse closer*
	Shouldn't be with. . . .	*to her.*
12	Hands on nose.	*Tom squeezes the back of*
		Jodie's neck.
13	Hands on lips.	*Tom pushes Jodie's back.*
14	Hands on eyes, hand on ears.	*Tom stamps his foot.*
15	Hands on heads, tricky one.	*Jodie points to Tom's foot.*
16	Hands behind head.	*Tom puts his foot on*
		Jodie's foot.
17	Mmm, very good, I didn't	*Tom taps his foot on Jodie's,*
	trick anybody.	*then exerts pressure. She*
		opens her mouth as if to yell.
18	Hands on feet Tom.	
19	Hands on feet, hands on knees.	*Jodie and Tom both bend*
		down to touch feet.
20	Hands behind backs.	*Tom pokes his finger into*
		Jodie's shoulder.
21	Hands in front.	*Jodie and Tom stare at one*
		another, she stands up, he
		remains crouched.
22	Hands on shoulders, hands on hips,	
23	where's your hips? Hands on hips.	
24	Hands on shoulders.	*Tom pulls Jodie's shorts.*
25	Hands on elbows, stand nice and	*Tom pulls Jodie's shorts*
26	tall, arms by your side.	*again.*
27	Do you know what I think Tom?	*Tom stands up. Jodie*
		watches.
28	Sshh, shh, shh!	*Jodie points across the*
		circle.
29	Do you know what I really think,	*Tom moves across the circle*
30	I think there are some people in	*away from Jodie to stand*
31	here who really need some	*beside Benjamin and*
32	practice in listening, because when	*the boys.*
33	I say something they don't always	

34	hear what I'm saying. So listen
35	very carefully, I hope I'm not
36	going to muck things up here, I
37	want you to go and stand behind
38	a chair, off you go.

Although Mrs. T represents Hands on Heads as a game (lines 6 to 9), like the songs, this is a childhood game being transformed into a technology of regulation, which Mrs. T will be able to call on during the course of the day, the month, the year to regulate the children's behavior.

Linguistically, the imperative "hands on heads" has been shortened or ellipsed from "put your hands on your heads," so that the comment *put* is omitted, the *hands* are thematized or come first, and the pronominal *your* is omitted so that the individual *heads* of the children become a singular collective target. This shifts the focus to the children's hands and away from both the instruction itself, *put*, and the person who is telling the children to move their bodies in prescribed ways, Mrs. T. We can diagram this linguistic transformation as follows:

- "Mrs. T says put your hands on your heads" becomes
- "Put your hands on head" becomes
- "Hands on head"

Linguistically, then, the children have agency, or rather their hands do, to act upon their own bodies, another instance of how technologies of power interact with technologies of self to produce self-surveillance. Writing in the actions of Jodie and Tom alongside the teacher imperatives in Text 4, however, reveals that such body disciplining is not simply taken up by the children and internalized. The linguistic/visual representation of Hands on Heads, in fact, allows us to produce different and more complex readings of this "game," whereby Hands on Heads transforms into Hands on Jodie.

Walkerdine (1981) notes that gendered relations of power and resistance are reproduced in the classroom, in continual struggle and constantly shifting. Here, alongside the authorized teacher discourse, we see Tom producing actions with his hands, as he is being commanded, but resistantly. Powerless within the domain of the teacher discourse, he positions Jodie and Ayse as subjects of other discourses of masculinist violence. He shoves Ayse as she returns to the circle (line 10) and targets a number of Jodie's body parts including her neck (line 12), her back (line 13), her foot (lines 16 to 17), her shoulder (line 20) and even the more taboo area covered by her shorts (lines 24 to 25). Although Tom is not a physically grown man, he can take the position of men through his actions on girls' bodies. His power is gained by refusing to be constituted as the powerless subject in the teacher discourse and recasting the girls as the powerless subject of his.

It is not the case, however, that Jodie simply accepts this positioning. She is the one, after all, who moves towards Tom in the first place. Although she returns momentarily to her initial place in the circle after being named by Mrs. T (line 5), she returns buoyantly, hands outstretched, tongue out, almost daring Tom. Significantly, Tom is positioned in the circle beside Bianca and Alice, two of the girls Jodie likes to spend time with. She may in fact move in order to sit near her friends and displace Tom to make a space for herself. Although she endures physical abuse from Tom, she remains an active participant and in the end Tom does leave the space. Jodie points in the direction of the boys (line 28) and Tom moves back across the circle to stand with Benjamin and the others (lines 29 to 30).

An important effect of this power struggle is the way in which Mrs. T interprets Tom's actions to lessen their oppressive effect. It is not clear, in fact, what she sees, as her attention is also directed at the twenty-three other children present. The first time she polices the disturbance, she names Jodie as the perpetrator, "Stand tall Jodie" (line 5), although Tom has been equally involved in the pushing. When Tom shoves Ayse with some force, it is Ayse, the victim, who is named, "Are you right there Ayse?" (line 11), rather than Tom, the perpetrator. When Tom is finally named (line 18), after he more obviously stamps his foot on Jodie's, the reprimand is realized linguistically through the imperative of the game, "Hands on feet Tom." Tom's resistance is thus seamlessly incorporated back into the domain of the teacher discourse, where he is less powerful. He is not reprimanded for what he has done and his violence remains unnamed, just a normal part of classroom life.

At the conclusion Tom is again named, "Do you know what I think Tom?" (line 27), but it is unclear whether Mrs. T is dissatisfied with his performance or with the whole group's, as she (lines 29 to 34) targets "some people" and "they" as the offenders, as the ones who don't listen, who "don't always hear what I'm saying" (lines 33 to 34). As a consequence, Mrs. T initiates a further session of body regulation (lines 34 to 38), where the children will be directed to stand behind, in front of, on and under the chairs, taking steps forward and backward to see if this time they can listen more carefully and get their bodies disciplined.

Constructing the transcript with the teacher imperatives on the left and the child actions on the right highlights the fact that in this interaction it is Mrs. T who controls the verbal domain. She talks, she speaks into existence a régime of regulation. The children do not speak, and any resistance takes place in the nonverbal domain, through the body. Thus it is that both the regulating and resisting occurs through bodily practices. This is not to say that the teacher's words do not have real effect. They target and surveil the body, limiting the range of subject positions made available to children. Subjectivity however, as Walkerdine (1987, p. 10) points out, is "not simply produced within single texts, but at the intersection of competing discourses and practices."

In this session of "Hands on Heads" the actions of Jodie and Tom put into play counter-discourses that break the surface of this regulation. Teacher discourse is a form of power that inscribes the collective student body, but the process of inscription is itself a struggle. While Mrs. T's discourse positions the children's bodies as object, the discourses of masculinity mobilized by Tom's actions target Jodie's body as object, and the discourses of femininity and female bonding mobilized by Jodie's actions compete with Tom's for supremacy. Without the visual representation of Jodie and Tom's actions, it would be possible to read these children, and the twenty-three others not discussed, as simply submitting to school-imposed disciplinary power. Such an analysis demonstrates the importance of reading the embodied text as well as the linguistic text, and of utilizing more complex frames for reading children's actions than are currently available to teachers in many classrooms.

Our analysis has attempted to make visible some of the seamless ways in which everyday school practices operate to discipline the student body. In his conceptualization of "kindergarten as academic boot camp," Harry Gracey (1962) notes that learning to live by the routines of school appears to be the principal content of the student role. Such notions are confirmed by this analysis of the set of ritualized songs, games, and routines put in place in Mrs. T's classroom during the first month of school.

While it was clearly Mrs. T's purpose to teach the children systems of rules and control, however, it was not her intention to construct gendered subjectivities through such practices. This raises serious problems about disciplining children's bodies. While it is commonly accepted that children need to be regulated in some manner if they are going to be schooled, how this is done is at issue. The fact that the process of regulation appears to be so deeply and yet invisibly gendered needs serious consideration by the teaching and research communities.

REFERENCES

Bourdieu, Pierre (1990). "Thinking about Limits," *Theory, Culture and Society*, Vol. 19, No. 1, pp. 37–49.

Christie, Frances (1989). *Language Education*. Geelong, Vic: Deakin University Press.

Foucault, Michel (1977). *Language, Counter-Memory, Practice*. Oxford: Basil Blackwell.

Foucault, Michel (1988). *Technologies of the Self*. L. H. Martin, H. Gutman, and P. H. Hutton (eds.). London: Tavistock.

Gracey, Harry (1962). "Learning the Student Role: Kindergarten as Academic Boot Camp." In *The Sociology of Education: A Source Book*. 3rd edition. H. R. Stub (ed.). Illinois: Dorsey Press.

Grosz, Elizabeth (1990). "Inscriptions and Body-Map: Representations and the Corporeal." In *Feminine, Masculine and Representations*. T. Threadgold and A. Cranny-Francis (eds.). Sydney: Allen and Unwin.

Luke, Allan (1992). "The Body Literate: Discourse and Inscription in Early Literacy Training," *Linguistics and Education*, Vol. 4, pp. 107–29.

Walkerdine, Valerie (1981). "Sex, Power, and Pedagogy." *Screen Education*, Vol. 38, pp. 14–24.

Walkerdine, Valerie (1987). *Surveillance, Subjectivity and Struggle: Lessons from Pedagogic and Domestic Practices*. CHS Occasional Papers No 11. Minneapolis: Center for Humanistic Studies, University of Minnesota.

Willis, Mary (1981). "Children Becoming Pupils: A Study of Discourse in Nursery and Reception Classes." In *Uttering Muttering: Collecting, Using and Reporting Talk for Social and Educational Research*. C. Adelman (ed.). London: Grant McIntyre.

12 The Visible Man

The Execution and Electronic Afterlife of Joseph Paul Jernigan

Joseph Paul Jernigan is a convicted murderer who "gifts" his body to medical science. After his execution by lethal injection, his body is frozen and minutely sliced and photographed in order to create a new digitized anatomical atlas. This digitized cadaver is celebrated by science as a new learning tool for the practice of medicine in the new century, applicable for both interns and experienced surgeons.

1. Think about the disciplinary interrelationships between all social institutions involved in the Visible Human Project. How do prison, medicine, religion, education, and family all interact after Jernigan's "gift" and execution? And most important, why is this significant?

2. Think about the different methods by which Jernigan and his body become and are maintained as an object under the control and authority of professionals. Why does he consent to this? Can you think of other similar methods in education? Religion?

3. Elias documented the historical and cultural transformation of the daily activity of blowing one's nose. In Jernigan's case, how does Victor Spitzer violate social taboos associated with the body? Why/how are they constructed within the article as acceptable?

From "The Visible Man: The Execution and Electronic Afterlife of Joseph Paul Jernigan," *Life* (February 20, 1997): 41, 44. © 1997 by Time Inc. Reprinted by permission of Time-Life Syndication.

4. Can you explain the relationship between the anatomical atlas, the panopticon of medicine, and the Visible Human Project as the "digital everyman"?

The prisoner sat on death row, hoping for life.

His had not been a good one so far. Booted out of the Army for drug use, Joseph Paul Jernigan of Waco, Texas, turned to robbery. When surprised in the act of stealing a microwave oven, Jernigan stabbed Edward Hale, 75, then killed him with Hale's own shotgun. "I know I did wrong," Jernigan said. "I have no one to blame but myself." Sentenced to death in 1981, he spent twelve years in prison before his final plea for clemency was denied. The next day, the thirty-eight-year-old ate his last meal—two cheeseburgers, fries, and iced tea. At 12:31 a.m. on August 5, 1993, a lethal dose of potassium chloride ran through a catheter into his arm. "I'm glad it's over," said his victim's nephew. "He won't be back on the street." But Jernigan is back. In an electronic afterlife, he haunts Hollywood studios and NASA labs, high schools, and hospitals. And in death, he may finally do something good for humanity.

The National Library of Medicine, in Bethesda, Maryland, boasts the largest collection of medical knowledge in the world. But in 1988 director Donald Lindberg realized that it was missing a significant reference tool: a computer model of the human body. Students of anatomy already had programs of body parts—knees, kidneys, brains—but no one had a whole virtual cadaver. And so the Visible Human Project was born. A hundred of the nation's medical schools competed for the grant to build the model. The project chief, Michael Ackerman, gave three finalists the task of picturing the abdomen of a guinea pig. One submission, photographs of cross sections, was more lifelike than the others. The men who had produced the pictures, Victor Spitzer and David Whitlock, professors in the University of Colorado's department of cellular and structural biology and radiology, won the $1.4 million contract in 1989. It sounded like a lot of money, but the project, which was run on a shoestring, would take five years.

First they needed a body. Actually, they wanted three men and three women so that a committee could pick the best representative of each sex, healthy specimens between twenty-one and sixty years old, and under six feet tall in order to fit into the scanning machines.

"We had to find a cadaver that was normal," says Ackerman. "That's an oxymoron—cadavers are not normal or they'd still be alive." Accident victims suffer damage, drug overdose victims are malnourished, heart attack victims have abnormal hearts. And should someone die in near perfect shape, fifty thousand desperately ill Americans are waiting for organs.

"In the end, the body came to us," says Ackerman. Prompted by a prison chaplain, several men on Texas' death row willed their bodies to science. They were young and pumped, but because the state executes by lethal injection, their organs could not be used for transplant. Those who knew Jernigan disagree about why he decided to donate his body. His mother says, "He told me he wanted to do something good." The DA who put him away says, "His family wasn't going to pay to bury him." A fellow convict believes Jernigan was hoping to star in a true-crime book and wanted to make a final, dramatic gesture. But Jernigan had no idea that his body would itself become a textbook.

"When we first heard that inmates were donating their bodies, we thought, 'Great,'" says Spitzer. "We know when and where. We could have the body in a short amount of time." The full-body scanning had to be done before the corpse was frozen, which changes the images. Spitzer, whose Ph.D. is in chemistry, is six feet four inches tall, with an oversize sense of humor. He was going to need it. He and his team of fifteen people—including his radiologist wife, their seventeen-year-old son and two nieces—experimented filling the arteries of practice cadavers with a red solution, the veins with a blue one, so they would show up in scans, but the blood vessels leaked. Storage was another problem. A Mobile-Mort freezer acquired from a mortician's catalog held only two bodies, so Spitzer bought a walk-in meat locker from a shopping mall at auction, disassembled it and moved it to his lab. Then there were no late-night flights from Texas to Colorado, so Spitzer asked Ackerman for permission to charter a Learjet for five thousand dollars. "We had the first guy in the plane about twenty minutes after the execution—I had to take off his tennis shoes," recalls Spitzer.

By the time Jernigan, the third volunteer, was to be executed, Spitzer says, "luckily, we had figured out it wasn't critical to have the body so soon. Jernigan's family decided to sit with him for a couple of hours after he died, and we would have seemed like vultures." The body was shipped air freight ($201.88) and unpacked within eight hours. At five feet eleven inches and 199 pounds, Jernigan had to be squeezed into the MRI machine; his elbows would not appear in the images. Scans of the three male cadavers were sent to the library for final selection. Although missing a tooth, a testicle, and its appendix, number 6022 was judged the best specimen. Jernigan would become the digital Everyman.

Now the hard part began: The body had to be cut into sections, then planed away in wafer-thin increments for photographs of cross sections. "Everybody said you can't do what we did, but I was too dumb to listen." says Spitzer, who attributes his can-do approach to his training as a blacksmith. To keep the body in the same position throughout the process, Spitzer ran rubber tubing along the cadaver, attaching it with Liquid Nails purchased at a local hardware store. To make the cuts even the tissue was frozen as hard as bone at –94° F for two days. Once quartered, the body was positioned in blocks of gelatin, bought in one-pound cans from the school's cafeteria and colored blue with food dye. Hollow cavities inside the body were filled with blue latex to keep their form. In February 1994, the slicing finally began.

"We started from the least important part, so we'd get some practice," says Spitzer. "Podiatrists won't like this, but we started with the foot block." Using an electric circular saw positioned overhead, dubbed a cryomacrotome (cryo for frozen, macrotome because a slice used to make microscope slides is called a microtome), two team members shaved one-millimeter slivers off the block. They checked for tissue that wasn't cleanly cut, sprayed cross sections with alcohol, attached labels and color strips to keep color consistent when developing film, then took pictures with three cameras. Between slices, they refroze the block with dry ice. They tried to plane at intervals of four to ten minutes and work in shifts for twelve hour days. Predictably, that was overambitious.

"Everything broke," says Spitzer. "The computer that collected the pictures broke. The machine that stored them broke. All the cameras broke. The saws and mechanical devices broke. I had to solve a crisis every day." By the time they reached the head, it was summer, and with no air conditioning, the block was thawing too quickly. They limited cutting to six hours a day. In the end, it took nearly nine months to produce pictures of all 1,878 slices.

It was time to boot Jernigan up. The raw data—photographs, CAT scans and MRIs—took up fifteen gigabytes of space. When the

Visible Human Project began, that would have filled fifteen thousand floppy disks; today, it can fit on twenty-three CD-ROM disks. In November 1994, Jernigan started doing time in cyberspace. It takes two weeks to download the raw data from the Internet, but some seven hundred individuals and organizations worldwide have applied for a free license to use the material in applications ranging from animation to virtual testing of crash helmets to planning surgical procedures. Most use it, however, to create images of the body. It has taken eighteen months to reformat scans and pictures to create the images on these pages. The two-dimensional photographs of the slices had to be stacked like pieces of bread to form a loaf in three dimensions, allowing a viewer to fly through any part of the anatomy. "Most medical students only get to explore the insides of one cadaver," says Spitzer. "We now have a stunt patient. We can dissect it, put it back together and start all over again. Our man in the machine allows everyone to explore a real human body."

When the Visible Man was finished, Spitzer began on the Visible Woman, a fifty-nine-year-old Maryland resident who died in September 1993 of a blockage to the heart that didn't affect the body's appearance. (Her family doesn't want her name revealed.) Spitzer was able to produce almost three times as many cross sections of her: 5,189. He hopes that someday doctors will be able to examine virtual patients of any age, sex, race, and body type. Spitzer, like his father before him, plans to donate his own body to medical science. "You should get the same respect as if you donated a million dollars," he says. "I'd love it if I became a Visible Human." If that were to happen, however, they'd have to design a bigger MRI machine. And find somebody else to fix the cryomacrotome.

Jernigan can be found on the Internet through the National Library of Medicine at http://www.nlm.nih.gov.

JESSICA R. JOHNSTON

IV | Resisting Bodies

How do we learn about the body? The preceding
sections have explored the various social mechanisms through which the body is conceptualized and disciplined.
The introductions to each section included topics such as the
Western tradition of the mind/body dualism, the persuasiveness of
advertising, and the discipline of medicine and psychotherapy while
the readings have highlighted gender determinations, etiquette, race,
and education. All of these social systems seem to bear down on the
individual, forcing people to think about their bodies in certain ways
and compelling them to mold their bodies to particular ideals. These
institutional languages have been presented as overdetermined, that
is, as totally interconnected and permitting only the single dominant
interpretation. The combined force of these institutional languages
does not appear to allow human beings to think "outside" the discourses of their culture knowledge systems. In the United States, the
authority of medical advice is integrated with advertisements for
commodities. Education reinforces gender displays. Psychotherapy
strengthens the mind/body dualism. All these institutions are interconnected so that people seem programmed to perceive their own
and others' bodies in predetermined ways. This overdetermined
interaction between institutional directives is termed "discourse
determinism." The entwined nature of these knowledge structures
suggests a powerful source of influence on our conceptualizations of
our bodies. Yet is resistance possible? Is there a way to think "outside

the square" of cultural dictates? How does one think beyond cultural knowledge systems?

Theorists analyzing Michel Foucault's interpretation of social structures suggest we cannot. According to Foucaultian theorists (see Rabinow, 1984; Seidman, 1994; Sheridan, 1980; Shumway, 1992; Wuthnow, 1984), language is not merely a tool to express a person's ideas but it is a system of ideas that creates the preconditions for expression. We are born into these structures, and are shaped through them as we grow, develop, and learn. Our knowledge and experience of our bodies is set before we can speak. The available language and ideas within that language imprison everyone, even as a person may seek to use language as a tool for resisting those imprisoning forces. Our language determines what we think about our bodies, how we think about them, even how we think about challenging those received ideas about them. We may be cognitively aware of and able to talk about our experiences and ourselves, but it is only through the constructions of our language. This theoretical orientation rejects the concept of "human agency" as merely a language construction.

Other theorists challenge the perspective that "agency" is merely a language construction (for an excellent summary, see Lears, 1985). According to this opposing framework, humans are not passive, and language is not an all-powerful medium that simply passes directly into the private mind of the speaker/thinker. Indeed, language can be seen as "overpopulated," proposing that within language and its meanings and messages, there are traces left by other speakers, and by other worldviews. Language then brings together a diversity of contradictory ideas and concepts.

These entangled qualities of language are especially relevant to the disciplining of bodies. Within a hegemonic structure, language must be flexible and adaptable, able to preserve a certain indeterminacy and open-endedness in order to be useful within negotiations for control. As a result, each visual or verbal exchange can become a many-sided struggle over meaning. A good example of the struggle over meaning is found in Emily Martin's article in this section, "Body Narratives, Body Boundaries," in which she analyzes a video for high school students about human reproduction. Instead of analyzing just the text itself, she also examines both the dominant and alternative readings produced by the children. Medical advice, advertising, gender displays, and educational videos can be fields of contention where interpretations are open and varied. Even though language may be shaped by structures of power, it is full of ambiguities that cannot be reduced to single meanings. While there may be large, overarching patterns of culture, reducing language to one interpretation denies its use by individuals as they challenge and resist those patterns. Thus the language that constructs the body is available for many interpretations and meanings.

Similarly, the discussion of the structures of power inherent in language should not be reduced to a single monolithic "voice" or source. Reducing power to a single identifiable entity denies the segmented, discontinuous character of society. Though dominant values may penetrate various knowledge systems deeply and thoroughly, not all expressions and attitudes towards the body can be pigeonholed as deriving from one dominant conceptualization. The Foucaultian assumption of a monolithic social control apparatus suggests there is a straight line linking beliefs, intentions, actions, and effects. Yet, in medical encounters, in education, even in advertising agencies, there are conflicts, power struggles, and negotiations between people and their positions. Attributing a single mentality to large institutions fails to see resistance and transformations that operate therein.

A classic example of these types of contradictions is displayed within the American economy. Theorists have demonstrated its tendency to seek, as workers, people who are ideal "producers" while simultaneously seeking, as customers, people who are ideal "consumers," though the two types can be seen as conflicting with each other. Essentially, producers are people who work hard, save, postpone their pleasure, develop discipline, concern themselves with efficiency, and know how to discipline their time and subordinate personal considerations to getting the job done. Ideal customers, however, do not postpone their satisfaction. They spend their time and energies consuming, maximally indulging their desires for immediate gratification.

Jackson Lears and Richard Fox suggest that the change from a production economy to a consumption economy at the turn of the twentieth century was reflected in changing attitudes toward the body and health (Lears & Fox, 1983). The Victorian attitude toward health rested on assumptions of physical and psychic scarcity. Children as well as adults were warned to conserve their energies. Even babies faced "psychic ruin" if they became overexcited while at play. Lears and Fox suggest that this older form of a healthy lifestyle expressed the persistent production orientation within the dominant culture. Frequently connected with the combined health/production orientation were money metaphors, such as the possibility of "bankrupting health" or "investing in one's health," with an associated insistence on careful disciplining of resources. Yet, by the 1890s there was a growing sense that health might not be exclusively a matter of moderation. Alongside the prudential "scarcity therapy," an exuberant "abundance therapy" began to appear. Charging that people were only half-alive, abundance therapy promised to reach untapped reservoirs of energy and open the way to a richer, fuller life. Increasingly, Americans were told they should not hoard savings but that they should spend. They were told they no longer lived in a world of scarcity but in one of abundance, and that they must develop new values in keeping with that new status. The body now became a vehicle for pleasure and sensation, an object to be spent upon and enjoyed.

These underlying contradictions of the American cultural knowledge systems are major determinants of problems displayed in attitudes towards the body. Under the old ethic, self denial was assumed to have virtue for its own sake. Under the self-fulfillment ethic, self-denial made no sense. The body became a site of contention as individuals attempted to conform to structural ambiguities, to the cultural mandates of both production and consumption values.

The heritage of those contradictions is evident in discussions about contemporary body image disorders. Bulimics and the overweight are seen to embody these contradictions as they attempt to fulfill the opposing sides of this duality. Real-world articulations of people attempting to negotiate and follow these opposing mandates are developed more fully in this section's article by Pirkko Markula, "Firm but Shapely, Fit but Sexy, Strong but Thin: The Postmodern Aerobicizing Female Bodies." Living with and articulating the dualities of conflicting cultural mandates is at times confusing and can be brutal as people try to simultaneously straddle opposing directives.

The cultural models of control and release played out in our own bodily experiences should not be understood then in a unitary fashion. Concepts of bodies and of health do not simply replicate cohesive or unitary cultural categories. Cultural meanings are not only shared or given; they are fragmented and contested. They are contested because social life is full of contradictions.

Theorists suggest that while we may recognize these large social mandates as conflicted, we also need to acknowledge that our individualized perceptions of those mandates are dissimilar. Symbols and ideas that may seem common to the entire society are still filtered through individuals at different places within a hierarchically arranged social structure. Because of those hierarchical relations, and the concrete experiences associated with one's position within them, people's perceptions of similar symbols, events, and ideas will be different. Because of these various positions within society, people not only internalize dominant codes, values, or categories differently; they have the capacity to resist them. They can substitute their own meanings, transforming them, often putting to "subversive" use symbols intended for quite another purpose. Thus, the body and the concepts used to describe bodily experiences are vastly different depending on age, gender, ethnicity, race, sexual orientation, and past experiences. The symbols inherent in ideals of self-control and/or release, for example, are "polysemic," meaning that they are interpretations that can be contested, resisted, and utilized for a variety of purposes. The body is not only a site for discipline and training, release and pleasure. It is also a site for resistance to and transformation of those conflicted systems of meaning.

A classic example of power struggles within large institutions is the patient/doctor encounter and their negotiations over the patient's body. Section Three suggested that medical practitioners have power because of their seemingly expert knowledge and the corresponding monopoly and authority with which that knowledge base is maintained. Yet, several theorists suggest that conceptualizing the doctor/patient relationship as one of a sovereign-type power exercising control over a patient's body is too simplistic (see Armstrong, 1987, pp. 69–70). Although the power relationship within the doctor/patient relationship is weighted towards the doctor, the patient makes the decision whether to: seek a doctor's opinion in the first place; consult a standard physician or seek alternative therapies; continue treatment or stop; discharge him or herself from the hospital against the doctor's recommendations; deviate substantially from prescribed regimens concerning medication and diet; and so on. The patient is not merely a passive object, a body without a mind, an entity to be manipulated. Theorists suggest that analysis of the doctor/patient relationship needs to acknowledge that while doctors do have power, and that the language structure supports their position within the hierarchy, negotiations for control of the body can be altered by various hierarchical positions: is the doctor newly qualified, or outdated; is the doctor female, young, nonwhite; is the patient terminally ill; is the patient a doctor or nurse with medical knowledge? Social class, age, ethnicity, gender, and past experiences will influence the relationship, affecting both resistance and accommodation to medical dominance.

There are thus significant socio-structural tensions embodied within individuals. Institutional structures, such as medicine, psychotherapy, education, and advertising, even as they are interrelated, are still full of contradictions. While all combine mandates for self-monitoring, self-control, and self-discipline and can emphasize the interconnectedness of the institutional structures, the inherent conflicts within and between institutions allow "spaces" where individuals can utilize alternative language structures and challenge dominant interpretations. While internalized community standards operating through the individual generate the seeming invisibility and indirectness of social control, the conflict between and within the institutions allows challenges. It is these conflicts in the micro-mechanisms of power, complexly interrelated throughout medicine, psychotherapy, education, and consumer mandates, that play a pivotal role in the management of individuals' lives through their direct action on their own bodies.

Dominant cultural notions may shape our concepts of the body, but they do so in complex relationships with meanings that emerge from our own physical, emotional, and social experiences. Our experiences do not simply conform to cultural mandates. This tension between inner and outer reality is a crucial factor motivating human behavior and action. For example, efforts at self-control do not always generate the benefits to the body expected or promised. And rejecting attempts at self-control or self-discipline may not generate the debased results threatened by cultural mandates.

An example of this bodily control issue is the discipline inherent in the transformation of the body in both bodybuilding and dieting to lose weight. Many analyses of bodybuilding and dieting suggest the transformed body should be interpreted as passive, as merely conforming to social control mandates. The method of bodily construction reveals a person who is, according to Foucault, "the object and target of power" (Sheridan, 1980, p. 128). Within the transformation process, self-mastery is seemingly confused with obedience. Yet, the commercial culture suggests a body that achieves appearance and health ideals is self-motivated, reflective of individual power.

Despite attempts at conforming to the ideals of health and/or attractiveness, theorists suggest that most individuals never feel they have made it. The young, healthy, thin, fit body is promoted as free and independent, however, as Featherstone suggested in his article in Section Two, the maintenance of that body imprisons the individual in disciplinary regimes. The intensity with which Americans keep trying to transform their bodies is presented as evidence of the unnaturalness of the effort. Americans are clouded by an ideology so insistently proclaimed and so well internalized as "natural" and "normal." Can we conceptualize the overweight or out-of-shape then as more aware of and having "clear" vision? Are they resisting cultural mandates, and in that sense free? Or does power come from beating our bodies into the shape our minds insist on? Are the out-of-shape merely seduced by other cultural mandates?

That the body is the site for both control and release should not be surprising. The mandates of control and release are experienced physically. Sobriety and intoxication, dieting and bingeing, plastic surgery and cosmetic pharmacology all suggest a constant contradiction between social control mandates and experience at the level of the body. The body/experience interface is thus an inevitable site of ideological struggle.

People can articulate critical insights into their own oppression. Their insightful critiques of society are embedded in their discussion of themselves and their life worlds. But their perceptions and condemnations of the larger structure are usually screened through a vocabulary and language that succeed in reinforcing their subordination. As was suggested in the third section, most individuals within a hegemonic culture find it difficult to translate the outlook implicit in their experiences into a conception of the world that will challenge that hegemonic culture (Lears, 1985, p. 569). If discrepancies between the two are observed, the larger social system is rarely held accountable. Instead, individuals use the language and vocabulary of permissible discourse that focuses on the individual as the problem in need of correction.

But this filter of responsibility does not negate the insights into and critiques of the cultural system. The challenges may be redirected and shunted into other passive and acquiescent forms, but the evaluative judgments are not suppressed. In fact, alternatives to "normal" interpretations of embodied "facts" can be put forth. For example, the assignment of a negative social label to the body is not necessarily accepted by either the society or the deviant. Organizations representing the blind, diabetics, paraplegics, and the overweight attempt to resist negative labeling by offering a more positive image of their lifestyles. By promoting themselves as "close to normal," such as the blind skiing or the obese dating, they identify themselves with cultural definitions of "acceptable."

Yet can identifying with cultural definitions of acceptability really be seen as an alternative to "normal" interpretations of the body or a critique of the social system? In that these groups are conforming to and displaying themselves in accordance with normal definitions, they are not rejecting the dominant cultural mandates. They are instead articulating their acceptability within various medical, therapeutic, and commodified visions of mental and physical health. They challenge negative labeling of their bodies through promotion of their acceptance of and agreement with chosen dominant value structures. So even those whose bodies are labeled negatively by society support the structures in their attempt to promote a more positive image of their lifestyle. They too want to be interpreted as "normal."

This promotion of normality even by those who are defined as abnormal is the living example of hegemony. Even those whose lives are constrained by the definitions of a "normal" body, give their support and their consent to the structures that exclude them. Even as they challenge the dominant definitions of their bodies as diseased, sick, or disabled, they attempt to conform to those same structures.

So, why does physically transforming the body usually bestow a new assertiveness and self-confidence to the individual? Do people achieve some political benefit from following cultural mandates? Or is the attempt to gain "control" of one's body a diversion from the real political concerns that people face? Is taking responsibility for one's body through health or fitness or self-care a political act in itself? Or are attempts at individual lifestyle transformations precisely what "power" requires of us at this historical moment?

Exploring the strategies by which individuals create meaning in interaction with and in resistance to dominant culture is currently one of the most productive strands of culture studies. The role of the essays in this final section is to show the viewpoint of those who challenge dominant culture interpretations of their bodies. These essays explore hidden knowledges and resistances as people confront dominant culture mandates and interpretations of their bodies. These essays also show how decisions that appear to be freely made are actually affected by and reproduce the social structure. Both resistances to, and accommodations of, the social structure are displayed as people confront the structures that determine their lives.

The point of analyzing these visions and the corresponding embodied struggles is to demonstrate how culture is a process of making meanings in which people actively participate. Assuming that culture is not a set of preformed meanings handed down to and imposed upon people, suggests the need to study the interpretive resources at the disposal of individual members of society. Analyzing the ideological contradictions and the embodied resistances can help all of us make meaningful sense of matters by redefining our relations with our bodies, with one another, and with the hierarchies of power that attempt to structure much of our lives. Resistance then is not futile. It is necessary for understanding the elements of social control. While Foucault suggests that rational understanding does not free us, it does provide choices and alternatives to the effects of those discourses.

EMILY MARTIN

13 Body Narratives, Body Boundaries

We are taught about the body in various institutional settings. The big question is, how do people
get outside the dominant, preferred interpretations of the body to resist "institutional" perspectives? How can children be taught to counter these
messages? Emily Martin examines the gendered
messages in an educational film about human
reproduction. She also investigates one successful
attempt to deconstruct those gendered interpretations attributed to sperm and eggs. A group of
high school students learn to question the taken-
for-granted assumptions inherent in the film.
These questions become a way to resist dominant
and overdetermined messages about the body.

My own work looks at scientific knowledge as
one purveyor of a view of the world from a par-
ticular vantage point. This knowledge is often able to masquerade as
"natural fact," a powerful means by which its vision of hierarchical
human relationships is learned and internalized. I am interested in
imagery conveyed in various ways—scientific and otherwise—which
depicts the body (in ever more fantastic magnification), and in how
visual and print media used to convey scientific information to the
public (ever more affordably) function within social processes. I
have been doing participant observation in a biological research lab,
participating as a volunteer in a community health education organization focused on HIV infection issues, and carrying out general

From Emily Martin, "Body Narratives, Body Boundaries" in *Cultural Studies*, ed.
Lawrence Grossberg, Cary Nelson, and Paula Treichler (New York: Routledge,
1992), 411–19. © 1992 by Routledge, Inc. Reprinted by permission of Routledge,
Inc.

fieldwork and interviews on health and work in three urban neighborhoods. Today I will focus on a particular incident that occurred in one of these urban neighborhoods, in which a group of young people watched a recent film about human reproduction called "The Miracle of Life." Before I describe that incident, let me introduce the kind of imagery and metaphors that occur throughout biology teaching materials used in textbooks as well as more popular publications, a lot of which is carried through into the film.

At a fundamental level, both male and female reproductive organs are metaphorically depicted in all major scientific textbooks as systems for the production of valuable things.[1] In the case of women, the monthly cycle is seen medically as preeminently designed to produce eggs, prepare a suitable place for them to be fertilized and grown, all, of course, to the end of making babies. Extolling production means that menstruation, which is seen as what occurs when the egg is not fertilized, carries with it an overlay of a productive system that has failed to be productive. Medically, menstruation is described as the "debris" of the uterine lining which is the result of necrosis or death of tissue. It also carries the idea of production gone awry, making products of no use, not to specification, unsalable, wasted, scrap. An illustration that accompanies a widely used medical text shows menstruation as a chaotic disintegration of the form, matching the many texts which describe it as: "ceasing" "dying," "losing," "denuding," and "expelling" (Guyton, 1984, p. 624).[2] These are not neutral terms, but ones that convey failure and dissolution.

In contrast, processes in male reproductive physiology are evaluated quite differently. In one of the same texts that sees menstruation as failed production, we learn that, "The mechanisms which guide the *remarkable* cellular transformation from spermatid to mature sperm remain uncertain. . . . Perhaps the most *amazing* characteristic of spermatogenesis is its *sheer magnitude*: the normal human male may manufacture several hundred million sperm per day" (Vander, Sherman, and Luciano, 1980, pp. 483–84, emphasis added). In the classic, *Medical Physiology*, edited by Vernon Mountcastle (1980), the comparison is explicit: "Whereas the female *sheds* only a single gamete each month, the seminiferous tubules *produce* hundreds of millions of sperm each day" (p. 1624, emphasis added). The female author of another text marvels at the length of the microscopic seminiferous tubules, which, if uncoiled and placed end to end, "would span almost one-third of a mile!" she comments, "In an adult male these structures produce millions of sperm cells each day" and wonders "How is this *feat* accomplished?" (Solomon, 1983, p. 678). None of these texts expresses such intense enthusiasm about any female processes, and it is surely no accident that the "remarkable" process of making sperm involves precisely what menstruation does not in the medical view: production of something deemed valuable.[3]

One could argue that menstruation should not be expected to elicit the same kind of response spermatogenesis does because it is not a biologically analogous process. The proper female analogy to spermatogenesis would be ovulation. Yet ovulation does not merit enthusiasm in these texts either. This could be partly because textbook descriptions stress that all the ovarian follicles containing ova are already present at birth. Far from being *produced* as sperm are, they seem merely to sit on the shelf, as it were, slowly degenerating and aging like overstocked inventory:

> At birth, normal human ovaries contain an estimated one million follicles [each], and no new ones appear after birth. Thus, in marked contrast to the male, the newborn female already has all the germ cells she will ever have. (Vander, Sherman, and Luciano, 1985, pp. 567–68)

What is striking about this description is the "marked contrast" that is set up between male and female, the male who continuously produces fresh germ cells and the female who has stockpiled germ cells by birth and is faced with the continuous degeneration of this material. The same goes for the egg and the sperm themselves. Even though each contributes almost exactly half of the genetic stuff to the new individual in fertilization, it is astounding how different their roles seem and how "femininely" the egg behaves and how "masculinely" the sperm.

The egg is seen as large and passive. It does not *move* or *journey*, but passively "is transported," "is swept" (Guyton, 1984, p. 619; Mountcastle, 1980, p. 1609), or even, in a popular account, "drifts" (Miller and Pelham, 1984) along the fallopian tube. In utter contrast, sperm are small, "streamlined," and inevitably active. They "deliver" their genes to the egg, "activate the developmental program of the egg" (Alberts, et al., 1983, p 796) and have a "velocity" which is always remarked on (Ganong, 1975, p. 322). Their tails are "strong" and efficiently powered (Alberts, et al., 1983, p 796). Together with the forces of ejaculation, they can "propel the semen into the deepest recesses of the vagina" (Guyton, 1984, p. 615). For this they need "energy," "fuel" (Solomon, 1983, p. 683), so that with a "whiplash-like motion and strong lurches" (Vander, Sherman, and Luciano, 1985, p. 580) they can "burrow through the egg coat" (Alberts, et al., 1983, p. 796) and "penetrate" it.[4]

In our cultural tradition, passivity is a quintessential female attribute, activity a male one. So one might imagine there is some cultural overlay on how egg and sperm are seen. But there is more. The egg is hidden behind a protective barrier, the egg coat, sometimes called its "vestments," a term used for sacred, religious dress. In addition the egg is said to have a "corona," a crown (Solomon, 1983, p. 700), and is accompanied by "attendant cells" (Beldecos, et al., 1988, pp. 61–76). The egg is evidently special, holy, set apart and above. As such the egg could potentially play queen to the sperm as king. In actuality her passivity dominates her royalty, which means she must depend on sperm to rescue her. Sperm have a "mission" (Alberts, et al., 1983, p. 796), which is to "move through the female genital tract in quest of the ovum" (Guyton, 1984, p. 613). An extravagant popular book, *The Facts of Life*, coauthored by Jonathan Miller (1984), the producer of the BBC series, "The Body in Question," has it that the sperm carries out a "perilous journey" into the "warm darkness," where some fall away "exhausted," but other "survivors" "assault" the egg, the successful candidates "surrounding the prize" (p. 7). The journey is perilous in part because it takes place in the vagina, which is called a "hostile environment."

But the egg's journey is also perilous: "once released from the supportive environment of the ovary, an egg will die within hours unless rescued by a sperm" (Alberts, et al, 1983, p. 804). The way this is phrased stresses the fragility and dependency of the egg, even though it is acknowledged elsewhere in this very text that sperm also only live a few hours (p. 801).[5]

In one photograph from the *National Geographic*, sperm are "masters of subversion": "human sperm cells seek to penetrate an ovum. Foreigners in a hostile body, they employ several strategies to survive their mission. . . ." (Jaret, 1986, p. 731). Sometimes the egg has her own defenses. In a "Far Side" cartoon, the egg is seen as a housewife besieged by clever sperm who try to get a foot inside the door. Sperm as postman says "Package for you to sign for, Ma'am."

Sperm as phone repairman says "Need to check your lines, Ma'am," and sperm as insurance salesman says "Mind if I step inside?"

There is another way sperm can be made to loom in importance over the egg, despite their small size. The article in which an electron micrograph of sperm and an egg appeared is called "Portrait of a Sperm" (Nilsson, 1975). Of course, it is harder to photograph microscopic sperm than eggs, which are just large enough to see with the naked eye. But surely the use of the term "portrait," a term associated with the powerful and the wealthy, is significant. Eggs have only micrographs or pictures, not portraits.

As far as I know there is only one cultural representation in Western civilization of sperm as weak and timid instead of strong and powerful. This occurs in Woody Allen's movie, *Everything You Ever Wanted to Know About Sex (But Were Afraid to Ask)*. Woody Allen, playing the part of a reluctant sperm inside a man's body, is afraid to go out into the darkness, afraid of contraceptive devices, and afraid of winding up on the ceiling if the man is masturbating. In biology texts, if there is an association between strong sperm and virility, it is never directly stated. But Allen makes explicit the link between weak sperm and the impotence of the man whose body he is in.

After getting to this point in my survey of scientific and popular materials, I looked extensively at very recent research coming out of labs investigating the sperm and the egg. To summarize briefly, the views I've just outlined have been overturned: scientists have found that the forward propulsive force of the sperm's tail is extremely weak, so that rather than strongly swimming forward with purpose, the sperm actually flail side to side, swim in circles, mill around. The current picture is that adhesive molecules on the surface of the egg capture the sperm and hold it fast; otherwise, its sideways motions would lead it to escape and swim away. (As an aside, nothing is simple: in this new research, the egg comes to be described as an engulfing female aggressor, dangerous and terrifying.)[6]

Nevertheless current scientific textbooks and journal articles continue to perpetuate the old stereotype. An article from a recent issue of the journal *Cell* has the sperm making, not a heroic fight for his love, but an "existential decision" to penetrate her. "Sperm are cells with a limited behavioral repertoire, one that is directed toward fertilizing eggs. To execute the decision to abandon the haploid state, sperm swim to an egg and there acquire the ability to effect membrane fusion" (Shapiro, 1987, p. 293–94). Is this perhaps the corporate manager's version of the sperm's activities—*executing decisions* while fraught with dismay over difficult options, limited choices carrying very high risk?

Other recent scientific work also draws on virile images, but ones that are working class rather than executive. In research designed to help couples with sperm-related infertility, methods are being developed to force an opening in the zona, the outermost covering of the egg, and so permit the sperm to "penetrate" it. In "Zona Blasters: There's More Than One Way to Crack an Egg," a review article in *Science News*, we find an unrevised version of the saga of egg and sperm:

> The microscopic human egg floats in its fluid-filled shell. Suddenly, thousands of tiny sperm bombard it. Lashing their tails to power their entry, they bore into the shell, a tough glycoprotein coating known as the zona pellucida. One particularly vigorous sperm pierces the zona barrier, setting off a chemical reaction that shuts the others out. Then, if all goes well, the winning sperm fertilizes the egg and the miracle of human life ensues. (Fackelmann, 1990, p. 376)

But trouble arises, given this view, when "the sperm can't whip their tails hard enough to bore through the tough outer shell" (p. 376). To handle this cause of infertility, "scientists are now developing imaginative methods of cracking, blasting or drilling tiny passageways through the zona envelope" (p. 376). In line with this imagery, the cover of this issue of *Science News*, captioned "Sperm at Work," shows a cartoon of three sperm ferociously attacking an egg with a jackhammer, a pickaxe, and a sledgehammer.[7] The undertone of violence in both words and picture scarcely needs comment.

And the same goes for popular publications that purport to represent the latest scientific knowledge. In a recent issue of *Life Magazine*, the dynamic activities of sperm and the passive response of the egg are presented yet again. In "The First Days of Creation," we read, "Although few will finish, about 250 million sperm start the 5–7 inch journey from the vagina to the uterus and then to the fallopian tubes where an egg may be waiting" (Milsson, 1990, p. 26). Two hours later, "like an eerie planet floating through space, a woman's egg or ovum . . . has been ejected by one of her ovaries into the fallopian tube. Over the next several hours sperm will begin beating their tails vigorously as they rotate like drill bits into the outer wall of the egg" (p. 28).

Other popular materials also do their part: the recent film *Look Who's Talking* begins with a simulation of a hugely magnified egg floating, drifting, gently bouncing along the fallopian tube of a woman who is in the midst of making love with a man. The soundtrack is "I Love You So" by the Chantals. Then we see, also hugely magnified, the man's sperm barreling down the tunnel of her vagina to the tune of "I Get Around" by the Beach Boys. The sperm are shouting and calling to each other like a gang of boys: "Come on, follow me, I know where I am, keep up, come on you kids, I've got the map." Then as the egg moves into view, they shout, "This is it, yeah, this is definitely it, this is the place, Jackpot, right here, come on, dig in you kids." And when one sperm finally pushes hard enough to open a slit in the egg (a slit that looks remarkably like a vulva), that sperm (as his whole self is swallowed up) cried out, "Oh, oh, oh, I'm in!"

When I got to this point in my research, I was already wondering what social effects such vivid imagery might be having. I thought perhaps this imagery might encourage us to imagine that what results from the interaction of egg and sperm—a fertilized egg—is the result of intentional "human" action *at the cellular level*. In other words, whatever the intentions of the human couple, in this microscopic "culture," a cellular "bride" (or "*femme fatale*") and a cellular "groom" (or her victim) make a cellular baby. Rosalind Petchesky (1987) makes the point that through visual representations such as sonograms, we are given "*images* of younger and younger, and tinier and tinier, fetuses being 'saved.'" This leads to "the point of viability being 'pushed back' *indefinitely*" (pp. 263–92). Endowing egg and sperm with intentional action, a key aspect of personhood in our culture, lays the foundation for the point of viability being pushed back to the moment of fertilization.

Why would this matter? Because endowing cells with personhood may play a part in the breaking down of boundaries between the self and the world, and a pushing back of the boundary of what constitutes the inviolable self.[8] In other words, whereas at an earlier time, the skin might have been regarded as the border of the individual self, now these microscopic cells are seen as tiny individual selves. This means that the "environment" of the egg and sperm, namely the human body, is fair game for invasion by medical scrutiny and intervention. It is not, of course, that the interior of our bodies was not the object of study and treatment until now. But we may be experiencing an intensification of those activities (made more potent by state support) which are understood as protecting the "rights," viability, or integrity of cellular entities.[9] It would not be that endowing cells with personhood by means of imagery in biology automatically *causes* intensification of initiatives in the legislature and elsewhere that enable protection of these new "persons." Rather, I am suggesting that this imagery may have a part in creating a general predisposition to think of the world in a certain way that can play an important role whenever legal and other initiatives do take place.

It is possible that in the 1990s what was the patient (or person) has itself begun to become *an environment* for a new core self, which exists at the cellular level. This change may be adding to our willingness to focus ever more attention on the internal structures of this tiny cellular self, namely its genes.[10] In turn, such a shift in attention may encourage us to permit dramatic changes in the "environment" of the genes in the name of maintaining their welfare.[11]

My thinking had gotten to this point, when, by one of the unpredictable twists of fieldwork, an unusual opportunity presented itself. It came about through John Marcellino, a largely self-educated man who is a community leader in the neighborhood he grew up in, a predominantly white neighborhood experiencing massive unemployment, a nearly 100 percent high school dropout rate, crime, health problems, and other adjuncts of persistent poverty. Several years ago, through John Marcellino's leadership and substantial community support, this neighborhood acquired—as a mortgage holder— a small rowhouse which it called the Community Survival Center. The center is the location for a food co-op; an alternative high school, where students who have dropped out of regular school can prepare for their high school equivalency degree; community meetings of various kinds; and liaisons with other groups they see as allies and as sharing the same conditions of life: residents of poor black urban neighborhoods, prisoners in Baltimore jails, and Native Americans in Baltimore or from other areas.

The group of high school students studying at the center had just watched a videotape about human biology called "The Incredible Human Machine." John (as they call him) and the kids (as he calls them) were very excited about the video and full of talk about it. So, building on that interest, we arranged to bring another biology video, called "The Miracle of Life," to the center. The class agreed that we would watch the video together, and then have a discussion, which we could tape record.

The video we took is made by Lennart Nilsson, one of the foremost purveyors of cell electron micrographs into popular media. It contains all the imagery I discussed a moment ago, the quest of the sperm for the egg, the thrust and penetration of the sperm, the hostile environment of the vagina which the sperm has to overcome, the passivity of the egg and the activity of the sperm, and so on. The film starts with a human couple in a swimming pool, and then moves inside the body. For fifty minutes, only the activities of cells and internal organs are shown, in technicolor fiberoptic photography, in real-time movement, and, for cells, in huge magnification. We see the egg released from the ovary and drifting down the fallopian tubes; we see sperm being produced in the testis, traveling down the various male ducts, being ejaculated inside the vagina. We then see the sperm struggling to travel up the vagina, through the cervix, to reach the goal—the egg. We see successful fertilization, implantation, and the growth of the fertilized egg in great detail into an embryo, through all the stages of pregnancy. Finally, in a shocking shift of perspective, in the last five minutes of the film we see a view of a woman in labor, from the perspective of the foot of her bed. She is undraped and unshaved, her husband at her shoulder. She pushes strongly, and the baby's head emerges, as often happens, purple, wet, slightly bloody, and covered with mucus and white vernix. The mother pushes a couple more times and the baby slides out altogether.

What I want to focus on is the use John and the students made of this film, remembering both my initial questions about the possibilities of envisioning other worlds, and my worries about the ideological effects of biological images. At first I thought my worries were entirely justified. During the movie John and the kids seemed entranced with the imagery of cells. There were innumerable exclamations of wonder and awe at this cell life. In contrast, the scene of the mother delivering her baby was met with strongly expressed teenage revulsion, mock vomiting, exclamations of "Gross!," and shrieks of disgust and dismay.

But this was before the discussion following the film. In the discussion, John and the students managed to analyze the implicit metaphors in the film, as well or better than any ethnographer, and then lead the rest of the class to see their implications. First John focused on the diversion in the film from the human environment to the environment of cells.

> *John:* Does it . . . change the way you might look at your-self or at other people?
>
> *The kids:* It kind of makes me feel bad for drinking and everything 'cause you see all the good things and like the miracles that's going on inside your body: and it kind of makes you feel bad for like messing it up when you drink, you know, all that stuff.
>
> *John:* That's what I was wondering, too . . . the only part that they tied in like *life* to that, or like *the life we live* to that, is when they were talking about the testicle in the man and heat, they talked about clothes, the environment and all that.
>
> *The kids:* Make sure you don't wear tight jeans.—It *was* dis-torted.
>
> *John:* Well I wish they could show . . . the woman: and all the stuff that a woman goes through; they only showed, you know, how it affected the sperm. And you know, like you say, if you drink here, or if, you, or like. . . .
>
> *The kids:* Drugs, drugs affect the baby.
>
> *John:* You know, maybe, like cleaning out the house, all the poisons that you have, you know, and when you clean your house and a woman breathes that in, how does that affect it and that kind of stuff.

The film focuses on boundaries within the body; John focuses on boundaries between the person and "the life we live." He continuously encourages the students to state where they can exercise agency.

Then the group takes on directly the implications of seeing embryos in the round, alive and moving at every stage of development.

> *John:* How many people thought about abortion?
>
> *Female student:* I did, 'cause I mean I never realized that the baby . . . has hands and even other things at that time, at eight weeks. And that kind of makes me

feel bad, I mean, but I guess it's somebody's own personal decision to make, but I personally don't believe in it, especially now, I feel more stronger about it.

John acknowledges her feelings but denies the film necessarily leads to this conclusion: "But you felt that way before you watched this." After some minutes of discussion, she agrees with him. She has her opinion but she had reached it independently of the film.

Next they tackle the metaphorical depiction of female-male relations in the guise of egg-sperm relations. During the movie itself, when the narrator described the hostile environment of the vagina, and showed how the woman's immune system tries to attack the sperm in the vagina, John blurted out "Just like our social studies!" Now, following up, he asks the class,

John: Did it raise any questions for you, watching it?

The kids: I never really knew they fought each other.—It was like revolutionary war.

John: What made you think it was like a war?

The kids: 'Cause it said it in the movie, they started fighting . . . when the man's semen, the cells and everything, they went into the woman, the acids and stuff was killing it off and they all had to stick together so it wouldn't kill them.

John: But it really made it seem like you're invading. I mean didn't it give you that impression? I mean you're watching and it goes into the hostile environment, like very aggressive, you know . . . like an invasion and you look at it and you go, damn, you know that's pretty serious. Because it isn't the way you think about . . . when you think about a baby you don't think about invasion, or it coming out of an invasion, you think about it coming together. At least that's the way I always thought about it.

The kids: Yeah you do, the boy and the girl meeting . . . —No, it seemed like the girl's egg was trying to hide from it or something. . . .

John: Yeah, it was trying to hide. It had all these defense mechanisms it said, the girl's got one egg and the guy's got, you know, three million sperm going

after it. You know attacking it, and she has all
these defenses and it . . . really made it seem like
the conception or the coming together was a hostile act but maybe a good thing comes out of it. It
sure made it seem like they weren't friends.

John and the group see these metaphors, jolt them into consciousness and so rob them of their power to naturalize social conventions.

Later I ask John how it would have been to see the movie without sound.

"If you look at that *without* the voice, like if we watched it the
first time without a voice or something and then the second time
with, I think you'd probably tell a different story, than looking at it
like an invading army . . . it seemed like there was this battalion, like
T.V. or something, you know. A mission, like . . . here's this army
and we're going after it and all this stuff, who's going to get through,
who's going to catch the one, you know. But I think it would be different if you watched it without the sound."

In Foucault's (1980) analysis resistance is usually held within
the boundary of power. This is partly because he stresses how techniques of power such as the gaze are taken on by the subject: "a gaze
which each individual under its weight will end by interiorizing to
the point that he is his own overseer, each individual thus exercising this surveillance over, and against, himself" (p. 155). Such resistance as there is is like the resistance of copper wire to an electric
current flowing through it, sometimes higher, sometimes lower, but
always enabling the current to flow along.

Foucault has a point: the production and dissemination of these
images has us thinking about the life of cells inside us, whether we
will or no. But if we can, as Marx thought, erect a structure in imagination before we erect it in reality, we can erect an imaginary structure around something like this film and frame it differently, jarring
it into another significance. This process amounts to redefining what
counts as political, moving "science education" from the "exposition
of natural facts" to revealing it as the imposition of a particular view
of the world.

In *Outline of a Theory of Practice*, Bourdieu (1977) chides
anthropologists for imagining that members of a culture who have
"practical mastery" of daily life operate as the ethnographer has to,
by means of maps and rules.

"Culture" is sometimes described as a *map*; it is the analogy which occurs to an outsider who has to find his way around in a foreign landscape and who compensates for his lack of practical mastery, the prerogative of the native, by the use of a model of all possible routes. (p. 2)

But although introducing this assumption into our description of a culture's daily life would be "pernicious," it would be equally pernicious to *miss* places, especially in stratified societies, where people deliberately introduce this kind of abstraction. Bourdieu describes the ethnographer this way:

In taking up a point of view on the action, withdrawing from it in order to observe it from above and from a distance, he constitutes practical activity as an *object of observation and analysis, a representation.* (p. 2)

But what happened at the Community Survival Center, I would argue, is that the group viewed a particular example of scientific discourse about the body from a distance, constituted it as an object of observation, drew a map to guide a way relatively unharmed through it. In a sense they are and see themselves as "outsiders who have to find their way around a foreign landscape," the landscape of the scientific body.

"The same institutions that legitimate the political economic domination of one class or gender simultaneously and contradictorily create the space for the expression of opposing discourses" (Gal, 1989 p. 360). In the case I have discussed, such a space was created first by the mass and variety of the materials that are produced for the dissemination of scientific information, materials that can give people a language they can use to talk *about* scientific images, even as they disseminate them. It was created secondly by the community's ownership of a space set apart from state schools and dedicated to enabling collective organization for the survival of threatened communities, in which such talk could take place.

There is a danger that I have created working-class heroes in the form of John and his community, heroes invested with a liberal humanist subjectivity and agency, consciousness, reason, and freedom (O'Hanlon, 1988). I might be trying to invest these heroes with the guts to stand up in a kind of virile strength against the forces which make my coffee-table authors, writing about the end of everything, knuckle under, thus creating these heroes in the image of what is lacking in a part of the world close to me. As a political role for ethnography this would probably be better than silence in the face of intellectual publications that foster a sense of inevitability in the face of the forces of global capitalism.

In conclusion, the incident I have discussed shows how scientific knowledge of the body, its dissemination enabled by new technologies, comes into contact with diverse interests and sites of resistance which "fracture and constrain it even as it exerts its conforming power" (O'Hanlon, 1988 p. 223). With Rosalind O'Hanlon, we can take issue with the "Swiss cheese" theory of hegemony which assumes that resistance can only crawl through the holes left by the incomplete imposition of hegemony. Instead we can argue that "hegemony does not spring fully-formed into being to be followed by a resistance which must always operate within its pregiven confines" (p. 223). By tracing the markings of the processes by which resistance is built into the construction of the hegemonic, in places like the Community Survival Center, we can see that there are many coexisting and contending knowledges of the body.

NOTES

1. The textbooks I consulted for this paper are the main ones used in classes for undergraduate premedical students or medical students, or held on library reserve for these classes, over the past few years at The Johns Hopkins University. Although this does not represent a complete survey of all existing textbooks, it does include all of the most widely used and highly regarded texts at universities like Johns Hopkins.
2. Mary Ellman (1968, pp. 74–78) characterizes the feminine stereotype of formlessness.
3. For elaboration of these points, see Martin (1987).
4. All biology texts quoted above.
5. For a literary version of some of these themes, see Barth (1968).
6. For a description of this research and references to relevant publications, see Martin (1991).
7. For another version of this story see Leary (1990).
8. In these remarks I have been greatly helped by conversations with Barbara Duden.
9. Court-ordered restrictions on a pregnant woman's activities to protect her fetus, refusal of abortion, fetal surgery, and amniocentesis, are all various facets of this process (Arditti, Klein, and Minden [1984]; Goodman [1987]; Lewin [1987]; Irwin and Jordan [1987].
10. Evelyn Fox Keller (1987) discusses how emphasis on individualism operates in biology to hold attention on genetic structures.
11. To cite only one recently patented method, a man's sperm can be screened and then "washed" to remove all those sperm containing a gene

complex encoding the human leukocyte antigens (HLA), which increase the susceptibility of the individual to certain diseases. This technique obviously profoundly affects and fragments the act of sexual intercourse for both men and women, replacing it with masturbation followed by chemical operations on the sperm and then artificial insemination (Bryant, 1987).

REFERENCES

Alberts, Bruce et al. (1983) *Molecular Biology of the Cell.* New York: Garland.

Beldecos, A. et al. (1988) "The Importance of Feminist Critique for Contemporary Biology." *Hypatia* 3, pp. 61–76.

Bourdieu, Pierre (1977) *Outline of a Theory of Practice.* Trans. R. Nice. Cambridge: Cambridge U. Press.

Fackelmann, Kathy (1990) "Zona Blasters." *Science News* 138 (24), pp. 376–79.

Foucault, Michel (1980) *Power/Knowledge: Selected Interviews and Other Writings: 1972–77.* C. Gordon (ed). Trans. C. Gordon, L. Marshall, J. Mepham, K. Soper. New York: Pantheon.

Gal, Susan (1989) "Language and Political Economy." *Annual Reviews of Anthropology* 18, pp. 345–67.

Ganong, William (1975) *Review of Medical Physiology,* 7th ed. Los Altos, CA: Lange Medical Publications.

Guyton, Arthur C. (1984) *Physiology of the Human Body,* 6th ed. Philadelphia: Saunders College Publishing.

Jaret, Peter (1986) "Our Immune System: The Wars Within." *National Geographic* 169 (6), pp. 701–35.

Miller, Jonathan & David Pelham (1984) *The Facts of Life.* New York: Viking Press.

Mountcastle, Vernon B. (1980) *Medical Physiology.* Vol 2. 14th ed. London: The C. V. Mosby Co.

Nilsson, Lennart (1975) "A Portrait of the Sperm." In *The Functional Anatomy of the Spermatozoan.* B. Afzelius (ed). New York: Pergamon, pp. 79–82.

O'Hanlon, Rosalind (1988) "Recovering the Subjects: Subaltern Studies and Histories of Resistance in Colonial South Asia." *Modern Asian Studies* 22 (1), pp. 189–224.

Petchesky, Rosalind (1987) "Fetal Images: The Power of Visual Culture in the Politics of Reproduction." *Feminist Studies* 13 (2), pp. 263–92.

Shapiro, Bennett M. (1987) "The Existential Decision for a Sperm." *Cell* 49, pp. 293–94.

Solomon, Eldra Pearl (1983) *Human Anatomy and Physiology.* New York: CBS College Publishing.

Vander, Arthur, James Sherman & Dorothy Luciano (1985) *Human Physiology: The Mechanics of Body Function.* 4th ed. New York: McGraw Hill.

PIRKKO MARKULA

14 Firm but Shapely, Fit but Sexy, Strong but Thin

The Postmodern Aerobicizing Female Bodies

The media send conflicting messages about appropriate body transforming activities for women. Pirkko Markula both analyzes these media messages and interviews women about how they negotiate the conflicts. Women do not passively accept media standards as their ideal. Instead, Markula demonstrates how women both critique the standards and ridicule themselves for attempting to follow those standards. The women's voices highlight both the overdetermined meanings produced by modern institutions and the attempts of individuals' resistance to that power. The question, though, remains: Is their resistance futile?

Introduction: The Feminine Beauty Ideal

She is fit . . . she's got an incredible body, she is completely tight, she has no fat on her body. (Anna)

Popular women's magazines are saturated with images of beautiful, thin, and tight models. These polished images are often accompanied

From Pirkko Markula, "Firm but Shapely, Fit but Sexy, Strong but Thin: The Postmodern Aerobicizing Female Bodies," *Sociology of Sport Journal* 12, no. 4 (1995): 424–31, 434–53. Reprinted by permission of Human Kinetics Publishers and the author.

with advice on how we readers can achieve a body that resembles these images. When the magazines motivate us to work toward the model look, they provide us with an opportunity for a positive change: to obtain our best body ever.

Many feminist scholars, however, consider this glossy festival of feminine beauty a disservice to women. They point out that women's bodies come in a variety of shapes and weights. Paradoxically, the media portray only thin and tight models. Therefore, these scholars conclude, this fashion ideal is oppressive precisely because of its singularity: If only slim and toned women are attractive, most women with normal figures are classified as unattractive (e.g., Bartky, 1988; Bordo, 1990; Coward, 1985; Martin, 1987; Spitzack, 1990; Wolf, 1990). Consequently, to look attractive in this society, the majority of us have to engage in activities—like dressing, applying makeup, dieting, exercising, or, most drastically, reconstructive surgery—to mask or alter our body shapes. Because the sole purpose of these practices is to change our bodies to resemble the narrowly defined beauty ideal, many feminists deem them as vehicles of oppression (e.g., Bartky, 1988; Bordo, 1989; Cole, 1993; Martin, 1989; Wolf, 1990).

Regardless of the feminist opposition to such practices, many women still engage in these potentially degrading activities. For example, they continue to read women's magazines for beauty tips or exercise to lose weight. Can one simply assume that most women are unaware of how they contribute to their own suppression through their everyday behavior? Or is a woman's everyday life a more complex phenomenon? Perhaps one's behavior is not purely a function of ignorance or lack of education. Although several researchers have examined the discourses surrounding feminine practices, few studies examine how individual women experience their bodies in everyday life. In this paper, therefore, I plan to investigate how women encounter and sense the body ideal in one potentially oppressive female activity, aerobics. I map women's body experiences within aerobics through an ethnographic study. Similar to other feminist scholars, I examine the body ideal, but I limit myself to the exercise context. Furthermore, I am interested in how women react to this body ideal. Are women single-mindedly occupied with improving their bodies in aerobics classes? Or do they celebrate their own figures ignoring the ideal imposed on them by the mass media? Or do they struggle to disregard the image but, at the same time, exercise to reshape their bodies?

First, however, I survey the literature examining women's need to become thinner by dieting and to become tighter by exercising. This journey will lead to my analysis of what kind of body ideal aerobics promotes and an interpretation of what some aerobicizing women think of this ideal.

"No Fat on Her Body"

Several writers have examined women's dieting in today's society (Arveda, 1991; Bordo, 1989, 1990; Chernin, 1981; Imm, 1989; Spitzack, 1990). Their findings suggest that women in general are more obsessed with dieting, body weight, and slimness than men are and that women's ideal slenderness also seems to be more narrowly defined than men's (Arveda, 1991; Bordo, 1990; Cole, 1993). Women diet to obtain the desired extremely slender body rather than accept the natural dimensions of their own bodies. Pamela Imm (1989) suggests that many women participate in aerobics because they are unhappy with their body shape and feel fat. She points out that particularly women who exercise excessively (six or more hours per week) view their bodies negatively although they are not heavier than the other participants. Why are women required to be so thin? Why do we submit to rigid, constant dieting regimes?

Carol Spitzack (1990) examines women's dieting practices from a Foucaultian perspective. She locates women's body reduction within the net of disciplining discursive power. Her main argument is that women accept the disciplining body control (diet) because it is masked under promises of liberation. In other words, women are persuaded to believe that after they lose weight their lives suddenly change and they can pursue new challenges, unobtainable earlier due to their excess weight. However, Spitzack (1990) proceeds, this voice of liberation only masks a continuous control over women by the dominant patriarchal and capitalist powers. This control process starts with individual confession that one has excess weight. After realizing her problem, a woman is capable of improvement; now she is ready to lose weight. This change requires, thus, individual initiative and willingness to take control of one's life. This confession mentality, Spitzack (1990) argues, also necessitates an ongoing surveillance and monitoring of one's own body. For example, women keep constantly looking for the excess fat that needs to be eliminated. The female body has become a site of constant self-scrutiny. Therefore, instead of liberating their lives, dieting practices increase the body discipline required from women. In this way, the dominant practice, without openly suppressing women, invisibly controls them.

Margaret Duncan (1994) applies Spitzack's formula to analyze women's body image in two issues of *Shape* magazine. She focuses her analysis on the text of "Success Stories," a recurring feature that introduces *Shape* readers to women who have successfully lost weight through diet and exercise. Duncan (1994) traces a similar pattern to Spitzack's (1990) study: *Shape*'s text urges individual readers to confess that they have a problem, advises them to take the initiative to change from fat and unhealthy to thin and healthy, and advocates how good they will feel after such a body change. Through the "Success Stories," Duncan (1994) concludes, *Shape* practices oppressive disciplinary control over women.

"She Is Completely Tight"

Dieting, thus, is an important part of the disciplinary practices designed to oppress women in this society. The desire to lose weight is maintained through the unobtainable female body ideal: Women are expected to be thin to be considered attractive and accepted in this society. Susan Bordo (1990) adds another component to this ideal: Now it is not enough to eliminate the excess, soft fat from our bodies; we are also required to achieve an athletic, tight look as well. Therefore, women must become more disciplined: In addition to dieting to lose weight, we now exercise to build muscle.

This new requirement—the tight athletic look—creates a paradoxical body ideal that oscillates "back and forth between a spare 'minimalist' look and a solid, muscular athletic look" (Bordo, 1990, p. 90). Slenderness, Bordo (1990) suggests, can be associated with reduced power and femininity, whereas muscularity symbolizes strength, control, willfulness, and masculinity. Therefore, these two ideals, Bordo (1990) continues, can promote different ideas about femininity in the same body: The muscularity could indicate women's liberation from the narrow definition of the female body as frail, whereas the thinness of this ideal restores the connotation to traditional femininity. This observation of such coexisting, disparate images characterizes many so-called postmodern studies examining the women's body ideal. If the women's body ideal simultaneously expands and limits the notions of femininity, it is no longer enough to label women's body practices only as disciplining or as empowering. Rather, in Helen Lenskyj's (1994) words, "a particular social practice cannot be understood purely as conformity or rebellion: rather, the ambiguities and contradictions need to be considered" (p. 258). Women's bodybuilding lends itself well to an analysis in which the disciplined exercise routine is interpreted both as oppressive and liberating (Lenskyj, 1994).

The Bodybuilding Body

Women's bodybuilding has captured many researchers' attention, because the bulging muscles of these competitors so clearly oppose the traditional frail feminine body ideal. These women lift weights to become visibly big. Hence, bodybuilding has clear potential to challenge the traditional notion of femininity. However, some research demonstrates that this emergent resistance has turned to serve the dominant power by sexualizing and objectifying the transgressive female bodybuilder body (Balsamo, 1994; MacNeill, 1988). Particularly, filmed or televised bodybuilding competitions that closely resemble beauty contests contribute to such an oppressive practice.

Other scholars have disengaged from debating whether bodybuilding is liberating or oppressing women. Rather, they argue that women's bodybuilding is a contradiction in itself: It simultaneously complies with and resists the dominant powers in the society (Bolin, 1992a, 1992b, 1992c; Daniels, 1992; Guthrie & Castelnuovo, 1992; Miller & Penz, 1991). Sharon Guthrie and Shirley Castelnuovo (1992) observe that women bodybuilders are compliant with the dominant discourse of feminine beauty in that they worry about their body shapes and invest tremendous energy to body care. In addition, their pink posing costumes, their blond, fluffy hair styles, and their feminine posing routines and music choices are in line with the traditional femininity. However, women bodybuilders resist the same femininity by actively creating a new female body shape. As a result, they do not feel compelled to model themselves after the more traditional feminine body form.

Anne Bolin (1992a, 1992b, 1992c) expands this analysis by locating the more compliant practices on the public—front stage—arena and the more resistant practices on the private—backstage—arena. When on the front stage during a competition, the women bodybuilders use the feminine accessories to comply with the judges' requirements of proper femininity. This, Bolin (1992a) demonstrates,

---

is necessary if one wants to win the competition, and bodybuilders are there to win. Therefore, enforced notions of femininity for them are simply a necessary means to a higher goal: a victory. On the backstage, outside of the competition, women bodybuilders do not worry about looking feminine. They train seriously to build more muscle mass in the hard-core gyms devoted only to bodybuilding. They wear training gear far from skimpy posing outfits: sweatpants, sweatshirts, baggy T-shirts, and shorts. Bolin (1992b) concludes,

> Theirs is a transformative experience. . . . The presentation of an appearance that the judges will regard as feminine is just a matter of strategizing one's training, diet, and accessorizing with insignias of femininity. This exposes femininity as a cultural construction with boundaries, while femininity as a lived attribute knows no such limits. (p. 395)

What about the aerobicizing body? Some bodybuilders consider that aerobics supports the dominant oppressive beauty ideal. For example, they regard "the aerobics instructor body" as a derogatory term when they discuss women bodybuilders like Cory Everson, who deliberately keeps her muscles smaller and softer to comply with the traditional femininity required by the media (Bolin, 1992a). Nevertheless, some scholars argue that aerobics, similar to bodybuilding, creates a double image that embodies traditional conceptions of both feminine and masculine characteristics.

The Aerobicizing Body

Margaret MacNeill (1988) observes that although aerobics helps to uphold a feminine look, it also promotes healthy life and vitality that assumes a tight, thin, and muscular body. Regina Kenen (1987) characterizes such an aerobics image as a "hybrid" of a patriarchal image (the feminine look) and a feminist image (strong, muscular look). Interestingly, Kenen (1987) argues that women need to obtain the feminine look to successfully manipulate the power source—the men. This form of resistance has provoked lively discussion among feminist scholars. They observe that instead of initiating open resistance women effectively obtain power through similar manipulation of the traditional channels (e.g., Abu-Lughod, 1990; Bolin, 1992a; Dubisch, 1986; Gottlieb, 1989; Strathern, 1981). Therefore, what looks like oppression to the researcher's eye might serve as a means for power for the women involved. Kenen (1987) also points out that the media equate the feminist image with sex appeal and turn it to serve the patriarchal powers. Here the aerobics image is truly ambiguous: The traditional feminine image is resistant, but the strong "feminist" image sexualizes women.

In their approach to the double image, Elizabeth Kagan and Margaret Morse (1988) place the aerobicizing body in the postmodern context. They concentrate on the images in Jane Fonda's exercise videotapes. Like Kenen (1987), they contend that Fonda's body incorporates the slender femininity with a new powerful self-determining subject in motion. However, these writers assume that women participate in aerobics basically to fight against their aging and sagging bodies. This preoccupation results in a compromising aerobics body image: The subjectivity and its will are delegated to shape the body to a commercially supported ideal of femininity. Like those who studied women's bodybuilding (Balsamo, 1994; MacNeill, 1988), Kagan and Morse (1988) conclude that the emergent potential for liberation is revisited to serve the purposes of patriarchy by linking women's physical activity to attractiveness.

Kagan and Morse (1988) like MacNeill (1988) focus on the body discourse transmitted through media. What about the everyday practice in aerobics classes? Do the aerobicizers there struggle to confront a contradictory body image? To find answers to these questions I set myself to listen to the voices of the aerobicizing women.

Method

Like Kagan and Morse (1988), I locate my research of aerobics within the postmodern cultural condition. Central to my study is the view that this culture is communication between different voices. Michael Bakhtin's (1981) examination of the dynamics of cultural dialogue serves as a foundation for my analysis.

In every dialogue, Bakhtin (1981) argues, several voices, some more dominant than others, struggle over each other to give meanings to cultural phenomena. Cultural dialogue, therefore, implies a certain authority and assumes certain power relations in its exchange. Bakhtin (1981) locates dominant voices in the public, official sphere, from where they claim the rights for the correct interpretation of the phenomenon at hand. For example, the magazines and aerobics videotapes are claiming the rights for public representation

of the perfect female body image. The private voices, like the aerobicizers', must use other channels available to them to replace the official interpretation with their own meaning. I believe, therefore, that
the meaning of aerobics in this culture is created by many voices
that contradict with each other and work to replace each other. All
these meanings, the public as well as the private, are produced
within cultural discourses.

For example, our understanding of the body is formed within
such discourses as health, medicine, and femininity. However, I
believe it is insufficient to examine the discursive construction of
the body ideal at the public arena. Like Spitzack (1990), I aim to
examine how the discursive dialogue of the public arena material-
izes in the women's everyday experiences. To find out, I have to listen to the voices of the individual women. I assume, along with
many other feminists, that women actively make sense out of their
social world and construct different meanings in different social contexts. In this paper, individual women engage in a dialogue with the
discursive representations: They strive to make sense of the "fit
body ideal." Here I focus on the ambiguities and contradictions in
women's body experience (Lenskyj, 1994), as I do not believe that
any experience can be classified as purely empowering or purely
oppressive. However, I believe, following Spitzack (1990), that aerobicizers' critical voices have the potential to alter the course of dominant practices.

I also assign an active role for myself when I aim to uncover
women's meanings about the aerobicizing body. The reported meanings are my subjective interpretations based on my fieldwork within
aerobics. In this study, therefore, the aerobicizers and I have negotiated a shared understanding of the aerobicizing body in American
culture. I also acknowledge that I am a human observer whose personal, social, and historical background structures research con-
siderably (e.g., Bruner, 1993; Clifford & Marcus, 1986; Denzin, 1992;
Rosaldo, 1989).

Fieldwork

I used several methods to reconstruct the dia-
logue surrounding the body image in aerobics: fieldwork, interviews, and media analysis. My research derives predominantly from
my ethnographic fieldwork among aerobicizers from 1990 to 1992.
Although ethnography is most often associated with anthropology,

today its methods have been increasingly used to study the state of Western society as the minutiae of everyday life (de Certeau, 1984) have attracted researchers across the social sciences. Many taken-for-granted, commonplace phenomena like aerobics are now considered especially fruitful topics, because they, in their popularity, unveil central aspects of our culture to a critical inquiry (Dunn, 1991; Featherstone, 1988; Foley, 1992; Johnston, 1986; McRobbie, 1994).

Aerobics handed itself quite easily to ethnographic fieldwork because aerobicizers gather regularly together in a public, yet well-defined place—the gymnasium. My field was mainly the university community in a small Midwestern town: Most aerobics classes were organized by the university and the participants were in some way associated with the university. This is only one context for aerobics classes. Kenen (1987) has found that the setting influences the aerobics praxis. For example, commercial health clubs exacerbate the negative, oppressive practices more than do public-sector classes like the YMCA. I do not intend to generalize my findings over the private aerobics sector (the health clubs) or different geographical regions of the U.S., although I attended private health clubs in the community and in other parts of the country to complete my ethnography. In this study I focus on women's experiences within a university community. On average, I participated in seven one-hour classes weekly.

In addition to my field observations, I conducted both informal and formal interviews to closely trace the individual experiences. I interviewed the aerobicizers informally whenever possible: before and after classes, in the locker rooms, in the street, in coffee shops, in the classes, or any other time I met one of the participants. The formal interviewing technique used in this study can be characterized after Michael Quinn Patton (1980) as open-ended topical interviews. I had prepared a list of topics instead of setting up detailed questions. I selected the topics—the structure and nature of an aerobics class, the body image, health, and nutrition—based on findings in the literature (Kagan & Morse, 1988; Kenen, 1987; MacNeill, 1988; Martin, 1987), an earlier pilot study, and my ongoing participant observation. Therefore, the discussion regarding the body was only one part of my larger research project on aerobics (Markula, 1993b). I wanted to adopt a conversational model (e.g., Spitzack, 1990) in which both the researcher and respondent assume equal responsibility for the discussion. Basically, we discussed the above-mentioned topics during each interview, but the conversation could also follow a particular concern of the interviewee. Body matters were such a concern for many of the aerobicizers, and we usually discussed body image extensively. The length of each interview varied from thirty minutes to two hours. I interviewed most participants once, but certain "informative" or verbal participants were interviewed twice. All the interviewees assumed anonymity, and I refer to them here by their pseudonyms. I interviewed thirty-five exercisers (thirty-three women and two men). This imbalanced gender ratio was common in the aerobics classes I participated in; the vast majority of the participants were women. Consequently, in this paper I focus on women's views. The exercisers in my study were mostly students but also were secretaries, staff members, and researchers. This research, therefore, is based on the experiences of a select group. The typical aerobicizer in my study was a white, well-educated, eighteen- to forty-five-year-old female, a description which—according to nationwide surveys—also characterizes an average aerobics exerciser around the U.S. (Rothlein, 1988).

In addition to recording the aerobicizers' private voices, I wanted to record the public voices constructing the aerobics body. Therefore, to support my investigation, I analyzed how aerobics was presented in the media. My research drew from images in aerobics videotapes but mainly I examined exercise images in such magazines as *Health, Women's Sport and Fitness, Shape,* and *Self.* I selected *Health* and *Women's Sport and Fitness* because they were likely to contain frequent articles on women's exercise. In addition, because they were available since 1979, I had a chance to examine the change in media representation of the female body through these magazines. I selected the other two monthly magazines, *Shape* and *Self,* because of their self-proclaimed specialization in women's fitness matters. For example, *Shape,* published by bodybuilding tycoon Joe Weider, promised to provide "mind and body fitness for women" (*Shape,* March 1994, p. 2). Moreover, individual aerobicizers I spoke with recommended these two magazines for me. I investigated issues of both magazines starting from 1986. In these magazines I focused specifically on articles about aerobics or women's exercise. Their topics varied from aerobics shoe and video guides to articles advising strength and toning exercises. I read the text of each article and examined the accompanying pictures, which I also compared to the text.

Several of the women I interviewed also exercised using video-tapes. I have, therefore, included the women's views about the video bodies in my study. Among the numerous exercise tapes available the women talked most about Jane Fonda's "Workout" series and Kathy Smith's exercise videos.

To analyze how the contradictory body image evolves in aero-bics, I first look at the meanings the magazines construct around the female body image. I then proceed to identify how these meanings materialize in aerobicizers' everyday experiences: How do the media discourses structure women's ideas about their bodies? In addition, I am interested in women's responses to the dominant media dis-courses: Do women question the media representation of the body? To conclude, I will explain why the media portray a certain female image and why women react to this ideal the way they do. I will start by sketching the ideal body of the exercising female in the media.

"Hot Moves to Shape Your Trouble Spots"

Magazines deepen the fragmented image when they assign special parts of our bodies as problem spots. Problem areas—abdomen, thighs, underarms, and the "butt"—are particularly resistant to manipulative toning, albeit they need it the most. Already in 1980, one article pointed out that "the main areas of con-cern for most women are the upper arms (batwings), abdomen (stretch marks and flab) and outer thighs (saddlebags)" (Stallings, 1980, p. 49). Fifteen years later these particular parts still trouble women. Jane Fonda, for example, advertised her 1992 video "Lower Body Solution" as "designed especially for the #1 problem areas for women; abs, buns, and thighs" (e.g., Self, March 1992, p. 178). In every issue magazines introduce workouts to "hit" one or more of these parts. A myriad of special exercises such as abdominal tight-eners, waist cinchers, lower belly flatteners, back-of-the-thigh hard-eners, seat shapers, bottom lifters, fanny firmers, hip slimmers, and front-of-the-thigh definers are designed to firm women's problematic body parts. These movements are promoted as simple, effective, and easy to perform. Therefore, even the busiest women can manage to fit exercise into her daily schedule.

Magazines advocate these workouts based on one assumption: Women need to look good. They assume further that their readers presently find their bodies imperfect. This imbalance results in great anxiety, which only their workout program can cure. In this sense, the magazines see themselves contributing to women's well-being.

> If you balk at pool-party invitations; if you lie awake at night wondering how to cover your thighs while keeping cool and looking great; if you seriously consider moving to Antarctica as soon as the hot weather sets in—this workout is for you. (Sternlicht, 1990c, p. 34)
>
> Weak triceps can make wearing a sleeveless shirt or evening dress an embarrassment. By adding triceps exercises to your workout, you can make the back of your arms shapely and strong. (Sternlicht, 1990a, p. 46)
>
> Both women and men alike are self-conscious of their derrieres, whether their buttocks are large or flat, high or low, round or saggy. But relax. It's fairly easy either to develop this area and give it more roundness or to firm it up and give it more sleekness. (Sternlicht, 1990b, p. 38)

One participant in my study also confirms that women exercise because their bodies are flawed:

> I think everyone there has a certain area that they want to work on; it's obvious to them or it's obvious to you, they wouldn't be there if they hadn't a complex about [some area]. They don't like something . . . like a stereotype, we don't like our arms, that's why we signed up . . . we are trying to get rid of our arms. (Sarah)

In the magazine texts, the problem spots cause the biggest anxieties; the thighs, the triceps (underarms), and the butts are what women are most embarrassed about. Are their predictions well placed? When I asked the aerobicizers to identify any problematic parts of their bodies, their answers resonate with the magazine discourse. The problem spots trouble the aerobicizer the most. For example, Jane, Cecilia, and Laura quickly identified their problem parts:

> *Pirkko*: Do you feel that you have certain problem areas in your bodies?
> *Jane*: My lower half, I sit all day.
> *Cecilia*: My stomach, that's the hardest part.
> *Laura*: After having a baby, stomach muscles are the worst.

Many aerobics classes I participated in included exercises for these particular parts. The instructors, like the magazines, presumed that women want to tackle those particular areas. I asked Becky, an aerobics instructor, to describe a typical toning session. She found that "a lot of them [the participants] want to work on their sides, the outer thighs or . . . the seats more . . . I think stomachs are probably one [problem area], hips, outer thighs, those are the main ones." When questioned why these areas are so problematic, she explained, "That's where we have most of our fat cells, that's where we store most of the fat." Obviously, storing fat is a highly undesirable, yet natural, process. The storage places are the problem spots whose fat levels women carefully monitor. These areas require special toning as they appear especially prone to excess fat and flab.

As other scholars, I contend that these spots "where we store most of the fat" are the very parts of our bodies that identify us as females: the rounded bellies, the larger hips, the thighs, the softer underarms. These "female parts" are also the ones we hate the most and fight the hardest to diminish. Logically then, we hate looking like women. Bordo (1990) argues that women grow up despising their feminine form, because the ideal feminine shape in this society resembles that of a young boy: wide shoulders, tight muscles, narrow hips (also Bartky, 1988; Chernin, 1981; Coward, 1985). The majority of women, regardless how hard they try, can never achieve this type of body. Most women simply are not born with male bodies. Kim Chernin (1981) adds that the unattainable boyish ideal is one of the major causes for women's anxieties with their bodies. The dissatisfaction with one's feminine shape can lead to an extreme fear of fat and consequently, a distorted body image. Ronda Gates (1991) reports that devoted aerobicizers and fitness professionals, more than anyone, have a distorted understanding of their bodies. They are afraid of fat: "If 22 percent of fat is optimum, 18 percent is better" (Gates, 1991, p. 28), these exercisers conclude (see also Imm, 1989). According to Chernin (1981), this attitude generates desperate attempts to control one's body weight that precede serious eating disorders like anorexia nervosa and bulimia nervosa.

Magazines advocate muscle tone as a vital feature of an ideal female body, and the aerobicizers seem to accept this model. Paradoxically, although they work hard to "sculpt" their trouble spots into the desired tone, they also question the meaning of the uncomfortable toning exercises. I examine next what is meant by toned muscles: What kind of muscle definition is desirable?

Sleek and Sexy

Although a "good female body" is a muscular body, the magazines discourage extreme muscularity. Exercise articles primarily promote a toned and shapely look. Magazine workouts, thus, aim to "tone" one's muscles, not to build muscles. One article puts a clear limit on female muscle size: "Strong muscles mean more shape in arms and shoulders, definition in the legs and a flat, but not concave middle" (Kaufman, 1989, p. 124). The ideal body is layered with long, sleek, unbulky muscles. Such muscles are also defined as "sexy." For example, workouts are advertised with such slogans as "The Ultimate Guide to Sexy Muscles" (*Self*, March 1991, cover), "Three Easy Ways to a Strong and Sexy Stomach" (*Self*, February 1991, cover), "Sculpted and Sexy" (Rover, 1992, p. 48), "Shoulders are Sexy" (Laurence, 1992, p. 103).

"Is It All Right for Women to Have Muscular Arms?"

Evidently, muscles—particularly the problem spots—need to be toned, tight, and firm. Most problem spots are located in the lower body. Toning the upper body in general and arms in particular is a more complex enterprise. Magazines encourage upper body workouts: "Firm Triceps and Shapely Biceps are in Vogue" (Sternlicht, 1991, p. 48) and "It's all right for women to have muscular arms" (Sternlicht, 1991, p. 48). For women in aerobics classes, however, muscular arms are not "all right." Many women fear large arm muscles if they do upper body workouts in their classes. Arm toning is complicated, because one of the problem areas is the triceps region, under the upper arm. Aerobicizers want firm triceps without bulking up. Sarah, for example, trains her arm muscles, but says, "I am afraid that I bulk up when I do arms. . . . I used to swim and I was huge, like bulky and I hated it." Sarah continues to explain why women hate "big arms":

> Girls don't really work out their arms, because if you work your arms, you get big arms, you look like a guy. It seems to be okay if you have strong legs, but if you are athletic and you have big arms, it's like she looks like a guy. It's more socially acceptable to have big legs than the arms.

Women do not want to look masculine, Sarah explains, and that is what muscular arms do to you: You end up looking like a guy.

Considering that the ideal female body nowadays "looks like a young guy" more than a woman, this distaste of big arms seems unjustified. Apparently, although women should possess broad shoulders, they should not be muscular.

Not only muscle size but also the location of the muscles defines the exerciser's femininity. Sarah in her earlier quote points out that muscular legs—firm thighs—are socially acceptable, unlike muscular arms. Kathy adds that tight legs are not only acceptable but desirable:

> I personally would like to work on my arms more, but it seems that a lot of girls would rather work on their thighs, their outer, inner thighs and their butt, but they don't feel that they need their arms built up. . . . The thing that guys look at or a lot of women are concerned, tends to be your butt or their thighs. They don't say, "I have fat arms" . . . and you don't have guys going by and saying, "Look at those sexy arms."

Well-toned legs are sought after because men notice them. Women do not urgently shape their arms because men do not care about seeing them. Obviously, arms are not as vital a part of an attractive woman as legs are. In addition, Kathy implies that women are exposed to a gaze that sets the standards of the desirable female form. We shape our bodies to please that gaze. Kathy clearly identifies the gaze as male; other aerobicizers do not really recognize a source for the controlling gaze. They are objects of a gaze that is just ubiquitously "societal": "It's a product of society" (Colleen): "It's socially acceptable" (Sarah). The preferences of this gaze often contradict the exercisers' own will, but they feel pressured to please the gaze. Most exercisers comply with, as Kelly puts it, what "most people presumably think women are . . . softer lines," and she continues, "which is too bad." Kelly indicates, hence, that she does not agree with such definitions of femininity. She weight trains herself, as do Andrea, Becky, Colleen, and Trisha. Trisha has even tried bodybuilding, and Kelly would like to start:

> I would like to do bodybuilding myself and we've [she and her bodybuilder husband] actually been in bodybuilding competitions . . . and I would like to do that. But I think I am a minority; a lot of women feel that's not the way a woman should look, but I wouldn't mind looking like that. (Kelly)

Interestingly she adds, "within reason, of course. I don't want to look like Arnold Schwarzenegger. I would like to build my muscles a little more than they are [now]." None of the women in my study desires to have big muscles, not even the exercisers who work out with weights. All the weight trainers also indicate that women cannot become too muscular even with the help of weights and definitely not without serious commitment and work. Becky and Colleen rely on a biological explanation: "I don't think women should worry about getting too muscular, because they just don't have the hormone" (Colleen), which Becky specifies as testosterone. Trisha reflects her own experience:

> It takes so much, I didn't realize . . . it's just really, very disciplined sport. . . . I think a lot of women have a misconception that if I go to the gym and lift weights I'll look like Rachel McLish, Cher or somebody, [but] it takes a lot. This one lady spent 40 hours a week in the gym—that's a career—but that is ridiculous and I think there are lot of people who think if you lift like six weeks you can see the difference. . . . I think women see men doing sit-ups, 100 sit-ups every day and their stomachs look like Rambo's; the women can do 100 sit-ups the rest of their lives and their stomachs still wouldn't look like that.

Although women do not want big muscles, everybody admires toned muscles. Most aerobicizers also admit needing more tone, also in their upper bodies. Kathy and Kelly indicate that they want to include more arm work in their classes but find themselves different from the majority of the women in this matter. Others, like Helen and Sarah, acknowledge that they benefit from arm exercises, although they prefer toning their legs to upper body work. Maria's comment summarizes the feelings of many exercisers in my study: "I just want my legs to be more toned and the upper arms, when you get older, you know, the little wonderful thing that flabs down here (points at her triceps area)." Maria is twenty-one years old, but already worries about how her aging body is changing. I discuss this concern more in depth later in this paper.

Some women, like Antoinette, Becky, Colleen, or Christy, do not want to appear muscular but still want to be strong. Antoinette reasons that it is good to be strong, because if I'm physically strong, I can do things that I want to do: I can unscrew jam jars—I don't have to ask some guys to do it for me—I can put the trash out; I can lift things. I don't like feeling weak and helpless and end up asking other people to do things for me.

Maria and Molly want to be strong to excel in the sports they love. For these women, it's not the appearance, the muscle size, that matters but the actual functionality of the muscles. Christy, a former competitive swimmer, likes to be strong and to have strong arms but believes that "you don't have to have muscle definition to have good strong muscles." Therefore, the aerobicizers might conform with the toned look of the ideal body, but for functionality, not only for looks.

"I Was Bulky and I Hated It!"

The aerobicizers admire other participants or instructors with tight and firm muscles, but built, big muscles are disliked. The muscle size, therefore, is an intricate matter. The women I interviewed define toned muscles quite differently from built muscles. For example, Kelly points out that "when you are toning you are just keeping the muscle firm and when you are body-building you are actually enlarging the muscle and building what they call definition, when you can see one muscle from the other." To the aerobicizers, toned muscles can be visible but not big and massive. Toned muscles are lean, in use, and tight. But when exactly does the tone turn into bulk? This, apparently, is a hard question to answer. Trisha considers that "there is a real fine line between looking good and being too muscular." Many women are perplexed: They begin to work out their muscles but end up feeling ashamed of their bodies. Andrea tells a story of a confused friend who started weight training but is not sure about the results:

> *Andrea:* We were going to go out and she was wearing a
> dress and she was like "I can't take off my
> jacket" . . . they [the arms] were definitely tight, but
> I don't think they were that unattractive, but she
> said she is always used to having great, thin arms,
> not the actual muscle, so I guess for some girls,
> maybe for the majority, it just is not very attractive.
> *Pirkko:* Why did she start lifting weights?

Andrea: I'm not sure. I think she did it because she was working on her upper body more, she just tried to get rid of her arm fat. I think eventually she started to work more on the arms, so she wouldn't over-work her legs.

Andrea's friend felt that she was unattractive; the never-resting eyes of society glanced at her arms disapprovingly. Some of the exercisers sense a contradiction here: They recognize that they want to be strong—it is good to be strong—but concurrently they feel bad about it. For example, Melissa is struggling with her feelings about being strong:

> It is really contradictory, because the very things that I do in aerobics, like my class always has this long session of push-ups, I'm strong and I feel uncomfortable with that, but at the same time I'm proud of that, not proud, that makes me feel good about myself to be strong, but I don't know. . . . I'm not satisfied and I don't know what I want to look better; it doesn't make sense.

Feeling simultaneous pride and shame does not make sense to Melissa. Many of these women can, thus, see the unfair expectation placed on them. It is, however, almost impossible to resist the societal pressure to conform. Aerobics does not seem to help women to expand the boundaries of the ideal feminine body to the same extent as, for example, women's bodybuilding does. However, Helen and Sarah compare aerobics to ice skating and ballet, physical activities they have been involved in earlier. They prefer aerobics because, unlike ice skaters or ballet dancers, aerobicizers can be proud of their muscles:

> I've been in ballet forever, and I prefer aerobics to it, because in ballet you are supposed to be skinny and have no muscles. I mean, muscles are not valued, just flexibility. In aerobics muscles are valued, because it shows that you've been doing aerobics for a while and if you have big calves. . . . [they think], "Oh, she is dedicated." (Sarah)

For these women, aerobics has been a liberating experience, because they no longer feel ashamed of their well-defined leg muscles. Both, however, express an added desire "to look thinner" (Helen).

Therefore, along with the refined regulations regarding ideal tone, the perfect female body is also required to be thin.

"I Like to Be Sort of Petite"

The connection between women's exercise and slimness dates back to the advent of aerobics. When aerobics began, its initial purpose was to facilitate weight loss (Cooper, 1968, 1970; Sorensen, 1979). Presently, weight loss is always listed as an advantage of a regular exercise program. Occasionally strength training is also sold to the audience by linking it with weight loss. Theoretically, increased muscle mass burns calories even at rest. Therefore, a muscular person will consume more calories in everyday life than her or his weaker counterpart (e.g., Barrett, 1991). This logic implies that women should build muscles to assist weight loss, not to increase strength.

Weight loss is important for the exercisers in my study, more so than the firm muscles. For example, one should first worry about being thin; once sufficiently thin, one can work on muscle tone. Cari's comment illustrates this sentiment:

> I'm trying to burn out some fat and just stay in shape, maybe if I got down to when I was satisfied [with my weight], maybe then I worked on shaping, but I'm a long way from there; right now, I'm just trying . . . to burn out some of those fat cells.

Cari supposes that shaped muscles are something slim exercisers work on; for her the ideal body is thin, and tone is a fringe benefit. The present body ideal is definitely slim. However, slimness does not mean soft, meatless flesh but requires firm, tight, and sleek muscle tone. Bordo (1990) confirms that "unless one goes the route of muscle building, it is virtually impossible to achieve a flab-less, excess-less body unless one trims very near to the bone" (p. 90). Consequently, Cari could not achieve a fashionably small body by only losing weight. Jiggling flesh, even on a thin body, feels loose—like fat. Hence, without toning one will always feel big. Magazine texts appeal to similar reasoning: They construct their strengthening exercises to reduce women's bodies like their diet regimens are designed to downsize their female readers. For example, Laurence (1992) reasons,

> Broad shoulders, squared and relaxed, create a regal, imposing carriage that signifies power and presence. They can also make

your waist seem smaller, more delicate, and the sight of silk sliding over a creamy shoulder carries its own potency. (p. 103)

Although broad shoulders signify "power and presence," above all, they make one's waist appear smaller. Some aerobicizers complete their toning exercises based on this rationale: Toned muscles actually will make one smaller. Even the much-feared arm exercises become acceptable when they, instead of strengthening, diminish women's arms. Eileen defends the arm exercises done in her aerobics class: "It's not that their arms are going to get bigger [by doing toning], they are just going to be tighter, they actually will look smaller, because they'll be tighter and not flabby."

Apparently, women do not want to be associated with big anything: Big muscles, big bones, and big bodies are generally feared. Somehow, we ought to fight the big body. This struggle to reduce the body is problematic. Sheila discusses a dilemma she has faced:

> *Sheila:* I tend to build muscle pretty fast, especially when I do biking. . . . I like to slim down my legs, most slim down the muscle. I do have a lot of muscle I could slim down.
>
> *Pirkko:* By doing what?
>
> *Sheila:* I don't know, it's hard. When I was a freshman, I managed to do it. I have a slow metabolism; I have to not eat, and I have to do more exercising. When I did I was only eating dinner as a meal, and I was trying to make it light and have a few snacks during the day.
>
> *Pirkko:* It didn't bother you to get more muscles by doing all those exercises?
>
> *Sheila:* You have to eat enough less, so that you are using more calories. It's hard to do for me. You have fifty pounds of equipment [when you play ice hockey] and you go skating around, it's going to build up my muscles unless I don't eat anything, so, I try to keep a balance so that I don't gain weight but it's hard, it's a battle. . . . I mean, I have a petite frame, I just don't have petite muscles.

Sheila tries to control her rebellious body—prevent it from becoming any bigger—by dieting and exercising, which creates a predicament:

Her muscles tend to develop due to her workout. She is trapped in a vicious cycle where only a strict diet, as she believes, can free her. An ascetic diet regime is the only way to reveal her petite frame. Her hobby, however, is ice hockey, which is not a sport for small and frail females. A hockey player, like Sheila, needs strong muscles. She, therefore, has to be strong and delicate, big and small all at the same time.

It is evident that aerobicizers' lived experiences reflect the double body image detailed by the scholars studying the aerobics image in the media (Kagan & Morse, 1988; MacNeill, 1988). Earlier studies also debated whether this image resists or complies with those in power. I believe that, like the bodybuilding body, it is an ambiguous image: It embraces potential for both empowerment and oppression. Similar to the women bodybuilders (Bolin, 1992a, 1992b), the aerobicizers aim to challenge the traditional beauty ideal by toning their muscles, but they also engage in oppressive feminine practices like dieting. Unlike bodybuilders, however, the aerobicizers dislike big muscles, especially in the upper body. Moreover, the aerobicizers aim to become smaller: they tone their muscles to look smaller when bodybuilders even diet to appear more muscular (Bolin, 1992b). Many aerobicizers think bodybuilders are disgusting:

> I've seen women's bodies that I find repulsive, because they are so muscular. (Cari)

> They have this huge bulging muscle that I think is really unattractive. (Molly)

> Women bodybuilders, that looks bad. (Eileen)

> I don't like . . . the women bodybuilders, to lift weights to become big, I personally don't like that. (Daedra)

The magazines support the aerobicizers' views regarding bodybuilding. For example, although the fitness articles promote upper body work, they clarify that their weight training will not result in bulging arm muscles (Barrett, 1991; Brick, 1990). Why this fear of big muscles?

Feminist research explains that such rejection of big muscles serves women's oppression in society. Namely, patriarchal domination over women is based on the assumption that men are naturally—biologically—stronger and bigger than women. Physically stronger males are also alleged to be naturally determined, intellectual, active leaders who should dominate the weak, passive, and small women. To retain this power arrangement in patriarchal society, it is necessary, thus, to define the female body differently from the male body: ideally, the weak female's muscles are sleek and firm, whereas the powerful male's muscles are visible and big. The aerobics body fits in this scheme nicely, whereas the bodybuilding body challenges this gender dichotomy, because it resembles the big, muscular male body and minimizes the biological gap separating the sexes (Holmlund, 1989). A simple conclusion would be that aerobics supports the patriarchal ideology but bodybuilding resists it. However, Bolin (1992b) adds an interesting dimension to this discussion.

She points out that not only bodybuilding but other sporting lifestyles can challenge and minimize the biological differences between the sexes. She uses triathlon, long-distance running, and rock-climbing as examples in which there is a considerable overlap in the contours of male and female physiques. It is noticeable that these athletic male bodies are small. Therefore, the resistant female body does not have to be bulky to challenge the patriarchal, dualistic definitions of gender. In this light, a well-toned aerobicizer's body could be seen to resemble a male athlete's body and defy the dominant patriarchy over the female body.

In addition to having toned muscles, the aerobicized body is thin. The aerobicizers accordingly are afraid of fat, more than they are afraid of big muscles. For example, Becky explains that she appreciates muscles, because they make "the person look very fit." However, when asked why she exercises, she answered, "I was once fat. I don't ever want to be fat again." Being overweight was a bigger concern for more of the aerobicizers than extensive muscles. As we know, bodybuilders also need to be unnaturally thin to show their muscle development. Therefore, even women bodybuilders, although challenging femininity through developing big muscles, do not aim to overcome the requirement of feminine thinness. Being fat is still probably the furthest from the ideal feminine body of the 90s. A strong, overweight woman, theoretically, would offer the most direct resistance to the patriarchal notions of femininity in this society, as her body would directly oppose the toned and thin ideal. If we define resistance only through clear binary oppositions like this, aerobics—or any other physical activity—would never offer an avenue for true resistance. I believe that instead of classifying women's practices exclusively into resistance or oppression, it is more fruitful to concentrate on the richness of everyday experiences.

Women in aerobics classes keep struggling to make sense of the contradictory requirements of the female body. There is an additional element in the ideal female body that needs to be analyzed. This ideal implies that besides being thin and toned, our bodies must stay young. This adds another component to our bodywork load.

"I Am Not Sure if It's Too Late"

The ideal female body is also a youthful body. Women over thirty seldom appear in fitness magazines. The flabless, firm muscles do not cover an old, wrinkly, bent, gray-haired body. Nevertheless, everyone will grow older, and the natural signs of aging are opposite to the requirements of the beautiful body. Some women in my study have turned to aerobics to specifically fight the effects of age: "I have this cellulite and these fat cells. I'm not sure if it's too late; at least I'm attempting to do something" (Cari). Cari feels somewhat optimistic about the power of exercise to overcome her aging body, although her late start worries her. Others feel that age exacerbates the problems they have with their body shapes. Some exercisers become desperate when their bodies show signs of old age. When the aging progresses, women have to work incredibly hard to obtain the ideal figure. Particularly, the problem areas—underarms, thighs, hips, and abdomen—seem to get flabbier and more resistant to shaping. This experience is tangible for some aerobicizers. Colleen, Ann, and Rosi describe their bodies:

> When you get older . . . your muscles aren't that dividing any more. . . . It seems relatively easy when you are a young person to have toned muscles. (Colleen)

> My body is getting older, it's harder to keep my weight in control, and I get really fat if I don't exercise. (Ann)

> You gain so much weight, you don't know how to get rid of it. (Rosi)

Why do we have to fight the naturally aging body so hard? To explain our urge to remain youthful, Mike Featherstone (1991) locates the body in the context of so-called consumer culture. He argues that in present consumerism the perfect body—youthful, physically beautiful, and healthy—makes its owner more marketable. For example, "good looks" increase a person's exchange value in the job market: A physically attractive person gets hired before someone else. Like the aerobicizers, Featherstone (1991) observes that the desired body shape can be achieved only with effort and body work. Cosmetic, beauty, fitness, and leisure industries have emerged to guide people in their quest for perfection. Sagging flesh, for example, should be treated in exercise programs provided by the fitness industry. But even with the help of specific programs, the consumer has to work hard for the results. Video queen and marketing master Jane Fonda (1981) emphasizes individual hard work as a means to a better body:

> Notice I've said "vigorous" and "exercise hard." I don't use these words idly. Namby-pamby little routines that don't speed up your heart beat and make you sweat aren't really worth your while. (p. 49)
>
> If you are serious about wanting to lose weight once and for all, about changing the shape of your body, about improving your self-image and your morale, you must get over being soggy. There are no short cuts. No sweatless quickies. You must be committed to working hard, sweating hard and getting sore. . . . You have to work for it. (pp. 55–56)

Fonda's own body demonstrates how effective vigorous work is. She, although over fifty, displays the ideal young boyish body discussed earlier: broad shoulders, narrow hips, long legs. Her body is "reminiscent of adolescence" (Coward, 1985, p. 41) in late middle age; it is a "version of an immature body" (Coward, 1985, p. 41) possessed by a mature woman. Spitzack (1990) reads two meanings in Fonda's fantastic teenager body. First, many women view Fonda in hopeful terms: Her body suggests that women over fifty can be viewed as attractive and can have a "good body." Consequently, older women are still attractive and maintain their marketability in consumer society. But second, women fear that this means an ongoing attention to appearance. Some had looked forward to middle age because of less focus on "looks," but now women need to continue monitoring their bodies to maintain an adolescent body, like Fonda's body, to a mature age.

In consumer society, we need to invest in body care to secure our positions in the market. Featherstone (1991) adds that this creates an expanding market for commodities that aid body work. Looking after one's body, he illustrates, is like looking after a car. As a car needs a whole array of things to function, the body needs products from soaps to diet teas to keep its shape. Such products as cosmetic surgery, diet pills, or cosmetic devices (Coward, 1985; Spitzack, 1990) are marketed particularly at women. I would place aerobics in this line of products: It is advertised to help women battle their aging, bulging, and sagging bodies in a manner similar to other body industry products. Evidently, if women start worrying about their bodies growing old at twenty, and aerobics is one of the solutions to discipline such a body, aerobics classes will be securely filled with customers, because we all will age and our bodies will need more and more work to resemble the ideal body.

Featherstone (1991) also points out that good looks are promoted by the media. Fitness magazines, TV programs, and exercise videos portray a stylized image of the body in consumer culture. Feminist research (Kagan & Morse, 1988: MacNeill, 1988) has found that these media images sexualize and objectify women as they emphasize appearance rather than fitness. The aerobicizers have obviously come face to face with the perfect media bodies in these sources. How do they find the media representation of the exercising women?

"You Don't See Them Sweating"

Women's ideas about exercise often resonate with the fitness discourse in the media: They work on their problem spots; they long for a toned body, but not for visible muscle definition; they struggle to fight fat and age, exactly as urged by the media texts. However, the same aerobicizers criticize the portrayal of exercisers in the media. Many women are consciously suspicious of this representation. To illustrate, Eileen, Anna, and Andrea consider the media exercisers unreal, even irritating:

> TV doesn't seem realistic; it's like they go out and get models to do it, because they are all tall and very skinny, in shape and kind of disgusting in a way; they have their hair perfectly done and their make-up is perfect; you don't see them sweating. It's the same image they project, very thin, lean . . . they are just generally thin, they are just models.

This portrayal makes the exercisers doubt the expertise of the demonstrators. They suspect that these "models" are there because of their looks, not because they know something about exercise. Christy verbalizes her skepticism: "They [the demonstrators] don't have to be necessarily fit, they could just be someone who looks good in a leotard and who are told, 'Put your body in this position.'" Christy refers to the way many exercises are presented in the magazine pictures: The demonstrator is in a still pose waiting for the camera to capture the moment. Often a series of these pictures is arranged on the page to illustrate a continuous exercise routine. The real-life aerobicizers feel, therefore, that even unfit, thin models can pose a couple of seconds for a beautiful picture, but they would not be able to follow a continuous aerobics class.

If my interviewees are skeptical of the magazine representations, they view exercise videotapes with an even stronger suspicion. Unlike the static pictures, a video shows a continuous aerobics class lasting thirty to sixty minutes. The video exercisers should, thus, demonstrate a good fitness level. The aerobicizers I interviewed are distrustful: The videotapes are a media trick because the video exercisers appear too perfect to be real. Sarah, for example, is annoyed with the exercise videos:

> It kind of makes me mad because I keep hearing that they stop, put on more make-up and jump another five minutes and then come back, wipe off the sweat, and you never see them really ugly; there is something wrong.

While being disturbed, women have also accepted that the media display only perfect bodies. For example, Daedra explains,

> I expect that anyone demonstrating any exercise in any magazine is going to have to be close to that ideal body. I don't think I expect anything but that.

Flawless models do not irritate all the aerobicizers. For some women, the perfect media exercisers are a positive incentive that keeps them exercising.

Regardless, many women in this study like to see "normal people" demonstrating the exercises. Or they prefer to follow a fitness expert who knows what she or he is doing. The body size is not as important as fitness level and professional instruction. These exercisers welcome a larger-size leader or participant in exercise class. Actually, a little "chunkiness" makes the person more human and easier to relate to. Therefore, the media class should resemble more closely the "real-life" classes they participate in. Sarah summarizes her requirements for an instructor:

> You can be an aerobics teacher and not have a body. My only requirements for an aerobics teacher are that they can do the routines with us and that they've got energy doing that. . . . I don't care if they are like 200 pounds, but if they can jump as high and are energetic . . . There is this picture in our minds like Jane Fonda, perfect body, [but] like [our teachers], they've got nice bodies, but are not beautiful, but as long as they can keep up with us, lead us, that's fine.

Sarah notices the discrepancy between the media images of an aerobicizer ("there is this picture in our minds like Jane Fonda, perfect body") and her instructors. She still prefers her instructors. Some exercisers have discovered that the recent exercise videos include different types of people in their model classes. For example, Fonda instructs some "overweight" exercisers in one of her latest tapes; in Kathy Smith's video class exercisers in different fitness levels aerobicize together. However, my interviewees regard these tapes as exceptional.

The interviewees do not like the thin and toned media ideal: It is too perfect, it is no longer real. This conscious rejection seems odd as the women keep working toward the same ideal in their aerobics classes. Therefore, women's relationship with the contradictory body ideal is ambiguous: Against their own judgment, many aerobicizers still desire to look like the flawless models. It seems a lot easier to judge the body image at the intellectual level than engage in the resistant action in real life. Recall how aerobicizers like Melissa or Sheila struggle to keep weight training. They choose to be strong, but when their bodies grow more muscular and less feminine, they find it hard to face the judgment of the policing gaze without shame. Likewise I, a feminist researcher, am petrified that I will become fat regardless of my knowledge that the ideal thinness is an unrealistic goal designed to keep women dieting. One has to be extremely secure to be able to confront the everyday challenges put forward by the dominant discourses and even more confident to engage in an openly resistant action. We struggle to resist the body ideal but are not able to ignore it or achieve it. Our bodies remain imperfect.

Many of my interviewees feel that they are continuously required to improve some part of their bodies. Occasionally—like

Antoinette here—they reflect their unhappiness with a touch of irony: "We talk about it [the body] a lot. My roommates and I sit around all the time, which is hilarious, because we are all in pretty good shape . . . but we think we are overweight or out of shape or we have too much fat." Antoinette and her friends realize that they actually look acceptable, but they still want to work on their bodies. Considering that the same women criticize the present body ideal for being unrealistically thin, their desire for change appears quite contradictory. Daedra is aware of her problematic relationship with the ideal body:

> I think it's [the body ideal] really unhealthy, but . . . the ideal
> body is the perfect woman . . . with no fat, a beautifully shaped
> body. . . . You have to work your butt off for that type of body . . .
> and a lot of people can just never look that way because of the
> way they are. I think a lot of girls have fallen into a trap that
> they have to look certain way. . . . I'm falling into that trap.

She recognizes how "unhealthy" and unrealistic the body ideal is but admits, at the same time, that she longs to have such a body herself. She is trapped into a false fight with her body. Why do we fall into the illusionary body ideal? Why do we need to change our bodies that really do not need a change? Why do women drive themselves for the image they find fallacious? In her discussion of dieting practices Spitzack (1990) connects the present beauty ideal to health. This connection provides a starting point for my discussion of women's antagonistic relationships with their bodies.

The Panoptic Power: Be Positive and You Can Change!

Spitzack (1990) first locates the body image in patriarchal consumer society. Her discussion confirms my notions that the present image of the perfect female body jointly serves visions of traditional femininity—women's muscles are toned and firm but not "hulkish," visible, or big—and the economic interest of consumer society. However, Spitzack (1990) argues further that the influence of these powerful agencies on the female body become more obvious when discussed in connection with the discourse of health.

Spitzack's key to understanding women's situation in society is the "aesthetics of health." Women's present beauty standard is defined through health: The "healthy look" and "natural beauty" are now fashionable, albeit culturally constructed, descriptions of a good-looking woman. Basically, a beautiful body in this society is a healthy body, not only a slender body as ten years ago. This shift away from thinness should provide more diverse models for women, but most descriptions of the healthy look still center on the requirements of physical attractiveness. In reality, the healthy body "mandates even greater restrictions on female bodies" (Spitzack, 1990, p. 37). For example, toned muscles now cast the required healthy glow on the slender women. Bradley Block's (1988) article in *Health* magazine can serve as a case in point. He proclaims that the great body today is a healthy body and, therefore, there is no single great body "look." The article introduces six women who demonstrate the growing diversity. However, when we take a closer look at these women, we find that they are all thin, young, and toned. The only variable is their height. Therefore, the healthy body is only a new, fashionable rubric for the physically attractive body.

Spitzack (1990) adds high self-esteem, self-confidence, and increased assertiveness to the measures of "the healthy look." This connection is evident in aerobics. Many women in aerobics classes assert that exercise makes them feel better not only about their physique but also about "themselves," much like the *Shape* "Success Story" heroines in Duncan's (1994) study. For example, Eileen tells how aerobics boosts her self-confidence:

> When I do aerobics, I feel toned; if I'm not even any more toned, at least I feel my muscles are tighter and I feel better about myself.

In this sense, aerobics indirectly makes the participants' self-confidence grow, which at first glance seems to empower the exercisers. Eileen, however, connects positive feelings about herself to her looks: When one looks better, one feels better. Here a conversation by Sarah and Helen further reveals how good looks and positive self-image are inevitably linked with each other:

> *Helen:* It feels better, when the jeans fit looser.
> *Sarah:* You can loosen your belt buckle . . . and you feel more confident . . . you can look better, you feel better . . .you look skinnier, you feel more confident about your body.

> *Helen:* The reason [to go to aerobics] is to look better, not just for a better body, but for self-image . . . you definitely see a difference in your body, maybe other people don't but you feel a lot better.
>
> *Sarah:* You just feel like you are doing your best for the body; this is straining, but it's also good for us, so you feel better.

Helen obviously believes that good looks consist not only of a "skinny" body but also of a good self-image, which again is a result of the improved body. Therefore, better self-confidence derives from an attractive body.

Similar to the aerobicizers, magazine texts connect self-confidence with good looks. Many articles claim that a better body ignites positive self-esteem. Magazines describe confidence and self-esteem to characterize the beauty ideal of the 90s. Now women who have confidence and a positive attitude look good. Furthermore, the new beauty reflects our growth and self-acceptance; women now "want to look and feel good" (Lazarus, 1991, p. 62). In one article Rita Freedman (1991), a psychologist, points out the unquestionable link between a woman's self-esteem and her body image: "Improving your body image is quite likely to improve your self-esteem—so working on self-esteem will usually improve your body image also. Body-loathing leads to self-loathing, while body-love leads to self-love" (p. 98). Consequently, women should not try to turn themselves into something they are not. Instead, magazines encourage readers to find their normal, healthy body weights and accept their current measurements. For example, magazines advise women to focus on the positive points of their mirror reflections, not the flawed parts (Freedman, 1991; Wise, 1990). In addition, exercise clothing—although quite revealing—can be designed to accentuate the positives about one's body: "Magicians do it with smoke and mirrors, but bodywear designers use lines, stitching, nips and cuts to improve upon reality. These exercise pieces perform their own magic to accentuate your positives" (p. 92) writes Kathleen Riquelme (1994) in *Shape* to introduce "the latest and greatest in figure-flattering bodywear" (p. 92). The article is named ironically "Grand Illusions" as if to acknowledge that women have to trick themselves to feel positive with bodywear magic. Women need magic to mask the real body like magicians need to create an illusion by hiding the traces of their tricks.

Partly, such a discourse sounds quite strange after readers are advised to accept themselves as they are. Why do we need illusions if we are to accept our "real" bodies? Is it something to do with the models wearing these clothes that create "larger-than-life" illusions? Their perfectly thin bodies are not imaginary; they are real. We readers know we don't look like them, but with the right clothing we can at least make the best of our "bottom-heavy-figures" (Riquelme, 1994, p. 92).

Partly, this discourse is very encouraging: Every woman should accept her body, feel confident about it, and derive increased self-esteem from her appearance even if it is achieved through clothing magic. These positive feelings and increased powerfulness can free women from the regulative mechanism of the masculine ideology and consumerism. Spitzack (1990) argues, however, that this seemingly liberating discourse is in itself an illusion.

Illusions surrounding the women's fitness movement have been tackled previously by other feminist researchers (Kagan & Morse, 1988; Lenskyj, 1986; MacNeill, 1988; Theberge, 1987). According to these scholars, as pointed out earlier, the potentially liberating impulses in aerobics have been turned to serve the masculine ideology by cementing the effects of exercise with an improved appearance. Spitzack (1990) agrees that such claims of liberation only "mask increasing control with a rhetoric of freedom" (p. 42). For example, to maintain a healthy body, women are required to detect their bodily flaws more carefully. While constantly scrutinizing, one has to appear assertive and confident about one's body. Rather than being free, women are prisoners of more detailed regulations of beauty. Why do women accept this controlling discipline?

Spitzack (1990) believes that this control is implemented over women through a confession that women have secret problems. As I demonstrated earlier, the magazine texts were indeed convinced that their readers all possessed hidden body anxieties. Similar to Duncan's (1994) and Spitzack's (1990) dieters, exercisers were urged to admit that their bodies are imperfect and then take action to change for the better. One article advises the reader to follow these exact steps: "The most important thing I have learned is that you have to accept the way you look now in order to make a change . . .

you have to think positively about yourself, your appearance and your ability to accomplish your goals" (Glenn, 1992, p. 13). Another article assures us that we women are not helping ourselves by self-disgust, which only "creates a feeling of punishment" (Weaver & Ruther, 1991, p. 81) and defeats our attempts to change through exercise or weight loss programs. To successfully change our female bodies, we have to enjoy the process.

In sum, self-acceptance in exercise discourse promotes only bodily change; feeling positive about oneself is a necessary precondition for a model body. One is to accept one's bodyshape only to reform it. Focus on women's psychological well-being disguises increased attention to women's appearance and makes a deeper obsession with the body possible. This practice, Spitzack (1990) observes, is analogical to the treatment of another obsession, alcoholism. For instance, similar to Alcoholics Anonymous (AA), Overeaters Anonymous (OA) is patterned to help overeaters overcome their addiction. Exercise discourse advocates similar logic. Curiously, unlike other addictions, the confession of body problems does not free one from the obsessive behavior. On the contrary, it precedes a more thorough internalization of the addiction. To further implement the logic of confession, magazines, as I interpret them, urge women to take responsibility for their change. The Foucaultian concept of panoptic power explains some meanings embedded in this discourse.

In his analysis of contemporary society, Foucault (1979) argues that the body is a target of subtle disciplinary practices that seek to regulate its existence. Different disciplinary practices—which Foucault ties to modern forms of the army, the school, the hospital, the prison, and the manufactory—produce "docile bodies" ready to obey the regimes of power in society. Each person has internalized the control mechanisms through the body discipline. Individual citizens are, therefore, governed not by visible and openly repressive power sources, but by themselves. Foucault (1979) illustrates this power arrangement with an analogy to the Panopticon, a model prison whose circular design leaves all inmates in their individual cells permanently visible for the invisible supervisor in the center tower. Each prisoner is disciplined through his or her awareness of the supervisor rather than the supervisor's actual presence. The inmates are controlled by their own awareness of power. Spitzack (1990) finds dieting practices effectively disciplining women's bodies. She adds that the power over them is the most effective and captivating when the dieting discourse persuades the individual women to control their bodies on account of society. This logic is evident in aerobics.

Individual aerobicizers have taken the responsibility to control their bodies. They, sometimes questioningly, aim to change to resemble the ideal body. In addition, women feel good when their body shapes begin to approximate the ideal. However, societal standards, not women's own standards, define this ideal. Therefore, even the heightened self-esteem derived from a better body ultimately serves the purposes of the powerful to continue the oppression of women in society. Aerobics, like dieting, is part of a complex use of power over women in postmodern consumer society. The panoptic power arrangement, whereby the individuals control themselves on behalf of the powerful while the power source itself remains invisible, ensures that women are so occupied with obtaining the healthy look that they do not have time to wonder why they are doing it. Such a conclusion sounds quite depressing. Is the power over us so extensive and does it penetrate so deeply into our lives that whatever we think we are doing for our own benefit is actually harnessed to serve the purposes of an invisible power?

Conclusion

The invisible discursive power seems to effectively shape our thoughts and our behavior regarding our bodies. But if this grip were complete, women would passively follow the confessional logic without ever questioning it. Aerobicizers in this study have an active voice. They do not quietly dedicate their lives to body reconstruction, but they question the body ideal and are particularly skeptical about the media presentation of exercising women. This questioning leaves many women puzzled: They want to conform with the ideal, but they also find the whole process ridiculous. As a result, women's relationship with the body ideal is contradictory. This awareness, nevertheless, demonstrates that women have not internalized the panoptic power arrangement entirely. Aerobicizers do not, however, visibly resist the patriarchal body ideal by actively aiming to build transgressive bodies like the women bodybuilders. Aerobics does not offer an avenue for a large-scale revolution, at least not in the public arena. Nevertheless, in aerobics, much like women's bodybuilding (Bolin, 1992a), the private setting is quite different from the official discourse and does not necessarily follow the practices set by the dominant powers.

Although many aerobics classes revolve around body shaping (e.g., the toning moves are designed to improve appearance rather than functionality; the muscles are built to increase the caloric expenditure, not to gain strength), many aerobicizers participate for reasons other than improving their bodies. For example, aerobics is a source of enjoyment and not only because of the improved body (Markula, 1993a, 1993b, in press); it provides a safe environment for being physically active (Markula, in press); it supplies women with increased energy to carry on with their work (Markula, 1993b); it allows women to spend time on themselves (Markula, 1993b); and it is an opportunity to meet and make friends (Markula, 1993b). All these reasons, whose resistant potential I have discussed in detail in other contexts, demonstrate that aerobics does not entirely serve as a vehicle for the oppressive dominant body discourses. Furthermore, the real-life aerobics class does not appear similar to the video classes. For instance, the instructors are not all picture-perfect (recall Sarah's earlier comment about her instructor); the aerobicizers themselves do not wear skimpy clothes like the video or magazine exercisers (Markula, 1992); and not all classes include nonfunctional moves geared around body shaping (Markula, 1993b).

Central to my examination of the body in aerobics has been the view that culture consists of communication between different voices. In this paper, individual aerobicizers' voices engage in a dialogue with the media voices of aerobics. Following Bakhtin (1981) I assume that cultural dialogue implies certain power relations: Some voices are public and more dominant than other, private, voices. For example, the voices of the magazines and aerobics videotapes can dominate the public representations of the perfect aerobics body. It seems obvious that this public discourse around the aerobics body is a voice of oppression. However, individual aerobicizers struggle to give different meanings to the ideal aerobicizing body. Like Spitzack's (1990) dieters, aerobicizers privately question the logic of this discourse whose contradictory beauty requirements leave many of these women confused. This leads me to ask, if the public voice authoritatively shapes the meaning of women's exercising bodies, are women's private voices heard? Bakhtin (1981) believes that individual voices can use alternative channels to replace the official meanings with their own meanings. I believe this study is one attempt to bring women's private voices to a public stage and give them the lines in the body dialogue they deserve. I hope these voices are loud enough to ignite a change.

REFERENCES

Abu-Lughod, L. (1990). The romance of resistance: Tracing transformations of power through Bedouin women. *American Ethnologist*, 17 (1), 41–55.

Arveda, K. E. (1991). One size does not fit all, or how I learned to stop dieting and love the body. *Quest*, 43, 135–47.

Bakhtin, M. M. (1981). Discourse in novel. In M. Holquist (Ed.), *The dialogical imagination* (pp. 259–442). Austin: University of Texas Press.

Balsamo, A. (1994). Feminist bodybuilding. In S. Birrell & C. L. Cole (Eds.), *Women, sport, and culture* (pp. 341–52). Champaign, IL: Human Kinetics.

Barrett, E. (1991, March). The ultimate guide to sexy muscles. *Self*, pp. 137–43.

Bartky, S. L. (1988). Foucault, femininity, and the modernization of patriarchal power. In I. Diamond & L. Quinby (Eds.), *Feminism and Foucault: Reflections on resistance* (pp. 61–86). Boston: Northeastern University Press.

Block, B. W. (1988, July). Great American body. *Health*, pp. 27–35.

Bolin, A. (1992a). Beauty or beast: The subversive soma. In C. Ballerino Cohen (Ed.), *Body contours: Deciphering scripts of gender and power* (pp. 54–77). New Brunswick, NJ: Rutgers University Press.

Bolin, A. (1992b). Flex appeal, food, and fat: Competitive bodybuilding, gender and diet. *Play & Culture*, 5, 378–400.

Bolin, A. (1992c). Vandalized vanity: Feminine physiques betrayed and portrayed. In F. Mascia-Lees (Ed.), *Tatoo, torture, adornment and disfigurement: The denaturalization of the body in culture and text* (pp. 79–99). Albany: State University of New York Press.

Bordo, S. (1989). The body and the reproduction of femininity: A feminist appropriation of Foucault. In A. M. Jaggar & S. R. Bordo (Eds.), *Gender/body/knowledge: Feminist reconstructions of being and knowing* (pp. 13–33). New Brunswick, NJ: Rutgers University Press.

Bordo, S. (1990). Reading the slender body. In M. Jacobus, E. Fox Keller, & S. Shuttleworth (Eds.), *Body/politics: Women and the discourse of science* (pp. 83–112). New York: Routledge.

Brick, L. (1990, May). The get set for summer workout. *Shape*, pp. 81–87.

Bruner, E. (1993). Introduction: The ethnographic self and the personal self. In P. Benson (Ed.), *Anthropology and literature* (pp. 1–26). Urbana: University of Illinois Press.

Chernin, K. (1981). *The obsession: Reflections on the tyranny of slenderness.* New York: Harper & Row.

Clifford, J., & Marcus, G. E. (1986). *Writing culture: Poetics and politics of ethnography.* Berkeley: University of California Press.

Cole, C. (1993). Resisting the canon: Feminist cultural studies, sport, and technologies of the body. *Journal of Sport & Social Issues*, 17, 77–97.

Cooper, K. H. (1968). *Aerobics.* New York: Simon & Schuster.

Cooper, K. H. (1970). *New aerobics.* Philadelphia: Lippincott.

Coward, R. (1985). *Female desires: How they are sought, bought and packaged.* New York: Grove Weidenfeld.

Daniels, D. B. (1992). Gender (body) verification (building). *Play & Culture*, 5, 370–77.

de Certeau, M. (1984). *The practice of everyday life.* Berkeley: University of California Press.

Denzin, N. (1992). *Symbolic interactionism and cultural studies: The politics of interpretation.* Cambridge, MA: Blackwell.

Dubisch, J. (1986). Introduction. In J. Dubisch (Ed.), *Gender and power in rural Greece* (pp. 3–41). Princeton, NJ: Princeton University Press.

Duncan, M. C. (1994). The politics of women's body images and practices: Foucault, the panopticon, and *Shape* magazine. *Journal of Sport & Social Issues,* 18, 48–65.

Dunn, R. (1991). Postmodernism: Populism, mass culture, and avant-garde. *Theory, Culture & Society* 8, 111–35.

Fairclough, E. (1980, May). Legs. *Women's Sports,* pp. 34–53.

Farah, A. D. (1984, January). Legs. *Health,* pp. 38–42.

Featherstone, M. (1988). In pursuit of the postmodern: An introduction. *Theory, Culture & Society,* 6, 195–213.

Featherstone, M. (1991). The body in consumer culture. In M. Featherstone, M. Hepworth, & B. S. Turner (Eds.), *The body: Social process and cultural theory* (pp. 170–96). London: Sage.

Foley, D. E. (1992). Making the familiar strange: Writing critical sports narratives. *Sociology of Sport Journal,* 9, 36–47.

Fonda, J. (1981). *Jane Fonda's workout book.* New York: Simon & Schuster.

Foucault, M. (1979). *Discipline and punish: The birth of the prison.* New York: Vintage Books.

Freedman, R. (1991, July). Mind over mirror. *Shape,* pp. 66–68.

Gates, R. (1991, March). Body image: The problem with trying to be perfect. *IDEA Magazine,* pp. 28–29.

Glenn, J. (1992, March 2). Healthy mind, healthy diet. *The Daily Illini,* p. 13.

Gottlieb, A. (1989). Rethinking female pollution: The Beng of the Cote D'Ivoire. *Dialectical Anthropology,* 14, 65–79.

Guthrie, S. R., & Castelnuovo, S. (1992). Elite women bodybuilders: Models of reistance or compliance. *Play & Culture,* 5, 401–8.

Holmlund, C. A. (1989). Visible difference and flex appeal. *Cinema Journal,* 28(4), 38–51.

Hoover, S. (1980, January). Exercise and all that jazz. *Women's Sports,* pp. 10–18.

Imm, P. (1989). *Exercise habits and perceptions of body image in female exercisers.* Paper presented at fourth Annual IDEA Conference, Los Angeles, CA.

Jacobs, C. (1991, March). Winning at the losing game. *Shape,* pp. 74–77.

Johnston, R. (1986). The story so far: And further transformations? In D. Punter (Ed.), *Introduction to contemporary cultural studies* (pp. 277–313). London: Longmans.

Kagan, E., & Morse, M. (1988). The body electronic: Aerobic exercise video. *The Drama Review,* 32, 164–80.

Kaufman, E. (1989, December). Put some muscle into it. *Self,* pp. 123–28.

Kenen, R. L. (1987). Double messages, double images: Physical fitness, self-concepts, and women's exercise classes. *Journal of Physical Education, Recreation, and Dance,* 58(6), 76–79.

Laurence, L. (1992, January). Shoulders are sexy, *Self,* pp. 102–5.

Lazarus, J. (1991, September). Beauty and the best. *Shape,* pp. 62–64.

Lenskyj, H. (1986). *Out of bounds: Women, sport and sexuality.* Toronto, ON: Women's Press.

Lenskyj, H. (1994). Sexuality and femininity in sport contexts: Issues and alternatives. *Journal of Sport and Social Issues, 18,* 356–76.

MacNeill, M. (1988). Active women, media representations, ideology. In J. Harvey & G. Cantelon (Eds.), *Not just a game* (pp. 195–212). Altona, MB: University of Ottawa Press.

Markula, P. (1992, November). *Bodywear that lets the body speak: Pleasures of fitness fashion in aerobics.* Paper presented at the Thirteenth Annual Conference of the North American Society for Sociology of Sport, Toledo, OH.

Markula, P. (1993a). Looking good, feeling good: Strengthening mind and body in aerobics. In L. Laine (Ed.), *On the fringes of sport* (pp. 93–99). Sankt Augustin, Germany: Akademia Verlag.

Markula, P. (1993b). *Total-body-tone-up: Paradox and women's realities in aerobics.* Unpublished doctoral dissertation, University of Illinois, Urbana-Champaign.

Markula, P. (in press). Postmodern aerobics: Contradictions and resistance. In A. Bolin & J. Granskog (Eds.), *Athletic intruders.* Newbury Park, CA: Sage.

Martin, E. (1987). *The woman in the body: Cultural analysis of reproduction.* Boston: Beacon Press.

Martin, E. (1989). The cultural construction of gendered bodies: Biology and metaphors of production and destruction. *Ethos, 3–4,* 143–59.

McRobbie, A. (1994). *Postmodernism and popular culture.* London: Routledge.

Miller, L., & Penz, O. (1991). Talking bodies: Female bodybuilders colonize a male preserve. *Quest, 43,* 148–63.

Patton M. Q. (1980). *Qualitative evaluation methods.* Beverly Hills, CA: Sage.

Riquelme, K. (1994, March). Grand illusions. *Shape,* pp. 92–97.

Rosaldo, R. (1989). *Culture and truth: The remaking of social analysis.* Boston: Beacon Press.

Rothlein, L. (1988, May). Portrait of an aerobic dancer. *Women's Sports and Fitness,* p. 18.

Rover, E. (1992, January). Biceps strengthener. *Self,* p. 48.

Sorensen, J. (1979). *Aerobic dancing.* New York: Rawson, Wade.

Spitzack, C. (1990). *Confessing excess: Women and the politics of body reduction.* Albany: State University of New York Press.

Stallings, J. (1980). Fantasy, fact. *Women's Sports,* p. 49.

Sternlicht, E. (1990a, January). Testing your triceps. *Shape,* pp. 46-48.

Sternlicht, E. (1990b, February). Behind every great shape . . . is a great behind. *Shape,* pp. 38–40.

Sternlicht, E. (1990c, July). Try this for thighs. *Shape,* p. 34.

Sternlicht, E. (1991, May). Up in arms. *Shape,* pp. 48–50.

Strathern, M. (1981). Culture in a netbag: The manufacture of a subdiscipline in anthropology. *Man, 16*(4). 276–92.

Theberge, N. (1987). Sport and women's empowerment. *Women's Studies International Forum, 10,* 387–93.

Tucker, S. (1990, July). What is the ideal body. *Shape,* pp. 94–112.

Weaver, G., & Ruther, K. (1991, March). Learning to love exercise. *Shape,* pp. 81–86.

Wise, E. (1990, July). Feeling fat. *Shape,* pp. 20–21.

Wolf, N. (1990). *The Beauty Myth.* London: Vintage.

DEBORAH GREGORY

15

Heavy Judgment

A Sister Talks about the Pain of "Living Large"

This article demonstrates the body as a site for discipline and training, while also being a site for resistance to and transformation of conflicted systems of meaning. Let's look at how much of this article can be interpreted as a resistance reading of weight consciousness in American society.

1. Please list the institutions or professions used to identify the overweight body as a problem. Now list the institutions used to challenge the conventional interpretation of overweight. On what topics do they speak with a monolithic voice? On what topics do they disagree? Are you convinced? Why or why not?

2. How does using the institutions that challenge the definition of overweight still support aspects of the status quo? For example, can you find sentences that reconfirm the legitimacy, power, and status of medicine as an institution to define what is healthy? Or as another example, how do the overweight within this article demonstrate discipline? Why is this important? Or how are gender performances reproduced?

3. How does this article portray African-American women and/or larger size women as having a "clearer" vision of American society? How do they challenge the discourse(s) that identify them as the "problem" that needs to be transformed?

4. What are some of the polysemic symbols, that is, symbols that can be interpreted differently? Describe *both* the standard and resistant meanings attached to these symbols.

From Deborah Gregory, "Heavy Judgment: A Sister Talks about the Pain of 'Living Large,' " *Essence* 25 (August 1994): 57–58, 105, 110–12. Reprinted by permission of the author.

Thirteen years ago I was a model in Europe. I was cramped inside a tiny fitting room in Paris, and a couturier's purse-lipped assistant put a tape measure around my hips, then screamed "Trop forte!" I didn't speak French, but I knew Madame wasn't delighted with my curvy proportions. The next day another designer called my agency and told them he wouldn't book me because I was too fat. The evidence in question: At five feet 11 inches tall I had the audacity to tip the scales at 140 pounds. Scandalous! It has taken me many years to forgive myself for not maintaining the rigid 125-to-130-pound model mandate—and to forgive the fashion industry for requiring mannequins to be paper-thin.

"Sashaying," however, isn't the only business practicing fat-cell-count discrimination: Monitoring women's size has become a weighty issue in the workplace. My favorite rationale is the film industry's hocus-pocus excuse that actresses used to be skinny because celluloid automatically adds ten pounds to their image. But, mind you, it's okay for hefty actors like Forest Whitaker (*A Rage in Harlem* and *The Crying Game)* to bare it all in love scenes. I have painfully discovered the extent of fat discrimination over the last ten years as I have vacillated between 140 and 235 pounds. I currently weigh around 200. What has come with the extra pounds is blatant professional and social discrimination, both to my face and behind my back—the kind that routinely dismisses my skills, talents, and God-given physical beauty.

The most recent example? A professional colleague, Tony J., was gracious enough to take a copy of my video reel to a television producer he knew at a network. Upon his return, Tony avoided my phone calls. When I finally reached him, he dillydallied before revealing, with much trepidation, that although the producer liked my "flavor" and was impressed with my journalistic credentials, he would only be interested in putting me on camera if I lost weight.

The toughest fact to swallow was that the producer in question is Black and the show is targeted to a Black audience. Has society's obsession with keeping women skinny bogarded its way into the Black community's psyche? The answer, painfully, is yes. Where once largeness was accepted—even revered—among Black folks, it now carries the same unmistakable stigma as it does among Whites.

Tipping the Scales of Equality

Since the 1960s, the Western standard of beauty for women has become drop-dead thin. Today the average American woman is five feet four inches tall and 145 pounds, yet models are 23 percent below the average weight, compared with only 8 percent 35 years ago. Who's hit hardest by these waifishly slim media images? We are. Black and Latina women are twice as likely to be overweight as White women. Forty-eight percent of Black women and 30 percent of Latinas are overweight, as compared with 26 percent of White women, according to the National Center for Health Statistics.

Pound for pound, women suffer enormous social and professional consequences for heftier proportions. Consider these chilling statistics: Large women are 20 percent less likely to marry than their thinner counterparts. They also have household incomes that average $6,710 lower and are 10 percent more likely to be living in poverty, according to an eight-year study led by Steven L. Gortmaker, Ph.D., of the Harvard School of Public Health and published in the *New England Journal of Medicine*. (The typical obese woman in Gortmaker's study was five feet three inches tall and weighed 200 pounds.)

On the other hand, the same research revealed that obesity had less impact on men. Although heavy men are less likely to marry (only by 11 percent, however), they are just as well off financially as their thinner counterparts.

Many a large sister can attest to the consequences of society's "fat phobia." Reveals singer Annette Taylor, who has been a size 16 for the past two years and is now a size 14, "I haven't gotten jobs because of my size. For example, I was highly recommended to an A & R executive at a major record company who was searching for a female singer. The first question he asked me over the phone was 'What size are you?' Needless to say, I wasn't even asked to audition. Another time, I auditioned for the female spot in C & C Music Factory. Even though my vocal style was a perfect match for the group, it was clear that I didn't get the part because of my size." Laments Taylor: "The entertainment business is *very* discriminatory against larger women. My manager even told me that I have to lose weight so I can be video-ready."

Adds E. K. Daufin, another large sister and an assistant professor of English and communications at Fort Lewis College in Durango, Colorado: "I've had students in my class hand me diets." Milana Frank, a television producer in Miami, Florida, makes an observation that sums up the woes of large women best: "Because of my size, I have experienced oppression, depression, and recession."

A Pound of Flesh

Who determines obesity? Frankly, it appears to be society at large with its ever-so-skimpy standards of how much "fat" is acceptable on a woman. Even at my heaviest weight (235 pounds on my nearly six-foot frame), I have never appeared or defined myself as fat. Large, yes. Fat, no. Yet every day I have to listen to people call me fat bitch, Fat Albert's wife, big-ass bitch, Heavy D, overweight lover. (At least Heavy D made money off the catchy tune of this same name!)

The medical community is currently involved in a "great weight debate," struggling to define obesity. Scientific surveys certainly don't tell the whole story; they usually deal in averages and don't reflect individual factors that influence a person's weight status.

In 1991, the federal government took a stab at developing a more meaningful way to assess weight. Dietary guidelines for Americans was produced jointly by the U.S. Department of Health and Human Services and the U.S. Department of Agriculture. The guidelines offer three criteria for determining the appropriateness of a person's weight: disease risk factors, weight tables (which group men and women together) and body-fat distribution. Of the three criteria, the government's weight tables have attracted the most attention by far, much to the frustration of C. Wayne Callaway, M.D., an associate clinical professor of medicine at George Washington University in Washington, D.C., who was on the advisory committee that developed the criteria.

"The weight tables are only *one* factor in assessing a person's weight-related health risks," Callaway states firmly. "The *most* important factor is whether the person has a medical condition that would improve with weight loss, such as high blood pressure or borderline high blood sugar, an early sign of diabetes." Obviously someone with conditions like these who is on the middle to high end of the acceptable range of the weight table should try to lose weight.

The Weight Scale: God or Guide?

It's sad but true that most of us determine our ideal size by the a-woman-can-never-be-too-thin mantra that has seized our society. And if we are in the dreaded category—a large woman—we are constantly on a diet or, at the very least, profoundly ashamed of our size. I have never failed to notice that when a few women get together, sooner or later the conversation turns to pound-

Dietary Guidelines for Americans

HEIGHT (WITHOUT SHOES)	WEIGHT, LB (WITHOUT CLOTHES)	
	AGES 19–34*	35 AND OLDER*
5'0"	97–128	108–138
5'1"	101–132	111–143
5'2"	104–137	115–148
5'3"	107–141	119–152
5'4"	111–146	122–157
5'5"	114–150	126–162
5'6"	118–155	130–167
5'7"	121–160	134–172
5'8"	125–164	138–178
5'9"	129–168	142–183
5'10"	132–171	146–188
5'11"	136–179	151–194
6'0"	140–184	155–199
6'1"	144–189	159–205
6'2"	148–195	164–210
6'3"	152–200	168–216

*Women or men. From the U.S. Department of Health and Human Services and the U.S. Department of Agriculture.

pondering, and inevitably even the thinnest in the group thinks she could stand to "lose a few pounds."

For too many women, the almighty scale rules our self-esteem. I used to weigh myself every morning—and I do mean before I drank *any* liquids, or even put on my perfume. In the final analysis, I found that I would be depressed no matter what the numbers were. Frustrated, I finally threw my scale out the window into the alley and heard it land with a resounding thud.

What is the root of society's obsession with women's body weight? In the PBS documentary *The Famine Within*, psychologist Catherine Steiner-Adair makes this astute observation: "I don't think it's a total coincidence that at exactly the same time women are being told they have equal rights and equal access to all professions and careers, there is a hidden clause that says, 'You can have equal opportunity as long as you have a body size that *very* few women can maintain.'"

You may be thinking, *Oh come on, we're much more accepting of large women in the Black community than Whites are.* "Black women are just as concerned about weight as White women," explains Shiriki Kumanyika, Ph.D., a professor of epidemiology at Pennsylvania State University College of Medicine in Hershey. "The more we try to emulate the mainstream image, the more the desire to be thin is mimicked and the higher the risk of eating disorders in our community."

Whose Fault Is Fatness?

One of the most cherished assumptions that many people have is that body size and shape are under the complete control of the individual—and anyone who is heavy, plump, overweight, or fat is greasin' around the clock. "This is a complete misconception," explains Sally E. Smith, executive director of the National Association to Advance Fat Acceptance in Sacramento, California. "A person's weight is determined by a number of factors, including genetics, metabolism and dieting history." Our denial of these factors is what fuels the $33 *billion* dieting industry that urges us to believe only willpower stands between us and the body of a runway diva! On many occasions I've been out with friends (or even people I don't know) and my menu choices have been scrutinized: "Maybe you should get a salad." "You know fish is less fattening than chicken." "How much do you eat?" I've grown very careful about what I order in public and often feel self-conscious about eating, period.

The truth is, it has been a long time since I've overeaten compulsively. Due to a long history of dieting, I can no longer afford that luxury because I am one of the many victims of the pitfalls of dieting. "You can actually diet your way up to fatness," says Smith.

I know firsthand. When I originally reached my first high weight (which was 190 pounds), I went on a low-calorie diet and lost 45 pounds in four months. After a few months at my lower weight, I went back to eating normally and not only gained the weight back but also reached a new high weight of 235 pounds. "With each period of low-calorie dieting, 95 to 98 percent of dieters can expect to gain back the weight and an additional 20 percent above that," claims Smith.

The question still remains: Why exactly are 48 percent of African-American women overweight? Part of it *is* genetics. "Black women have always been endowed with large hips, buttocks, legs and breasts," explains Monica Dixon, a dietician and image consultant in San Francisco. "This tendency dates back hundreds of years and is probably an adaptation to famine control. Historically, those who were able to maintain their adipose tissue [a layer of fat beneath the skin and around various internal organs] were the ones who survived the periods of famine in African countries." Therefore the genetic body type of women that prevailed in Africa became those with bigger hips and larger buttocks. As a matter of fact, in some parts of Africa, women who are well endowed are considered a prize, explains Mavis Thompson, M.D., a holistic practitioner in Brooklyn and author of *The Black Health Library Guide to Obesity* (Owl Books).

Another crucial factor: Black women may use food and body size to fight personal trauma. "When it comes to body weight, discrimination based on race, class, poverty and sexual orientation affects African-American women tremendously," says Thompson. While men may act out their rage through violence, sex, alcohol, or drug addiction, women tend to eat as a way of coping—or to obliterate pain.

Used to Abuse

Some experts believe that discrimination against overweight individuals is so profound that Congress should consider extending legal protection to ensure their civil rights. "Discrimination against fat women seems to be the last fashionable form of overt prejudice people can safely indulge in without remorse," says Albert J. Stunkard, Ph.D., a professor of psychiatry at the University of Pennsylvania.

Last winter, in what could be a major legal precedent, an overweight Rhode Island State mental-institution attendant, Bonnie Cook, won back her position and $100,000 in damages when she was turned down for the job because of her weight.

There isn't a day that goes by that I don't have to endure comments about my weight from coworkers, people in elevators and even my tax accountant ("Have you been to Weight Watchers yet?" he queried on my last visit). Brothers leer at me on the street and describe my proportions in exact detail. And well-meaning professional colleagues *constantly* make remarks about my appearance.

Fat women jokes have also become the stock and trade of every stand-up comic's repertoire. On his album *Talkin' Shit*, comedian Martin Lawrence makes the timely observation that "women are always worrying about their weight!" But then the risqué Martin goes on to poke fun at us: "People make excuses for their weight. Ain't no excuses. It's my metabolism. No, it's not. It's them *Twizzlers* in your goddamn back pocket! Let the Reese's Cups go. Get out of the Haagen-Daas line! If you are weighing over 250, stay the f—- out of Spandex!"

Why is it still okay to abuse large women? Explains Julia Boyd, a psychotherapist in Seattle and author of the book *In the Company of My Sisters: Black Women and Self-Esteem*, "We are very threatened by large-size women because they represent our worst fears—our own hidden fears of being overweight and rejected. They also disturb the status quo of the acceptable image that society has diligently enforced on women."

Living Large and *Healthy*

The real issue for large women is being *healthy*. Each of us must find our *own* body weight based on our genetics and height–body-mass index (small, medium, or large frame). We should feel fit and flexible and be able to run for buses and bound up flights of stairs. We must make the commitment (and stick to it!) to take care of ourselves by exercising and eating properly. If weight is really causing a health problem, we *must* address that. I exercise three to four times a week, am in excellent health (I visit my physician twice a year and have complete blood workups once a year) and adhere to a fairly healthy diet.

Basically, I feel great. What causes me a great deal of emotional anxiety is the glaring fact that society doesn't embrace women like me as readily as it does my thinner counterparts. All around me I see large women who are beautiful, stylish, glowing, healthy and fit. But I also see too many who reject themselves, make themselves sick by dieting dangerously and desperately try to live up to an impossible beauty ideal.

Perhaps, most important, large women need to reject body size as the chief determinant of competence. We must spend time taking care of ourselves and developing professional and social skills that will offer true fulfillment. The bottom line: *Any* woman who relies solely on her looks for self-esteem will always be at someone else's mercy!

GLOSSARY

Accommodation: Adaption or adjustment practiced by an individual or a group seeking admission or assimilation into a larger group, culture, or social body. A process in which an individual or group goes along with current interpretations or actions.

Agency: The state of being in action or exerting power usually in reference to the self. A person is said to have agency when they exert power for their own best interests.

Ahistorical: Generally, that which is outside history, not concerned with history or historical development.

Androgynous: Not clearly male or female, or (specialized) having both male and female features. Showing or possessing both characteristics of male and female traits.

Anthropomorphism: The representation of nonhuman objects, whether real or fictitious, in human form; the ascription of human attributes, characteristics, and/or preoccupations to nonhuman beings.

Commodification: To turn into or treat as a commodity or a mass-produced, unspecialized product. To transform one into a product ready for exchange or exploitation within a market.

Commodity feminism: Political discourses inherent in feminism re-framed into a style and product to be purchased. Advertisements suggest that women's emancipation is attainable through the consumption of a product. Power imbalances are redressed in terms of consumption.

Commodity fetishism: A preoccupation with the status possessions afford to their owners, and their exchange value independent of their worth. The fetishism of commodities, in Marx's sense, covers all commodities. It is basic to the commodity form in which social relations are hidden or disguised.

Cosmetic pharmacology: The use of drugs to transform personalities in order to meet cultural ideals. The culture constructs a psychological ideal of the mind and then manufactures additional substances for those who have trouble attaining those standards. Individuals then medicate themselves as the troubled entity, as if they are the problem in need of change. Ignored are the larger cultural forces that generate the display of symptoms and a pharmacological industry dedicated to profiting from eradicating them.

Cyborgs: Science fiction creation that is part human and part machine or, more loosely, sometimes a robot in human form. Examples are developed in the *Terminator* films and *RoboCop*. By transgressing the boundaries between body and machine, cyborgs display symbolic crossing of other borders: production and reproduction, artificial and real, nature and culture, and the individual and "the collective."

Depoliticize: To cause to have no political connections. When one discusses an artwork or any other thing without reference to the political and social circumstances informing its creation, one depoliticizes it. This is a particular problem when the only concern is aesthetics. To remove the political aspect from; remove from political influence or control.

Determinism: A belief system that suggests behavior is predestined or driven by prior causes to such a degree that free will is largely an illusion.

Disciplinary technologies: Concept originated by Michel Foucault, they are the techniques used by society to discipline individuals' minds and bodies. As opposed to the direct effect of torture and punishment, they are in many ways indirect and invisible.

Discourse: A type of language constructed through and by an ideology. It is used by and between particular individuals, groups, or professions for specific effects. Discourse is not an absolute, but a relative term in which linguistic structures help to guide perception, descriptions, evaluations, and the maintenance of a specific social reality. A scientific discourse would mean the language with which a particular group constructs its conception of objective and reproducible truth as the paramount reality.

Docility: In contemporary social theory, when a person is quiet and easily controlled, the person becomes voiceless.

Dystopia: The opposite of utopia; an extremely disagreeable place construed as an era, a political state, or even a state of mind. Dystopias are usually obvious, as in Orwell's *1984* or Huxley's *Brave New World*.

Embodiment: To represent in bodily or material form. To deprive of abstractness, to give tangible or discernable form to. To make part of a system or whole; to incorporate.

Empowerment: The gaining of economic, political, or cultural power by a group or individual that was previously oppressed.

Epidermal hierarchy: Specific physical features of the body become visual markers, translating seemingly neutral physical differences into geographies, politics, and ideologies. This seeming "natural" reading of the body's physical display is placed within a sociocultural context.

Essentialism: Concept that refers to the primacy of essences, that is, the seemingly permanent, unchanging, "real" identities that lie "behind" appearances. Gender and ethnicity are two areas where essentialist concepts are challenged. Essentialism is frequently attacked by postmodernists in writings that are thought to have been produced by unreflective racists or sexists.

False consciousness: Any belief, idea, ideology, et cetera, that interferes with an exploited and oppressed person or group being able to perceive their oppression and the source of their oppression.

Fetishized: To create a sense that a material object, an idea, a person, or an institution may have powers seemingly unrelated to commonly assumed qualities.

Hegemony: Predominant influence. A type of social control or coercion that wins consent to its rule from those it subjugates. A process in which a governing power establishes a pattern of domination that is perceived as desirable, universal, natural, and inevitable. The maintenance of hegemony is dependent upon this effect, which makes the power of the dominant class appear desirable and natural. This in turn makes the meanings chosen by the dominant group appear to be universal. Hegemonic power does not operate through direct physical punishment or codes of law but is invisible and indirect, operating through a control that is internally legitimated. The power relationships are produced, negotiated, and reproduced through "micro-powers" inherent in social relationships. Hegemony is, however, not a stable entity but what Antonio Gramsci called a "moving equilibrium" in which power positions are ceaselessly revised. Power is thus not totally possessed by a specific group once and for all, but is realized through a series of shifts of power, sometimes across groups and alliances. Hegemony is thus constantly being reconfigured and resymbolized to maintain the consent of those who are ruled.

Ideology: A pattern of beliefs superimposed onto the world by identifiable social groups, that guides a particular interpretation of that world. The result, particularly in Marxist thought, is a distortion of reality to maintain authority over it. These patterns of beliefs are communicated through institutional representations. An ideology is made intelligible to individuals through their interactions with and within institutions. For example, capitalism as a pattern of beliefs that supports consumption, is experienced through the institution of the family. Via allowances, children are taught how to save and spend, and learn the meaning of value in commodity relationships so that these relationships seem natural.

Infrastructures: The basic structures that organize and direct processes within an ideology or culture.

Jouissance: More than mere enjoyment, an enjoyment with a sexually orgasmic connotation. In some meanings, the idea of taking pleasure in something, with an implicit analogy drawn between demand and desire.

Legitimation: The process by which a power comes to be at least tacitly accepted as an authority. Consent to authority.

Marginalization: Existing at the edges of a social structure, institution, or culture. When individuals or groups are assigned to the border, with correspondingly fewer rewards from the dominant group. To make others feel less important by associating them with what one considers dispensable or superfluous is to marginalize them. The opposite of central: in the margins, peripheral, or nonessential.

Medicalization: Redefining a behavior as an illness or disease.

Metaphor: A comparison without using the words "like" or "as." Generally, a metaphor conveys an impression about something relatively unfamiliar by drawing an analogy between it and something familiar. A metaphor is never innocent, but always implies an undercurrent of political meanings.

Negotiation: A relationship in which meaning is not imposed but arises from an interaction.

Normative: Conforming to standards or conventional patterns.

Objectification: The process of turning something into an object. The term is very commonly used to describe the dehumanizing oppression of women, visible minorities, and other marginalized groups.

Oppositional: Attempting to resist a dominant theory or practice.

Other: A view of another person, or group of people, as being opposite, dissimilar, excluded, alien, inferior to. Also included in some meanings, a projection of negative feelings or fears, arising from the individual's own issues, onto images of other people.

Panoptic: A comprehensive or panoramic view that provides self-control through an internalized system of observation. Jeremy Bentham's Panopticon was a model for an ideal prison in which a minimum number of guards in a shuttered guard tower could observe a maximum number of prisoners. Prisoners disciplined their own behavior as if they were under constant surveillance by guards in the tower. Michel Foucault appropriated the idea as a metaphor for the scientific point of view, which can supposedly survey everything objectively.

Panoramic: Pertaining to a panorama—that is, an unobstructed view in every direction. Figuratively, then, "panoramic" indicates comprehensiveness or thoroughness in the presentation of a subject. By extension it can mean any of several types of visual presentations that endeavor to represent an unobstructed view.

Paradigm: The methods, theories, facts, hypotheses, instrumentation, standards, production, and dissemination that make up a system of knowledge. An example, pattern, or standard. By extension, the term also refers to the basic structure of given mind-sets or models of knowledge.

Patriarchy: Literally, the rule of the father. A social organization in which men are the heads of their families, and descent and inheritance are reckoned in the male line. Feminism characterizes patriarchy more generally as socially sanctioned male dominance.

Phenomenology: Both a methodology and a philosophy that views the individual as active in constructing meaning in and through his or her own experience. Phenomenology challenges the assumption of an objective detached observer as being able to get outside of social experience. Instead, it is an approach that focuses on the individual's experience as the primary evidence of reality. It is a theory and philosophy that supports a reality that is directly apprehended by the senses.

Phrenology: The physiological hypothesis that mental faculties and traits of character are shown on the surface of the head or skull; craniology. A theory that linked mental functions to particular parts of the skull and asserted that the size and shape of the skull indicated the strength or weakness of particular mental faculties.

Polysemic: Having more than one meaning.

Postindustrial: Characterizing a society moving from economic dependence on heavy manufacturing to one more centered on information exchange.

Power: One of the crucial conceptions of much postmodern thought. Forces that are taken for granted as given, but do not have objectively verifiable existence. For Foucaultians, these forces are determined by knowledge systems that are peculiar to given social groups who have managed to suppress rival groups' belief systems.

Praxis: Employing theory and critical methods in a particular way that connects action, activity, and ideological insight. Highlights the indissolubility of action and significance.

Reification: The act of making something abstract into something concrete. In Marxist terminology, reification usually means treating human actions, characteristics, and relations as if they were objective things with an independent existence. Femininity, for example, is treated as something inherent in lace. Through purchasing and wearing lace, a person appears feminine. Lace appears to have the "concreteness" of femininity. See False consciousness.

Resistance: An attempt to oppose a dominant force, by direct or indirect means.

Subject: In contemporary social theory, there are two meanings of the word "subject." A person can be subject to someone else by control and dependence. For example, in feudalism, a person was a subject of the king. The second meaning is oriented toward how a person is connected to his or her own identity by a conscience or self-knowledge. See Subjective. Both meanings suggest a relationship of power, of someone or something that subjugates or overwhelms, and makes subject to influences.

Subjective: Characteristic of reality as perceived by a specific individual. The perspective of objects and events experienced in a manner peculiar to a particular individual and therefore not reproducible, in the manner of an "objective" scientific inquiry. This is what most speakers mean when they say that interpretation, for example, is purely subjective. But is it?

Subvert: To undermine fixed or unquestioned assumptions usually associated with a particular ideology.

Utopia: A perfect, remote, and almost unthinkably ideal "place" construed as location, an era, a political state, or even a state of mind and therefore the opposite of dystopia.

REFERENCES

Armstrong, D. (1983). *The Political Anatomy of the Body*. New York: Cambridge University Press.

———. (1987). Bodies of Knowledge: Foucault and the Problem of Human Anatomy. In G. Scambler (ed.), *Sociological Theory and Medical Sociology*. London: Tavistock.

Balsamo, A. (1996). *Technologies of the Gendered Body: Reading Cyborg Women*. Durham: Duke University Press.

de Beauvoir, S. (1989). *The Second Sex*. New York: Vintage Press. (Originally published 1952.)

Bourdieu, P. (1984). *Distinction: A Social Critique of the Judgement of Taste*. London: Routledge.

———. (1986). The Forms of Capital. In J. Richardson (ed.), *Handbook of Theory and Research for the Sociology of Education* (pp. 241–58). New York: Greenwood Press.

Burnham, J. (1989). The Quest for Health as the History of Modernization. *Reviews in American History* 17, 357–63.

Butler, J. (1990). *Gender Trouble: Feminism and the Subversion of Identity*. New York: Routledge.

Douglas, M. (1970). *Natural Symbols: Explorations in Cosmology*. New York: Pantheon Books.

———. (1984). *Purity and Danger: An Analysis of the Concepts of Pollution and Taboo*. London: Routledge.

Foucault, M. (1973). *Madness and Civilization: A History of Insanity in the Age of Reason*. New York: Vintage Press.

———. (1979). *Discipline and Punish: The Birth of the Prison* (trans. A. Sheridan). New York: Vintage Books.

Goldman, R. (1992). *Reading Ads Socially*. New York: Routledge.

Gowaty, P. A. (1997). *Feminism and Evolutionary Biology: Boundaries, Intersections, and Frontiers*. New York: Chapman & Hall.

Grosz, E. A. (1994). *Volatile Bodies: Toward a Corporeal Feminism.* Bloomington: Indiana University Press.

Irigaray, L. (1991). *The Irigaray Reader* (ed. M. Whitford). Cambridge, MA: Basil Blackwell.

Jonas, H. (1970). The Nobility of Sight: A Study in the Phenomenology of the Senses. In S. Spicker (ed.), *The Philosophy of the Body: Rejections of Cartesian Dualism.* Chicago: Quadrangle Books.

Kimmel, M. (1987). Rethinking "Masculinity." In M. Kimmel (ed.), *Changing Men* (pp. 9–24). Beverly Hills: Sage Publications.

Kirkpatrick, J., & G. White (1985). Exploring Ethnopsychologies. In *Person, Self, and Experience: Exploring Pacific Ethnopsychologies* (pp. 3–32). Berkeley: University of California Press.

Kuletz, V. (1998). *The Tainted Desert: Environmental and Social Ruin in the American West.* New York: Routledge.

Lears, T. J. J. (1985). The Concept of Cultural Hegemony. *American Historical Review* 90, pp. 567–93.

Lears, T. J. J, and R. W. Fox, (1983). *The Culture of Consumption: Critical Essays in American History, 1880–1980.* New York: Pantheon Books.

Locust, C. (1995). The Impact of Differing Belief Systems between Native Americans and their Rehabilitation Service Providers: Spirituality, Disability, and Rehabilitation. *Rehabilitation Education* 9, pp. 205–15.

Lupton, D. (1994). *Medicine as Culture: Illness, Disease and the Body in Western Societies.* London: Sage Publications.

Merleau-Ponty, M. (1962). *Phenomenology of Perception.* (trans. C. Smith). London: Routledge.

Mishkind, M. (1987). The Embodiment of Masculinity. In M. Kimmel (ed.), *Changing Men* (pp. 37–52). Beverly Hills: Sage Publications.

Nietzsche, F. (1967). *The Will to Power* (trans. W. Kaufmann). New York: Random House. (Original work published 1901.)

———. (1997). *On the Genealogy of Morality* (ed. K. A. Pearson, C. Diethe, trans.). New York: Cambridge University Press. (Original work published 1887.)

O'Neill, J. (1985). *Five Bodies: The Human Shape of Modern Society.* Ithaca: Cornell University Press.

Rabinow, P. (1984). *The Foucault Reader.* New York: Pantheon Books.

Sapir, J. D., and J. C. Crocker. (1977). *The Social Use of Metaphor: Essays on the Anthropology of Rhetoric.* Philadelphia: University of Pennsylvania Press.

Scheper-Hughes, N., and N. Lock. (1986). The Mindful Body: A Prolegomenon to Future Work in Medical Anthropology. *Medical Anthropology Quarterly* 17, 5, pp. 6–41.

Schur, W. (1987). Women and Appearance Norms. In E. Rubington & M. Weinberg (eds.), *Deviance: The Interactionist Perspective* (pp. 66–72, 77–81). New York: Macmillan.

Seidman, S. (1994). *The Postmodern Turn: New Perspectives on Social Theory.* New York: Cambridge University Press.

Sheridan, A. (1980). *Michel Foucault: The Will to Truth.* New York: Tavistock.

Shumway, D. R. (1992). *Michel Foucault.* Charlottesville: University Press of Virginia.

Slater, D. (1998). Trading Sexpics on IRC: Embodiment and Authenticity on the Internet. *Body & Society* 4, 4, pp. 91–117.

Spallone, P. (1998). The New Biology of Violence: New Geneticisms for Old? *Body & Society* 4, 4, pp. 47–65.

Springer, C. (1993). Muscular Circuitry: The Invincible Armored Cyborg in Cinema. *Genders* 18, Winter, pp. 87–101.

Stein, H. (1985). *The Psychoanthropology of American Culture*. New York: The Psychohistory Press.

Stepan, N. (1990). Race and Gender: The Role of Analogy in Science. In D. T. Goldberg (ed.), *The Anatomy of Racism* (pp. 38–57). Minneapolis: University of Minnesota Press.

Turner, B. (1984). *The Body and Society: Explorations in Social Theory*. New York: Basil Blackwell.

Wiegman, R. (1995). *American Anatomies: Theorizing Race and Gender*. Durham, NC: Duke University Press.

Williams, R. (1968). *Communications*. Harmondsworth: Penguin.

Wuthnow, R. (1984). *Cultural Analysis: The Work of Peter L. Berger, Mary Douglas, Michel Foucault, and Jurgen Habermas*. London: Routledge.

SUGGESTIONS FOR FURTHER READING

OVERVIEWS

Hargreaves, J. (1987). The Body, Sport and Power Relations. In J. Horne, D. Jary, and A. Tomlinson (eds.), *Sport, Leisure and Social Relations* (pp. 139–59). London: Routledge & Kegan Paul.

The body is analyzed as a major site of social struggle. Hargreaves's analysis is both historical and contemporary, using sport in Britain to illustrate how discipline is achieved. Focusing on issues of class, physical education, and consumerism, sport is shown to be another arena of hegemonic control over the body.

Scott, S., and D. Morgan (1992). *Body Matters: Essays on the Sociology of the Body*. London: Falmer Press.

This compilation of readily accessible essays gathers together a variety of investigations of the body. The book includes topics such as dance, sex therapy, infant bodies, masculinity issues, and bodybuilding, highlighting the range of topics that focus on the body in the social sciences and humanities.

Seltzer, M. (1992). *Bodies and Machines*. New York: Routledge.

Looking at the industrial culture at the turn of the nineteenth century, Seltzer examines America's double fascination with both nature and technology. Using a range of literary, naturalistic, and scientific discourses from 1850 to the 1920s, Seltzer analyzes the development of the interface between conceptualizations of the body and of the machine.

Shilling, C. (1993). *The Body and Social Theory*. London: Sage Publications.

This book is a tightly woven theoretical examination of the body. Shilling goes beyond traditional social constructionist theories to analyze the new sociological literature on the body, including Bourdieu and Elias. It is comprehensive, broad-ranging, and accessible.

Staples, W. G. (1994). Small Acts of Cunning: Disciplinary Practices in Contemporary Life, *The Sociological Quarterly* 34, pp. 645–64.

Discipline and surveillance are demonstrated to flow from the prison into the world of the nondeviant. Reviewing the panoptic prison structure and the social isolation of the prisoner, Staples suggests that the change to electronically monitored home confinement and drug testing are new forms of surveillance adapted to the postmodern era. The gaze established and internalized within the panoptic prison is a central aspect in his analysis of drug testing. Control of the body is accomplished through individual accountability.

Stern, P. (1997). *Fat History: Bodies and Beauty in the Modern West.* New York: New York University Press.

By analyzing cultural attitudes in both France and the United States, Stern explores the historical timing and development of America's obsession with weight. The comparative analysis highlights the various cultural influences of ideal body size and, as such, challenges biological factors.

Turner, B. (1984). *The Body and Society: Explorations in Social Theory.* New York: Basil Blackwell.

Critiquing sociology's portrayal of people as unembodied social actors, the chapters in this book use contemporary social theory to relocate the body as central to the analysis of society. The book explores the social control of individuals through their bodies, encompassing debates on Cartesian dualism, gender relations under a system of patriarchy, social regulations in a system of mass consumption, and medicine and religion as forms of social control.

Woodward, K. (ed.), (1997). *Identity and Difference (Culture, Media and Identities).* London: Sage Publications.

The body is intimately linked to the construction of our identity. This book has three chapters specifically on the body, focusing on the interaction of class, sexuality, and gender issues. Combined, these three chapters are in many ways another reader on the body, with additional articles and exercises included within the selections. They are theoretical yet accessible.

CYBORGS

Balsamo, A. (1996). *Technologies of the Gendered Body: Reading Cyborg Women.* Durham, NC: Duke University Press.

From Harraway's cyborgs to women bodybuilders to virtual bodies in cyberspace, this book examines the interaction of gender identity, technology, and the human body. The first chapter, "Reading Cyborgs, Writing Feminism: Reading the Body in Contemporary Culture," is especially effective at reviewing the current literature on the body and gender in accessible language. Using Foucault, Laqueur, Douglas, and Harraway, it explains the central tenets of each theorist without jargon.

Featherstone, M., and M. Burrows (1995).*Cyberspace/Cyberbodies/Cyberpunk: Cultures of Technological Embodiment.* London: Sage Publications.

This collection of essays examines the social and cultural forms of the human body in relation to concepts inherent in cyberspace. Representations of technological embodiment in literature and film, gender issues and technology, embodied pleasures and virtual reality are all investigated.

Genders, (1993). 18, Winter.

This entire issue of *Genders* focuses specifically on the interactions of gender and technology in film and literature. Cyberpunk fiction and the novels of William Gibson are examined along with films dealing with technology. Topics such as morphing, cyborgs, virtual motherhood and humanism, and theories of postmodern identity, "the real," and gender determinants are examined.

DISABILITY STUDIES

Mairs, N. (1990). *Carnal Acts: Essays.* New York: Harcourt Perennial.

Written by a woman with multiple sclerosis, these essays discuss the embodied experience of living with a disability. Readily accessible through her lived experience, the autobiographical narratives Mairs weaves serve as illustrations of many theoretical positions of the body concerned with the mind/body duality, the medical profession, stigmas, and gender.

Michael, O. (1990). Disability Definitions: The Politics of Meaning. In *The Politics of Disablement: A Sociological Approach* (pp. 1–11). New York: St. Martin's Press.

In the opening chapter of his book, Michael demonstrates the "real world" consequences corresponding with various definitions of disability. He effectively highlights the social and political results of disability oppositionally perceived as either a civil rights issue or as a personal or individual "tragedy."

Thomson, R. G. (1990). Speaking about the Unspeakable: The Representation of Disability as Stigma in Toni Morrison's Novels. In J. Glasgow & A. Ingram (eds.), *Courage and Tools*: *The Florence Howe Award for Feminist Scholarship, 1974–1989.* New York: The Modern Language Association of America.

This essay is an examination of the representation of women with physical disabilities or anomalous markings in five Toni Morrison novels. Thomson draws upon anthropology, sociology, feminism, African-American literary criticisms, and narrative analysis to focus on the stigma attached to denigrated flesh, and highlights the corresponding positive "enabling models" Morrison portrays.

Thomson, R. G. (1995). Anne Petry's Mrs. Hedges and the Evil, One-Eyed Girl: A Feminist Exploration of the Physically Disabled Female Subject. *Women's Studies* 24, pp. 599–614.

Beginning with the reading of a fairy tale to her daughter, Thomson analyzes the negative images attributed to women with disabilities. Drawing on Mary Douglas's *Purity and Danger* and Mikhail Bakhtin's notion of the grotesque, the article highlights the socially constructed nature of "disabled." More important, the article also draws upon Gloria Anzaldúa's transgression of borders and Donna Harraway's analysis of cyborgs to "recast" the concept of "disabled" from the master narrative of deviance and its related concepts of normalcy, wholeness, and conventional womanhood. The disabled body is "reimagined" as positively transgressive.

GENDER ANALYSIS

Berger, M., B. Wallis, and S. Watson (1995). *Constructing Masculinity*. New York: Routledge.

Challenging legal, biological, and gender analyses, these essays suggest that masculinity is not a monolithic entity, but an interplay of social factors that implicate women as well as men. The essays are written from a variety of perspectives, the personal and the theoretical, the literary and the scientific, and are both accessible and informative. It is a compilation concerned with both how and why masculine identities are constructed around the body.

Brumberg, J. J. (1988). *Fasting Girls: The Emergence of Anorexia Nervosa as a Modern Disease*. Cambridge, MA: Harvard University Press.

Looking at the issue of class and women's resistance through food, the book is an investigation of the cultural significance of women's self-starvation. Brumberg uses materials drawn from mostly historical and some contemporary medical publications and archives to examine the modern interpretation of women's emaciation and food refusal.

———. (1997). *The Body Project: An Intimate History of American Girls*. New York: Random House.

Drawing on diary excerpts and media from 1830 to the present, the essays in this book examine the transformation of Victorian concerns with character and morality to the late-twentieth-century focus on appearance. Girls' changing attitudes toward menstruation, breast size, clothing, hair, and virginity are analyzed through a critical exploration of a supposed evolution of personal freedom and choice.

Charmaz, K. (1994). Identity Dilemmas of Chronically Ill Men. *Sociological Quarterly* 35, pp. 269–88.

Charmaz conducted forty in-depth interviews with twenty men who faced life-threatening illnesses. The article analyzes the threats to their masculinities and their reevaluation of masculine stereotypes. Frightened by the sense of their bodies failing, these men reveal how their identities are shaped through their definitions of their bodies as disabled and/or ill.

Conboy, K., N. Medina, and S. Stanbury (1997). *Writing on the Body: Female Embodiment and Feminist Theory*. New York: Columbia University Press.

This is a comprehensive compilation of some of the best and most recent feminist writing on the body. Drawing from a range of disciplines and authors, the topics included focus on the classic and contemporary issues of rape, pornography, anorexia, maternity, class, race, and sexuality.

Craig, S. (1992). *Men, Masculinity and the Media: Research on Men and Masculinities*. Newbury Park, CA: Sage Publications.

The editor has brought together historical and contemporary perspectives on the analysis of masculinity, including appearance issues. Though no chapter focuses on the male body specifically, most chapters develop aspects of male, embodied concerns through the analysis of advertisements, television shows, films, and sporting displays.

Grosz, E. (1994). *Volatile Bodies: Toward a Corporeal Feminism*. Bloomington: Indiana University Press.

Grosz argues that traditional Western philosophy is patriarchal, phallocentric, and misogynistic. By separating the mind from the body, and identifying women with body, the body and women are doubly marginalized. Grosz instead suggests a politics of the body that elaborates a "corporeal feminism," and thus a transformative philosophy and politics. The book is highly theoretical, but well worth the effort.

Orbach, S. (1979). *Fat Is a Feminist Issue*. New York: Berkley Books.

One of the classics of the feminist movement, this book analyzes the oppression of body image. Interactions of gender with perceptions of excess weight and patriarchal social structures are analyzed along with the corresponding self-disgust, loathing, and shame that large women experience. Orbach then juxtaposes this self-rejection with the advertisers who "court us to eat more and more" and the "slimming columns, doctors, fashion magazines, friends who counsel those overweight to curtail their food intake." Orbach suggests that a vicious cycle of compulsive eating and dieting is rooted in the social inequality of women. She also proposes that fat represents an attempt to "break free of society's sex stereotypes." Dieting is unsuccessful because fat serves a "protective" function for women, one method they use to adapt to and assert themselves in an oppressive and exploitative system.

Wiegman, R. (1995). *American Anatomies: Theorizing Race and Gender*. Durham, NC: Duke University Press.

Focusing on the presumed biological and cultural bases of race and gender, these essays delve into the historically constructed hierarchies that ground our current perceptions of racial difference and identity. Moving from the Renaissance through the Black Power movement, from Toni Morrison novels to the buddy films in the 1980s, Wiegman investigates how white racial supremacy, based on interpretation of the body, has been and is currently institutionalized within American culture.

Young, I. M. (1990). *Throwing Like a Girl and Other Essays in Feminist Philosophy and Social Theory*. Bloomington: Indiana University Press.

The entire book is an accessible exploration of the social theory of the body. The chapter "Pregnant Embodiment: Subjectivity and Alienation" is especially good in analyzing medical interpretations of pregnancy and juxtaposing the "outsider" view with a woman's sense of both something within her and yet not her. Drawing on Merleau-Ponty, this chapter complicates the distinctions and seeming exclusivity between dualistic categories of inner and outer worlds of the body.

MEDIA AND THE BODY

Bernardi, D. (1998). *Star Trek and History: Race-ing toward a White Future.* New Brunswick, NJ: Rutgers University Press.

By highlighting the socially constructed visible markers of race, Bernardi demonstrates how *Star Trek* reflects cultural assumptions of white superiority. Though not analyzing the body specifically, this book investigates the production of whiteness/race as displayed on the body. The chapters illuminate how the display of race is embodied and institutionalized through examination of representational, narrative, and production values.

Bordo, S. (1995). *Unbearable Weight: Feminism, Western Culture, and the Body.* Berkeley: University of California Press.

In an easily accessible style, this book comes to grips with the major theoretical developments surrounding the body. Exploring the mind/body dualism, medicine, gender constructions, reproductive rights, and the media, Bordo applies feminist and postmodern theoretical orientations in a refreshingly transparent language. The last section is especially effective at reassessing the notion of resistance.

Goldman, R. (1992). *Reading Ads Socially.* New York: Routledge.

While giving an excellent overview of how to interpret advertisements, the techniques Goldman highlights also focus attention on how the body is used in advertising to convey information. The chapter development illuminates the "logic of commodities" and how this "logic" has the potential to influence the way we think about our bodies, our relationships, and ourselves.

MEDICINE AND THE BODY

Lupton, D. (1994). *Medicine as Culture: Illness, Disease and the Body in Western Societies.* London: Sage Publications.

Lupton brings together a critical and accessible examination of the influence of medicine both as a form of knowledge and as an interactional practice. The chapters include theoretical perspectives on medicine and the health of the body, including AIDS, sex, gender, fitness, and cleanliness as well as the commodified and the dead body. The chapters on the power relations inherent within medical encounters, and feminist critique of medical power, are especially good.

Martin, E. (1987). *The Woman in the Body: A Cultural Analysis of Reproduction.* Boston: Beacon Press.

The essays in this book highlight the influence of patriarchal interpretation of the human body. Reexamining the constructions of sperm and egg production, menstruation, labor, birth, and menopause, Martin vividly illuminates how medicine is not a value-neutral science, but is deeply enmeshed within patriarchal systems of knowledge.

Scheper-Hughes, N., and M. Lock (1986). The Mindful Body: A Prolegomenon to Future Work in Medical Anthropology. *Medical Anthropology Quarterly* 17, pp. 6–41.

The distinct but interrelated academic discourses on the body—philosophical, textual, and political—are examined. The authors demonstrate how academic analyses of the body have failed to incorporate an integrated "unhyphenated" investigation of entwined cultural influences. Both Western and non-Western examples of conceptions of "health" and medicine are given.

Medical Anthropology Quarterly, and *Social Science and Medicine*.

These journals are good vehicles for juxtaposing Western medical interpretations of the body with non-Western orientations, while exploring the many-faceted social and political constructions of those interpretations.